THE INTERNATIONAL LINKAGE OF NATIONAL ECONOMIC MODELS

CONTRIBUTIONS
TO
ECONOMIC ANALYSIS

78

Honorary Editor

J. TINBERGEN

Editors

D. W. JORGENSON

J. WAELBROECK

NORTH-HOLLAND PUBLISHING COMPANY – AMSTERDAM • OXFORD
AMERICAN ELSEVIER PUBLISHING COMPANY, INC. – NEW YORK

THE INTERNATIONAL LINKAGE OF NATIONAL ECONOMIC MODELS

Edited by

R. J. BALL

London Graduate School of Business Studies

NORTH-HOLLAND PUBLISHING COMPANY – AMSTERDAM • OXFORD
AMERICAN ELSEVIER PUBLISHING COMPANY, INC. – NEW YORK

Library of Congress Catalog Card Number: 72 88287

North-Holland ISBN Series 0 7204 3100 x
North-Holland ISBN Volume 0 7204 3182 4
American Elsevier ISBN 0 444 10464 x

Publishers:

NORTH-HOLLAND PUBLISHING COMPANY – AMSTERDAM
NORTH-HOLLAND PUBLISHING COMPANY, LTD. – OXFORD

Sole distributors for the U.S.A. and Canada:
AMERICAN ELSEVIER PUBLISHING COMPANY, INC.
52 VANDERBILT AVENUE
NEW YORK, N.Y. 10017

First edition 1973
Second printing 1975

213779

PRINTED IN THE NETHERLANDS

3-1303-00054-6482

INTRODUCTION TO THE SERIES

This series consists of a number of hitherto unpublished studies, which are introduced by the editors in the belief that they represent fresh contributions to economic science.

The term economic analysis as used in the title of the series has been adopted because it covers both the activities of the theoretical economist and the research worker.

Although the analytical methods used by the various contributors are not the same, they are nevertheless conditioned by the common origin of their studies, namely theoretical problems encountered in practical research. Since for this reason, business cycle research and national accounting, research work on behalf of economic policy, and problems of planning are the main sources of the subjects dealt with, they necessarily determine the manner of approach adopted by the authors. Their methods tend to be 'practical' in the sense of not being too far remote from application to actual economic conditions. In addition they are quantitative rather than qualitative.

It is the hope of the editors that the publication of these studies will help to stimulate the exchange of scientific information and to reinforce international cooperation in the field of economics.

THE EDITORS

EDITOR'S PREFACE

This volume is the product of many people from many countries joined together in an international research project to integrate national econometric models and so obtain better predictions of world trade and deeper understanding of the transmission of international fluctuations. It contains a first analysis of the conceptual framework within which such an integration may take place and illustrations of the empirical work that underlies the project as a piece of applied research. A second volume will contain details of the econometric models of the countries concerned in the project.

In preparing this volume I am indebted to my editorial committee, Chikashi Moriguchi, Jack Sawyer and Jean Waelbroeck for discussion and advice. Indispensable help has been given by my colleague Brian Boatwright with regard to the editing of the volume and preparation of the index. I am greatly in his debt. My thanks are also due to my secretary, Ann Adams for carrying the burden of typing and retyping the manuscript. Lastly, I am grateful for the patience of my colleagues in Project LINK in dealing with the demands made upon them by the editor.

May 1972   R.J. Ball

To Robert Aaron Gordon, wise counsellor and friend, this volume is respectfully dedicated by his colleagues for his service to model building, economics and Project LINK.

CONTENTS

Editor's preface   vii

Chapter 1   B.G. Hickman, L.R. Klein and R.R. Rhomberg,
Introduction   1

Part I: The theory of international linkage

Chapter 2   R.R. Rhomberg, Towards a general trade
model   9

Chapter 3   B.G. Hickman, A general linear model of world
trade   21

Chapter 4   J. Waelbroeck, The methodology of linkage   45

Part II: The general models of Project LINK

Chapter 5   R.J. Ball, The economic models of Project
LINK   65

Chapter 6   UNCTAD Staff, Models for developing countries   109

Chapter 7   G.B. Taplin, A model of world trade   177

Part III: Models of trade capital and services

Chapter 8   G. Basevi, Commodity trade equations in
Project LINK   227

Chapter 9   A. Amano, International capital movements:
Theory and estimation   283

Chapter 10   J.A. Sawyer, The invisible components of the
current account of the balance of international
payments   329

Part IV: Applications of bilateral linkage

Chapter 11 C. Moriguchi and M. Tatemoto, An econometric analysis of a bilateral model of international economic activity: Japan and U.S.A.   367

Chapter 12 J.F. Helliwell, F.W. Gorbet, G.R. Sparks and I.A. Stewart, Comprehensive linkage of large models: Canada and the United States   395

Part V: The operation of total linkage

Chapter 13 L.R. Klein and A. Van Peeterssen, Forecasting world trade within Project LINK   429

Index   465

1. INTRODUCTION

B.G. HICKMAN, L.R. KLEIN and R.R. RHOMBERG

The Committee on Economic Stability of the Social Science Research Council (USA) has had some success in sponsoring and stimulating group research ventures across university and other institutional lines. The S.S.R.C. – Brookings Econometric Model and Federal Reserve Board-MIT-Pennsylvania (now MIT-Pennsylvania-SSRC) Model projects are outstanding examples. It was not an unusual step, then, for the Committee to foster the establishment of Project LINK in 1968.

The problem posed to the Committee by one of its members, Rudolf Rhomberg, was to initiate research on the international transmission mechanism. The first steps, supported by Committee members, R.A. Gordon, Bert Hickman (Chairman) and Lawrence Klein, were to inquire about the interest of possible foreign participants and to convene a small working group in Stanford, California, during August 1968.

The original thought was to work through existing, maintained econometric model projects in various study centres (Tokyo, Toronto, Philadelphia, London, The Hague, Brussels and Bonn), the idea being that national models could be *linked* through their trade equations. The 1968 founding meeting proved to be productive in many respects:

It was agreed

(i) in principle to proceed with the organisation of a linkage project, with full cooperation of all the participants;

(ii) to work through an explanation of imports in each national model and to estimate exports from trade shares;

(iii) to disaggregate imports according to certain SITC groupings in each national model;

(iv) to find consistent world solutions that preserved accounting identities between exports and imports.

The research mode adopted was not unlike that used in the early stage of the SSRC – Brookings Econometric Model project. Once each year, participants would convene for a lengthy working seminar (one week or more), report on contemporary research and lay group plans for the next year's tasks. Regional meetings in Eastern and Western hemispheres would be held between annual meetings. This has proved to be a workable format. A central facility at the University of Pennsylvania would coordinate the linkage calculations and serve as a secretariat. Model proprietors responded by sending data files, programs, current input values and equation specifications to LINK Central, where simultaneous solutions of national models and implied trade patterns have been obtained.

Two major financing sources were obtained, in addition to separate contributions in kind and in cash from the individual participating centres. The International Monetary Fund and the U.S. National Science Foundation each made generous research grants that enabled the various project activities to be carried out. The IMF grant was originally for three years and the NSF grant for two years. The latter was renewed in 1971 and the former in 1972. In order to support the growing scope of LINK activities, additional research support will be sought.

A guiding philosophy in LINK has been that each model builder knows his own country best. The project was not based on the standardised construction of national models and trade equations at one remote research centre, but on the effective integration of large existing models with some international standardisations acceptable to all participants. In addition to the original group of participating model builders, the project has added Australia, Austria, Finland, Italy and Sweden. The Socialist countries and developing countries have been modelled for LINK by UNCTAD. The other developed countries are presently represented by small models built by research groups at the International Monetary Fund and Stanford University. In the course of time, other large scale national models represented by ongoing research projects will also be included, but expansion at this stage is limited by project ability to coordinate diverse interests and sources of information.

France and Italy are key countries among industrial nations. In the first year, to fill a gap caused by the absence of working models of these economies available to the project, LINK Central constructed some simple income determination models for these two countries. After one year, a research team at the University of Bologna started the construction of an Italian model. It will soon be used within the LINK system. After three years, the project started its own construction of a French model at the Free University of Brussels. In the near future, it is expected that a larger working French model will be functioning within LINK.

In the first three years, LINK has been successful in deriving world trade solutions and projections within a consistent framework of individual country performance at the national level. It has been possible to make projections over a two-year horizon, and a future goal will be to make longer-term projections – up to five years. The ultimate world model will never be built. No matter how good any approximation might become, there is always a possibility of improvement. There are many ways of improving individual models or the treatment of the world trading system. Mainly, however, success has been achieved so far, in a modest way, at the trade level covering both price and quantity movements. The next major thrust of LINK will be at the balance of payments level. The Canadian model of the Bank of Canada, the Japanese model and the Australian model all have equations for the main capital flows in the balance of payments.

The Canadian and Japanese models are being studied in bilateral linkage experiments with the U.S.A. Also, the U.S. balance of payments has been modelled for the Brookings Econometric project, and this work will be drawn upon for the eventual incorporation of the balance of payments sector in the U.S. model for LINK.

In order to account for capital flows, many variables from money and credit markets must be endogenously treated in individual country models. This has stimulated much thinking and research within LINK to develop more complete monetary sectors in those models that lacked such coverage. This is, in large part, preparatory to balance of payments modelling at the international level.

The reader of this volume will find many of the preceding ideas developed more fully in separate chapters by LINK participants. He should also see clearly the need for extension in the directions mentioned — towards including more countries, more types of countries (e.g., developing and socialist), longer time horizons, better treatment of fluctuations in the coefficients of the world trade matrix, monetary variables and capital flows. The esprit de corps and international cooperation that has already been achieved in the working team of LINK participants has been gratifying. There is every reason to expect this spirit to continue as the new and more difficult problems are successively tackled.

The papers are grouped into five sections. The first part consists of three papers on the theory of international linkage. The chapter by Rudi Rhomberg outlines the specification of the model for internationally traded goods. Bert Hickman, in ch. 3, presents an explicit approach to linkage through a trade shares matrix, whilst in ch. 4, Jean Waelbroeck stresses the practical problems of this approach. The second part of the book is concerned with the general models of Project LINK. Ch. 5 by Jim Ball surveys the models of the industrialised countries in the Project, comparing their approaches to modelling different sectors of the economy, whilst the chapter presented by UNCTAD outlines the approach taken towards building models for the developing countries and their incorporation within Project LINK. Ch. 7 by Grant Taplin, outlines a model of world trade developed at the IMF, the results of which may be compared to those given in ch. 13.

The third part of the book is concerned with empirical studies of trade, services and capital flows. Georgio Basevi, in ch. 8, deals with the commodity trade equations used in the industrial countries of Project LINK. Akihiro Amano, in ch. 9, presents various models for the flow of international capital and results from Japanese data. Ch. 10 by Jack Sawyer, is a survey of the models currently being used to explain the invisible component of the balance of payments.

Part four of the book presents two applications of bilateral linkage. The first of these, ch. 11 by Chikashi Moriguchi and Masahiro Tatemoto, presents the results of the linking of the Japanese and U.S. models, whilst the second by John Helliwell and others concentrates on the practical problems of reconciling two models used for Canada and U.S.A. Finally, the last part of the book on the operation of total linkage presents a paper by Larry Klein and Alain Van Peeterssen, which gives an outline of the methods currently used in Project LINK in order to forecast world trade, with some results using both "Mini" and "Maxi" LINK approaches.

Project LINK participants

Australia: Reserve Bank of Australia.
Austria: Institute of Advanced Studies, Vienna.
Belgium: Free University of Brussels.
Canada: Institute for the Quantitative Analysis of Social and Economic Policy, University of Toronto.
Finland: Bank of Finland Institute for Economic Research.
West Germany: University of Bonn.
International Monetary Fund: Washington D.C.
Italy: Istituto di Scienze Economiche, University of Bologna.
Japan: Institute of Economic Research, Kyoto University.
Netherlands: Central Planning Bureau, The Hague.
Sweden: National Institute of Economic Research, Stockholm.
United Kingdom: Econometric Forecasting Unit, London Business School.
United Nations: New York.
U.S.A.: Economic Research Unit, Wharton School of Finance and Commerce, University of Pennsylvania.
Research Center in Economic Growth, Stanford University.

Part I

THE THEORY OF INTERNATIONAL LINKAGE

2. TOWARDS A GENERAL TRADE MODEL *

R.R. RHOMBERG

1. Introduction

National economies are linked to one another through the exchange of goods, services and capital assets (including international
reserve assets). Economic change in any country may, in principle,
affect the flows of goods, services and assets among all countries,
as well as the prices at which they are exchanged. A full description of the entire interdependent system of the world economy,
including all the adjustment mechanisms that are at work, is still
beyond present capabilities of model construction and estimation.
Simplification is achieved, at the present stage of the project, by
regarding certain variables as exogenous. In particular, policies of
governments and central banks, including exchange rate policies,
are taken to be exogenously determined, even though they may at
times be induced by developments in the balance of payments or
the domestic economy. Moreover, capital movements will initially
be considered exogenous, but it is hoped that this limitation of the
model can be removed at a later stage of the project. [1]

Taking account of these limitations, the international model
presently envisaged can be described as follows. The regions to be
linked may be individual countries or groups of countries. A set of
exogenous variables operating in the various regional economies
determines developments in the domestic economies of each region to the extent that these developments are described in the
various regional models, as well as the quantities and prices of

* I am grateful to B.G. Hickman, L.J. Lau and P.J. Verdoorn for comments on an
earlier draft of this chapter.
[1] See chs. 11 and 12 in this volume.

merchandise exports and imports and the receipts and payments for internationally exchanged services. The current account balances of all regions determined in this manner together with exogenously determined capital movements yield, on the assumption of given exchange rate policies, the overall balance of payments and the change in international reserves of each region of the model. The purpose of this chapter is to outline the manner in which that part of the model which determines the quantities and prices of internationally traded goods (the "trade model") could be specified.

2. An ideal trade model

Although limitations of data and resources make it necessary to start actual model construction with highly simplified approaches, it may be best to begin this methodological discussion by setting forth the principal features of what might be considered an "ideal" trade model and to compare approaches that might be practical in the near future with these ideal standards.

For the sake of concreteness we may envisage a model of trade among some 30 regions (some of which are individual countries and others geographic areas). Total merchandise trade among these regions would be divided into a limited number of commodity classes; but regardless of whether as few as 4 or as many as 20 such commodity classes are distinguished, this division can never be fine enough to result in a set of homogeneous goods. The first strategic decision, therefore, concerns the question of whether it is more appropriate to approximate reality by treating the commodity classes distinguished in the model as if they are homogeneous goods or whether the exports recorded in a particular commodity class that are produced by different regions should be regarded as different goods. [2] The specification of the trade model is quite different in the two cases.

If the trade flows reported under a particular commodity class were considered to constitute trade in an homogeneous good for

---

[2] For a discussion of this question, see Leamer, E.E. and R.M. Stern, *Quantitative International Economics*, Allyn and Bacon, 1970.

which, in the absence of transportation costs or other trade barriers, there could be only one price in the world market, the appropriate specification of the trade model would be as follows. For each region, there would be a demand schedule for each good indicating the dependence of quantities demanded on income, or on some other measure of economic activity in the region, and on the price of the good relative to prices of other goods. Similarly, for each region there would be a supply schedule for each good indicating the relation between quantities of the good supplied and the price of the good as well as other factors influencing the ability or willingness of residents of the region to supply the good in question. Summation of the demand and supply schedules for all regions would yield schedules of world demand for, and world supply of, each good. The intersection of these schedules would determine the price of the good and its global output and consumption. At this equilibrium price, every region is demanding either a larger or a smaller quantity of the good than it is itself supplying, and it is, therefore, either an importer or an exporter of the good in question. Its imports or exports would be measured by the difference between the quantities demanded and supplied at the world equilibrium price. In practical applications, this analysis would have to be modified in the traditional manner to allow for the existence of transportation costs, tariffs or other trade barriers.

This model has a number of awkward features. First, it implies that every region will, in general, either import or export a particular good, but not both. In fact, however, most countries record both imports and exports under particular commodity classes, not only when broad commodity groups such as manufactures or raw materials are considered but also when fairly narrow subclasses such as textiles or steel products are examined. It would be possible to reinterpret the model to mean that each region will be either a net importer or a net exporter of a particular good depending on whether its demand for the good exceeds or falls short of its domestic supply at the world price level. But this reinterpretation begs the question of how the gross trade flows, exports and imports, are actually determined. Second, in this model prices for the same good in different regions can diverge only because of transportation costs and other trade barriers. Independent price movements in different regions would be confined to the sector of non-traded goods — an implication of the model that is at variance with observed price behaviour in many commodity classes. Third, there is a practical difficulty that net imports or net exports in a particular commodity class are not only smaller than the corresponding gross trade flows but may be particularly small relative to domestic consumption and production. Estimates of net exports or net imports would have to be based on the difference between separate estimates of total demand and supply, and relatively small errors in these estimates would cause large proportionate errors in the estimate of net trade.

The alternative approach is to regard commodities of a particular class produced in different regions as different economic goods. Manufactured products, and some others as well, are sufficiently differentiated as between different producing countries to justify this procedure. When relatively broad classes of commodities are being considered, the commodity bundles reported under the particular class heading by various exporting regions may contain few, if any, goods that are identical as between regions and these bundles would, in any case, differ in composition. Even if one were to go to a rather fine commodity classification containing such classes as coffee, cotton or steel pipe, it would be found that qualitative differences among the products produced by various regions under one of these class headings are so large as to cause an effective separation of markets and the persistence of price differentials.

The trade model appropriate to this approach is somewhat more complex than that which could be constructed on the assumption that each commodity class constitutes an homogeneous good, regardless of the region of production. [3] It will be convenient to

---

[3] Such a trade model was developed by Armington, P.S., 'A Theory of Demand for Products Distinguished by Place of Production', *IMF Staff Papers*, March 1969 and 'The Geographic Pattern of Trade and the Effects of Price Changes', *IMF Staff Papers*, July 1969, in which an analysis of the demand side of such a model is developed, and his 'A Many-Country Model of Equilibrating Adjustments in Prices and Spending', Appendix to Rhomberg, R.R., 'Possible Approaches to a Model of World Trade and Payments', *IMF Staff Papers*, March 1970, where the complete model is outlined.

refer to commodity classes as "goods" and to the output of a "good" produced in a particular region as a "product"; for instance, manufactures may be one of the goods distinguished in the model, while French manufactures, U.S. manufactures, etc., are products. [4] For every region there is a set of demand functions for the products of each region, including the home region. For n regions and m traded goods there are nm products and thus $n^2 m$ demand functions for traded products. In addition, there will be one or several demand functions in each region for the non-traded products of that region. These demand functions would depend on economic activity and various other non-price factors, as well as on all prices in the system, i.e., the prices of all products entering into trade as well as the prices of non-traded products in the home country. For each region, there is a supply schedule for each product produced by that region, so that there are nm supply schedules for traded products, as well as one or several additional supply schedules for non-traded products in each region. [5] In other words, it is assumed that, while buyers differentiate between the products of different regions, sellers offer their products to all potential purchasers and do not discriminate between residents of different regions. [6]

The n regional demand functions for each of the nm products can be summed to obtain nm world demand schedules for these products. World demand for one of the products of a particular region and that region's supply of the product determine the quantity sold and its price. The world price level of any good is the weighted average of the prices of the corresponding regional pro-

---

[4] This is the terminology used by Armington, in the references cited above.

[5] The specification of supply schedules implies that products are assumed to be produced under competitive conditions. Monopoly elements could be introduced, where appropriate, by substituting for these supply schedules the familiar analytical apparatus of pricing under conditions of monopoly or monopolistic competition.

[6] This assumption — namely, that discriminating monopoly is absent — may not be entirely realistic. Pricing for the export market, where competition may be stronger, often differs from pricing for the home market, where it is less strong. In a more elaborate model, this differentiation could be taken into account, since separate price indices for exports and for domestic sales exist or can be constructed. However, there are generally no data on differences in prices of exports going to different destinations. The simplifying assumption in the text is, therefore, introduced even at the stage of discussing the "ideal" model and will undoubtedly have to be retained, entirely or in part, in any practical application.

ducts. It is to be noted that in this approach producers of a particular good in the home region are represented as competing for the
home market and for markets abroad with producers of the good
situated in other regions. The solution of the model determines at
the same time the domestic sales of domestically produced products and the bilateral trade flows from each region to every other
region (and thus each region's global exports and imports).

Traditional import demand functions are typically based on an
hybrid approach. Imports are considered to be a product that is
different from domestic output of similar commodities, so that
there can be a differential of prices between imports and home
production to which the demand for imports responds. At the
same time, all foreign suppliers of the good in question are considered to produce an homogeneous product, so that it is not necessary to distinguish separate demand schedules for the exports of
various foreign regions. In some models separate functions are
estimated for imports originating in two or three different regions,
say, in one or two principal trading partner countries and in the
rest of the world. But even where this is done, foreign regions that
are individually treated are typically selected on the basis of the
size of their market shares in the importing region rather than by
the criterion of the degree of product homogeneity. [7]

What has been described here as the "ideal" trade model is thus
a Walrasian model of the world economy in which track is being
kept of the country of residence of the purchasers, as well as of
that of the sellers, of each good. In practice, it would be difficult
to construct a workable trade model strictly along these lines by
linking existing national models together. In the first place, a full
articulation of a Walrasian world economic model would present
each of the various demand and supply functions, especially the
former, as depending on a large number of prices; for instance, if
four traded goods are distinguished and if there are 20 countries,
then 80 products enter into international trade and the demand
for each depends in principle on all 80 prices, as well as on the

---

[7] There are exceptions to this. Where total merchandise imports from industrial and
primary producing countries are separately estimated, a crude separation of exporting
regions by product homogeneity is in fact achieved (manufactures vs. primary products).

prices of the non-traded products. Clearly, some fairly drastic simplifications must be introduced to make this system of equations
manageable for either econometric estimation or policy simulation. Second, national models emphasise the determination of
overall economic activity and price levels, but do not typically deal
with demand for, and supply of, the products of the various industrial subdivisions or the determination of relative prices by industry. They are, therefore, not well suited to being linked in an
essentially Walrasian framework. The remainder of this chapter
deals with the question of how the two difficulties just mentioned
may be overcome.

3. Practical problems of model construction

The first problem concerns the simplifications that could be introduced for the purpose of reducing the number of price variables
occurring in each of the demand functions. Armington has shown
that, under relatively weak assumptions, the competitive effects of
changes in product prices (i.e., supply prices of various regions) on
the demand for a given product can be separated from the effects
of changes in the prices of goods (i.e., average world price levels
for various commodity classes) on the demand for a given good. [8]
This means that the dependence on price and income factors of a
region's demand for a product – say, Italy's demand for U.K.
machinery – can be expressed in two steps: (1) Italy's demand for
machinery in general depends on Italy's income (total expenditure) and on the "world price levels" of machinery and other
commodity classes; (2) Italy's demand for U.K. machinery depends on Italy's demand for machinery in general and on the ratios
of U.K. export prices of machinery to the export prices of each of
the other countries that produce machinery (including Italy itself).

---

[8] Armington, P.S., 'A Theory of Demand...', *loc. cit.* The assumptions mentioned in the
text are (1) that buyers' preferences for products in a particular commodity class are
independent of their purchases of products pertaining to another commodity class and (2)
that the distribution of the demand for a good over the component products varies only
with the relative prices of those products.

A further simplification can be achieved by making the assumptions (a) that elasticities of substitution in any market between products pertaining to one commodity class are constant and (b) that these elasticities are the same for all pairs of products competing in that market. [9] The demand for a product in a particular region can then be expressed as a constant share of the region's demand for the good in question, multiplied by a single relative price term. This price term is the ratio of the price of the product to the weighted average price of the good (i.e., the weighted average of the product prices) in the region, raised to a power which represents the elasticity of substitution. This formulation leads directly to a market shares approach of trade model construction. For each region, the demand for each product can be represented as a constant fraction of that region's demand for the good, modified by the price term just mentioned.

Realised (ex post) market shares will be equal to these ex ante shares only if prices are assumed to clear the markets. To the extent that markets are not cleared through equilibrating price movements, the influence of non-price factors affecting the utility of the product to the purchaser, such as delivery lags, will cause realised market shares to diverge from those that would be expected on the basis of actual (non-equilibrium) prices. Moreover, observed prices would in principle have to be corrected so as to reflect changes over time in the price equivalent of costs or benefits to the purchaser arising from the purchase of particular products, such as those related to tariff preferences, preferential credit terms or the quality of service. Such corrections are necessary only if these costs or benefits, expressed as percentages of the observed prices, have changed during the period studied; otherwise they

---

[9] See Armington, P.S., 'A Theory of Demand...', *loc. cit.* The assumption under (b) in the text is not as easily accepted as the other simplifying assumptions so far introduced. It might be more plausible to consider that the elasticity of substitution between particular products is the same in all markets than to make the assumption stated in the text. For two countries that mainly export coffee, the elasticity of substitution in the commodity class "food" will tend to be high in all markets; and for a coffee-producing country and a wheat-producing country, this elasticity of substitution will tend to be low in all markets. Unfortunately, this alternative assumption does not yield a suitable simplification of the problem.

may simply be absorbed into the set of qualitative differences among products that cause the substitution elasticities between pairs of products to be less than infinite.

If the model is to be constructed on the working assumption that pure competition prevails, supply functions for the products produced by each country can be derived from production functions and the postulate of profit maximisation. In the short-run, with capital equipment and the number of firms in each industry held constant, the quantity of a product that is supplied depends on the price of the product and the costs of the inputs, namely, labour, products bought from another domestic industry and imported products. In the long-run, the cost of capital must be included in the determinants of supply.

In the absence of changes in prices, wages and the cost of capital, the quantities supplied of all products would tend to vary with the amounts of the productive resources — labour and capital — available in the economy. This consideration suggests a form of the supply function for a product in which the quantity supplied (a) is proportional to the potential output of the regional economy as long as all prices of inputs and products remain unchanged and (b) responds to changes in the ratios of the price of the product to wages and to the prices of other factor inputs (produced at home or imported) as well as to any special supply factors (droughts, strikes, innovations, etc.) operating in the sector producing the product.

In a model based on the demand and supply framework just outlined, the prices and quantities of the various home products determined by world demand and domestic supply would, after proper allowance for indirect taxation and interindustry (input —output) relations, yield each region's gross national product. The model would have to be completed by specification of (i) the relation between gross national product and expenditures on the various classes of goods distinguished in the model, (ii) the determination of wages and other factor prices, and (iii) a number of ancillary relationships. The model could then, in principle, be solved for the endogenous domestic and foreign trade variables of all regions.

A model of this type could be regarded as a simplified version of the "ideal trade model" in the sense that it preserves the integrated treatment of domestic economic activity and external trade. This is achieved by considering domestic producers in any region as being in (imperfect) competition with producers in each of the other regions in the domestic market as well as in the markets of other regions. This feature distinguishes the model from conventional models of international trade and of national economies. Trade models are not typically concerned with domestic production for the domestic market; and national models do not ordinarily determine gross national product as the aggregate value of output of various industries each of which is calculated as the resultant of interaction of an industry supply schedule with a world demand schedule for the industry's product. To adapt existing national models to this approach would require, as a minimum, the specification and estimation of national demand and supply functions for the commodities distinguished in the trade model and for non-traded goods and services. As already mentioned, this requirement may be considered impractical by national model builders. Their models are constructed on Keynesian lines, and the Walrasian features of a trade model do not fit well into the traditional structure of existing national models.

For these reasons it may be necessary, at least initially, to operate the trade model, and the regional models linked by it, in a less than fully integrated manner. The following procedure may provide a feasible approximation to the ideal model. Each regional model would contain an import demand function and an export supply function for every commodity class — rather than total demand and supply functions, which would be required under the ideal approach. The import demand functions could be constructed on the lines that would be appropriate under the ideal method if there were only two regions, the home economy and the rest of the world. In addition to income and other variables determining expenditure on the good in question (whether produced at home or abroad), they could thus, in principle, contain two price ratios: (1) the price of the good relative to the average price level of other goods — regardless of the origin, domestic or foreign, of these goods — and (2) the price of the imported product relative to the price of the competing home product pertaining to the same commodity class. [10] Since the effect of domestic capacity utilisation on imports is not, then, indirectly covered through domestic supply equations for products competing with imports, these effects may have to be introduced directly into the import functions, albeit at the cost of making somewhat of a hodgepodge of demand and supply factors.

The export supply functions could be estimated in the form of export price equations. Since exports are ordinarily only a small part of total domestic output, export prices would tend to depend closely on prices charged in the domestic market by the industries producing for export. They could be estimated as a function of these prices or, if that is not feasible, as a function of the general level of prices and wages in the economy. Moreover, they should contain as additional arguments the volume of exports relative to a scale variable, such as the total potential domestic output of the commodity, except where the price elasticity of supply of exports is infinite, and a time trend to reflect the difference, if any, between the rate of productivity growth in export production and that in the economy in general.

The trade model could then be solved in the manner described earlier for the entire model. For each commodity group, the demand for imports in each regional model would be determined along conventional lines, except for the distinction between the effects of changes in relative prices of goods (food vs. manufactures) and of products (domestic vs. imported). [11] The world demand for each region's export products would be derived from the demands for imports of all regions through an analysis in terms of traditional market shares modified by relative export prices. Simultaneously, world demand for each export product and its supply price would determine export prices and quantities, and thus also import prices, for every region.

---

[10] In any market, the weighted average of the two prices mentioned under (2) equals the (average) price of the good in question mentioned under (1).

[11] When only a few broad commodity groups are distinguished, as in the present project, the effect of relative prices of goods may be negligible.

Models of the sort discussed in the preceding paragraphs are set out in greater detail in ch. 3; an illustrative application is given in ch. 7.

3. A GENERAL LINEAR MODEL OF WORLD TRADE *

B.G. HICKMAN

1. Introduction

The trade model presented in this paper is a mathematically explicit approach to the linkage of national models through a trade shares matrix. For reasons stressed in other chapters in this volume by Rhomberg and Waelbroeck, this line of attack offers the most promise for Project LINK. My basic purpose is to generalise the shares approach by embedding it in an explicit supply and demand framework which simultaneously satisfies domestic and world constraints and provides an endogenous explanation of changes in market shares over time. The problems of implementing such a system empirically are formidable, but not insolvable, and it may provide an appropriate long-term goal for Project LINK.

In the interests of brevity and clarity, many of the practical problems involved in operating the central LINK system are neglected in this chapter. The theoretical model is presented in linear form in order to clarify the relationships between the trade and country models in complete systems solutions, leaving discussion of the solution procedures employed in the actual nonlinear LINK system to the chapters by Waelbroeck and by Klein and van Peeterssen. Similarly, I assume that there is only one category of traded goods, and in that sense, the discussion is less general than in Rhomberg's

* I have benefitted markedly from a study of Rudolf R. Rhomberg's general principles of trade model construction, as set forth in his chapter in this volume and in earlier writings, as well as from his specific comments and suggestions on this paper. Comments by Lawrence J. Lau and P.J. Verdoorn led to significant improvements in the interpretation of key assumptions and are gratefully acknowledged.

theoretical contribution or in the actual LINK system of four-fold
commodity disaggregation. Finally, I abstract from the c.i.f.-f.o.b.
valuation problem by assuming that imports as well as exports are
measured f.o.b., and from the currency conversion problem by
assuming that exchange rates are constant and that all variables are
measured in units of a single currency. [1]

The organisation of the paper is as follows. Sect.2 defines the share
coefficients and introduces a nonlinear relative price expression of
their determination which is analogous to a theoretical formulation
of Armington. [2] The demand and supply framework for traded
goods is specified in sect. 3. An export demand function for each
country is derived by a process of linearisation and aggregation of
the underlying nonlinear shares expression. The outcome of these
procedures is an export demand function in which the weights of all
price indices are explicitly derived from base period market shares
and substitution elasticities and in which the base period market
shares appear as one determinant of current export demand. The
hypothesis is also generalised to incorporate non-price demand
determinants. The framework is completed by specifying a general
export supply function and import demand function for each country. The import supply function is suppressed on the assumption of
an infinitely elastic supply to each country.

The structural trade functions for each country as specified in
sect. 3 could be solved for the partial equilibrium values of export
and import quantities and export price. In a general equilibrium solution, however, account must be taken of trade-determining variables in the structural functions which are themselves endogenous in
either the national or the world models. In sect. 4 the reduced form
solutions for the endogenous trade variables are derived for each
country model in terms of domestic and foreign predetermined
variables. Finally, in sect. 5, the reduced form trade equations of the

---

[1] I have discussed these last topics in 'Prices and Quantities in a World Trade System',
Project LINK Working Paper Number 1, LINK Central: Economic Research Unit, University of Pennsylvania, September 1971.

[2] Armington, P.S., 'A Theory of Demand for Products Distinguished by Place of
Production', *IMF Staff Papers*, March 1969.

several countries are incorporated into a series of four complete world trade systems of increasing endogeneity and generality.

The first two systems allocate imports over exports solely by use of the base period shares matrix, with no allowance for the effects of induced changes in market shares as trading occurs. Models 3 and 4 incorporate the complete demand and supply framework for foreign trade, however, and take direct account of induced changes in market shares in the solution. It is shown that the world trade constraints are automatically satisfied in all four model solutions, and that the last two models explain endogenous changes in market shares as well as in total imports and exports of the various countries or regions.

2. The matrix of market shares

The centrepiece of all the models described below is a world trade matrix which permits the calculation of market shares. Let x_{ij} be total merchandise exports from region i to region j. These elements may be arranged in an $n \times n$ matrix of export flows, where n is the number of regions to be distinguished in the model. Then total imports of region j are given by the column sums $m_j = \Sigma_i x_{ij}$. Total exports of region i are found as the row sums $x_i = \Sigma_j x_{ij}$. Total world exports (or imports) are given by $x = \Sigma_i = \Sigma_j x_{ij}$. The value of x_{ii} will be zero if region i is a single country but will contain the value of "intra-trade" if it consists of several countries. For present purposes, we simplify the discussion by assuming that all x_{ii} are zero.

The matrix of market shares, α_{ij}, is obtained by dividing each column by its column sum: $\alpha_{ij} = x_{ij}/\Sigma_i x_{ij} = x_{ij}/m_j$. Thus α_{ij} is the share of the total imports of country j that is supplied by country i, and $\Sigma_i \alpha_{ij} = 1$.

For some purposes it is also useful to define a matrix of coefficients $\lambda_{ij} = x_{ij}/\Sigma_j x_{ij} = x_{ij}/x_i$. The λ_{ij} define the regional distribution of the exports of country i, with $\Sigma_j \lambda_{ij} = 1$.

In principle, the α_{ij} can be expected to change over time with changes in relative export prices of competing countries. [3] As emphasised by Rhomberg [4], however, it is necessary to reduce the large number of relative prices entering the export demand functions if an empirically manageable system is the goal. My point of departure is a market share expression of the following form:

$$\alpha_{ij} = \frac{x_{ij}}{m_j} = \alpha_{ij}^0 \left(\frac{p_{ij}^x}{p_j^m} \right)^{-\sigma_j} \tag{1}$$

In this expression p_{ij}^x is the price of exports from country i to country j and p_j^m is the import price index for country j, i.e., a weighted average of the export prices of all countries supplying the jth market. Thus α_{ij} is assumed to be a function of only one relative price term involving a single import price index instead of n relative price terms involving pairwise comparisons of all export prices. Both p_{ij}^x and p_j^m are assumed to be measured on the same base period, so that α_{ij}^0 is the market share in the base period. Finally, σ_j is the elasticity of the real market share with respect to relative export prices and is assumed to be the same for all suppliers in the jth market.

Eq. (1) may be regarded as an approximation to Armington's elegant theoretical formulation of an export demand equation. [5] Strictly speaking, however, his formulation cannot lead directly to a real market share expression like eq. (1). This is because the basic import "good" for market j in his model is not the sum of the x_{ij} over all i (m_j is this notation) but rather a CES function of the x_{ij}, assuming a single, constant elasticity of substitution between all x_{ij} in the jth market. That is, his import good is defined by a quantity-index of the exports supplied by various countries rather than by the aggregate quantity itself. Correspondingly, his import price index is of the CES form rather than the linear form specified below (eq. 3).

---

[3] Other, non-price, factors may also affect market shares. A method of generalising the approach to allow for such factors will be developed below.

[4] Ch. 2, this volume.

[5] Armington, *op. cit.*

Despite these differences, the market share approach to export demand represented by eq. (1) clearly preserves the spirit of Armington's formulation. Aggregate imports in market *j* are regarded as a composite good, the real demand for which is determined by the corresponding import price index and other relevant variables. The exports of the supplying countries are regarded as imperfect substitutes in the composite import bundle, with the share of each depending ultimately on all relative export prices, as summarised in the import price index. The use of linear approximations to Armington's CES indices of price and quantity does some violence to the assumptions underlying the partitioning of the export demand equations in his model. In empirical applications the approximations are likely to be quite close, however, and the present approach is clearly superior in complete trade model solutions. This is because, as is shown below, it leads directly to a world trade solution in which the adding up properties that

$$m_j = \sum_i x_{ij} \, , \quad x_i = \sum_j x_{ij} \, , \quad \sum_i x_i = \sum_j m_j$$

are automatically preserved. This would not be a property of a CES system.

One final remark needs to be made regarding eq. (1). In subsequent sections, the parameter σ_j will be called the elasticity of substitution rather than the share elasticity. The elasticity of substitution is the underlying structural demand parameter, and σ_j would be a direct measure of the substitution elasticity if m_j and p_j^m were CES functions of x_{ij} and p_{ij}^x. Assuming that the linear approximations in the present model are close to the correct specifications, however, it is reasonable to regard σ_j as the substitution elasticity.

3. Demand and supply framework for traded goods

Each country model must contain structural demand and supply functions for exports and imports. A general import demand function for country i will contain the relative price of imported and domestic goods, plus other demand determinants, such as income and capacity utilisation. In order to specify the import demand function in a linear form with separable price terms, use is made of the approximation $(p_i^m/p_i) \cong (1 + p_i^m - p_i)$, where p_i^m and p_i are indices respectively of import and domestic prices with base period values of unity. It is also necessary to distinguish between those determinants of import demand which are endogenous in the complete macroeconomic model for country i, and those which are not. On the assumption that the supply of imports to any individual country is perfectly elastic, the import price index for country i is an exogenous variable in the country model, whereas the domestic price index is endogenous. Thus the structural import demand function of the ith country is written as:

$$m_i = a_{i1}p_i + b_{i1}p_i^m + \sum_{p=2}^{r} a_{ip}y_{ip} + \sum_{q=2}^{s} b_{iq}z_{iq}, \quad i = 1,...,n \qquad (2)$$

In this expression the a_{ij} are coefficients of the r endogenous variables y of the complete country model, with the domestic price index $(p_i \equiv y_{i1})$ separately distinguished from the $(r-1)$ other endogenous variables. Similarly, the b_{iq} are coefficients of the import price index $(p_i^m \equiv z_{i1})$ and the $(s-1)$ other predetermined variables z of the country model. Many of the a_{ip} and b_{iq} will be zero, since the corresponding variables of the complete model will not enter the import demand function. Finally, $|a_{i1}| = |b_{i1}|$ and $a_{i1} < 0$, since the indices are entered as the difference $(1 + p_i^m - p_i)$ with a single coefficient, prior to being separated into the exogenous and endogenous groupings. [6]

Because of the assumption that imports are in infinitely elastic

---

[6] The coefficient of the unitary term from the price variable is absorbed into a constant term – the coefficient of one of the z_{iq} which is a unit vector – in eq. (2).

supply at the price p_i^m, no explicit supply functions need be written down.[7] Given p_i^m, and the other variables in (2), m_i is fully determined. It remains to define the import price index to complete the discussion of the demand and supply framework for imports to a single country. The index is defined as a weighted average of the export prices of all other countries to country j:

$$p_j^m = \sum_i \alpha_{ij} p_{ij}^x , \qquad j = 1, ..., n. \tag{3}$$

In this expression, p_{ij}^x is the price of exports from country i to country j and α_{ij} is the share of country j's imports that is supplied by country i. Recall that here, as well as elsewhere in the paper, the $\alpha_{ii} = 0$, so that the summation over all i in equation (3) excludes the export price of country j itself, as indeed it should. Notice also that the α_{ij} are themselves a function of the p_{ij}^x and p_j^m in any period other than the base period for the price indices, as may be seen from eq. (1) above, unless the p_j^m are to be treated as fixed-weight indices, in which case the weights are given by the base period market shares.

Let us now turn to the export side. Eq. (1) determines the demand for the exports of country i to country j for given relative prices and total import demand in country j. The demand function for the total exports of country i is simply the sum of the x_{ij} for all j markets. The exact expression for x_{ij} in (1) is nonlinear, however, and the linear sum would not lend itself to convenient analytical solutons. Moreover, the linear sum of a logarithmic transformation of (1) would not be useful either, because it would be equivalent to a geometric average of the x_{ij} rather than their sum. It is therefore desirabie to linearise the demand function (1) as follows:

---

[7] An alternative view is to assume that (2) is a *mutatis mutandis* demand function which allows for any induced change in import price that may result from an exogenous change in, say, the income of the importing country. It is then unnecessary to assume a perfectly elastic supply in order to suppress the import supply function, but it is also then incorrect to treat the import price index as an exogenous variable in the import demand function of a single country, as is typically done in national models.

$$x_{ij} = \alpha_{ij}^0 (p_{ij}^x/p_j^m)^{-\sigma_j} m_j \qquad \text{(rearranging eq. (1))} \qquad \text{(1a)}$$

$$x_{ij} \cong \alpha_{ij}^0 [1 - \sigma_j(p_{ij}^x - p_j^m)] m_j \qquad \begin{array}{l}\text{(linearising the price} \\ \text{expression)}\end{array} \qquad \text{(1b)}$$

$$x_{ij} = \alpha_{ij}^0 m_j - \sigma_j \alpha_{ij}^0 p_{ij}^x m_j \qquad \text{(separating terms)} \qquad \text{(1c)}$$
$$+ \sigma_j \alpha_{ij}^0 p_j^m m_j$$

$$x_{ij} = \alpha_{ij}^0 m_j - \sigma_j \alpha_{ij}^0 m_j^0 p_{ij}^x \qquad \begin{array}{l}\text{(linearising cross-} \\ \text{products)}\end{array} \qquad \text{(1d)}$$
$$+ \sigma_j \alpha_{ij}^0 m_j^0 p_j^m$$

where the α_{ij}^0 are the base-period market shares (i.e., the shares where $p_{ij}^x = p_j^m = 1$) and the m_j^0 are the base period imports. [8]

The total demand for the exports of country i is obtained by summing (1d) over all the j markets:

$$x_i = \sum_j \alpha_{ij}^0 m_j - \sum_j \sigma_j \alpha_{ij}^0 m_j^0 p_{ij}^x + \sum_j \sigma_j \alpha_{ij}^0 m_j^0 p_j^m , \qquad (4)$$

$$i = 1, ..., n$$

The first term shows how the exports of country i would vary with the total import demands in its j markets if its realised market shares were the same as in the base period — that is to say, if *relative* prices remained constant so the second and third terms cancelled. The effects of changes in relative prices on the realised exports of country i depend on the elasticities of substitution σ_j between the exports of all competing countries in each of the j markets as well as on the base period exports ($x_{ij}^0 = \alpha_{ij}^0 m_j^0$) of country i to its j markets.

As it stands, eq. (4) relates export demand to $2(n-1)$ price variables, and would not be a useful specification in applications in-

---

[8] An export demand equation of the same general form as (1d) has also been suggested by Waelbroeck (without taking Armington's theory as a point of departure or introducing the substitution parameter) as a method for generalising the shares approach to trade model construction (see ch. 4, in this volume).

volving more than a few countries. However, a more useful form can be derived on the basis of further simplifying assumptions. Thus the second term in (4) is a weighted sum of the p_{ij}^x. In the absence of discriminating monopoly in export markets, however, the same price would be charged by country i in all j markets, and there are compelling practical reasons to assume that is the case. The j subscript may, therefore, be dropped from the export price variable and its coefficient becomes a constant: $\Sigma_j \sigma_j \alpha_{ij}^0 m_j^0 = \bar{\sigma}_i x_i^0$. This last expression for the constant is obtained by use of the identity $\alpha_{ij}^0 m_j^0 = \lambda_{ij}^0 x_i^0$ and the definition $\bar{\sigma}_i = \Sigma_j \sigma_j \lambda_{ij}^0$, or the weighted average elasticity of substitution in the export markets of country i.

The third term of (4) may also be simplified. Let us define an index of prices competitive to the exports of country i as follows:

$$p_i^{xc} = \frac{\Sigma_j \sigma_j \lambda_{ij}^0 p_j^m}{\Sigma_j \sigma_j \lambda_{ij}^0} = \sum_j (\sigma_j / \bar{\sigma}_i) \lambda_{ij}^0 p_j^m \tag{5}$$

with weights summing to unity. In this expression, p_j^m is a weighted index of the prices charged by all exporting countries in market j (see eq. (3) above) and the p_j^m are in turn weighted by the relative elasticities of substitution and the shares of the j markets in the total exports of country i, to yield an overall index of prices competitive to the exports of country i.[9] Given the foregoing assumptions and definitions, eq. (4) may be rewritten with transformed second and third terms as:

$$x_i = \sum_j \alpha_{ij}^0 m_j - (\bar{\sigma}_i x_i^0) p_i^x + (\bar{\sigma}_i x_i^0) p_i^{xc} . \tag{6}$$

Export demand is related to only two price indices with constant coefficients instead of the $2(n-1)$ prices involved in the more

[9] It is important to stress that, unlike the import price index, the weights for the export competitive price index include relative substitution elasticities as well as market shares. Only if the substitution elasticities are the same in all importing markets will the relative substitution elasticities drop out of the expression for p_i^{xc}.

general specification given in (4). This considerable simplification, however, is achieved at the cost of ignoring export price discrimination and possible differences in substitution elasticities over time.

The preceding development was based on the formulation of the market share function as specified in eq. (1). One difficulty with that formulation is that it makes no allowance for the effects of terms of sale other than product price on market shares. Delivery times in particular must be a factor in selecting among suppliers of close substitutes. Allowance for non-price factors may be made by conceiving of an "effective price" which reflects the positive or negative value of ancillary sales conditions as well as the market price itself. Thus the effective export price might be thought of as a multiple of the market price: $p_{it}^{xe} = k_{it} p_{it}^{x}$. Conceivably many factors could influence k_{it}, but a convenient, though possibly crude, assumption is that it varies in proportion with the rate of capacity utilisation in the exporting country: $k_{it} = k_i \bar{u}_{it}$, where $\bar{u}_{it}$ represents the percentage utilisation rate. Finally, since p_i^x is an index with a value of unity in the base period and p_i^{xc} should be placed on the same base, we may define

$$p_{it}^{xe} = u_{it} p_{it}^{x} , \tag{7}$$

where u_{it} is an index of the utilisation rate of exporting country i (equal to 1 in the same base period as the export price index) and the constant k_i divides out of the expression. [10]

How does recognition of the fact that effective export price may systematically diverge from measured price modify the previous specifications of the import and export demand functions? First, an effective import price index must be defined as:

---

[10] A capacity utilisation index for export-based industries would be more appropriate, but on the present level of aggregation it would scarcely be distinguishable from the economy-wide index. In a recent article, Gregory, R.G., 'United States Imports and Internal Pressure of Demand: 1948–68', *American Economic Review*, March 1971, the concept of effective price is employed in connection with import demand. The present development generalises the concept to include the export side and places it in a general equilibrium framework.

$$p_j^{me} = \sum_i \alpha_{ij} p_i^{xe} = \sum_i \alpha_{ij} u_i p_i^x \,, \qquad (8)$$

where the time subscripts have been eliminated to simplify the notation. This is the same expression as in the earlier definition of p_j^m given in (3), except for the substitution of p_i^{xe} for p_i^x in forming the weighted average of export prices, and the elimination of the j subscript on the export price index in recognition of our simplifying assumption that the export price charged by country i is the same in all j markets.

If the effective import price index as defined in (8) is to be included in the relative price term of the import demand function, it should be compared with a similarly constructed effective domestic price index. Just as before, however, it is desirable to linearise the expression for p^{me} itself as follows:

$$p_j^{me} = \sum_i \alpha_{ij} u_i p_i^x \cong \sum_i \alpha_{ij} (u_i + p_i^x - 1) = u_j^m + p_j^m - 1 \,, \qquad (9)$$

where $u_j^m = \Sigma_i \alpha_{ij} u_i$ is the weighted average utilisation index of all countries exporting to country j, and p_j^m is the measured import price index previously defined in eq. (3). The weights for the two indices are identical, as they should be, since both indices by hypothesis are components of the effective import price index. A corresponding linearisation of the domestic effective price is also in order, so that $p_i^e = u_i + p_i - 1$.

Upon making use of these definitions and linearisations, the new version of the import demand function of the ith country becomes:

$$m_i = a_{i1} p_i + a_{i2} u_i + b_{i1} p_i^m + b_{i2} u_i^m + \sum_{p=3}^n a_{ip} y_{ip} + \sum_{q=3}^n b_{iq} z_{iq} \qquad (10)$$

$i = 1, ..., n \,.$

Corresponding to the earlier version (2), the first four coefficients have the same absolute value but the first two carry a negative sign. By separating the price and utilisation variables, one is able to distinguish clearly between the two sources of a change in the effective import price: those due to alterations in market price and those related to changes in non-price sales conditions.

The export demand function requires similar modifications to allow for non-price factors affecting market shares. Expression (1) is unchanged in general form, but the original export and import price indices are replaced by p^{xe} and p^{me}. The same general linearisation procedure as before results in a slightly more complicated expression for the export demand function.

$$x_i = \sum_j \alpha_{ij}^0 m_j - (\bar{\sigma}_i x_i^0) p_i^x - (\bar{\sigma}_i x_i^0) u_i + (\bar{\sigma}_i x_i^0) p_i^{xc} + (\bar{\sigma}_i x_i) u_i^{xc} . \quad (11)$$

In this expression p_i^{xe} is represented by its components p_i^x and u_i, and correspondingly p_i^{xce} is represented by p_i^{xc} and an average utilisation index which is defined as:

$$u_i^{xc} = \sum_j (\sigma_j / \bar{\sigma}_i) \lambda_{ij}^0 u_j^m \qquad (12)$$

and which will be called the export competitive utilisation index by analogy with the export competitive price index (5). Upon rearranging the terms in (11) we obtain:

$$x_i = \sum_j \alpha_{ij}^0 m_j - (\bar{\sigma}_i x_i^0)(p_i^x - p_i^{xc}) - (\bar{\sigma}_i x_i^0)(u_i - u_i^{xc}) . \qquad (11a)$$

Thus the quantity of exports demanded responds to a change in either the market price or the intensity of capacity utilisation of the exporting country relative to the weighted average of its competitors in its various export markets.

It is apparent that the import and export demand functions in measured prices alone, given by (2) and (6), can be considered as special cases of the more general specifications in (10) and (11). If changes in nonprice supply factors, as proxied by changes in the intensity of capacity utilisation, do not appreciably affect import

and export demands, the utilisation terms may be eliminated from
(10) and (11), leaving the functions as originally specified in (2)
and (6). Another possibility is that the non-price factors are the
effective determinants of demand and that market prices themselves are unimportant, in which case the measured price terms
would drop out of (10) and (11).

It remains to specify the export supply function of the ith
country. A general linear specification would be:

$$p_i^x = a'_{ir} x_i + \sum_{p=1}^{r-1} a'_{ip} y_{ip} + \sum_{q=1}^{s} b'_{iq} z_{iq} . \tag{13}$$

As in the analogous import demand function, the y_{ip} are the r
endogenous variables in the complete country model, with $x_i \equiv y_{ir}$
separately distinguished, and the z_{iq} are the s predetermined variables. Of course, many of the a'_{ip} and b'_{iq} will be zero. The supply
function could include domestic input and product prices among
the endogenous variables, and possibly capacity utilisation as well.
The function has been normalised on the export price instead of
quantity because exports conceivably could be in perfectly elastic
supply, eliminating x_i from the equation.

Eqs. (11) and (13) are market demand and supply functions for
the export of country i. They can be solved for the partial equilibrium values of p_i^x and x_i for given values of the other included
variables. This would still be two steps removed from a general
equilibrium solution, however, since some of the export-deter-
mining variables are themselves endogenous in the complete country model, and others, although exogenous to the country model,
are endogenous in the complete trade model. A similar remark
applies to the import side.

4. The reduced form trade equations

The first step towards a general solution is taken by solving the ith
complete country model for the reduced form equations for m_i
and x_i, p_i^x and u_i as functions of only predetermined variables.

These solutions may be written as follows:

$$m_i = \beta_{i1} \sum_j \alpha_{ij}^0 m_j + \beta_{i2} p_i^m + \beta_{i3} p_i^{xc} + \beta_{i4} u_i^m + \beta_{i5} u_i^{xc}$$

$$+ \sum_{q=6}^{s} \beta_{iq} z_{iq} \qquad\qquad i = 1, ..., n \qquad (14)$$

$$x_i = \eta_{i1} \sum_j \alpha_{ij}^0 m_j + \eta_{i2} p_i^m + \eta_{i3} p_i^{xc} + \eta_{i4} u_i^m + \eta_{i5} u_i^{xc}$$

$$+ \sum_{q=6}^{s} \eta_{iq} z_{iq} \qquad\qquad i = 1, ..., n \qquad (15)$$

$$p_i^x = \gamma_{i1} \sum_j \alpha_{ij}^0 m_j + \gamma_{i2} p_i^m + \gamma_{i3} p_i^{xc} + \gamma_{i4} u_i^m + \gamma_{i5} u_i^{xc}$$

$$+ \sum_{q=6}^{s} \gamma_{iq} z_{iq} \qquad\qquad i = 1, ..., n \qquad (16)$$

$$u_i = \pi_{i1} \sum_j \alpha_{ij}^0 m_j + \pi_{i2} p_i^m + \pi_{i3} p_i^{xc} + \pi_{i4} u_i^m + \pi_{i5} u_i^{xc}$$

$$+ \sum_{q=6}^{s} \pi_{iq} z_{iq} . \qquad\qquad i = 1, ..., n \qquad (17)$$

The five externally-determined exogenous trade variables are separately denoted in the reduced forms. I shall refer to $\Sigma_j \alpha_{ij}^0 m_j$ as the external demand index. The β_{iq}, η_{iq}, γ_{iq} and π_{iq} are the reduced form coefficients, or impact multipliers, for m_i, x_i, p_i^x, and u_i. The domestic predetermined variables are included in the z_{iq}, along with any exogenous foreign variables not explicitly specified in the discussion of export and import markets.

In general, and unlike the underlying structural functions, the reduced form equations depend on all the predetermined variables in the model, and the reduced form coefficients are mixtures of all the structural parameters. In particular, the external demand variable appears in all the reduced form equations, even though it was absent from the structural import demand function. Similarly, the import price and utilisation indices appear in the export equations and the export-competitive price and utilisation indices appear in the import equations.

In the following sections the reduced form trade equations of the several countries, or less general variants of them, are incorporated into complete world trade systems of differing degrees of endogeneity and generality.

5. A family of linear trade models

5.1. Trade model 1

Let us begin with the simplest case by assuming that, for each country, real exports are externally determined and are independent of the measured export price and utilisation levels of the country. This assumption might be justified either on the basis that substitution elasticities are negligible in all export markets or that all effective export prices move so closely together that relative price changes are small enough to neglect. Having gone this far, we may as well assume also that real import demand is independent of effective import prices, either because substitution against domestic products is negligible or because effective import prices move closely with domestic prices. On these assumptions, the only structural trade equation for country i would be the import demand function, and it would exclude the price and utilisation variables that appear in the more general specification given by eq. (10) above. However, the exogenous volume of exports would appear in the reduced form equation for imports through its effects on other import determinants such as national income. The particular form of the reduced form equations for imports of the n countries on these assumptions is:

$$m_i = \beta_{i1} x_i + \sum_{q=2}^{s} \beta_{iq} z_{iq}, \qquad i = 1, ..., n .$$ (18)

Although exports are exogenous to each country model, they are endogenous in the trade model. The export function for country i in the trade model is:

$$x_i = \sum_j \alpha_{ij}^0 m_j , \qquad i = 1, ..., n \tag{19}$$

where the α_{ij}^0 are base period market shares.

The $2n$ import and export equations may be expressed in matrix form as:

$$m = Bx + z \tag{20}$$

$$x = Am \tag{21}$$

where m and x are the $(n \times 1)$ import and export vectors, B is the $(n \times n)$ diagonal matrix of the export multipliers β_{i1}, A is the $(n \times n)$ base period market share matrix and z is an $(n \times 1)$ vector of scalars representing the weighted sums of the domestic predetermined variables $(= \Sigma_{q=2}^s \beta_{iq} z_{iq})$ of the n countries.

Upon substitution of (21) into (20) and employing the $(n \times n)$ identity matrix I, the solution for imports is obtained as

$$m = (I - BA)^{-1} z \tag{22}$$

which in turn leads to

$$x = A(I - BA)^{-1} z . \tag{23}$$

What are the properties of this simultaneous solution?

First, it automatically satisfies the world trade constraint that total exports $(\Sigma_i x_i)$ must equal total imports $(\Sigma_i m_i)$, since the solution vector m in (22) is exhaustively allocated over the x vector in (23) by use of the export shares matrix A.

Second, the solution also satisfies all the individual country models. For the given domestic predetermined variables for country i, consistency is guaranteed between the endogenous value of imports and the domestically exogenous value of exports. More-over, upon substitution of the x_i calculated from the trade model into the reduced form equations for the other endogenous varia-bles, a complete set of country forecasts for domestic variables can be derived, and those will also be consistent with the calculated trade flows.

Third, in a forecasting application, the model makes systematic use of information about the geographic distribution of world trade in the export projections for each country, and it does this in a way which also yields consistent solutions for the individual country models.

Fourth, the solution yields a supportable level of world trade, in the sense that each country can absorb the calculated imports, given the consistent solution values for income and other endoge-nous variables appearing in its structural import demand function. It is merely implicitly assumed, however, that sufficient export capacity exists in each country to provide the calculated exports.

Fifth, in this linear case, the general solution can be found with a single calculation, provided that no policy or technical con-straints are violated in the solution. If such constraints are violated — for example, if the forecast trade balance were outside a tolera-ble range in one or more countries — the exogenous variables or parameters for those countries could be adjusted to yield new reduced form equations and a new world solution tested for con-sistency with the policy constraints.

5.2. Trade model 2

In this model the price of imports is allowed to influence the quantity demanded. On the export side, however, we retain the assumption of Model 1 that the quantity demanded from country i is externally determined and is independent of its export price or utilisation levels. The export supply price, on the other hand, may depend on the quantity demanded if the supply function is not perfectly elastic. Thus the structural import demand function of the ith country is as specified in eq. (2) and the export supply function is given by (13), but the price and utilisation terms are omitted from the general export demand function (11). These assumptions imply a situation in which the overall quantity of the imported good (product bundle) depends on its average price, but the allocation of purchases among the regional products comprising the bundle is independent of their prices.

Since both import prices and the quantity of exports are exogenous to each country model, the reduced form equations for imports and the export price level become:

$$m_i = \beta_{i1} x_i + \beta_{i2} p_i^m + \sum_{q=3}^{s} \beta_{iq} z_{iq} , \qquad i = 1, ..., n \tag{24}$$

$$p_i^x = \gamma_{i1} x_i + \gamma_{i2} p_i^m + \sum_{q=3}^{s} \beta_{iq} z_{iq} , \qquad i = 1, ..., n . \tag{25}$$

The model is completed by adding the definitional equations for the n import price indices, as given by (3) above, and the n export distribution eqs. (19).

In matrix notation, the complete system of $4n$ equations is:

$$m = B_1 x + B_2 p^m + z' \tag{26}$$

$$p^x = \Gamma_1 x + \Gamma_2 p^m + z'' \tag{27}$$

$$p^m = A' p^x \tag{28}$$

$$x = Am \tag{29}$$

where B_1 and B_2 are diagonal matrices of the β_{i1} and β_{i2} coefficients, Γ_1 and Γ_2 are the corresponding matrices of the γ_{i1} and γ_{i2} coefficients, A' is the transpose of A and the other symbols follow previous definitions.

The four eqs. (26)–(29) are sufficient to determine the unknown vectors m, x, p^x, p^m, although the algebraic solutions are cumbersome and will not be reproduced here. The system is a substantial advance over the first model, since it allows endogenous market forces to affect export and import prices and import quantities. It also retains the property of automatically satisfying the world trade constraint that $\Sigma \, x_i = \Sigma \, m_i$, since eq. (28) again exhaustively allocates the solution vector m over x. The principal deficiency of the model, of course, is that the export shares remain fixed at base-period values despite changing export prices. As observed in the discussion of Model 1, such stability in the market shares *could* result from negligible elasticities of substitution in all import markets or from common movements of prices in all markets. Either of these assumptions can be challenged as unduly restrictive, however, and the purpose of our next model is to allow export prices to affect the market shares.

5.3. Trade Model 3

This model incorporates the complete demand and supply framework specified earlier for the foreign trade sector of each country, on the assumption that measured and effective prices are the same. The underlying structural functions for each country consist of the import demand function (2), the export demand function (6) and the export supply function (13). The reduced forms for imports, exports and export prices are given by eqs. (14)–(16) with the external utilisation indices deleted. To these are added the definitional equations for the indices of import prices (3) and export competitive prices (5). The complete trade system in the customary matrix form is:

$$m = B_1 Am + B_2 p^m + B_3 p^{xc} + z' \tag{30}$$

$$x = H_1 Am + H_2 p^m + H_3 p^{xc} + z'' \tag{31}$$

$$p^x = \Gamma_1 Am + \Gamma_2 p^m + \Gamma_3 p^{xc} + z''' \tag{32}$$

$$p^m = A' p^x \tag{33}$$

$$p^{xc} = \Sigma_1 \Lambda \, \Sigma_2 \, p^m \, . \tag{34}$$

In this system B_1, B_2 and B_3 are diagonal matrices of the corresponding reduced form coefficients, similar definitions hold for the H_i and Γ_i matrices, Λ is the matrix of the λ_{ij}^0 $(= x_{ij}^0/x_i^0)$ coefficients defining the regional distribution of the exports of country i in the base period, Σ_1 is a diagonal matrix of the reciprocals of $\bar{\sigma}_i$, Σ_2 is a diagonal matrix of the σ_j and the other symbols are as defined earlier.

The complete system may be solved for the unknown vectors m, x, p^x, p^m and p^{xc}. This is a general equilibrium solution, in which the n export prices clear the export markets of the n countries and the corresponding prices and quantities of imports satisfy the import demand functions of the n countries. Moreover, the equilibrium trade values are also consistent with the domestic activity levels of all n countries, since the latter, just as the former, are functions of the same predetermined variables, including the equilibrium values of the indices of external demand, import prices and export competitive prices.

The system is only in short-run equilibrium, however, for two reasons. First, the country models may contain lagged endogenous variables in their domestic or foreign sectors, so that the reduced form equations yield only single period solutions. Second, nothing in the general solution prevents disequilibria in the payments balances of the various countries. Even if the national models were not dynamic, the equilibrium merchandise trade balances might be inconsistent with the balance of payments objectives in one or more countries, leading to policy reactions in subsequent periods which would alter the predetermined policy variables and lead to a new short-term equilibrium for the complete system. As discussed in connection with Model 1, in a forecasting context the discovery of excessive trade disequilibria in the complete solution could lead to a re-examination of the assumptions on exogenous policy variables or parameters in the various national models. Since trade prices are endogenous in Model 3, exchange rates would be included among the policy instruments that could be varied in the search for a general solution consistent with national and international policy objectives. [11]

[11] Although exchange rates have not been introduced explicitly in any of the models discussed herein because of a desire for expositional simplicity, it would not be difficult to do so.

Worth stressing also is the fact that the solution to Model 3 necessarily satisfies the world trade constraint. This is not as transparent as in the earlier models, in which the base period shares matrix was used explicitly to allocate imports completely to exports. Nonetheless, Model 3 accomplishes the same result *by implicitly allocating imports to exports according to current market shares as determined endogenously in the model.* Thus, the solution yields an equilibrium set of market clearing export prices. Weighted averages of these export prices form the import price indices which determine import quantities through the structural import demand functions (2). The same export and import prices and quantities satisfy the export demand functions (6), with the import prices entering as weighted averages forming the export competitive price indices. Finally, since the export demand functions were obtained by linear aggregation of the n current market share equations of each country (1d), the export total for each country is implicitly obtained as the sum of its current shares in all markets, and since this is true for every country, the world trade constraint is satisfied. [1][2]

---

[1][2] A rigorous proof of this proposition may be developed as follows. First, recall that the export demand function (6) was obtained as a specialisation of the original specification given in (4), which in turn was derived by summing the market share equations (1d). An equivalent way of writing (6) is:

$$x_i = \sum_j \alpha_{ij}^0 m_j - \sum_j \sigma_j \alpha_{ij}^0 m_j^0 p_i^x + \sum_j \sigma_j \alpha_{ij}^0 m_j^0 p_j^m . \tag{a}$$

(This expression is obtained from (6) by eliminating p_i^{xc} in terms of its definition as given in (5) and by using the relationships $\lambda_{ij}^0 x_i^0 = \alpha_{ij}^0 m_j^0$ and $x_i^0 = \sum_j \alpha_{ij}^0 m_j^0$. It differs from the more general function (4) because of the simplifying assumption of a single export price for country i.) Upon summing the export demand functions (a) for all countries, an expression for total world exports is obtained and seen to be equal to total world imports:

$$\sum_i x_i = \sum_i \sum_j \alpha_{ij}^0 m_j - \sum_i \sum_j \sigma_j \alpha_{ij}^0 m_j^0 p_i^x + \sum_i \sum_j \sigma_j \alpha_{ij}^0 m_j^0 p_j^m$$

$$= \sum_j m_j \sum_i \alpha_{ij}^0 - \sum_j \sigma_j m_j^0 \sum_i \alpha_{ij}^0 p_i^x + \sum_j \sigma_j m_j^0 p_j^m \sum_i \alpha_{ij}^0$$

$$= \sum_j m_j - \sum_j \sigma_j m_j^0 p_j^m + \sum_j \sigma_j m_j^0 p_j^m = \sum_j m_j \tag{b}$$

where use has been made of the relationships $\sum_i \alpha_{ij}^0 = 1$ and $p_j^m = \sum_i \alpha_{ij}^0 p_i^x$.

It also follows that once the complete set of import prices and quantities and export prices has been obtained for all countries from the simultaneous solution, the current export shares matrix can easily be calculated by returning to the underlying market share eq. (1d), and hence the geographic distribution of trade is fully determined. [13]

Thus, Model 3 comprises a general equilibrium approach to the endogenous explanation of changes in market shares as well as in the total imports and exports of the n countries or regions. Whether it would provide a good explanation of actual changes in observed market shares is uncertain and depends on several factors: principally, these are the extent to which the basic share hypothesis of eq. (1) is valid, the extent to which the approximations involved in the linearisation and aggregation of the share equations may introduce error, the extent of specification error in the domestic sectors of the underlying national models, and the importance of random disturbances not incorporated in the deterministic solution. These empirical questions lie outside the scope of the present paper.

5.4. Trade Model 4

This is the last and most general of the models to be presented in this chapter. It differs from Model 3 only in incorporating the hypothesis that effective prices may differ from market prices because of non-price factors affecting conditions of sale and delivery. The underlying structural equations in the national models include the import and export demand functions (10) and (11)

---

[13] Thus (1d) may be rewritten as:

$$x_{ij} = \alpha_{ij}^0 m_j - \sigma_j \alpha_{ij}^0 m_j^0 p_j^x + \sigma_j \alpha_{ij}^0 m_j^0 p_j^m \qquad (c)$$

upon imposing the assumption of a single export price. Given the model solutions for m_j, p_i^x and p_j^m, the values of the x_{ij} are fully determined, and so are the current market shares $\alpha_{ij} = x_{ij}/m_j$. Also, of course, the row sums of the x_{ij} add up to the x_i as can be seen by summing eq. (c) over j and comparing it with eq. (a) of the preceding footnote, and the column sums of the x_{ij} add up to the m_j, as can easily be shown by using general procedures of the preceding footnote.

and the export supply function (13). The reduced forms for imports, exports, export prices and the domestic capacity utilisation index are given by eqs. (14)–(17), and to these we add the definitional identities for p_i^m, u_i^m, p_i^{xc} and u_i^{xc} as given in (3), (9), (5) and (12). The complete model in matrix form is:

$$m = B_1 Am + B_2 p^m + B_3 p^{xc} + B_4 u^m + B_5 u^{xc} + z' \tag{35}$$

$$x = H_1 Am + H_2 p^m + H_3 p^{xc} + H_4 u^m + H_5 u^{xc} + z'' \tag{36}$$

$$p^x = \Gamma_1 Am + \Gamma_2 p^m + \Gamma_3 p^{xc} + \Gamma_4 u^m + \Gamma_5 u^{xc} + z''' \tag{37}$$

$$u = \Pi_1 Am + \Pi_2 p^m + \Pi_3 p^{xc} + \Pi_4 u^m + \Pi_5 u^{xc} + z'''' \tag{38}$$

$$p^m = A'p^x \tag{39}$$

$$u^m = A'u \tag{40}$$

$$p^{xc} = \Sigma_1 \Lambda \Sigma_2 p^m \tag{41}$$

$$u^{xc} = \Sigma_1 \Lambda \Sigma_2 u^m \tag{42}$$

As usual, the B_i, H_i, Γ_i and Π_i are diagonal matrices of reduced form coefficients. The vector of domestic utilisation indices is represented by u, whereas u^m and u^{xc} are the vectors of the u_i^m and u_i^{xc}. All other symbols are as defined earlier.

Thus, allowance for non-price factors affecting the behaviour of market shares has increased the size of the system from the $5n$ equations of model 3 to $8n$ equations in Model 4. This involves no difficulties in principle, however, and the complete linear system may be solved for the unknown vectors m, x, p^x, u, p^m, u^m, p^{xc} and u^{xc}.

The formal structure of the system is identical to Model 3, and all the properties of the latter model carry over to the new one. It, too, is a general equilibrium system which automatically satisfies the world trade constraint and determines not only the total import and export flows of all countries but also their geographic distribution.

4. THE METHODOLOGY OF LINKAGE *

J. WAELBROECK

1. Introduction

A substantial number of models of the world economy have been built since the war.[1] These models were built from scratch and, hence, the representation therein of the national economies tends to be stereotyped. The explanation of world trade was a major preoccupation of the authors and, accordingly, the international trade equations tend to be the centrepiece of the models. No consistency problem arises, as it is easy when building from scratch to avoid the inconsistencies which arise when existing models are combined.

The LINK project is the first to undertake the building of a world model by combining existing national short-run models. This approach has the advantages of both harnessing a fund of detailed knowledge of the national economies and of accumulated empirical research, which is vastly greater than could be marshalled by a single research team working within the constraints of a research project. The disadvantage lies in the fact that it is not easy to build up a consistent whole out of pieces which are built up by separate groups of researchers pursuing different objectives.

The fusion of country models into a workable model of the world economy will necessarily be a gradual process. It is neces-

---

* I have derived much benefit from study of Rhomberg's recent article on this subject – Rhomberg, R.R., 'Possible Approaches to a Model of World Trade and Payments', *IMF Staff Papers*, March 1970, which was originally presented to the Hakone meeting of Project LINK.

[1] See, for instance, an excellent survey of the subject by Taplin, G.B., 'Models of World Trade', *IMF Staff Papers*, November 1967.

sary to get the system working as soon as possible, as only from
real experience will it be possible to judge how serious each of the
many problems which could be foreseen at the start really are, and
to discover which serious problems had not been foreseen initially.

This justifies a flexible strategy, with room for alternative solutions of the linkage problem, and for both "quickie" solutions
which make it possible to put LINK on the computer with as little
trouble as possible, and more elaborate and theoretically satisfactory solutions whose implementation is, however, more time con-
suming. As will be seen, the theory of linkage is not complicated;
the main problems are data gathering, estimation of the relevant
equations and the even more formidable problem of putting the
system on the computer. Accordingly, this paper will stress the
practical problems rather than the theory.

2. Direct linkage procedures

2.1. A trial and error approach

The simplest approach is the trial and error approach used in the
"Mini-LINK" exercise completed early in 1970. [2] This implies
solving country models for alternative levels of world trade, given
a fixed level of world prices, and computing the corresponding
levels of world imports. The solution of the system is that for
which world imports and exports balance.

This quickie solution proved both cheap and interesting in
shedding light on important properties of the national models. It
also seems to have provided surprisingly satisfactory forecasts of
trade. It, however, reflects only one type of linkage between economies, via the total volume of international trade, to the neglect,
for instance, of price and direction of trade effects. Even balance
between total imports and exports is not assured in a true sense.
For although total computed imports do match the assumed volume of international trade, nothing in the procedure guarantees

---

[2] See ch. 13 in this volume for a discussion of the "Mini-LINK" exercise.

that the volume of international trade also equals the sum of computed exports of individual countries.

2.2. Simultaneous solution of a set of national models

A more elaborate approach is to combine national models into a large world model in which variables which in country models are treated as foreign exogenous variables become endogenous. Before this can be done, it is necessary to iron out minor inconsistencies in the formulation of different country models; thus if the Japanese model uses as a foreign exogenous variable a U.S. aggregate which is not computed in the Wharton model, it is necessary either to reformulate the Japanese equation, or to add to the U.S. model an appropriate equation.

The resulting world model is very large. The present LINK model, is a 600 equation system which contains numerous non-linearities. This could be solved by brute force. It is far more efficient to exploit the special structure of the system to obtain a solution more cheaply.

The structure of the system may be brought out as follows. In the discussion I will assume that the model dealt with is linear, in order to take advantage of the clarity of matrix notation, but the argument is quite general. Each country model can always be written in the form

$$A_i y_i + \sum_j B_{ij} y_j = C_i z_i , \qquad (1)$$

where A_i is the endogenous matrix of the model of country i, y_i and y_j are endogenous variables in models of countries i and j, B_{ij} are matrices of coefficients of variables of third countries in equations of the model of country i, C_i is the matrix of coefficients of exogenous variables in country i's model which are not endogenous in models of other countries and z_i the vector of those variables. Writing the model in this form requires minor adjustments. As mentioned above, minor adjustments may be necessary to ensure that foreign variables used in the model of a country are in fact defined by the model of the other country. If "world variables" are used – e.g. world imports in the export equation – they should be decomposed into country variables using the relevant definitional equation.

A formulation of the system for the three country case is given below.

$$
\begin{bmatrix} A_1 & B_{12} & B_{13} \\ B_{21} & A_2 & B_{23} \\ B_{31} & B_{32} & A_3 \end{bmatrix}
\begin{bmatrix} y_1 \\ y_2 \\ y_3 \end{bmatrix} =
\begin{bmatrix} C_1 & z_1 \\ C_2 & z_2 \\ C_3 & z_3 \end{bmatrix} . \tag{2}
$$

It is inefficient to solve such a system by inverting the endogenous matrix and computing the reduced form and solution in the usual way. In practice it turns out that in each country model only a small number of equations, which I will call the "linkage equations", contain variables endogenous in models of other countries. Sometimes only the export equation contains such variables. The other equations, the "domestic equations", contain no variables endogenous in other country models.

Attaching a * to variables and coefficients of linking equations, and a ** to the variables and coefficients of domestic equations, the model may be rewritten as

$$
\begin{bmatrix} A_1^{**} & 0 & 0 \\ 0 & A_2^{**} & 0 \\ 0 & 0 & A_3^{**} \\ A_1^{*} & B_{12}^{*} & B_{13}^{*} \\ B_{21}^{*} & A_2^{*} & B_{23}^{*} \\ B_{31}^{*} & B_{32}^{*} & A_3^{*} \end{bmatrix}
\begin{bmatrix} y_1 \\ y_2 \\ y_3 \end{bmatrix} = Cz \tag{3}
$$

where C and z are the matrix and vector of all exogenous variables. This exposes the fact that a large part of the endogenous matrix is quasi-diagonal. The C matrix likewise is nearly quasi-diagonal: most exogenous variables in the equations that relate to a country do not appear in equations for other countries; there are only a few exceptions, for instance time trends.

Call the variables defined by the linking equations the "linking variables". Then an efficient computational procedure is to:

(a) express the domestic variables as functions of the linking and exogenous variables by an appropriate reduced form.

(b) using these reduced forms, substitute for the domestic variables in the linking equations in terms of the linking and exogenous variables, and solve the resulting system for the linking variables in terms of the exogenous variables.

(c) using the reduced form obtained, substitute for the linking variables in terms of the exogenous variables in the equations of the reduced form obtained by solving each country's domestic equations.

In the linear case, a solution is obtained in three steps without the need for iteration. In the non-linear case it will as usual be necessary to assume appropriate initial values of all the endogenous variables and to iterate. In the non-linear case in particular, it may be important to take account of special features of the linking matrix. For instance, as certain U.S variables appear in the Canadian and Japanese models without any reciprocal dependence of the U.S. on the Canadian and Japanese economies, these U.S. variables should be calculated before the Canadian and Japanese equations are solved. It may turn out that there is blockwise dependence between the economies of the Common Market countries, and this will likewise have to be taken account of in solving the system. Finally, it is clear that the pattern of solution can vary. The pattern described is the clearest one from a didactic point of view, but the model structure can be exploited efficiently by many solution patterns, all based on the same principle.

2.3. Linkage via international variables

A slightly different formulation may be advantageous in certain cases; it is a generalisation of the trial and error approach described above. Instead of expressing endogenous variables of country models as functions of endogenous variables of other models and exogenous variables, they can be expressed as functions of world variables and exogenous variables. Each country model is written as

$$A_i y_i + D_i w = C_i z_i \qquad (4)$$

and an international submodel is added which defines world variables. Some will be true world variables — e.g. world imports or world prices. In other cases a country variable is relabelled as a world variable: thus if U.S. GNP plays a role in a Canadian equation the international submodel is thought of as containing an equation defining the world variable GNPUSw = GNPUS (in the computer programme there will be an expression relabelling the variable, which will not change the size of any matrix which is to be inverted).

The world model then takes the form

$$
\begin{bmatrix}
A_1 & 0 & 0 & D_1 \\
0 & A_2 & 0 & D_2 \\
0 & 0 & A_3 & D_3 \\
E_1 & E_2 & E_3 & I
\end{bmatrix}
\begin{bmatrix}
y_1 \\ y_2 \\ y_3 \\ w
\end{bmatrix}
=
\begin{bmatrix}
C_1 & z_1 \\
C_2 & z_2 \\
C_3 & z_3 \\
C_4 & z_4
\end{bmatrix}
\qquad (5)
$$

where I is the unit matrix, E_i are the matrices of coefficients of the equations defining world variables as functions of country endogenous variables and C_4 is the matrix of coefficients of country exogenous variables which appear in the definition of the world variables. w is the vector of world variables and z_4 is the vector of country exogenous variables which appear in their definitional equations.

The model can be solved by a three stage procedure which is similar in principle to that applied to eq. (3). As before, in the linear case, a solution is obtained in three steps without iteration. In the non-linear case, it is necessary to start from proper initial values and to iterate.

From a computational point of view, the formulation (5) is advantageous if the same world variables appear in the model of several countries. Then the E_i matrices will have fewer rows than the A_i^* matrices taken together, and the system of equations solved at step (b) of the procedure will be smaller. The trial and error approach described in sect. 2.1 is a special case of a system of type (5) in which only one world endogenous variable is defined.

2.4. Omitted definitions and consistency of the model

In trial and error linkage, the search for a solution is simplified by treating such variables as world prices as exogenous instead of defining them by appropriate equations; there is inconsistency between the values of world variables and the values of the corresponding country variables. Even the more elaborate solution procedures described in sects. 2.2 and 2.3 do not assure complete consistency of the solution of the world model. This is because a world model must satisfy balance equations which are not required in country models. These equations are the balances between total exports and imports.

There is no guarantee that solving the model (3) will yield export and import figures for countries which balance at the world level. If it is desired to assure this balance, then the procedure described must be modified.

It may be argued that the problem is unimportant, because the discrepancy is likely to be small. If builders of country models have used consistent international trade data this will be true for the sample period over which their models were estimated; but it is well known that international trade figures produced by different countries are not consistent. In any case there is nothing which guarantees consistency for forecasts outside of the sample period and for simulation runs of LINK.

From a theoretical point of view, inconsistency between imports and exports implies that there is a discrepancy between aggregate resources and expenditures: it is as though there was net borrowing from, or lending to, the planet Mars. Via the multiplier and accelerator this imaginary extra-terrestrial lending may have a substantial effect on changes in world income and expenditures.

The easiest way to patch over the difficulty is to calculate one country's exports as a residual; but this makes the results of LINK meaningless for that country. It seems preferable to allocate the discrepancy to all countries in proportion to their exports, or according to any other reasonable criteria. This implies adding to the models (3) and (5) equations defining the discrepancy between imports and exports as calculated by the equations of country models, and adding to exports as calculated by each country's equation an appropriate fraction of the discrepancy. The reformulated model can be solved by the three step procedure already outlined.

2.5. The direction of international trade and its importance

One of the striking features of the world economy is the existence of blocks of closely interdependent countries. U.S. fluctuations are immediately transmitted to Canada, but economic trends in North America and in Europe have often diverged. It is essential to catch this feature of the world economy in LINK.

The answer lies in defining world imports in each country's export equation as an index weighted according to the commodity and geographic structure of the country's exports. This procedure recognises that an increase in French imports means much more to Germany than to Canada. The use of unweighted imports would imply that increased French imports have the same effect on Canada's exports as an equal increase in imports of the United States.

This implies that in linkage of country models, it will be necessary to define a weighted world import total for each country. For an identical reason, it will prove desirable to define for each country a "competing exports" price index. The number of world variables in the final version of LINK will thus be large. As the choice between the linkage schemes (3) and (5) depends on the comparison between the number of linking equations in (3) and of world variables in (5), this means that the formulation (3) will in the long-run prove to be the best, to the extent at least that direct linkage is not abandoned as a method of solving LINK.

3. Bilateral linkage

Direct linkage is the procedure which best meets the basic objectives of Project LINK of using as basic building blocks real models built to solve problems of policy and forecasting in individual countries, and kept alive on a continuing basis by re-estimation and amendments inspired by everyday usage of the models. This distinguishes the project from other world models, which made good journal articles but were never tested on real problems. This philosophy makes it desirable to alter the models as little as possible, so that the models subjected to the test of LINK simulations are really the models used by country teams in their own work as forecasters and policy advisers.

The drawback of direct linkage is that it does not lead to a logically satisfactory picture of the mechanisms which link countries together. There are import and export functions, and re-weighting of world imports on the basis of the export structure of each country does establish a connection between exports and the geographic and commodity pattern of imports. But the connection between exports and imports of individual countries is not very clear, and is further obscured by the fact that the discrepancy between exports and imports computed according to the model equations has be distributed between exporters.

From a theoretical point of view, the ideal way to link economies together by foreign trade is to specify equations explaining each bilateral trade flow. For reasons which have been convincingly set out by Rhomberg [3], however, this is not practicable. Information on the value of bilateral trade flows is hard to come by, information on the corresponding volume and price indices even more so. It also seems that bilateral trade flows can adequately be explained only by equations containing a large number of variables reflecting the many factors which influence trade between every pair of countries.

Bilateral linkage is not practicable as a general approach to linkage. It may, however, be worth experimenting with it in attempts to study the relations between such closely inter-dependent groups of countries as Canada, the U.S.A. and Japan, or the Common Market countries. That this is feasible is indicated by several studies of U.S.-Canadian trade and U.S.-Japanese trade, as well as

---

[3] Rhomberg, *op. cit.*

recent work by Barten on intratrade of the Common Market countries. [4]

This idea raises the problem of combining the bilateral approach used for part of the trade flows, with some other approach applied to the rest of international trade. This leads to the mixed approach to linkage which is briefly described in sect. 5.

4. Linkage by means of an import allocation model: The shares approach

Far more practicable as a method of linkage is what Rhomberg [5] has termed the "shares approach". Whereas in direct linkage exports and imports are computed independently and brought into balance by an ad hoc adjustment, in the shares approach computed imports are allocated to individual exporters by appropriate functions designed so that the total amount allocated to exporters equals imports.

The best known version of this approach is the Tyszinski [6] method of forecasting exports, in which it is assumed that the share of each exporter in the imports of a commodity by a country is constant. This has been tested empirically with convincing results which suggest that most of the variation of exports can be explained by a combination of a trend with a Tyszinski term. [7] Little export variation is left to be explained by other variables.

In spite of this empirical success, the constant shares approach cannot be used except possibly in preliminary work on linkage, because it does not reflect changes in competitive strength. Fortunately, it is not difficult to design versions of the shares approach which take account of the effect of prices and other factors affect-

---

[4] Barten, A.P., 'An Import Allocation Model for the Common Market', *Cahiers Economiques de Bruxelles*, No. 50, 1971.

[5] *Ibid.*

[6] Tyszinski, H., 'World Trade in Manufactured Commodities 1889–1950', *Manchester School*, September 1951.

[7] Tims, W. and F.M. Meyer zu Schlochtern, 'Foreign Demand and the Development of Dutch Exports', *Cahiers Economiques de Bruxelles*, No. 15, 1962; see also Waelbroeck, J., 'La demande à l'exportation et l'évolution des exportations belges', *Cahiers Economiques de Bruxelles,* No. 15, 1962.

ing competitivity on the shares of individual exporters in a country's imports. In the linear case, the exports from country i to country j would be equal to

$$E_{ij} = s_{ij}M_j + \sum_k t_{ijk}(R_{ik} - R_{wjk}) \tag{6}$$

where E_{ij} is exports from i to j, s_{ij} is a coefficient satisfying $\sum_i s_{ij} = 1$, the t_{ijk} are appropriate coefficients, R_{ik} is the kth factor determining export competitivity and

$$R_{wjk} = \sum_i t_{ijk}R_{ijk} / \sum t_{ijk}$$

is the average competitiveness of countries. If a constant term r_{ij} is included, then it must be true that $\sum_i r_{ij} = 0$. It is reasonable to require that for each k the t_{ijk} have the same sign, and that the s_{ij} be positive.

The approach can be extended to non-linear formulations of the export equations, for instance to elasticity of substitution schemes, the formulae being complicated, though computable.

The procedure achieves consistency between exports and imports by two devices:

(a) the form of the functions is such that doubling imports in a given market doubles total exports to that market.

(b) the form of the export functions dictates the definition of the variables which measure average competitiveness of exporters to a given market.

More refined formulations have been proposed in the literature on estimation of consumer demand curves which guarantee, in addition to the additivity and homogeneity properties of the approach defined above, that demand curves are compatible with utility functions for each country. This would be a gain if it were believed that the conditions for existence of community welfare functions are satisfied in practice.

From a practical point of view, the chief difficulty is that it will be difficult to estimate import allocation functions for each commodity group imported by each member of LINK. In the initial stage, at least, it will be necessary to use parameters chosen a priori in the light of the work of McDougall [8], Ginsburg [9], Junz and Rhomberg [10], Waelbroeck [11], and others, on measuring the elasticity of substitution between exports of different commodity groups by pairs of countries.

The task of estimation would be much simplified if the shares approach was applied to total world imports instead of to imports of each country. It would be sufficient to estimate equations allocating total world imports to individual suppliers. This is not a good solution, however, as such functions are not capable of taking account of direction of trade effects of the type discussed in sect. 5. Such a linkage technique could not account for the fact that the Belgian economy moves more closely in step with that of other European countries than with the economy of the United States.

A realistic appraisal of what can be accomplished within the time and money constraints of LINK suggests that the grand task of estimating, in a truly proper manner, all the parameters involved in the full version of the shares approach cannot be completed. It will be necessary to merge together pieces of information gathered in partial studies of elasticities of substitution, pressure of demand effects on exports and Tyszinski effects. The requirements of LINK will suggest the need for additional research on these problems. The estimation problems raised by the shares approach do reduce its attractiveness, but do not warrant abandonment of the approach.

---

[8] MacDougall, G.D.A., 'British and American Exports, a Study Suggested by the Theory of Comparative Costs', *Economic Journal*, December 1951, and September 1952.

[9] Ginsburg A., *American and British Regional Export Determinants*, North-Holland, 1969.

[10] Junz, H.B. and R.R. Rhomberg, 'Prices and Export Performance of Industrial Countries 1953–1963', *IMF Staff Papers*, July 1965.

[11] Waelbroeck, J. and E. Rosselle, La Demande à l'Exportation pour les Pays du Marché Commun', *Cahiers Economiques de Bruxelles*, No. 38, 1968.

5. A mixed approach

The approaches described above are not incompatible; it is quite feasible to combine them if this seems advantageous. In particular, there is great interest in studying closely the transmission of fluctuations within the U.S.-Canada-Japan and Common Market zones. This makes it desirable to have a way of separating trade within these zones from the rest of the world trade, and perhaps to use a different linkage technique to account for intra and extra zone trade. From the computing point of view, there is no difficulty in solving a model in which, for example, U.S.-Canada-Japan trade is handled by the bilateral approach, Common Market intra-trade by the shares approach, and the rest of the world trade by direct linkage. In practice the computer programme would solve the models of countries belonging to the same trading zones in blocks, the blocks being linked together and to third countries by a distinct set of linking equations. Such a programme structure has great attractiveness for study of the forecasting and policy problems of members of such zones. The way in which international trade data is published in statistical publications makes it possible to obtain the trade data broken down by regions which is required to implement the mixed approach.

6. Missing links

Perhaps the most interesting question raised by the LINK project is whether simulation of the completed world model will reproduce convincingly the synchronised up and downswings of economic activity of different countries which are such a striking feature of the world business cycle. The answer depends on whether the links established between countries by the export and import equations of the present models are sufficiently powerful to account for this feature of economic acitivity.

The first results of the "Mini-LINK" exercise suggest that the answer may well be negative. Solving country models for different levels of world trade suggests that the "reflection elasticities" which measure the sensitivity of a country's imports to a 1% increase in world trade are not very high in some of the present models. This means that the impact of an impulse originating in one country will be quickly dissipated as it spreads throughout the world economy. Of course "Mini-LINK", which covered a single period and involved drastic simplifications of linkage mechanisms, cannot settle the issue definitively.

My experience in building and working with a national model leads me to suspect that a reason for this apparent bias may be that national model builders have much better access to data on their own country than to foreign data. This may lead them systematically to include domestic variables in their equations, and exclude foreign variables, whenever this is not obviously a gross distortion of reality. As there is such a striking parallelism between economic developments in different countries, this does not prevent model builders from obtaining good fits for their equations.

It is therefore worth while giving some thought to the question of whether existing models do reflect all the links which exist between the economies of different countries. "Missing links" may be of two types:

(a) they may be terms which are wrongly omitted from export and import equations, whose inclusion would strengthen or alter the nature of the linkage established between the economies of different countries by foreign trade.

(b) they may be mechanisms linking economies together other than via foreign trade.

Study of the models built up by members of Project LINK and of recent quantitative research on forecasting trade gives some indications on what these missing links may be.

As to links via foreign trade, it is necessary to keep in mind the possibility that the current specification of export functions may be quite wrong. Anyone who has experience in estimating such functions knows that the process is an unholy one in which the econometrician, wedded to the idea that the price elasticity of demand is definitely less than -1, keeps trying new specifications until persistence and luck bring what he desires. This is not a recommendable procedure, and the poor forecasting accuracy of present export functions suggest that it is also not an effective one.

The problem may be one of poor data instead of poor specification, and recent work by Kravis and Lipsey [12] points to this. Perhaps errors of observation swamp the true price variability; biasing hopelessly any estimates. The remedy is then to follow their example and gather price data directly from firms instead of relying on unit values, and this is something that statistical institutes should be able to do.

It is interesting, however, to take stock of ideas about new ways of specifying export equations in LINK models and elsewhere. This survey leads to the table on the next page.

Even more interesting questions are posed by the possibility that linkages might operate in other ways than via international trade flows. Non-trade linkages have not been reflected in the LINK model so far, but research is under way to clarify the issues involved.

A very obvious type of linkage is via capital and monetary markets: recent monetary events are witness of the forces which are unleashed by interest and exchange arbitrage and dramatically multiplied by speculation. Proper modelling of such interactions requires extensive research to construct monetary sectors in the individual country models, and to clarify the logical issues involved. Extensive monetary sub-sectors have been developed in the U.S., Canada, Italy and Belgium, while the paper by Amano on capital flows in this volume deals with the problem both from a theoretical and empirical point of view.

The response of policy makers to surpluses or deficits, originating either in current or capital transactions, also affects in a vital way the international transmission of fluctuations. It should be recognised that the speed and timing of transmission depends in a complex way on the decision rules followed by policy makers.

A third issue is that some variables can perhaps not be properly explained by a world model of the LINK type, built up by adding

[12] Kravis, I.B. and R.E. Lipsey, *Price Competitiveness in World Trade*, Studies in International Economic Relations, No. 6, N.B.E.R., 1971.

Table 1
Specifications of export equations

Determinants of competitivity	Status of problem
Pressure of demand: appearance of excess capacity within a country enables its producers to beat their competitors by offering quicker delivery dates. This leads to an increase in exports and a drop in imports. This strengthens sharply international linkage and changes its time pattern, by making the current balance more sensitive to changes in demand and by causing an immediate impact of demand on exports before it has had time to affect wages and prices.	This is by now accepted by most model builders, though the idea has as yet found little reflection in international trade theory.
Export prices and domestic costs: this amounts to introducing supply elements into the export function in a way which is reasonable if domestic markets are not perfectly competitive. Introduction of such terms into the export function also obviously strengthens linkage between countries.	Such a term appears in the export equation of the Dutch model.
Export prices depend on the domestic pressure of demand and on world prices: This can be justified either by inelasticity of export supply or by the presence of imperfect competition. Introduction of a pressure of demand term strengthens linkage, introduction of a world price term weakens it, except in conjunction with an export price – domestic costs discrepancy term in the export function.	The Japanese and Belgian export price equations have pressure of demand terms; in addition, the Belgian equation has a world price term. The need to introduce a world price term is strongly suggested by the recent research of Kravis and Lipsey[a] on effective export prices.
Purchasing power parity effects: Changes in exports become a function not of changes in relative prices, but of the absolute discrepancy between domestic prices of exportables. This is the most drastic amendment of the specification of the export function, as it implies that the long term price elasticity of demand for exports is infinite. This changes not only the strength of linkage but its dynamic modus operandi.	Positive results obtained by Van der Beld[b], but further research seems needed.

[a] Kravis and Lipsey, *op. cit.*
[b] Van der Beld, C.A. and D. Van der Werf, 'A Note on International Competitivity', *Economia Internazionale,* May 1966.

together individual country models. A chief example is commodity prices: here there is clearly a need for estimation of world behavioural equations.

A last thought which comes to mind is that there may well be "psychological" linkages. In this age of media, fears of inflation and shortages, waves of optimism or pessimism may well cross frontiers without being transmitted by observable variables. The likelihood of such invisible linkages is enhanced by the growth of multinational corporations who plan their strategy on a world basis. Research on this topic was initiated by Grinwis [13], who studied the correlation matrix of residuals from behavioural equations in different countries to detect the possible influence of such common invisible factors. The results were negative, however, except for investments.

7. Concluding remarks

This paper has examined from a practical point of view the different methods of linkage which may be used to build a world model by connecting together existing country models. We have discussed the range of alternative linkage techniques which are to be experimented with. Experience acquired so far shows that solving LINK is a big task in computer programming, but certainly not an insoluble one. As sect. 6 of the paper shows, there is a wide range of unsolved problems in the study of the international transmission of fluctuations on which Project LINK promises to shed new light.

[13] Grinwis, M., 'Bestaan er Psychologisch Schakels Tussen de Ekonomie van de Verschillende Landen', *Cahiers Economiques de Bruxelles*, No. 49, 1971.

Part II

THE GENERAL MODELS OF PROJECT LINK

5. THE ECONOMIC MODELS OF PROJECT LINK *

R.J. BALL

1. Introduction

Project LINK is concerned with the integration of economic models of particular countries in order to generate forecasts of world trade and payments, and to enable simulation work to be carried out in connection with the international transmission of business cycles. Its building blocks are the economic models of member countries in combination with models for the developing countries which have been estimated by UNCTAD. In this chapter we survey the models of the developed countries that are being used in the project. [1] An account of the work carried out by UNCTAD appears as ch. 6 in this volume.

The models under review are those which are at the time of writing being used in exercises of the "Mini-LINK" and "Maxi-LINK" type described in ch. 13 below. This means that we exclude from the discussion the Bank of Canada quarterly model of the Canadian economy which is used in the bilateral analysis of trade and payments between the Canadian and United States economies and which appears here as ch. 12. In several of the countries concerned in Project LINK there are, of course, other econometric models on a national scale. But this survey is confined to those

* In preparing this chapter I am much indebted to my colleague Brian Boatwright for help in organising the material. I have also benefited from the comments of the LINK model builders, whose patience and support has been much appreciated. Any remaining errors of fact and interpretation are my responsibility alone.
[1] By the time this volume is published there will be other models operating in the LINK project. This survey is limited to those available at the time of writing.

that are serving as inputs into the LINK system. In addition, it should be pointed out that there is an important omission from the list of country models in the shape of France. This is because currently no indigenous model of the French economy has been developed that will fit the general Project LINK format. Models in use at an official level in France have been directed primarily to other longer term objectives and no university or research institute project is as yet underway to fill the gap. This is an unfortunate lacuna in the present LINK system which it is hoped to fill at the earliest possible opportunity. The survey is therefore confined to eleven developed countries as follows: Austria, Belgium, Canada, Finland, Germany, Italy, Japan, Netherlands, Sweden, United Kingdom and the United States. [2]

The models themselves are under the auspices of university departments, research institutes and official bodies. Those for Belgium, Canada, Germany, Italy, Japan, United Kingdom and the United States are essentially university sponsored. The models for Austria and Sweden are based in research institutes. The model for Finland is based on an official project of the Bank of Finland, while the Dutch model is the latest in a long line of familiar models which have been developed at the Central Planning Bureau.

When all the models are written down they amount inevitably to several hundreds of equations, so that space precludes a complete specification of all the models being included here. A complete equation and data source listing will therefore appear in a companion volume. This raises the question of what is the most helpful way to organise the material available in the absence of complete equation listings to which the reader may readily refer. With the publication of the second model volume this difficulty will disappear. However, there is much to be said for making this survey as independent and complete as possible and so its organisation does not depend essentially on the complete equation listings being available.

One approach to the problem is to write surveys of the models for each of the countries separately which would then be pres-

---

[2] A full list of institutions is given in the Appendix.

ented seriatim. Such a catalogue, however, does not make it easy to bring out significant points of comparison between the different systems. The approach followed here, therefore, is to begin with a general overview of the models in terms of a general set of parameters relating to their design and operation and to follow this with some detailed comparison of their treatments of particular equation sectors that are commonly found in all of them. To facilitate comparison the key features of the treatment of each sector are summarised in a series of tabular presentations which seek to encapsulate the specific characteristics of each model. Apart from a general survey we treat the models in terms of the following sectors:

consumption
business fixed investment
residential investment and stocks
production, employment and unemployment
incomes and prices
the monetary sector.

International trade items are dealt with in other chapters.

It must be emphasised that in this survey one can only indicate the flavour of the work that the models represent. It is impossible to do proper justice to each of them separately. The survey can only indicate the general character of the models used in Project LINK.

2. The models in general

It must be borne in mind that Project LINK was begun in circumstances which found a number of models for individual countries operating as going concerns. The Project itself may be thought of as a dynamic process in which advances are made continually toward a more effective integration of the building blocks out of which it is fashioned. The models that existed at the outset represent the initial conditions at the start of the process which are changing and developing over time as the Project proceeds. An important by-product of the research itself consists in the exchange of experience between members of the Project, with resulting improvements and developments in the individual country models. In the course of the Project, therefore, standardisation is taking place along a number of dimensions, including notation, computing and solution methods, estimation procedures and the specification of particular sectors of the models. At the outset much of the standardisation with regard to specification has been confined to the trade sectors of the models, which are now in the process of being extended to include services and the capital account of the balance of payments. It is also being extended to important details of individual internal sectors which relate to external trade and payments. A good example of this is the insistence on the development of a monetary sector, which it will be seen does not exist in some of the models.

However, while a movement toward standardisation is discernible, it should be made clear that the philosophy of the Project is that individual member countries are obviously immediately responsible for their models, and are in the best position to judge which particular specifications and treatments of sectors of their economies are most appropriate. There is no attempt being made to slavishly follow any particular general model pattern for each individual country, thereby possibly destroying the flexibility required to model each country separately and successfully. The fact that many similarities between models occurs is a function of the universality of economic theory, which is found to have general application, rather than the adherence to any set format.

It would in any case be difficult in practice to impose a completely general format for the purposes of Project LINK alone. The availability of data varies from country to country, both in terms of the degree of disaggregation that is possible in specific sectors and in terms of the time unit in which data appear. This means that inevitably, if progress is to be made, it is necessary to work with a mixture of both annual and quarterly models. In the main, all the models surveyed here are primarily intended to serve short-term forecasting purposes, which one might argue requires quarterly rather than annual data. For Italy, Japan, the United Kingdom and the United States quarterly models exist that are used in the project solutions. The models of the Bank of Finland and the University of Toronto are also being constructed on a quarterly basis. The remaining models are all annual. Efforts are being made, notably at the Central Planning Bureau and at the Free University of Brussels, to build quarterly models to replace for LINK purposes the annual ones at present in use for the Netherlands and Belgium. But the data problems are severe. It must be anticipated that a mixed annual-quarterly system will prevail in Project LINK for some time to come. In addition, one must remember that each country may have specific purposes to which it wishes to put its model, which may require specification and treatment which cut across the objectives of Project LINK. For many internal purposes a more detailed disaggregation of particular sectors may be desirable than is either required for Project LINK purposes, or indeed is even feasible. A more detailed treatment of a particular sector is multiplied up many fold in terms of model size when one looks at the LINK system as a whole. At some point management and computer handling constraints become significant. This means that countries may have to — and some already have — run special versions of their total systems for LINK purposes only. The survey in this chapter is confined to the LINK versions of models where any difference arises.

An overall look at the country models is given in table 1. The details of each model will be picked up in the succeeding discussion of the individual sectors. The Austrian and Dutch models are both expressed in terms of relative first differences and it is clear that the Dutch work has influenced the Austrian development. The Austrian model comes from the Institute for Advanced Studies in Vienna while the Dutch model is the official model used in the Central Planning Bureau in the Hague. The Canadian TRACE model, emanating from the Institute for the Quantitative Analysis of Social and Economic Policy at the University of Toronto, is by far the largest and most sophisticated of the annual models, more detailed than some of the quarterly systems. The Belgian model, estimated at the Free University of Brussels, is also annual and is

Table 1

General characteristics of LINK models

Country	Total number of equations	Behavioural equations	Identities	Exogenous variables	Of which dummy variables	Data base	Sample period
Austria	37	16	21	31	5	annual	
Belgium	38	19	19	24	0	annual	1953–1968
Canada	221	73	148	143	9	annual	1926–1940 and/or 1947–1968
Finland	133	62	71	60	9	quarterly	1958–1969
Germany	130	56	74	*	0	annual	1955–1968
Italy	61	31	30	36	10	quarterly	1957–1970
Japan	117	62	55	53	4	quarterly	1955–1968
Netherlands	87	13	74	51	0	annual	1923–1938 and/or 1948–1966
Sweden	134	79	55	101	0	annual	1957–1969
U. Kingdom	93	54	39	63	30	quarterly	1959–1970
U.S.A.	203	68	135	102	25	quarterly	1954–1969

* All exogenous variables (e.g. world trade, foreign price levels etc.) are endogeneised by estimating them as functions of time.

about the same size as the Austrian, although estimated in the levels of variables primarily rather than relative first differences. The German model, from the University of Bonn, represents the other annual system which includes more behavioural relations in the Government sector than is found elsewhere.

The quarterly systems of Italy, Japan, the United Kingdom and the United States reflect broadly the same structural and theoretical approach, although there are manifest differences in disaggregation and scale. The Italian model, built especially for Project LINK by a research group at the University of Bologna, has some data problems, including an inability at present to separate consumption and inventory data. The Japanese and U.K. models are both fairly standard Keynesian developments, carried out at the University of Kyoto and the London Business School respectively. The United States model is the Wharton School quarterly model, which is the largest and most detailed of the quarterly systems at present in use in Project LINK. The Finnish model, built by the Bank of Finland, is a large quarterly system, but the size stems mainly from a particularly detailed breakdown of production by categories and a substantial wage and price sector. The expenditure categories are not disaggregated as far as the size of the model might suggest. In this respect it is similar to the Swedish model estimated at the Konjunkturinstitutet, in which there is also a very large industrial breakdown which inevitably generates a large number of additional equations, since not only production but also stocks are disaggregated by industry.

Generically these models might be broadly said to reflect model building in the post-Keynesian tradition, although there are specific differences worth noting that will be illustrated subsequently. As indicated above they may all be essentially regarded as short-term, although some of them have been used for medium-term exercises.

3. The consumption functions

The theory of consumers expenditure has occupied a key place in economic research since the Keynesian consumption function first came on the scene. The realisation that current income alone was insufficient to account for the behaviour of consumers expenditure in most countries, lead to two intertwined developments, the search for alternative specifications of the income effect, and the introduction of assets together with income as an explanatory variable. These developments, pioneered by Duesenberry, and reaching perhaps their peak in the work of Friedman and Ando and Modigliani, are reflected in the majority of the formulations of the empirical consumption function that we see today. [3]

The issues between the contributors to the massive literature on the consumption function are by no means totally resolved. The question, for example, as to whether non-human or wealth variables should appear explicitly in the consumption function together with some measure of income is still open to debate. As shown by Ball and Drake and Spiro [4], it is possible to develop a consumption function where consumption can be made to depend on income only, although the underlying behavioural hypothesis relates the level of consumption to net worth. Thus the explicit omission of a wealth variable from the estimated consumption relationship does not necessarily imply that wealth does not affect consumers' expenditure. In practice the empirical relationships estimated by individual investigators are often consistent with more than one specific theory of consumers expenditure. This proposition evidently applies to the consumption equations that appear in the various models of the LINK project.

The treatment of income in the consumption functions of the member countries is dominated by versions of the permanent income hypothesis, which is caught by expressing consumption initially as a geometrically weighted sum of past levels of income.

---

[3] Duesenberry, J.S., *Income, Saving and the Theory of Consumer Behaviour*, Harvard University Press, 1949; Friedman, M., *A Theory of the Consumption Function*, Princeton University Press, 1957; and Ando, A. and F. Modigliani, 'The Life-Cycle Hypothesis of Saving', *American Economic Review*, March 1963.

[4] Ball, R.J. and P.S. Drake, 'The Relationship between Aggregate Consumption and Wealth', *International Economic Review,* January 1964; and Spiro, A., 'Wealth and the Consumption Function', *Journal of Political Economy*, August 1962.

Where income is treated in this way, the equation is transformed and the lagged level of consumption appears as an explanatory variable. This is the case for Canada, Germany, Japan, Sweden, the U.K. and the U.S.A. The Finnish model uses a simple moving average of income rather than an average with declining weights. The consumption equation for Belgium is the simplest of all being an equation that simply relates the level of consumption to the level of disposable income, with no lags at all. It should be pointed out that the Belgian model is based on annual data, which may have obscured the short-run nature of lagged behaviour and heightened the degree of collinearity between the level of income and lagged consumption. The Italian consumption function differs in formulation from the main stream in that the dependent variable is the average propensity to consume, rather than the level of consumption, but this is also assumed to be a geometrically distributed lag function of its arguments. As already pointed out, the Italian group face the difficulty of being unable to separate consumption and inventory data and this clearly affects their specification of the relationship and its interpretation.

For the most part the effects of either a functional or size distribution of income are not explicitly taken into account in the consumption functions. The exceptions to this are firstly in the Austrian and Dutch models which are specified similarly to allow for different effects of wage and non-wage income, with discrete rather than continuous lags in the relative first differences of the variables. The Dutch model corrects the bias due to past shifts in income distribution, in that the coefficients of the two income variables are multiplied by the share of consumption attributable to each type of income in the previous year. Secondly, in the case of the U.K. model a special assumption is made with regard to the effects of income on non-durable consumers expenditure, in that for this type of expenditure the propensity to consume out of Government grants is assumed to be unity. The rationale for this restriction is that the consumption effects of changes in such income elements as unemployment benefit and pension payments by Government are believed *a priori* to have very different effects on consumption than, for example, changes in the overall level of disposable income due to changes in standard rates of income tax.

The degree of disaggregation in the consumption sectors varies from country to country, as one would expect given amongst other things differences in the availability of data. For Austria, Belgium, Germany, Italy, Japan and the Netherlands there is only one equation for total private consumption. The Canadian and U.K. models draw a distinction between durable goods and non-durable goods. For Finland there is a tripartite breakdown between autos, other goods and services, for Sweden a four way split between food, other non-durables, durables and services, and for the U.S. a division into autos, other durables, non-durables and services. Thus practice varies a great deal from country to country. There is on the whole general agreement that a minimum split into durables and non-durables is desirable where the appropriate data exist, but probably less agreement on the desirability of further disaggregation if interest is focussed on the problem of forecasting aggregate consumption for LINK purposes rather than on individual components which have special interest for particular countries and for other purposes.

Monetary variables occur in the consumption sectors of some of the models, although here the treatment is not in any way uniform. Finland, Italy, the Netherlands and the U.S. all introduce a liquidity effect into consumption behaviour (although in the Italian case the effect observed may also be related to stocks). In the first three instances the stock, or change in the stock, of liquidity is introduced, while in the case of the U.S. model a money supply variable is deflated by the level of disposable income. Interest rate effects are built into the models for Canada, Italy, the Netherlands and the U.S. for some of the equations, while specific policy variables relating to hire purchase occur in the U.K. equation for durables. On balance the monetary effects, while not appearing as strongly as a convinced monetarist might like, nonetheless are sufficiently widespread in these models to suggest that continued work on trying to identify such effects is both valuable and necessary if a more complete explanation of consumers expenditure is to be derived. Its particular relevance to Project LINK stems from the linkages between balance of payments and money supply, which provides another source of linkage other than directly through income effects and the foreign trade multiplier.

In the consumption sectors for Finland, Sweden and the U.S. price variables appear in particular disaggregated consumption equations. The vast majority of the countries produce consumption functions that are consistent with the hypothesis that consumption demand is not subject to money illusion, the significant exceptions here being Austria and the Netherlands. Both these countries allow the absolute price level to affect consumer demand so that money illusion is presumed to exist.

The main features of the consumption sectors described above are set out in tabular form in table 2. The broad conclusion that emerges is that, while obviously income plays a major role in all models, practice with regard to the degree of disaggregation and the inclusion of other variables varies considerably from model to model.⸴

4. Business fixed investment

While in the consumption sectors of the LINK models some differences of detail occur between different countries, one may hazard the view that there are probably no fundamental differences in broad viewpoint with regard to consumption theory. This is much less evident when we turn to the treatment of fixed private investment, excluding investment in residential construction. It is useful, therefore, to begin with some brief review of the main issues in investment theory in order to structure the discussion of the empirical findings as represented in the models of the individual countries in Project LINK.

Clarification of the distinction between the marginal efficiency of investment and the marginal efficiency of capital results in an analogous distinction between the theory of investment and the theory of the demand for capital. Within this framework of thought, we may conceive of the theory of investment as being concerned with the dynamics of the adjustment of the actual to

R.J. Ball

Tab
Consump

Country	Income variables	Income distribution	Assets	Monetary variables
Austria	disposable income	labour and non-labour income		
Belgium	disposable income			
Canada	first difference in disposable income {			long-term rat of interest
Finland	disposable income {	ratio of invest-ment income to wages and salaries {	time deposits {	
Germany	disposable income			
Italy	first differences in disposable income		first differences in private liq-uid assets	first differen in long-term of interest
Japan	disposable income			
Netherlands	disposable income	labour and non-labour income	stock of bank deposits	long-term rat of interest
Sweden	disposable income {			
U. Kingdom	disposable income {	government grants and other income {		new credits {
U.S.A.	disposable income {		ratio of money supply to income {	rate of intere

tive prices	Other variables	Lag structures	Disaggregation
		discrete	total private
		—	total private
		geometric {	durable goods other
of cars to total	rate of unemployment {	moving averages {	motor cars other goods services
		geometric	total private
		distributed lags	total private plus stockbuilding
		geometric	total private
		discrete	total private
) of other non- able to total {		geometric { —	non-durable goods and services durable goods
		— geometric	durable goods other
) of respective price rice of consumption {	unemployment residential investment { time	geometric {	cars other durable goods non-durable goods services

the desired or optimal capital stock, and the theory of capital demand as concerned with the determinants of the desired stock.

On the whole there is less disagreement about the theory of investment than the demand for capital stock. Various forms of the flexible accelerator have been proposed and tested which take into account such factors as inertial and information lags, and technical constraints such as the gestation period of capital goods in determining the form of the lag structure relating the rate of investment to the difference between actual and desired capital stock. In a number of formulations of the investment function that have appeared over the years financial variables have been introduced relating to the flow of funds available for investment, but it has not always been made clear whether financial factors enter in as a constraint on the rate of investment (or the speed of adjustment), rather than as determining the desired stock of capital. It is, of course, possible that the availability of funds merely acts as a constraint on the speed of adjustment rather than as a determinant of desired capital stock. Thus, for example, it is possible to postulate a simple hypothesis that the desired capital stock is simply a function of the expected level of market demand and yet to include financial variables relating to the supply of funds in the investment function. Even the simplest accelerator theories of the demand for capital are not inconsistent with the appearance of financial variables in the investment function.

For this reason, if for none other, it is not particularly helpful to try and categorise theories of the demand for capital into two broad groups, as has often been done in the past, depending on whether output or profits appear as the central motivating variables in investment functions. Equally it is not useful to divide theories into those which depend on profit maximisation as a rationale of capital demand and those which do not, since even those formulations of the investment function which depend essentially on output variables alone may be quite consistent with the profit maximisation assumption. [5] For example, if the produc-

---

[5] Locke Anderson, W.H., 'Business Fixed Investment: A Marriage of Fact and Fancy', in: *Determinants of Investment Behaviour*, Universities National Business Conference Series No. 18, Columbia University Press, 1967. Also Meyer, J.R. and E. Kuh, *The Investment Decision*, Harvard University Press, 1957.

tion function facing the firm is assumed to be of the fixed proportion type, and the supply of funds to the firm is perfectly elastic at the ruling rate of interest, a profit maximising stock of capital may exist determined solely by the level of expected demand, given a fixed price of output independent of the size of capital stock. Such a model suggests that a more useful way of classifying models of capital demand is to consider the alternative sets of hypotheses about the nature of production functions, the nature of the considerations governing the supply of funds to the firm, and the limitations imposed by expectations about the level of market demand. Whether profit maximisation is assumed or not, these factors are likely to receive implicit or explicit treatment in most theories of capital demand, but since as implied above probably most plausible formulations of capital demand can be shown to be consistent with profit maximisation under some set of simplifying assumptions about the three factors, acceptance of the principle of profit maximisation, as a basis for deriving a positive theory of the demand for capital, is unlikely to be unduly restrictive.

It has already been pointed out that financial variables may enter into the investment function as constraints on the rate of investment itself. In principle this will only occur when the market for funds is imperfect in some way, either because some form of rationing is implicit in the system or because imperfections are explicitly introduced from time to time by the monetary authorities. The point may be made another way by saying that in the absence of rationing, funds may always be obtained at a price, so that in this event it is the cost of capital alone that is relevant to the demand for capital stock. In that case the cost of capital determines the optimal or desired capital stock, together with other relevant factors. Where, however, rationing exists (or is partly self-imposed by the constraint of an external/internal funds ratio) both the cost of capital and the availability of funds may legitimately appear as arguments of the investment function.

Assumptions about the nature of the underlying production function can largely be divided into those which allow substitution between the factors of production and those which do not. The critical issue here is whether relative factor prices should appear as determinants of optimal capital stock. In between the extremes of production functions with fixed factor proportions and those with perfect substitutability between factors of production in the short-run, we have the vintage capital approach which may permit features of both to appear in the short-term demand for capital.

It is difficult to see how any model of capital demand based on profit maximisation (or any other plausible model that is not) can ignore the level of market demand. Differences that arise between particular specifications of the demand for capital on this account may tend to arise from different specifications of the precise impact of market demand, ranging from assuming some simple relationship between the demand for capital stock and the current level of market demand and more complex formulations of the concept of expected market demand as an argument of the demand for capital function.

Within the context of these broad theoretical considerations, it is possible to generate many specific formulations of private fixed investment functions. It is, therefore, perhaps not surprising that in specific terms the investment functions developed by the individual LINK model builders vary widely. A summary of the characteristics of the equations used by different countries is given in table 3. Generalisation is also made difficult by the rather different disaggregation patterns that occur.

It may be seen that all countries include some output effects on investment. Output effects enter in through direct, or indirect, proxies related to utilisation, through the level of output in some cases, and through changes in the level of output in particular forms such as the special formulation of changes in output, modified by the cost of capital, as in the family of models of the type developed by Jorgenson. [6] The nature of the underlying production functions is not always clear, and in some cases the availability of finance in the short-run becomes the dominant factor. In

---

[6] Jorgenson, D.W., 'Capital Theory and Investment Behaviour', *American Economic Review*, Papers and Proceedings, May 1963.

short the estimated functions range over the whole gamut of possibilities that the previous theoretical discussion opens up.

The annual equations developed for Austria, the Netherlands and Germany all lay stress on the flow of funds emanating directly from corporate profits. In the case of the Netherlands the equation also includes an additional liquidity variable and the equation is basically thought of as a 'finance' equation. Thus, while a capacity utilisation variable based on unemployment is also included, attention is focussed for the most part on the effects of financial constraints on investment. The Austrian model divides the investment function into two, one for equipment and one for construction, so that both residential and business construction are aggregated together. The forms of the equations are however similar. In all these cases the nature of the underlying production function, as it affects investment decisions, is not clear. The German equation for business investment includes retained profits, a measure of capacity utilisation and a variable based on the level of Government expenditure. The underlying production function is of a CES form with an elasticity of substitution between labour and capital of one half.

The annual Belgian model and the quarterly U.K. model both draw directly on the work of Jorgenson. In the case of Belgium there is a single equation for industrial investment, but in the U.K. case investment is divided partly by sector and partly by type of asset purchased. For the U.K. there are separate equations for investment in plant and equipment for the manufacturing and for the distributive and other commercial sectors. There is also an aggregate equation for investment in new building and vehicles which covers both sectors. Both the Belgian and the U.K. approaches are consistent with an underlying production function that is Cobb-Douglas. The cost of capital enters as in the standard Jorgenson model and no allowance is made directly for the effects of the availability, or non-availability, of finance. The Japanese model also allows implicitly for factor substitution insofar as it includes the level of real wages as an explicit explanatory variable. It also includes both the rate of return on capital and the rate of interest on bank loans as well as an output utilisation factor. In a

Ta
Private f

Country	Demand variables	Flow of funds	Monetary variab
Austria	output {	disposable non-labour income {	commercial cred
Belgium	gross domestic product deflated by the user cost of capital		rate of interest
Canada	capacity utilisation {	after tax profits divided by the capital stock {	long-term rate of interest {
Finland	private consumption { industrial production {		bank debt to credit ratio {
Germany	capacity utilisation ratio of government to total expenditure	retained profits	
Italy	gross domestic product { capacity { utilisation	profits to output ratio {	long-term rate of interest {
Japan	capacity utilisation	rate of profit on capital stock divided by the rate of interest on bank loans	
Netherlands	pressure of demand (unemployment)	disposable non-labour income	bank deposits
Sweden	industrial production		ratio of bank cre to capital stock
U. Kingdom	industrial production deflated by the user cost of capital { industrial production		equity dividend y
U.S.A.	output { capacity utilisation {		long-term rate of interest {

Investment

Stock levels	Other variables	Lag structures	Disaggregation
		discrete	equipment construction (including residential)
capital stock lagged one period	tax rate on business depreciation allowances	distributed lags	total industrial
capital stock lagged one period	capital cost allowances	discrete	machinery and equipment non-residential construction
		geometric	machinery and equipment non-residential construction
		discrete	total private
		distributed lags	machinery and equipment construction (including residential)
	ratio of price of labour to output	discrete	total private
	investment permits	discrete	total private
capital stock lagged one period		discrete	total manufacturing
capital stock lagged one period	government tax allowances tax rate on business	distributed lags	machinery and equipment 1. manufacturing 2. distributive trades industrial buildings and vehicles
capital stock lagged one period	depreciation allowances	distributed lags	machinery and equipment 1. manufacturing 2. regulated 3. commercial

sense the Japanese model looks more immediately Keynesian than the other two. There is one equation in the Japanese quarterly model covering all business investment (other than inventories).

Business investment in the U.S. quarterly model is divided between manufacturing and mining, regulated and commercial investment, the treatment of each being slightly different. Investment in manufacturing and mining is related to utilisation, the level of sector output and the user cost of capital divided by the deflator of sector output with different lag structures. The equation for regulated investment is similar, except that the capital stock appears explicitly in place of the utilisation rate. Finally, the equation for the commercial sector differs from that for regulated in that it is the changes in output level and real user cost that appear rather than the levels. This latter equation bears some similarity to the family of Jorgenson models referred to earlier. The theoretical form of the Italian investment function for machinery and transport equipment seems similar to the Wharton model equation for manufacturing and mining, since it includes the level of output, a utilisation variable and the ratio of profit to output, which appears to play a similar role to the user cost of capital. The treatment of lags is rather different but the spirit of the relationship appears much the same.

The Canadian annual model differs in form from the others in that the dependent variable is the percentage change in capital stock in the investment equations. A distinction is made between investment in machinery and equipment and investment in non-residential construction by the business sector. The basic form of the two equations is similar in that they are essentially distributed lag functions of the cost of capital and the utilisation rate for the business sector, and are derived from a CES production function following a modification of the Jorgenson approach. The Swedish model includes an equation for gross investment in manufacturing which depends on the level of industrial production, the level of fixed capital stock and the ratio of changes in bank credits to the stock of fixed capital. Finally, the quarterly model for Finland has two equations for private fixed non-dwellings investment, one for equipment and one for construction. Each one is a distributed lag function of an activity variable and a credit variable, which takes the form of the ratio of the central bank debts to total bank credits.

The foregoing brief review of the investment functions of the LINK model builders makes it clear that no neat and tidy summary is possible. As pointed out at the outset of this chapter, in the main, the view has been taken that each model builder knows his own country and his own data best and that some sort of complete standardisation is neither to be expected nor to be desirable. There are, of course, many points of similarity that exist between the model treatments but a survey of this kind suggests that, despite differences which may be idiosyncratic to individual countries, there is as yet no uniformity with respect to theory of the kind that broadly exists with regard to consumers expenditure. The disparate treatments of lagged behaviour and differences in the degree of disaggregation and data unit all make comparison difficult. Nevertheless, it is interesting to observe the extent to which most of the model builders, in some form or another, have attempted to construct investment models which allow for the effects of monetary policy on investment. The method of treatment varies from country to country but the impact of monetary changes, in some cases through direct credit flows and in others through interest rate effects on the cost of capital, is present in the majority of cases. The nature of this connection between the monetary and investment sectors is of obvious importance when at a later stage the LINK programme is concerned with simulation.

5. Housing investment and stockbuilding

As is already apparent, not all the LINK model builders are able to achieve a minimum investment breakdown between fixed investment other than housing, housing and stockbuilding. In the case of the Netherlands and Sweden residential construction is treated as exogenous, in Austria residential housing is aggregated with total construction, while in Italy there is no explicit stockbuilding function since inventory data cannot be separated from consumption data. This heterogeneity of treatment must be regarded as to some extent unsatisfactory, and it is to be hoped that in future it will be possible to achieve at least some minimum breakdown across countries of the type suggested above.

Thus as far as residential construction is concerned only the Belgian, Finnish, Japanese, U.K. and U.S. models have explicit equations for private residential investment. The information relating to investment in residential construction is summarised in table 4. From that it will be seen that broadly speaking the main factors taken to affect housing investment are some measure of purchasing power, credit availability and the cost of funds. In the case of the U.S. model allowance is made for substitution between house purchase and renting. The most common purchasing power variable used is real disposable income, although in Finland use is made of wages and salaries, and in Belgium of the flow of private saving. The Belgian function is in terms of current rather than constant prices.

The most elaborate housing sector model is to be found in the U.K. model, which relates housing investment initially to housing starts, which are in turn related to income and the flow and cost of funds. [7] The flow of funds, primarily from building societies, is then determined through a series of equations which account for the inflow and outflow of funds from the mortgage market. Starts are also used to predict housing investment in the Canadian model, where starts are disaggregated into single and multiple starts, but the lag structure chosen results in housing investment being essentially predetermined for the year ahead. [8]

The treatment of stockbuilding in the LINK models exhibits a

[7] An approach to determining starts is to be found in Maisel, S., 'Fluctuations in Residential Construction Starts', *American Economic Review*, June 1963. A similar approach to the analysis of the relationship between starts and investment is to be found in Helliwell, J.F., H.T. Shapiro, G.R. Sparks, I.A. Stewart, F.W. Gorbet and D.R. Stephenson, 'The Structure of RDX2', Bank of Canada Staff Research Studies No. 7, 1971.

[8] In Canada it has been goverment policy to set target levels for the number of housing starts, so that when the system is simulated more than one year ahead, the number of starts is taken as an exogenous policy instrument. Governmental financial policies are followed to make the target number of starts feasible.

Country	Income	Credit	Starts	Monetary variables	Other variables	Lag structures	Disaggregation
Austria	←						included in fixed investment ↑
Belgium	private saving					discrete	total private
Canada			current and lagged (exogenous)			discrete	single and multiple completions
Finland	wages and salaries	ratio of bank debts to credits			building permits	discrete	total
Germany	←					↑	included in fixed investment
Italy	←					↑	included in fixed investment
Japan	disposable income					geometric	total private
Netherlands	←		——— exogenous ———				
Sweden	←		——— exogenous ———				
U. Kingdom	disposable income	advances by building societies and local authorities	lag over five quarters	bank rate	ratio of the price of housing to all prices	distributed lag on starts	total private
U.S.A.	disposable income			excess of bond yield over the prime commercial rate	ratio of the price of housing to rents	distributed lag	total non-farm

broader degree of uniformity than either business fixed investment or investment in residential construction. By and large the underlying theory is that of the flexible accelerator, although the precise specification varies from country to country.

The inventory equations for Canada, Japan and the U.K are all variants of the simple flexible accelerator model with output and a lagged stock of inventories appearing but with rather different lag specifications. The Japanese and Canadian models both include an additional cyclical variable, in the former case the four quarter change in GNP and in the latter the deviation between the actual and trend rate of expenditure on consumer durables. The German inventory equation also includes income, lagged income and lagged inventory variables but is expressed in current rather than constant prices. For Belgium there is a simple relationship on an annual basis relating the lagged change in output and the inverse of unemployment to the rate of change in inventory stock.

The inventory equation in the Netherlands model also starts from a stock adjustment principle, but builds in carefully the existence of a signalling lag which reflects the time taken before a behavioural reaction occurs with respect to the desired stock of inventories, and a gestation lag which reflects the average delivery time. In addition, a profit variable, expressed as the standard profit per unit of output, is also included and the possibility of speculation with regard to import prices is also allowed for, which explains the appearance of the import price level. By and large speculative effects are not directly allowed for in the majority of the LINK models. Because the Netherlands model is estimated over a sample period including pre-war, a time trend also appears which reflects the long term downward trend in the desired inventory stock/output ratio.

The Wharton model for the U.S. deals with the level of stock holding, rather than its rate of change, and disaggregates non-farm inventories between manufacturing and non-manufacturing. The basic form is a geometric distributed lag in the level of gross private output in manufacturing together with a number of expenditure GNP categories. The rationale for this is that the identity between inventory change and production and sales may be empirically approximated with positive coefficients for production and negative coefficients for components of expenditure. The Wharton model is the only one to make any extensive use of order statistics, which are not generally available for the other countries concerned. Order statistics, such as manufacturers net new orders, are not related directly to inventory behaviour but enter in via the determination of gross private manufacturing output, whose determining equation thus takes on the form of an output decision function.

The Swedish model is exceptional for its degree of disaggregation. Inventory holding is broken down by industrial sector as well as by the stage of the production process, i.e. raw materials, work in progress and finished goods. The transaction motive, expressed in terms of production or demand variables, is the dominant explanatory variable throughout.

6. Production, employment and unemployment

The previous sections have discussed the treatment of the main endogenous expenditure items in the LINK models, with the exception of items relating to trade and payments which are discussed elsewhere in this volume. We now turn to some examination of the supply side of the LINK systems. Here there are a number of specific issues to consider, the determination of the GNP, the determination of sector outputs where relevant, the demand for labour and the explanation of unemployment.

In most of the econometric models that have been built on basically Keynesian foundations, the GNP expenditure identity completes the system with respect to the GNP itself. Expenditure determines output in such a system in this particular sense. In some systems an aggregate production function is postulated relating output to labour and capital stock, so that given the existence of an investment equation the role of the production function is to complete the system with regard to the determination of the level of employment. But even in a system of this type, where the supply of labour may be assumed to be perfectly elastic up to the limit imposed by the labour force, it is still not strictly true that it can be regarded as purely 'expenditure' determined. The reason for this lies in the nature of the inventory function which reflects a joint decision about the level of output and the level of stockholding. [9] It is possible, for example, to look at the question from the other side of the coin, by writing down an explicit production decision equation allowing the rate of inventory investment to be determined by the GNP identity. This is not usually done although it was the case in earlier versions of the U.K. LINK model. For the LINK models generally the GNP identity completes the system with respect to GNP and explicit inventory functions are formulated.

In some of the LINK models sector outputs also have to be determined. Here the most common practice is to derive the particular sector output from expenditure categories which are generated by the models – the procedure being equivalent to a quasi input–output analysis in which the intermediate steps are missed out.

In earlier econometric models as pointed out, the aggregate production function completed the system with regard to the level of employment. Until recently a great deal of attention was bestowed on the demand for capital but comparatively little on the demand for labour. However, during the last ten years a considerable literature has grown up with regard to the demand for labour, with particular emphasis on the behaviour of the demand for labour in the short-run. This literature has three strands to it. The first is the realisation that the short-run demand for labour is a complex phenomenon that is related to expectations, the costs of hiring and firing, and the general problem of labour hoarding that has been a phenomenon in a number of industrial countries over the last twenty five years. The second, that has grown out of the first, is the application of capital theory to the demand for labour, which has emphasised the demand for labour as a stock rather than as a flow of services that are directly consumed in production. It has

---

[9] Johnston, J., 'An Econometric Study of the Production Decision', *Quarterly Journal of Economics*, May 1961.

been recognised that the flow of labour services fluctuates much more than the level of employment, so that the utilisation of a given stock of labour will fluctuate over the cycle of economic activity. The development of the concept of human capital has led to a number of insights in various areas of economics, and with particular reference to the demand for labour evokes by analogy with physical capital, the concepts of investment, replacement costs and stock adjustment. The third strand relates to the interest in the problem of making a distinction between the short-run and long-run behaviour of labour productivity. This is not only of interest in its own right but also has important implications for pricing policy and the behaviour of factor shares in the short and long-run. [10]

This literature leads us towards a general theory of the demand for factors of production, pricing policies and factor shares. The application of capital theory to the demand for labour as a stock opens up a distinction familiar in investment and capital theory between the determinants of the desired stock of labour and the mechanism of adjustment of the actual to the desired stock. An approach of this kind is to be seen in many of the LINK models although, as in other areas, there are detailed differences of treatment.

If a labour force equation is explicitly postulated the level of unemployment may then be derived by identity. However, the level of unemployment is often a small difference between two large numbers such that, although employment and the labour force may be predicted with relative accuracy, the forecast error of unemployment may be very large indeed. Thus in some cases in the LINK models the labour force equation is dropped and the level of unemployment estimated directly.

The majority of the LINK models incorporate the stock adjustment principle with regard to the demand for labour, or can be interpreted as such. The principal differences, therefore, relate to the specification of the equilibrium or desired stock of labour. In

---

[10] Killingsworth, M.R., 'A Critical Survey of Neoclassical Models of Labour', *Bulletin of the Oxford University Institute of Economics and Statistics,* May 1970.

some cases the equilibrium stock of labour is derived from the
existence of a long-run production function so that arguments of
the long-run production function itself, such as output and capital
stock from the inverted form, appear explicitly in the employment
function. The simplest case of this is the employment function in
the Belgian model in which the underlying long-run production
function is assumed to be Cobb-Douglas. Thus, after substituting
the long-run production function in inverted form in the labour
stock adjustment function, the short-run level of employment is a
function of output, capital stock and the lagged level of employment. Neutral technical progress is also assumed so that a trend
term is included. A rather more elaborate version of the same idea,
without the assumption of neutral technical progress, is also apparent in the demand for labour in manufacturing and mining in the
U.S. model. In the U.S. equations for employment in the regulated
and commercial sectors, however, the equilibrium level of employment is related to the outputs of those sectors alone.

Generally speaking, most of the models relate the equilibrium
level of labour demand to an output variable. The main differences
in additional specification turn on whether the equilibrium stock
of labour is derived by substituting the production function in the
adjustment equation or whether profit maximisation is being assumed, so that the desired stock of labour is essentially derived
from the marginal productivity conditions. The Japanese, Finnish
and Austrian models, for example, include the real wage level
together with the output level which can be interpreted as a quasi
representation of the marginal productivity conditions. The Netherlands demand for labour equation is aggregate and represents a
mixture of both approaches since it includes a variable which allows for embodied technical progress and profit factors represented by the profit per unit of output, import costs and a credit
variable. The U.K. model determines employment from an essentially production function approach in which, however, the effects
of capital accumulation together with technical progress are sub-
sumed into a trend term. In this model the ratio of employment to
output is taken as the dependent variable − i.e., the inverse of
output per man is directly explained. Thus the long-run rate of

productivity growth is taken as given in this model and the short-run fluctuations in employment modelled about it. The Canadian model has a similar equation for business employment, except that capital productivity is also included as a variable. It is derived from a Cobb-Douglas production function with a partial adjustment between desired and actual demand for labour occurring in each period. In the Italian model the demand for labour is split between the industrial sector and the construction sector. Both functions can be interpreted as being of the stock adjustment type, although for the industrial sector a special variable is included that is related to man hours and there is a trend term in the equation for construction. The German model has a very detailed employment sector, in which employment measured in working hours is derived from the level of production, taking into account technical progress and the degree to which production is capital intensive. There are also equations to explain average working hours per week offered by the working population and the development of the working population.

Many of the models have equations for man hours, sometimes on a disaggregated basis. However, since the general principles followed have already been exemplified in the discussion of employment, much of it would be repetitious and so we pass over these relationships here. It remains to make some comment about unemployment. Roughly speaking the main difference here is between those countries which specify an equation for unemployment and those that do not. Specific unemployment equations exist for Austria, Belgium, Germany, Japan, Italy, the Netherlands and the U.K. Unemployment is determined by identity in the Canadian, Finnish and U.S. models. The Swedish model determines a labour demand variable which is the difference between vacancies and unemployment. Again discussion of these relationships would add little to the general flavour of the discussion of employment.

By and large there is a considerable communality in the approach to the determination of output and employment in the LINK models given the level of expenditure. There is broad acceptance it appears of a capital theory approach to the demand for

Tab
Employm

Country	Output	Income	Hours	Capital st
Austria	squared function of total output	labour income per employee	working hours	
Belgium	gross national product			industrial ital stock unlagged
Canada	business output divided by capital stock			
Finland	gross domestic product	wages and salaries		
Germany	gross national product { government expenditure {		working hours per employed person {	
Italy	gross domestic product of industrial sector		monthly hours worked per man	
Japan	output { consumption {	real wage { earnings {		
Netherlands	output	gross trading profits per unit of output		ratio of investmen to output
Sweden	manufacturing output investment in buildings consumption paper production			
U. Kingdom	gross domestic product		normal weekly hours	
U.S.A.	output of respective sector {			capital sto lagged one perio

* E = Employment, Q = Output, K = Capital Stock, W = Wage.

...er variables	Equation form *	Lag structures	Disaggregation
	linear	discrete	private sector
	$E = Q^\alpha K^\beta E_{-1}^\lambda$	geometric	total
...e	$\dfrac{E}{Q} = \dfrac{E_{-1}^\alpha}{Q}\dfrac{Q^\beta}{K}$	geometric	business non-agricultural sector
	$E = Q^\alpha W^\beta E_{-1}^\lambda$	geometric	total
...ome and wage ...el abroad {	subsystem of nonlinear equations {	discrete {	private sector / government sector
	linear	geometric	industrial sector
	$E = Q^\alpha W^\beta E_{-1}^\lambda$ {	geometric {	manufacturing / other industries
...mployment ...rgin between im-...t and output prices ...k of bank deposits	linear (dependent variable expressed in man years)	discrete	private sector
	proportionate change (dependent variable expressed in man hours)	discrete	{ industrial / building / trade / forrestry
...our taxes ...e	linear (dependent variable E/Q)	geometric	total
...e {	$\dfrac{E}{E_{-1}} = Q^\alpha K^\beta E_{-1}^\lambda$ { $E = Q^\alpha E_{-1}^\lambda$ {	geometric {	manufacturing / regulated sector / commercial sector

labour, which allows one to draw a clear distinction between the
stock of labour and its utilisation in terms of man hours. It also
leads to a further distinction between the desired stock of labour
and the adjustment process by which it is achieved. There remain
differences between the ways in which the desired stock of labour
is specified, which we have categorised broadly into two approaches, the one which explicitly introduces the arguments of the
production function into the labour stock adjustment equation
without either explicitly or implicitly assuming profit maximisation and those that essentially derive the desired stock of labour
from the profit maximising conditions. Some resolution of the
issues here is required to achieve further standardisation of approach between the LINK model builders. A summary of the characteristics of the employment equations used by different countries is given in table 5.

7. Incomes and prices

The income side of the LINK models may perhaps be most con-
veniently discussed in terms of prices, wages and other incomes. In
principle this whole sector might be expected to be amenable to
treatment theoretically in terms of a general theory of income
determination, but there is little evidence from a cursory study of
the LINK systems that this is generally true. The treatment of
prices and wages, for example, in the models contains a number of
ingredients that are derived from the gamut of theories and pieces
of empirical work on a partial basis that have been presented in
recent years.

As the degree of disaggregation of econometric systems grows
the number of individual prices that need to be determined grows
rapidly. Where the number of prices to be determined is relatively
small the approach is often to explain each price in terms of cost
factors, demand factors, etc. separately. Where the number of
prices becomes relatively large, however, an alternative procedure
which is used in varying degrees in many models is to select a
price, or a small subset of prices, that are explained directly, and

then to "pivot" the explanation of the remaining prices around these, adding in any special factors that may be expected to cause the individual price to diverge from the pivot price. This kind of procedure, for example, is followed in the U.S. model where the wholesale price of manufactures and the commercial and regulated sector prices serve as direct inputs into other consumption and investment price equations. The choice of pivot price is not the same in all models. For example, in the case of the U.K., it is the price of final expenditure that serves as the pivot price to which other prices are geared. Where production is highly disaggregated an alternative approach to generating a large set of sector prices is to follow an input—output scheme as in the case of Finland.

The heterogeneity of the detailed treatment of prices that are directly explained in the sense of the above makes a convenient summary difficult, and a detailed exposition inordinately lengthy. There are, however, a number of common elements that underlie the rather detailed treatments. Virtually all the models start by relating prices that are directly determined to unit labour costs. [11] Differences arise with regard to the form of the cost variable used. The "normal cost" hypothesis suggests that price setting behaviour relates to normal or standard costs rather than actual costs. In the case of Italy and the U.K. this is treated by smoothing the acutal cost data as an approximation to standard costs. However, the same effect may be captured by including actual costs as an explanatory variable and adding in a cyclical variable such as the unemployment or utilisation rate. In some cases this makes it difficult to interpret the meaning of a demand variable of this kind that appears in the pricing equation. Some of the models (for example the Dutch) interpret this relationship as a flexible mark up but it is also quite consistent with the normal or standard cost

---

[11] On the treatment of cost items see for example Eckstein, O., 'A Theory of the Wage—Price Process in Modern Industry', *Review of Economic Studies,* October 1964; Eckstein, O. and G. Fromm, 'The Price Equation', *American Economic Review,* December 1968; Neild, R.R., *Pricing and Employment in the Trade Cycle,* Cambridge University Press, 1963; Ball, R.J. and M. Duffy, 'Price Formation in European Countries', to be published in the proceedings of a conference on pricing sponsored by the Federal Reserve Board, Washington, November 1970.

hypothesis. If actual costs and a utilisation rate are used and the normal cost hypothesis holds, one would expect that as the utilisation rate falls, actual costs will rise above normal costs, and so with a negative coefficient on the utilisation rate there will be offsetting effects on the price level. Formally speaking, this could also mean that a flexible mark up holds such that, as costs rise and the utilisation rate falls, the mark up on actual costs is reduced, and vice versa. A further approach, that may also be regarded as representative of the normal cost hypothesis, is to specify the price level as depending upon a geometrically weighted average of past unit labour costs, which can be interpreted as the normal cost variable. This interpretation is consistent, for example, with the procedure followed in the U.S. model for the sector prices in manufacturing, commercial and regulated sectors, that essentially form the pivot subset referred to above in this model. In the models for Austria, Belgium, Japan and Sweden actual unit labour costs are used, and in the absence of other relevant variables cannot be interpreted as consistent with the normal or standard cost hypothesis. The central price equation in the Canadian model for business output, which can be interpreted as the pivot price in that system, also follows a distributed lag approach rather than using actual costs by themselves, and in the sense discussed can also be interpreted as consistent with a normal cost hypothesis. The principal German price equation for private output is also a mark up on actual unit labour costs. Thus, while all the models use unit labour costs as an explanatory variable in price formation, there is no general agreement on detailed specification.

A second factor that appears in many of the models is the level of import prices. In some cases, where appropriate for individual disaggregated prices, the import price variable is itself disaggregated. Leaving this detail on one side, one can say that import prices are significant in accounting for internal price movements in Austria, Belgium, Canada, Finland, Germany, the Netherlands, Sweden and the United Kingdom. Import prices do not appear in price equations for the United States or the other remaining countries. It is perhaps not very surprising that import prices have little or no effect on the price level in the United States, nor that they are a significant factor affecting the internal price level in an economy as open as the Netherlands. One would expect that the smaller and more open the economy, the greater the likely impact of import on domestic prices, and it is perhaps surprising that for a number of countries, import price effects do not appear. These prices evidently play an important role in the transmission of inflationary pressures from one country to another. None of the LINK models postulates any direct effect of monetary factors on prices, with the exceptions of the Netherlands and Canada, where for the former the interest rate is assumed to affect the consumer price level, whilst in the latter model during periods of floating exchange rates, balance of payments effects change the exchange rate and thus directly affect domestic prices. Thus, there are no general direct linkages between balance of payments, the money supply and price levels. Price level effects from the balance of payments must work indirectly through the money market and expenditure mechanism.

Finally, there is the question of direct effects of demand on prices. In some of the models pressure of demand effects appear in particular equations. For example, in the U.S. and German models a utilisation variable helps to explain the price level in the manufacturing and private sectors respectively. A similar variable is included in the equation for the price of residential construction in the Canadian model and the same is true of the equation for industrial wholesale prices in Italy. In the Dutch model, the pressure of demand affects all prices, but in particular consumption prices. However, across the board of the LINK model builders, these are relatively sporadic influences. In the main cost variables predominate in the price formation equations of the system.

Turning now to income formation on the wage side, in most cases the level of wage income in the LINK models is determined from the identity between the wage bill, average earnings and the level of employment or man hours. Employment was discussed in the last section, so we confine ourselves here to the determination of average earnings. In some models there is an important distinction between the wage rate and average earnings. In the U.K. and Finnish models the wage rate is treated as exogenous and average earnings determined by what is essentially an equation (or set of equations where relevant) for the wage drift. The Belgian model draws an explicit distinction between earnings and rates and explains them both endogenously. The German model explains the rate of growth of the nominal wage rate by the rates of growth of labour productivity and GNP and by the deviation of actual from "normal" man hours. The remainder of the systems deal directly with what corresponds to earnings.

The information relating to wages and salaries is summarised in table 6. There is a considerable degree of uniformity in the LINK models with regard to the determination of average wages, since most of them are representative of some version of the Phillips curve. The Belgian wage rate function makes the change in rates depend only on unemployment, and the change in earnings is then related simply to the change in rates. In the U.K. and Finnish drift equations, pressure of demand variables are introduced. Of the LINK models, those for Austria, Belgium, Canada, Italy, the Netherlands and the U.S. all make use of unemployment in this connection. The Swedish model makes use of a more sophisticated labour demand variable also involving vacancies, while the Japanese model makes use of a special variable which essentially amounts to expressing vacancies as a per cent of employment. For Austria, Canada, Italy, Japan, the Netherlands and the U.S., consumer prices, as a cost of living effect, are also introduced. Productivity appears in the equations for the Netherlands and for Japan. To this there is very little of significance to add, save for the fact that it is worth observing that a number of (although not all) the models reported here are using equations estimated before the major upsurge in world prices at the turn of the decade. In the U.K. at least it is arguable that the Phillips curve relationship has broken down for this period. It will, therefore, be of considerable interest to observe the extent to which the almost universal adherence to the Phillips curve in the other country models will be sustained as new data become available. On the whole, rates of inflation throughout the world in 1971 were underestimated by most forecasters unless their equations were adjusted for past errors. The resolution of this problem has considerable significance for future simulations in the LINK project, designed to throw light on the international inflationary mechanism.

Disposable income for an individual country will have many other components other than wage income for which equations are provided in the LINK models. However, they do not raise any particular points of general interest, and may, therefore, be passed over here. What remains, however, of particular interest, is the determination of corporate income. The most common approach to generating corporate income is via an income identity. This is the case for Austria, Germany, Italy, the Netherlands and the U.S. There are no equations in the Belgian, Finnish or Swedish models for corporate income. For Canada, Japan and the U.K. there are explicit equations for corporate income, rather than exact identities. None of these appears to reflect any significant theory of income determination. The Canadian equation relates gross profits to the difference between business income and business salaries, plus a utilisation term. The U.K. formulation is intended to capture the same idea, while the Japanese model does not include any cost variables but relates profits to the national income, the investment/income ratio and a utilisation factor.

8. The monetary sector

It has been evident at a number of points in this survey that monetary effects are to be found in many parts of the LINK models. The revival of monetarism in the last fifteen years has increased the effort to establish significant monetary effects on the expenditure side of econometric models, and the current set of LINK models testifies to this increase, in both interest and activity. General conclusions about the effectiveness of monetary policy are not likely to be helpful, since the institutional conditions that face individual model builders in this field differ considerably. The LINK models themselves reflect a broad spectrum of institutional conditions, ranging from countries with a relatively sophisticated set of financial markets and institutions to those where bond and equity markets are virtually non-existent. In addition, traditional

Ta▮
La▮

Country	Output	Prices	Labour market con▮
Austria	total output	consumer price index	number unemploye▮
Belgium			inverse of the numb▮ unemployed
Canada		consumer price index	inverse of the rate of unemployment
Finland	productivity in sector i less national productivity	total price index	rate of unemployme▮
Germany	gross national product in private sector: labour productivity		
Italy		consumer price index	moving average of t▮ inverse of rate of "adjusted" unemplo▮ ment
Japan	production multiplied by employment {	consumer price index {	job offer − application ratio employment index
Netherlands	productivity	consumer price index	unemployment
Sweden			vacancies less unemployment {
U. Kingdom	capacity utilisation		
U.S.A.		consumer price index {	rate of "potential" unemployment {

* Agriculture
  Other non-competing goods production

Gas, Electricity and Water
Construction

›nre

er variables	Equation form	Dependent variable	Disaggregation
	proportionate change	gross wage bill	private sector
	ratio of current to previous value	wage rate	total
	ratio of current to previous value	average wage per hour	business non-agricultural
	levels	wage rate drift	eight sectors *
...ation of actual from ...rmal" man hours	proportionate change	wage rate	private sector
	proportionate change	gross hourly earnings	total industrial sector
...o of farm workers ...otal population ...ings in manufac-...ng	proportionate change { levels {	wage earnings {	manufacturing other industries
...ernment direct taxes	proportionate change	average gross wages per standard year	total
...e increase for ...ustrial workers {	proportionate change {	negotiated wage increase {	industrial building sector industrial (salaried) trade sector other sectors
...mal hours	proportionate change	wage drift	total
...e rate in manufac-...ng	average proportionate change { first difference {	wage rates {	manufacturing regulated sector commercial sector

...vices   Competing Industries producing semi-finished goods
...mpeting Raw Materials Industries   Other Competing Industries

patterns of financial behaviour themselves are different from country to country. In some countries, investment expenditure is heavily dependent on borrowing from the banks in the form of loans,
while in others the equity content of investment finance is relatively high. Such differences are likely to affect the leverage of
particular monetary policies.

The significance of the monetary sector, and of monetary policy in particular, to Project LINK is evident, since through the
balance of payments an important possible inter-country linkage
exists via the supply of money. The obvious potential importance
of this linkage has resulted in the decision that all LINK models
must have monetary sectors relating to the quantity of money and
interest rate levels. At the time of writing, research is already
underway in those countries for which adequate monetary sectors
do not exist, some of which may be completed by the time that
the models are published in a companion volume to this one. We
summarise here, therefore, the models for which work already
exists.

For Austria, Germany and Sweden there is no monetary sector.
Monetary variables do not enter into the systems. For the U.K.
interest rates affect both business investment and investment in
residential construction, but all monetary influences are made to
depend ultimately on exogenous monetary instruments. In the
Belgian model, the rate of interest influences business investment
but is treated as an exogenous variable. No equations for the general level of interest rates or the money supply are currently in
these systems. In the Canadian model, interest rates appear in both
consumption and investment equations, with the main impacts on
interest rates in Canada being made to come from the U.S. short-
term rate and the velocity of circulation. This is made to affect the
Canadian bill rate which in turn helps to determine the Canadian
long-rate.

The Netherlands model makes extensive use of bank deposits in
a number of the expenditure equations of the system, and there is
one equation explaining the level of such deposits. The equation
itself may be interpreted as a mixture of demand and supply influences, therefore serving essentially as the reduced form of a

more complex underlying structure. Recent developments in monetary theory and empirical practice have focussed on the problem of endogeneising the supply of money in econometric systems rather than treating the quantity of money as essentially predetermined, leaving the demand function to determine the interest rate. [12] In the Netherlands equation for bank deposits, we find the balance on current and capital account of the balance of payments and a variable reflecting "inflationary" Government spending. These may be clearly classified as money supply variables. However, total expenditure at current prices and the central bank discount rate also appear with the signs one would expect if the equation were a money demand equation. The central bank discount rate appears at a number of points in the Netherlands model but is treated as exogenous. No interest rates are determined endogenously.

The monetary sector of the Finnish model reflects the rather special conditions operating in Finland. In a sense, the Finnish monetary sector is very simple because of the fact that since the early 1960's interest rates have been relatively fixed and, therefore, have played little or no role in affecting expenditures, particularly as the real rate has remained very low. Consequently, the formulations of the demand functions for time and demand deposits do not contain interest rate variables, only income type variables. Since the main control weapon of the authorities over the banks has consisted in the control of central bank lending, the monetary variable used in the Finnish investment equations has been the ratio of central bank credit to total bank credit in the private sector.

The Japanese treatment of the monetary sector starts from the call loan rate which is made to depend in part on supply factors, since the equation includes the ratio of central bank loans to city banks to required reserves. The call rate, the central bank redis-

---

[12] Teigen, R., 'Demand and Supply Functions for Money in U.S.A.: Some Structural Estimates', *Econometrica*, October 1964; Goldfeld, S.M., *Commercial Bank Behaviour and Economic Activity*, North-Holland, 1966. See also Crouch, R.L., 'A Model of the United Kingdom's Monetary Sector', *Econometrica*, October 1967.

count rate and the flow of "investible" funds (measured as corporate savings plus private sector capital consumption allowances)
then determine the long rate or rate on bank loans. The model
then determines the supply of bank loans to firms, the time and
deposit holdings of firms and the deposit holdings of households.
The deposit equations are properly interpreted as demand equations. The supply of money is not directly modelled. No direct
balance of payments effect can, therefore, enter in through the
supply of money.

The Italian and U.S. models contain the most fully articulated
attempts to model both the supply and cost of money, although
the Italian model contains rather less equations. Moreover, there
appear to be significant differences in the underlying logic of
the two models, representing two rather different traditions. In
the U.S. model the level of interest rates can broadly be conceived
of as the result of the interplay between the decisions of the banks
to hold free reserves, thus affecting the supply of money, and the
decisions of transactors to hold money, or the demand for money.
If the money supply were, for the sake of argument, made exogenous, the demand for money equation would complete the U.S.
system with respect to the interest rate. This is made even clearer
by the fact that the rate of interest is made the regressand in the
demand for money equation in the post-Keynesian tradition. The
Italian model, on the other hand, specifies equations for demand
and time deposits and an additional equation to determine the
interest rate. This latter equation is essentially a demand equation
for free reserves by commercial banks, normalised for the rate of
interest. Since the Italian system also includes an equation for
commercial bank borrowing from the central bank, the interest
rate equation cannot be interpreted as a supply equation.

9. Postscript

The preceding sections as explained at the outset are intended to
serve as a broad indication of the character of the economy
models relating to the developed countries that are included in the

LINK system. Like all good statistical models they must be regarded as organic rather than mechanical, developing over time in response to new data and new ideas. What has been presented is, therefore, no more than a series of snapshots of a system that is changing and will continue to change over time. The joint involvement of the model builders in a common activity in itself results in important by-products for the individual model builders. The development of an economy wide econometric system is in itself an important type of learning process. The joint activity of the model builders is an important contribution to this learning process which will be continued. As this survey has indicated there are many points on which the individual models diverge. For some purposes this will no doubt always be the case insofar as institutional conditions vary from country to country. However, it is to be hoped and expected that the common enterprise will serve to assist in the process of improving and standardising approaches to various problems where the possibilities exist.

Appendix. LINK Proprietary institutions *

Austria: Institute for Advanced Studies, Vienna.
Belgium: Free University of Brussels.
Canada: Institute for the Quantitative Analysis of Social and Economic Policy, University of Toronto.
Finland: Bank of Finland Institute for Economic Research.
West Germany: University of Bonn.
Italy: Istituto di Scienze Economiche, University of Bologna.
Japan: Institute of Economic Research, Kyoto University
Netherlands: Central Planning Bureau, The Hague.
Sweden: National Institute of Economic Research, Stockholm.
United Kingdom: Econometric Forecasting Unit, London Business School.
U.S.A.: Economic Research Unit, Wharton School of Finance and Commerce, University of Pennsylvania.

* As of August 1971 and as referred to in the text.

6. MODELS FOR DEVELOPING COUNTRIES

UNCTAD STAFF

1. Introduction

At the first session of the United Nations Conference on Trade and Development (UNCTAD) a recommendation [1] was made calling for an examination of individual developing economies to determine the feasibility of rates of growth higher than those experienced in the past and to indicate measures to achieve them. In pursuance of this recommendation quantitative studies of individual developing countries were undertaken by the UNCTAD secretariat with a view to assessing (a) the feasible range of target growth rates for each developing country consistent with its historical performance and its absorptive capacity and (b) the external resource requirements consistent with those target rates of growth. About forty developing countries were taken up for study, accounting for the bulk of the income and trade of the developing countries. The scope and depth of these studies varied from country to country due to limitations of data and resources. Eighteen of these countries were studied in some detail. Based on these country studies, projections were made of the external resource requirements of individual developing countries consistent with the target growth rates. These were then aggregated to obtain regional and global estimates of external capital requirements. The results of these studies were presented in a secretariat study submitted to the second UNCTAD at New Delhi in 1968. [2]

[1] UNCTAD, Proceedings of the United Nations Conference on Trade and Development, Volume 1: *Final Act and Report*, United Nations Publication, Sales No. 64.II.B.11, 1964, annex A.IV.2.
[2] UNCTAD, 'Trade Prospects and Capital Needs of Developing Countries', United Nations Publication, Sales No. E.68.II.D.13, 1968.

In general, the methodology followed was based on the well known two-gap approach which distinguishes between the resource gap, measured as the excess of investment requirements over savings possibilities for a given level of income, and the trade gap, measured as the excess of import requirements over export possibilities consistent with the same level of income. The two-gap analysis gives rise to certain theoretical and measurement problems and is, therefore, not generally accepted. However, there seems to be some agreement on the conceptual usefulness of distinguishing between the two gaps insofar as they indicate the presence of structural rigidities.

While the two-gap model provides a useful point of reference in the analysis of the development assistance needs, it is too simple to be able to handle the analysis of the effects of alternative national and international policies needed for the purpose of Project LINK simulations. This requires comprehensive general equilibrium models, work on which has already been taken up in the UNCTAD secretariat. The nature and scope of these models are discussed in the following section.

2. Type of macroeconomic models for development planning

In referring to models for developing economies, it is not implied that all developing countries are alike. On the contrary, the differences in structural characteristics and institutional elements are as varied as those among the industrially advanced countries. What we are looking for are some broad characteristics shared by all the developing countries and which differentiate them from the developed countries.

A prior question, i.e., whether model building for developing countries is useful for their planning purposes and whether it is a worth while effort at all, has been raised by Vernon. [3] He was highly sceptical of this kind of work and three main points of his

---

[3] Vernon, R., 'Comprehensive Model Building in the Planning Process: The Case of the Less Developed Economies', *Economic Journal*, March 1966.

criticism were: (i) the multivalent nature of the objectives behind national plans; (ii) poor data base and (iii) the high opportunity cost of skilled resources needed for this kind of work. These criticisms are not without merit but the highly pessimistic attitude of Vernon might tempt one to counter it by the argument that the non-econometric methods cannot do any better. Refraining himself from such a temptation, Conrad [4] counters the criticism of Vernon with positive arguments on the usefulness of econometric models, with examples of actual case studies. One of the main points made by Conrad is "that econometric models need not pretend to specify unambiguously social welfare functions nor attempt to impose a welfare function upon the decision-makers. Rather, they offer the possibility of trade-offs among the several objectives that must somehow be reconciled in the planning process". As regards unreliability of data and the costs of model building, the problems mentioned by Vernon are quite real but the continuing effort being made at the national and international levels and resources devoted to such modelling work at the UN and other international agencies should help remove the sting out of Vernon's criticism.

Turning to the features to be incorporated into the models for developing countries, one would naturally look into the abundant literature on the modelling of developed countries in order to examine which parts of these models could be carried over and which need to be modified. In an important paper on this subject, Klein [5] comes to the conclusion that while substantial parts of the models of the developed countries could be carried over, the supply side should be given much greater emphasis in the models for

---

[4] Conrad, A.H., 'Econometric Models in Development Planning', in: Papanek, G.F. (ed.), *Development Policy, Theory and Practice*, Harvard University Press, 1968.
[5] Klein, L.R., 'What Kind of Macroeconometric Model for Developing Economies?', reprinted in: Zellner, A. (ed.), *Readings in Economic Statistics and Econometrics*. On this subject, see also Behrman, J. and L.R. Klein, 'Econometric Growth Models for the Developing Economy', in: Ellis, W.A., M.F.G. Scott and J.N. Wolfe (eds), *Induction, Growth and Trade*, Clarendon Press, 1970 and Beltran del Rio, A. and L.R. Klein, 'Macroeconomic Model Building in Latin America: The Mexican Case', mimeographed, 1971 and Behrman, J., 'An Annual Macroeconomic Model of Post-War Chile, 1954–1965', mimeographed, 1971.

developing countries. The short-run versions of the models for developed economies are, by and large, based on the Keynesian theory of effective demand. Since productive capacity is fairly large, the emphasis is on the expenditure side of the national accounts, the problem being to create the necessary effective demand. Recent trends in econometric model building for these countries involve substantial extensions of the basic Keynesian model; the emphasis is on making the models more dynamic, incorporating both long-run growth aspects and the short-run cyclical features and laying greater emphasis on the institutional factors. If the models for developing countries were to be useful for planning of trade and development, it is necessary to adopt a similar pragmatic and institutionalised approach.

Thus, the general criteria to be adopted for building macroeconomic models for developing countries are the following. First, the models should reflect the dual nature of these economies and their internal rigidities. Second, they should incorporate both long-run growth aspects and short-run cyclical swings in output and prices. Third, the level of disaggregation and detail should be such as to permit an evaluation of the trade-offs which are of special relevance to the developing economies. To mention a few, the trade-off between price stability (particularly for countries with relatively high rates of inflation as in some of the Latin American countries) and growth, the trade-off between sectoral balance and overall growth on the one hand and domestic savings rate and external capital requirements on the other and the trade-off between current external capital needs and the constraint which debt service imposes in the future, are of importance. Fourth, fiscal and monetary sectors and the specific country institutional factors should be explicitly taken into account. Finally, the size of the models should not be out of proportion to the degree of interdependence and the available data base.

In the following section, estimated models for three countries, one from Latin America (Argentina), one from Asia (India) and one from Africa (Nigeria) are presented as illustrative case studies and their distinctive features in comparison and contrast to those of developed market economies are briefly discussed. The basic data and the results of simulation are not presented as the purpose is only to indicate the type of models being built.

3. Three case studies

3.1. Model of the Argentinian economy, 1955–1969

Unless otherwise specified, variables are measured in billion pesos, 1960 prices, except those followed by the symbol($'$) which are in million dollars 1960 prices, and those followed by an asterisk, which are in current prices. Index variables are preceded by the letter (i) and are in base 1960 = 100; variables preceded by (f) are measured in first differences and those preceded by (r) are in annual percentage rates of growth. All price variables are in index form, 1960 = 100. All variables are measured annually and refer to the current time period unless otherwise indicated by subscripts.

3.1.1. Endogenous variables

ACO	= Area seeded with corn, in million hectares
AFX	= Area seeded with flaxseed, in million hectares
AWH	= Area seeded with wheat, in million hectares
$AYCO$	= Average yield of corn per hectare, in kilograms.
$AYFX$	= Average yield of flaxseed per hectare, in kilograms
$AYWH$	= Average yield of wheat per hectare, in kilograms
BEQ	= Total production of beef – slaughtering plus increase in stocks – in thousand heads
$BESL$	= Slaughtering of bovine cattle in thousand heads
$BEST$	= Stock of bovine cattle in thousand heads
$CAME$	= Domestic consumption of meat
CG^*	= Government consumption expenditures
$CMFDY$	= Private consumption of manufactured goods, dynamic industries
$CMFVG$	= Private consumption of manufactured goods, vegetative industries
COT	= Other private consumption

CP	=	Total private consumption expenditures.
CUDY	=	Capacity utilisation, dynamic industries, expressed as a percentage
CUMF	=	Capacity utilisation, total manufacturing, expressed as a percentage
CUVG	=	Capacity utilisation, vegetative industries, expressed as a percentage
E	=	Total employment, in millions
EMF	=	Employment in manufacturing, in millions
EMFC	=	Employment in manufacturing for full utilisation of capacity, in millions
FAN'*	=	Net foreign assets
FPN'*	=	Net factor income payments abroad
FPNI'*	=	Net interest payments on the external debt
FPNP'*	=	Net direct foreign investment income
GDF*	=	Government deficit
GDP	=	Gross domestic product
GIN*	=	Interest payments on the public debt
GSU*	=	Government subsidies
GTF*	=	Government transfer payments
IFMF	=	Gross fixed private investment in manufacturing
IFP	=	Total gross fixed private investment
IG	=	Government investment
ISBE	=	Change in the stock of bovine cattle
ISOT	=	Change in other stocks
L*	=	Total money supply (money plus quasi-money)
M'*	=	Total imports of goods and non-factor services
MF'	=	Imports of fuels
MI'	=	Imports of investment goods
MR'	=	Imports of raw materials and intermediate goods
MSV'	=	Imports of services
N	=	Total population, in millions
NU	=	Urban population, in millions
P	=	Implicit GDP price deflator
PAG	=	Implicit price deflator of value added in agriculture
PCAME	=	Implicit price deflator of meat consumption
PCMDY	=	Implicit price deflator of consumption of manufactured goods, dynamic industries

PCMVG	=	Implicit price deflator of consumption of manufactured goods, vegetative industries
PCOFX	=	Weighted average of corn and flaxseed prices
PCOT	=	Implicit price deflator of consumption of other goods
PCP	=	Implicit price deflator of private consumption
PFXWH	=	Weighted average of flaxseed and wheat prices
PIF	=	Implicit price deflator of gross fixed investment
PM	=	Unit value index of imports in domestic currency
PMF	=	Implicit price deflator of value added in manufacturing
POT	=	Implicit price deflator of value added in sectors other than agriculture and manufacturing
PWHCO	=	Weighted average of wheat and corn prices
PX	=	Unit value index of exports in domestic currency
QCO	=	Output of corn in thousand tons
QFX	=	Output of flaxseed in thousand tons
QWH `	=	Output of wheat in thousand tons
RO*	=	Non-tax current government revenue
T*	=	Total tax revenue
TD*	=	Total direct tax revenue
TI*	=	Total indirect tax revenue
TM*	=	Import tax revenue
TO*	=	Other tax revenue
TX*	=	Export tax revenue
VAG	=	Value added in agriculture
VCEFX	=	Value added in the production of cereals and flaxseed
VCROT	=	Value added in other crops
VIF	=	Value added in infrastructure (non-residential construction, transport and communications and public utilities)
VLVFI	=	Value added in forestry, hunting and fishing
VMF	=	Value added in manufacturing
VMFC	=	Value added in manufacturing at full capacity
V2VG	=	Value added in vegetative industries
V2VGC	=	Value added in vegetative industries at full capacity
V3DY	=	Value added in dynamic industries
V3DYC	=	Value added in dynamic industries at full capacity

VOT	=	Value added in other sectors
W*	=	Average annual earnings per worker in thousand pesos
WFC	=	Total output of wheat, flaxseed and corn in thousand tons
WMF*	=	Average annual earnings per worker in the manufacturing sector, in thousand pesos
X'*	=	Exports of goods and non-factor services
XCO'*	=	Exports of corn
XCR'*	=	Total exports of crops
XDYNT'	=	Non-traditional exports of manufactures, dynamic industries
XFX'	=	Exports of linseed oil
XLVME'	=	Exports of livestock, including meat
XME'	=	Exports of meat
XQU'*	=	Exports of quebracho extract
XSV'*	=	Exports of non-factor services
XVGNT'	=	Non-traditional exports of manufactures, vegetative industries
XVGT'	=	Traditional exports of manufactures, vegetative industries (excluding meat)
XWH'*	=	Exports of wheat
XWOG'*	=	Exports of greasy wool
Y*	=	Gross domestic product at factor cost
YDP*	=	Gross disposable income
YN*	=	Total non-wage income
YNMF*	=	Non-wage income in the manufacturing sector
YW*	=	Total wage income

3.1.2. Exogenous variables

CRG*	=	Total credit to the government sector
CRP*	=	Total credit to the private sector
*D*1	=	Dummy variable to represent the impact of the Latin American Free Trade Association, taking the value of 0 for the years 1955–1961 and a time trend for the ensuing eight years

ER	=	Average implicit merchandise (exports plus imports) exchange rate in pesos per dollar
EREF	=	Annual effective exchange rate applicable to non-traditional exports of manufactures, i.e., the nominal exchange rate adjusted upward for 'reintegro' and drawback subsidies and deflated by the Argentine industrial price index relevant for the particular non-traditional export group
FBN'*	=	Net foreign borrowing
FDN'*	=	Net direct foreign investment
GKO*	=	Capital expenditures of the government sector other than in fixed investment
MC'	=	Imports of consumer goods
PBE	=	Annual average wholesale price for bovine cattle in the Liniers market
PCO	=	Average quoted prices of corn in Buenos Aires during the commercialisation of the corn harvest
PFX	=	Average quoted prices of flaxseed in Buenos Aires during the commercialisation of the flaxseed harvest
PM'	=	Unit value index of imports in dollars
PPU	=	Implicit price deflator of value added in public utilities
PUSMF'	=	Industrial wholesale price of the U.S.
PWH	=	Average quoted prices of wheat in Buenos Aires during the commercialisation of the wheat harvest
PX'	=	Unit value index of exports in dollars
RBE	=	Index of rainfall in the cattle breeding areas
RCO	=	Index of rainfall in the corn producing areas
RFX	=	Index of rainfall in the flaxseed producing areas
RWH	=	Index of rainfall in the wheat producing areas
t	=	Time trend
TRN	=	Average tax rate on non-wage income
TRW	=	Average tax rate on wage income
VMI	=	Value added in the mining sector
XSU'*	=	Exports of sugar

3.1.3. Predetermined variables

CFDN' *	=	Cumulative net direct foreign investment
CGDF *	=	Cumulative government deficit
CIG *	=	Cumulative government investment
CIFMF	=	Cumulative investment in manufacturing
*ED' * *	=	Total external debt in year 0 plus cumulative net foreign borrowing

3.1.4. Estimated equations

I.   **Production**

   A.   *Agricultural sector*

   A.1. Wheat

1. $$iAWH = 50.980 \left(\frac{PWH}{PCOFX}\right)_{-1} + 0.477\ iAWH_{-1} + 14.45$$
$$ (2.158) \phantom{\left(\frac{PWH}{PCOFX}\right)_{-1}} (2.419) \phantom{+ 0.477\ iAWH_{-1} +} (0.51)$$

   $$\bar{R}^2 = 0.444, \quad s = 11.4 \quad \text{Mean} = 119.0 \quad DW = 1.92$$

2. $$AYWH = 643.690\ \frac{PWH}{PCOFX} + 6.556\ iRWH - 241.06$$
$$ (1.884) \phantom{\frac{PWH}{PCOFX}} (3.480) (0.52)$$

   $$\bar{R}^2 = 0.409 \quad s = 155.3 \quad \text{Mean} = 1162.8 \quad DW = 1.85$$

   A.2. Flaxseed

3. $$iAFX = 60.810 \left(\frac{PFX}{PWHCO}\right)_{-1} + 0.410\ iAFX_{-1} - 2.12$$
$$ (2.018) \phantom{\left(\frac{PFX}{PWHCO}\right)_{-1}} (2.035) \phantom{+ 0.410\ iAFX_{-1} -} (0.08)$$

   $$\bar{R}^2 = 0.476 \quad s = 15.8 \quad \text{Mean} = 90.9 \quad DW = 1.68$$

4. $$AYFX = 207.150\ \frac{PFX}{PWHCO} + 2.273\ iRFX + 7.951\ t +$$
$$ (1.812) \phantom{\frac{PFX}{PWHCO}} (2.419) (1.991)$$
$$ + 5.86$$
$$ (0.04)$$

   $$\bar{R}^2 = 0.449 \quad s = 67.0 \quad \text{Mean} = 549.3 \quad DW = 2.51$$

A.3. Corn

5. $iACO = 21.440 \left(\dfrac{PCO}{PFXWH}\right)_{-1} + 1.252 \; iACO_{-1} - 48.672$

    $\quad\quad\quad\;\; (2.301) \quad\quad\quad\quad\quad\quad (16.911) \quad\quad\quad\quad (2.790)$

    $$\bar{R}^2 = 0.969 \quad s = 4.0 \quad \text{Mean} = 117.5 \quad DW = 1.50$$

6. $AYCO = 5.589 \; iRCO + 45.253 \; t + 279.86$

    $\quad\quad\quad\;\; (4.711) \quad\quad\quad (5.114) \quad\quad (1.51)$

    $$\bar{R}^2 = 0.740 \quad s = 162.4 \quad \text{Mean} = 1491.8 \quad DW = 1.67$$

A.4. Other crops

7. $iVCEFX = 0.322 \; iQWFC + 0.279 \; iVCEFX_{-1} + 35.17$

    $\quad\quad\quad\quad\;\; (4.612) \quad\quad\quad\quad (1.711) \quad\quad\quad\quad (1.95)$

    $$\bar{R}^2 = 0.653 \quad s = 9.4 \quad \text{Mean} = 103.2 \quad DW = 2.91$$

8. $iVCROT = 2.278 \; t + 74.80$

    $\quad\quad\quad\;\; (6.376) \quad (13.41)$

    $$\bar{R}^2 = 0.739 \quad s = 5.0 \quad \text{Mean} = 109.0 \quad DW = 1.36$$

A.5. Beef

9. $iBESL = -46.801 \; \dfrac{PBE}{P} + 2.036 \; iBEST -$

    $\quad\quad\quad\quad (4.501) \quad\quad\quad (2.377)$

    $\quad\quad\quad\;\; - 0.264 \; iRBE - 14.30$

    $\quad\quad\quad\quad (1.965) \quad\quad\quad\quad (0.14)$

    $$\bar{R}^2 = 0.873 \quad s = 5.2 \quad \text{Mean} = 122.3 \quad DW = 2.49$$

10. $iBEQ = 24.801 \left(\dfrac{PBE}{P}\right)_{-1} + 1.259 \; iBEST - 50.81$

    $\quad\quad\quad\; (4.475) \quad\quad\quad\quad\quad (3.303) \quad\quad\quad\quad (1.28)$

    $$\bar{R}^2 = 0.768 \quad s = 2.9 \quad \text{Mean} = 97.8 \quad DW = 1.06$$

A.6. Other livestock

11. $VLVFI$ = 1.975 t + 65.93
      (3.039) (6.26)

$$\bar{R}^2 = 0.507 \quad s = 5.0 \quad \text{Mean} = 97.5 \quad DW = 2.31$$

B. *Manufacturing sector*

B.1. Total value added in manufacturing, actual and capacity

12. VMF = 1.297 $CUMF$ + 0.297 $(CIFMF_{-1}) \dfrac{CUMF}{100}$ +
     (50–63) (4.070)   (26.009)

       + 0.149 EMF − 147.49
        (7.099)   (5.63)

$$\bar{R}^2 = 0.991 \quad s = 4.8 \quad \text{Mean} = 248.5 \quad DW = 2.52$$

13. $VMFC$ = 0.297 $CIFMF_{-1}$ + 0.149 $EMFC$ − 17.75

B.2. Vegetative industries

14. $V2VG$ = 0.642 $V2VGC$ + 0.437 VAG +
      (2.588)   (1.860)

       + 0.238 $f\left(\dfrac{CRP^*}{iWMF}\right)$ + 0.775 $(MR + MF)$ − 78.05
        (1.684)   (3.526)   (3.68)

$$\bar{R}^2 = 0.890 \quad s = 5.6 \quad \text{Mean} = 148.3 \quad DW = 1.52$$

B.3. Dynamic industries

15. $V3DY$ = 0.912 $V3DYC$ + 1.337 $(MR + MF)$ +
      (35.254)   (6.182)

       + 0.110 $f\left(\dfrac{CRP^*}{PM}\right)$ − 72.77
        (1.316)   (6.27)

$$\bar{R}^2 = 0.990 \quad s = 6.4 \quad \text{Mean} = 171.8 \quad DW = 1.99$$

16. $V3DYC$ = $\quad$ 0.816 $\quad VMFC -$ 97.48
$\qquad$ (123.382) $\qquad\qquad$ (41.11)

$$\bar{R}^2 = 0.999 \quad s = 1.8 \quad \text{Mean} = 189.5 \quad DW = 0.51$$

C. $\quad$ *Other sectors*

C.1. Infrastructure

17. VIF $\qquad$ = $\quad$ 0.145 $\quad CIG_{-1} +$ 1.496 $\quad MF + 69.64$
$\qquad\qquad$ (10.625) $\qquad\qquad$ (2.740) $\qquad$ (6.68)

$$\bar{R}^2 = 0.933 \quad s = 6.2 \quad \text{Mean} = 132.7 \quad DW = 1.77$$

C.2. Rest

18. VOT $\qquad$ = $\quad$ 0.530 $\quad VMF +$ 1.713 $\quad CG + 52.70$
$\qquad\qquad$ (12.232) $\qquad\qquad$ (4.617) $\qquad$ (2.48)

$$\bar{R}^2 = 0.988 \quad s = 5.4 \quad \text{Mean} = 376.7 \quad DW = 1.36$$

II. $\quad$ Consumption and investment

A. $\quad$ *Private consumption*

A.1. Aggregate

19. CP $\qquad$ = $\quad$ 0.738 $\dfrac{YDP^*}{PCP} +$ 164.450 $\dfrac{(1-TRW)\ YW^*}{(1-TRN)\ YN^*} -$
$\qquad\qquad$ (20.580) $\qquad\qquad\qquad$ (2.859)

$\qquad$ $-$ 52.62
$\qquad\quad$ (0.95)

$$\bar{R}^2 = 0.968 \quad s = 20.3 \quad \text{Mean} = 803.5 \quad DW = 1.68$$

A.2. Agricultural goods

20. $CAME$ $\qquad$ = $\quad$ 0.076 $\quad CP -$ 28.330 $\dfrac{PCAME}{PCP} +$ 36.31
$\quad$ (50–63) $\quad$ (15.417) $\qquad$ (11.149) $\qquad\qquad$ (20.93)

$$\bar{R}^2 = 0.956 \quad s = 1.3 \quad \text{Mean} = 65.5 \quad DW = 1.74$$

A.3. Manufactured goods

21. $CMFVG = 0.284\ CP - 98.510\ \dfrac{PCMVG}{PCP} + 180.85$

     (50–63)   (6.528)   (1.720)   (4.14)

        $\bar{R}^2 = 0.794 \quad s = 9.5 \quad \text{Mean} = 275.8 \quad DW = 0.94$

22. $CMFDY = 0.282\ CP - 125.910\ \dfrac{PCMDY}{PCP} + 68.52$

     (50–63)   (6.832)   (2.890)   (0.79)

        $\bar{R}^2 = 0.987 \quad s = 7.4 \quad \text{Mean} = 118.3 \quad DW = 0.99$

B. *Private investment*

23. $IFP = 0.261\ \dfrac{YN^* - T^*}{PIF} + 0.636\ r\left(\dfrac{CRP^*}{PIF}\right) + 19.43$

         (7.626)   (2.578)   (1.10)

        $\bar{R}^2 = 0.827 \quad s = 16.4 \quad \text{Mean} = 153.9 \quad DW = 1.19$

24. $IFMF = 0.477\ IFP + 88.201\ \dfrac{YNMF^*}{VMF^*} + 62.15$

         (5.074)   (2.104)   (4.28)

        $\bar{R}^2 = 0.944 \quad s = 5.8 \quad \text{Mean} = 45.2 \quad DW = 0.94$

III. Government

A. *Current revenue*

A.1. Direct taxes

25. $\dfrac{TD^*}{P} = 0.060\ Y_{-1} + 44.910\ \left[\dfrac{(1-TRW)\ YW^*}{(1-TRN)\ YN^*}\right]_{-1} -$

         (4.117)   (2.557)

        $- 0.298\ rP - 0.58$

         (3.265)   (0.03)

        $\bar{R}^2 = 0.696 \quad s = 7.7 \quad \text{Mean} = 83.3 \quad DW = 1.54$

A.2. Indirect taxes

26. $TM^* = \underset{(18.957)}{0.168} \ M^* - \underset{(0.40)}{0.98}$

$\bar{R}^2 = 0.962 \quad s = 6.3 \quad \text{Mean} = 33.4 \quad DW = 1.34$

27. $TX^* = \underset{(6.209)}{0.085} \ X^* - \underset{(0.94)}{3.88}$

$\bar{R}^2 = 0.728 \quad s = 10.7 \quad \text{Mean} = 15.0 \quad DW = 1.31$

28. $\dfrac{TO^*}{P} = \underset{(4.421)}{0.240} \ VMF_{-1} - \underset{(1.254)}{0.194} \ rP + \underset{(1.068)}{19.335}$

$\bar{R}^2 = 0.597 \quad s = 13.1 \quad \text{Mean} = 88.3 \quad DW = 0.90$

A.3. Other revenue

29. $RO^* = \underset{(20.074)}{0.003} \ Y^*_{-1} - \underset{(0.05)}{0.02}$

$\bar{R}^2 = 0.966 \quad s = 1.1 \quad \text{Mean} = 5.6 \quad DW = 2.16$

B. *Current expenditures*

B.1. Government consumption

30. $CG^* = \underset{(45.453)}{0.108} \ Y^* - \underset{(0.28)}{2.17}$

$\bar{R}^2 = 0.993 \quad s = 20.5 \quad \text{Mean} = 250.2 \quad DW = 1.18$

B.2. Subsidies

31. $GSU^* = -\underset{(1.62)}{69.46} \ \dfrac{PPU}{P} + \underset{(7.052)}{1.118} \ GSU^*_{-1} + \underset{(1.74)}{73.70}$

$\bar{R}^2 = 0.871 \quad s = 7.7 \quad \text{Mean} = 32.3 \quad DW = 1.47$

B.3. Transfers to households

32. GTF^* $= 27.237\ NU + 0.896\ GTF^*_{-1} - 365.91$
　　　　　　　(1.914)　　　(6.244)　　　　　　(1.84)

$\bar{R}^2 = 0.962\quad s = 25.9\quad \text{Mean} = 137.5\quad DW = 1.20$

B.4. Interest payments on the public debt

33. GIN^* $=\ 0.031\ CGDF^*_{-1} + 3.60$
　　　　　　　(7.614)　　　　　　(2.09)

$\bar{R}^2 = 0.803\quad s = 4.9\quad \text{Mean} = 12.5\quad DW = 0.63$

C.　Government investment

34. IG $=\ 0.028\ GDP_{-1} - 0.859\ rGDP_{-1} - 0.136\ rP$
　　　　　　(1.596)　　　　　(1.722)　　　　　　(1.354)

$\bar{R}^2 = 0.540\quad s = 8.4\quad \text{Mean} = 46.9\quad DW = 1.87$

IV. Population and employment

A.　*Population*

35. $\ln N$ $=\ 0.017\ t + 2.84$
　　　　　　(61.612)　　(747.27)

$\bar{R}^2 = 0.996\quad s = 0.0\quad \text{Mean} = 3.1\quad DW = 0.50$

36. NU $=\ 0.818\ N - 2.94$
　　　　　　(141.811)　　(23.66)

$\bar{R}^2 = 0.999\quad s = 0.03\quad \text{Mean} = 14.6\quad DW = 1.37$

B.　*Employment demand*

37. E $=\ 2.620\ GDP - 1752.960\ \dfrac{W^*}{PIF} + 4053.82$
　　　　　　(5.487)　　　　　(2.240)　　　　　　(22.40)

$\bar{R}^2 = 0.890\quad s = 98.9\quad \text{Mean} = 5821.5\quad DW = 1.1?$

38. $EMFC$ = 1.565 $VMFC$ − 582.680 $\dfrac{WMF^*}{PIF}$ + 1438.03
    (4.342) (2.482) (16.97)

$$\bar{R}^2 = 0.591 \quad s = 57.9 \quad \text{Mean} = 1489.2 \quad DW = 1.07$$

V. External sector

A. *Exports*

A.1. Agriculture

39. $iXWH$ = 0.707 $iQWH$ + 0.409 $iXWH_{-1}$ − 16.61
    (2.751) (1.813) (0.42)

$$\bar{R}^2 = 0.398 \quad s = 27.6 \quad \text{Mean} = 108.7 \quad DW = 1.84$$

40. $iXCO$ = $\overline{iXCO}$

41. XCR'^* = 1.120 $(XWH'^* + XCO'^*)$ + 56.03
    (56−67) (29.055) (4.53)

$$\bar{R}^2 = 0.990 \quad s = 15.0 \quad \text{Mean} = 392.4 \quad DW = 2.14$$

42. $iXME$ = 0.578 $iBESL$ + 0.696 $iXME_{-1}$ − 25.84
    (1.776) (3.221) (0.52)

$$\bar{R}^2 = 0.484 \quad s = 21.4 \quad \text{Mean} = 141.0 \quad DW = 2.14$$

43. $XWOG'^*$ = − 2.336 t + 0.804 $XWOG'^*_{-1}$
    (1.470) (2.233)

$$\bar{R}^2 = 0.443 \quad s = 21.6 \quad \text{Mean} = 78.9 \quad DW = 1.76$$

44. $XLVME'^*$ = 1.106 $(XME'^* + XWOG'^*)$ − 9.29
    (56−67) (20.374) (0.44)

$$\bar{R}^2 = 0.974 \quad s = 9.6 \quad \text{Mean} = 415.1 \quad DW = 1.03$$

A.2. Vegetative industries

A.2.1. Traditional

45. $XVGT' = 6.818\ t - 0.093\ CMFVG' + 518.05$
$(55-66)\quad (2.711)\quad (2.305)\quad\quad\quad (3.75)$

$\bar{R}^2 = 0.393\quad s = 22.6\quad \text{Mean} = 229.0\quad DW = 1.48$

A.2.2. Non-traditional

46. $XVGNT' = 0.138\ iEREF - 0.380\ CUVG_{-1} +$
$(55-66)\quad (2.108)\quad\quad (2.155)\quad\quad\quad\cdot$

$+ 4.276\ D1$
$\quad (5.737)$

$\bar{R}^2 = 0.824\quad s = 3.1\quad \text{Mean} = 16.9\quad DW = 2.34$

A.3. Dynamic industries

A.3.1. Traditional

47. $iXFX' = 1.354\ iQFX + 0.91$
$\quad\quad (4.855)\quad\quad (0.04)$

$\bar{R}^2 = 0.634\quad s = 21.6\quad \text{Mean} = 103.8\quad DW = 3.04$

48. $iXQU = \overline{iXQU}$

A.3.2. Non-traditional

49. $XDYNT' = 0.073\ V3DY' - 2.000\ CUDY_{-1} + 118.27$
$(55-66)\quad (12.329)\quad\quad (3.623)\quad\quad\quad (2.27)$

$\bar{R}^2 = 0.923\quad s = 13.7\quad \text{Mean} = 91.4\ DW = 1.16$

A.4. Non-factor service receipts

50. $XSV'^* = 14.470\ t + 36.96$
$\quad\quad (4.049)\quad (0.95)$

$\bar{R}^2 = 0.524\quad s = 59.8\quad \text{Mean} = 181.7\quad DW = 0.54$

B. *Imports*

B.1. Fuels

51. MF' $= 0.070$ $VMF' - 1.50$ $VMI' + 113.17$
    (5.222)   (10.120)   (3.44)

    $\bar{R}^2 = 0.929$ $s = 16.1$ Mean $= 149.7$ $DW = 1.40$

B.2. Other intermediate goods

52. MR' $= 0.076$ $VMF' + 2.338$ $rVMF' +$
    (53–66) (3.114)   (1.007)

    $+ 1.799$ $f\left[\dfrac{FAN'*}{\sum\limits_{i=1}^{3}(M'^*_{-i}/3)}\right] + 192.88$
    (1.619)   (2.11)

    $\bar{R}^2 = 0.709$ $s = 54.0$ Mean $= 463.0$ $DW = 2.30$

B.3. Investment goods

53. MI' $= 0.371$ $IF' - 0.193$ $V3DY' +$
    (6.543)   (3.771)

    $+ 1.032$ $f\left[\dfrac{FAN'*}{\sum\limits_{i=1}^{3}(M'^*_{-i}/3)}\right] - 69.33$
    (1.130)   (1.10)

    $\bar{R}^2 = 0.906$ $s = 44.1$ Mean $= 450.9$ $DW = 1.60$

B.4. Non-factor service payments

54. $MSV'*$ $= 26.299$ $t - 54.44$
    (6.887)   (1.31)

    $\bar{R}^2 = 0.768$ $s = 63.7$ Mean $= 207.8$ $DW = 1.30$

C. *Net factor income payments*

55. $FPNP'*$ $= 0.201$ $CFDN'^*_{-1} + 711.400$ $\dfrac{YNMF*}{VMF*} - 380.35$
    (4.504)   (1.786)   (1.71)

    $\bar{R}^2 = 0.607$ $s = 48.8$ Mean $= 91.1$ $DW = 1.86$

56. $FPNI'^* \quad = \quad 0.025 \ ED'^*_{-1} \ - \ 5.09$
    $\qquad\qquad\quad (5.892) \qquad\qquad (0.68)$

$\qquad\qquad\quad \bar{R}^2 = 0.707 \quad s = 8.9 \quad Mean = 36.6 \quad DW = 1.80$

VI.   Wages and prices

A.   *Wages*

57. $rW^* \qquad = \quad 0.511 \ rPCP + 181.840 \ \dfrac{YN^*}{Y^*} + 1.056 \ CUMF -$
    $\qquad\qquad\quad (4.616) \qquad\qquad (2.005) \qquad\qquad (2.144)$

    $\qquad\qquad - \ 191.58$
    $\qquad\qquad\quad (2.23)$

$\qquad\qquad\quad \bar{R}^2 = 0.689 \quad s = 8.2 \quad Mean = 28.0 \quad DW = 2.29$

58. $rWMF^* \quad = \quad 0.470 \ rPCP + 160.610 \ \dfrac{YNMF^*}{VMF^*} +$
    $\qquad\qquad\quad (4.711) \qquad\qquad (2.882)$

    $\qquad\qquad + \ 1.049 \ CUMF - 182.46$
    $\qquad\qquad\quad (2.233) \qquad\qquad (2.62)$

$\qquad\qquad\quad \bar{R}^2 = 0.694 \quad s = 7.6 \quad Mean = 28.2 \quad DW = 2.41$

B.   *Prices*

59. $PAG \qquad = \quad 0.387 \ PX + 0.736 \ PAG_{-1} + 11.571$
    $(57\text{–}69) \qquad (1.937) \qquad (3.963) \qquad\qquad (1.136)$

$\qquad\qquad\quad \bar{R}^2 = 0.984 \quad s = 20.0 \quad Mean = 219.1 \quad DW = 1.34$

60. $rPMF \qquad = \quad 0.175 \ rPM + 0.668 \ rWMF^* + 0.362 \ rPAG -$
    $(57\text{–}69) \qquad (3.001) \qquad (3.821) \qquad\qquad (3.572)$

    $\qquad\qquad - \ 8.306$
    $\qquad\qquad\quad (1.853)$

$\qquad\qquad\quad \bar{R}^2 = 0.951 \quad s = 5.7 \quad Mean = 27.43 \quad DW = 2.51$

61. $rPOT \qquad = \quad 0.725 \ rPMF + 0.197 \ rPPU + 3.60$
    $\qquad\qquad\quad (14.045) \qquad\quad (1.665) \qquad (2.11)$

$\qquad\qquad\quad \bar{R}^2 = 0.980 \quad s = 2.7 \quad Mean = 26.6 \quad DW = 1.53$

62. $PCAME$ = $0.949 \ PAG - 3.39$
    $(32.415) (1.49)$

$\bar{R}^2 = 0.989 \quad s = 0.054 \quad \text{Mean} = 0.517 \quad DW = 1.19$

63. $PCMVG$ = $0.722 \ PMF + 0.383 \ PCMVG_{-1} - 1.61$
    $(18.123) (7.999) \phantom{PCMVG_{-1} -} (2.45)$

$\bar{R}^2 = 0.999 \quad s = 0.015 \quad \text{Mean} = 0.603 \quad DW = 1.87$

64. $PCMDY$ = $1.048 \ PMF + 0.70$
    $(85.642) (0.71)$

$\bar{R}^2 = 0.998 \quad s = 0.024 \quad \text{Mean} = 0.645 \quad DW = 1.20$

65. $PCOT$ = $0.737 \ POT + 0.343 \ PCOT_{-1} + 2.31$
    $(7.688) (2.951) \phantom{PCOT_{-1} +} (1.84)$

$\bar{R}^2 = 0.997 \quad s = 0.037 \quad \text{Mean} = 0.671 \quad DW = 2.01$

66. $rPIF$ = $0.724 \ rPMF + 0.112 \ rPM$
    $(10.142) (3.142)$

$\bar{R}^2 = 0.943 \quad s = 5.2 \quad \text{Mean} = 25.6 \quad DW = 1.38$

VII. Definitions and identities

A. *Production*

A.1. Agricultural sector

67. $BEST$ = $BEQ - BESL + BEST_{-1}$
68. VAG = $0.227 \ iVCEFX + 0.562 \ iVCROT + 0.376 \ iBEQ + VLVFI$
69. $iQWFC$ = $[47.923 \ iAWH(AYWH) + 12.280 \ iAFX(AYFX) + 30.620 \ iACO(AYCO)]/107.7$
70. QWH = $AYWH \ (AWH)$
71. QFX = $AYFX \ (AFX)$

72. $QCO \quad = AYCO\,(ACO)$

73. $PCOFX \quad = 0.773\,PCO + 0.227\,PFX$

74. $PWHCO \quad = 0.614\,PWH + 0.386\,PCO$

75. $PFXWH \quad = 0.156\,PFX + 0.844\,PWH$

76. $ISBE \quad = BEST - BEST_{-1}$

A.2. Manufacturing sector

77. $VMF \quad = V2VG + V3DY$

78. $VMFC \quad = V2VGC + V3DYC$

79. $CUMF \quad = \dfrac{VMF}{VMFC} \times 100$

80. $CUVG \quad = \dfrac{V2VG}{V2VGC} \times 100$

81. $CUDY \quad = \dfrac{V3DY}{V3DYC} \times 100$

A.3. Total production

82. $GDP \quad = VAG + VMI + VMF + VIF + VOT +$

$$+ \dfrac{TI^* - GSU^*}{P}$$

B. *Consumption*

83. $CP \quad = CAME + CMFVG + CMFDY + COT$

C. *Government*

84. $TI^* \quad = TM^* + TX^* + TO^*$

85. $T^* \quad = TD^* + TI^*$

86. $GDF^* \quad = CG^* + GSU^* + GTF^* + GIN^* + IG\,(PIF) +$

$$+ GKO^* - (TD^* + TI^* + RO^*)$$

D. *Income and income distribution*

87. $YW^* = E(W^*)$

88. $YN^* = Y^* - YW^*$

89. $YNMF^* = VMF(PMF) - EMF(WMF^*)$

90. $Y^* = GDP^* - TI^* + GSU^*$

91. $YDP^* = Y^* + GTF^* - TD^* - FPN^*$

E. *External sector*

92. $X'^* = XCR'^* + XLVME'^* + (XVGT' + XVGNT' + XFX' + XQU' + XDYNT)PUSMF + XSV'^*$

93. $M'^* = (MC' + MR' + MI')PM + MSV'^*$

94. $FPN'^* = FPNP'^* + FPNI'^*$

95. $FAN'^* = FAN'^*_{-1} + X'^* - (M'^* + FPN'^*) + FDN'^* + FBN'^*$

F. *Money and prices*

96. $fL^* = fFAN^* + fCRP^* + fCRG^*$

97. $PCP = 0.088\,PCAME + 0.421\,PCMVG + 0.211\,PCMDY + 0.280\,PCOT$

98. $PX = PX'(iER)$

99. $PM = PM'(iER)$

100. $P = [(VAG)PAG + (VMF)PMF + (VMI + VIF + VOT)POT]/(GDP - (TI^* - GSU^*)/P)$

101. $P(ISOT) = P(GDP) - PCP(CP + CG) - PIF(IF) - PBE(ISBE) - X(PX) + M(PM)$

3.1.5. Supply equations

Eqs. (1) to (18) relate to the supply side which is disaggregated into four broad sectors: agriculture, manufacturing, infrastructure and services. Each sector is in turn divided into a number of sub-sectors, the choice of disaggregation being determined by their importance as either suppliers or users of foreign exchange resources. Thus, in the agricultural sector, four major commodities are individually considered, namely, wheat, corn, flaxseed and beef, which together account for about 45% of the export earnings of Argentina over the period under study.

In explaining the supply of cereals and flaxseed (eqs. (1) to (6)), acreage under each of these crops and yields per hectare are considered separately. For each crop, total seeded area is related to the price level of the respective crop lagged one year relative to a weighted average of the prices of the closest substitutes in production. In addition, each equation allows for a lag in response due to possible rigidities. Although the explanatory power of the equations for both wheat and flaxseed acreage is rather weak, the coefficients of the relative price variables are statistically significant in all three cases. The level of rainfall, which refers to the six months immediately preceding planting, shows a significant impact on the yields of each crop. Although the coefficients of the relative price variables in the yield equations have the expected sign, their t-ratios are not highly significant. In the case of corn, the significant upward trend mainly reflects the impact of the increasing use of hybrid seeds, particularly during the latter years of the period under study. The equations discussed above can be improved substantially by the introduction of additional explanatory variables to account for the interrelationship of crop production and cattle raising, price expectations and the impact of government support prices, all of which have been omitted at this stage of the analysis.

Eqs. (9) and (10) relate to the supply of beef. The slaughtering of bovine cattle is related to the relative price of beef, to the stock of bovine cattle at the beginning of the year and to an index of rainfall in the cattle breeding region. Total production of beef, which includes, in addition to the slaughtering of beef, the increase in the stock of beef, is related to the relative price of beef lagged one year and to the stock of beef at the beginning of the year. These equations show that given the stock of beef a negative short-term price elasticity of beef slaughtering (−0.46) is consistent with a positive short-term price elasticity of total beef production (0.24). This is due to the fact that the beef output is at the same time an input in the production of beef and that there is a technological relationship limiting the amount of beef which can be produced with a given stock. Other things being equal, an increase in the relative price of beef increases the profitability of investment in beef production, thus leading beef producers to decrease slaughtering in the short-run to build up stocks. Although the coefficient of the rainfall index is not highly significant, it points in the expected direction. In effect, since Argentina supports cattle almost exclusively on natural pastures, any decrease in the rainfall that reduces pasture production results in herd liquidation.

Eqs. (12) to (16) relate to the supply of manufacturing output. In the case of this sector, a distinction is made between capacity output, measured from a trend through peak values, and actual output. Actual output originating in the manufacturing sector depends on utilised capital [6] and labour. Since actual output is determined later in the model, this equation actually determines employment in the manufacturing sector. Eq. (13) uses the same coefficients as eq. (12) but introduces total available capital and full capacity employment as the independent variables. This gives a measure of full capacity output for manufacturing which can then be related to actual output to form an index of capacity utilisation. To determine actual output, two groups of manufacturing industries are distinguished, namely, a relatively slow-growing group highly dependent on agricultural inputs and traditionally referred to as vegetative industries, and another relatively

---

[6] Cumulative investment in the manufacturing sector is used as a proxy for the capital stock in this sector. The equation is estimated for the period 1950–1963, since data on investment by sectors of destination is not available for later years.

fast-growing group highly dependent on imported inputs and traditionally referred to as dynamic industries. [7] The deviations of actual from capacity output in the first group depend on agricultural output, on credit to the private sector relative to the level of manufacturing wage income per worker (as a measure of wage cost), and on the availability of intermediate imports. Deviations in the output of dynamic industries depend similarly on the availability of intermediate imports, and on credit to the private sector relative to import prices (as a measure of the cost of imported inputs). Imports of intermediate goods appear to have been the most important factor determining deviations of actual from capacity output in both groups. The estimated coefficients imply an average mean elasticity of value added in manufacturing with respect to intermediate imports of about 0.28 for vegetative industries and 0.41 for dynamic industries for the period 1955—1969.

3.1.6. Domestic demand equations

Eqs. (19) to (22) comprise the private consumption functions. Aggregate private consumption depends on disposable income and on income distribution between wage and non-wage earners. Since data on direct tax collections disaggregated by each of these two income components is not available, the income variables are expressed in gross terms for estimation, but the coefficients are adjusted by marginal direct tax rates for purposes of simulation. [8] Several lag structures were tested but the results were not statistically significant. The estimated marginal propensity to consume of 0.74 is consistent with other studies of Argentine consumption patterns. Sectoral consumption functions required to determine the exportable surpluses are estimated for meat and manufactured goods originating in both vegetative and dynamic industries. They are all related to aggregate consumption and to the corresponding relative prices.

---

[7] Vegetative industries include ISIC groups 2 minus 27 plus 39; dynamic industries include ISIC groups 3 plus 27 minus 39.

[8] A similar approach is followed by Behrman and Klein, *op. cit.*

In eq. (23), aggregate gross private fixed investment depends on gross disposable non-wage income and on the rate of growth of real credit. The coefficients of both variables are statistically significant, reflecting the dependence of private investment on both internal funds and credit availability. [9]

Gross private fixed investment in manufacturing, eq. (24), is related to aggregate investment and to the share of non-wage income in total manufacturing income.

3.1.7. Government sector

Current government revenue is disaggregated into five components: direct taxes, import and export taxes, other taxes and non-tax revenue (eqs. (25) to (29)). Direct taxes in real terms depend on real income lagged one year (since direct taxes are assessed on the previous year's income), on the distribution of income between wage and non-wage earners (also lagged one year) and on the rate of inflation. The latter variable is a proxy for the differential between the rate of inflation and the interest rate charged on unpaid taxes. The interest rate was so low (2% per month up to 1964) relative to the rate of inflation (25 to 30% per year), that during most of the period under study it was cheaper to borrow from the Government by non-payment of taxes than to borrow from the market at interest rates of up to 4% per month. Foreign trade taxes are related to the corresponding foreign trade variables and other taxes in real terms, comprising mainly sales and value added taxes, are related to value added in the manufacturing sector and to the rate of inflation.

On the expenditure side (eqs. (30) to (34)), four components are distinguished in the current account. Government consumption depends on income, government subsidies depend on a distributed lag of the prices of public utilities, government transfer payments to households depend on urban population, and government interest payments are related to the cumulative deficit of the govern-

---

[9] Time series data of the breakdown of investment between corporations and unincorporated enterprises are not available.

ment lagged one year. Eq. (34) determines real government investment as a function of *GDP* and the growth rate of *GDP*, both
lagged one year, the rate of inflation and lagged government investment. Although the standard errors of the coefficients are relatively high, their signs are as expected. Given the level of income, a
fall in the rate of growth leads the government to increase public
investment in the following year, but an acceleration in the current rate of inflation tends to increase the government deficit and,
therefore, results in a cutback of public investment expenditures.

3.1.8. Population and employment

Total population is simply determined at this stage as a logarithmic function of time, and urban population is related to total
population.

Aggregate employment demand depends on the level of output
and on the wage rate relative to the price of investment goods.
Since employment demand in the manufacturing sector is determined earlier in the model, eq. (38) actually determines full capacity employment in manufacturing.

3.1.9. External sector

Eqs. (39) to (50) determine exports of goods and services. Adequate explanations of export behaviour, particularly of exports of
agricultural origin, are difficult to find. Several foreign demand
factors as well as relative prices, were tested as explanatory variables in most export equations, but without success. It is not
unreasonable to consider Argentine exports of rural goods as supply determined, being equal to the difference between the domestic supply and demand of exportable rural goods. However, since
the definitions of the production and consumption variables used
in this model are not strictly comparable, this approach could not
be followed at this stage. Instead, simple equations were estimated
for the quantum of wheat and meat exports relating them to
output and to the dependent variable lagged one year, on the
assumption that given output, farmers adjust to an equilibrium

level of exports. The quantum of corn exports, on the other hand, has fluctuated widely and is tentatively assumed to be equal to its average value for the period.

Exports of manufactures are disaggregated into two broad categories, namely, traditional and non-traditional, under each of the two industrial subsectors considered. Although the traditional exports of both industrial groups embody a considerable amount of value added by manufacturing, they are essentially processed agricultural goods. The exports of vegetative industries are mainly hides and skins, dairy products, wheat flour, washed wool, cotton ginning and edible oils. The dynamic industries, on the other hand, export two traditional goods, namely, linseed oil and quebracho extract. A time trend and domestic consumption of goods of the vegetative industries determine traditional exports of the first group. Exports of linseed oil are simply related to the output of flaxseed, while exports of quebracho extract which have remained virtually constant during the recent past are assumed to be equal to the average for the period of observation.

In determining non-traditional exports (eqs. (46) and (49)) Felix's approach is followed.[10] They are assumed to depend on an index of the effective exchange rate, i.e., the nominal exchange rate adjusted upward for export subsidies and deflated by the Argentine industrial price index relevant for the particular non-traditional export group, on the annual rate of utilisation of industrial capacity lagged one year and on a dummy variable to represent the impact of the Latin American Free Trade Association (LAFTA). In the case of the export equation for the vegetative industries, the coefficients of the three variables are statistically significant and have the expected sign. For the exports of dynamic industries, the exchange rate variable was not statistically significant and hence it was dropped; moreover, the LAFTA variable, represented by a suitable time trend, seemed to capture mainly other effects in addition to the expansion of non-traditional exports to LAFTA countries and it was, therefore, replaced by the

[10] Felix, D., 'Subsidies, Recession and Non-Traditional Industrial Exporting in Argentina', mimeographed, 1968.

output of the dynamic industries which turned out to be highly significant.

Merchandise imports are disaggregated by economic use into four broad groups: consumer goods, fuels, other intermediate goods and investment goods (eqs. (51) to (53)). On the whole, imports of consumer goods did not show any clearly discernible trend, amounting on the average to less than ten per cent of total imports and to less than one per cent of total consumption. They are, therefore, taken as exogenous in the present model. Fuel imports reached a peak in 1957, when they accounted for about one quarter of total merchandise imports. An intensive process of import substitution in fuels began by the end of 1958, as a result of which fuel imports declined drastically, and by the end of the period under study they accounted for less than ten per cent of total merchandise imports. The demand for fuel imports is, therefore, considered to depend on both a demand variable, the level of value added in manufacturing, and an import substitution variable, the level of value added in mining, the coefficients of which are both highly significant and have the expected sign, implying mean partial elasticities of demand for fuel imports of 1.79 with respect to industrial production and of -1.54 with respect to mining production.

About one half of the import bill of Argentina is accounted for by raw materials and other intermediate goods. The industrial sector absorbs all imports of intermediate goods, and it is thus assumed that demand for such imports depends on the level of manufacturing production. However, it has been observed that the intermediate import elasticity with respect to manufacturing output tends to increase with an acceleration in the rate of growth, suggesting a non-linear relationship between intermediate imports and output. Therefore, the demand for intermediate imports is assumed to depend not only on the level of manufacturing production but also on its rate of growth. In addition, since exchange controls and other quantitative restrictions have been applied to control imports during the period of observation, the lagged changes in the ratio of the level of net gold plus foreign exchange reserves to a three-year average of total imports has been included in the demand equation for intermediate imports as a proxy variable for changes in the intensity of import restrictions. [11a]

Imports of investment goods tended to decline as a proportion of fixed investment from 1955 to 1958 but increased sharply during the years 1959 to 1963 mainly due to investment in the petroleum and car industries. By the end of the period the ratio has regained the relatively low 1958 level. The demand for imports of investment goods is determined by gross fixed investment, by an import substitution variable represented by the level of value added in the dynamic industries and by the same proxy variable for quantitative restrictions (unlagged) included in the demand equation for intermediate imports. The coefficients of all three variables are of the correct *a priori* sign, but only two are statistically significant. They imply an elasticity of demand of investment goods imports of 2.45 with respect to investment and −1.24 with respect to value added in dynamic industries.

Two components of net factor income payments are distinguished, namely direct foreign investment income and interest payments on the external debt. The former is determined by the stock of private foreign capital, represented by cumulative direct foreign investment lagged one year, and by the share of profits in manufacturing income. Interest payments, on the other hand, are related to the total external debt lagged one year. The coefficient of the external debt variable implies an average interest rate, at the margin, of 2.5%, which appears to be extremely low in the light of the rather high interest rates that Argentina had to pay on new foreign loans in the recent past.

3.1.10. Wages and prices

The next set of eqs. (57) to (66) relate to the determination of wages and prices. [11b] The rates of increase in the national average wage rate and in the wage rate prevailing in the manufacturing sector are related to the rates of increase in the prices of consumer

[11a] Cf. Diaz Alejandro Carlos, *Essays on the Economic History of the Argentine Republic,* Yale University Press, 1970, Chapter 7.
[11b] See Maynard, G. and W. van Rijckeghem, 'Stabilisation Policy in an Inflationary Economy – Argentina', in Papaneck, *op. cit.*

goods, i.e., the deflator of consumer expenditure, the degree of capacity utilisation and the corresponding shares of non-wage income in total income. The dollar prices of Argentinian exports, a substantial part of which consists of agricultural goods, are considered to be exogenous. With the exception of beef, the share of the agricultural exports of Argentina in the corresponding total world exports is not large. The export price level valued in terms of domestic currency is, therefore, taken as the principal determinant of the domestic price level of agricultural goods making allowance for a lag in adjustment between the domestic and export price level (eq. (59)). The rate of change in the price level of manufactured goods is simply related to the rates of change in wages and the costs of domestic and imported inputs. The two basic sectoral price levels, agricultural and manufactured goods, being determined in this way, all other sectoral price levels are related to these prices (eqs. (61) to (66)). The overall price level (the *GDP* deflator) is determined as a weighted average of the sectoral prices from the accounting identity in eq. (100).

It will be noted that the level of cash balances with the public has no direct effect on the level of prices in the above model and there is no separate equation explaining the demand for money. It is implicitly assumed that the demand for money by the public is always met and is thus determined endogenously. However, the monetary authority could vary the allocation of credit between the domestic private sector and the government sector. The credit made available to the private sector, as mentioned earlier, is a significant factor influencing their investment expenditures.

The remaining eqs. (67)–(100), are accounting relationships and definitions. Eq. (101), which determines inventory investment as a residual, requires an explanation. This equation is essentially an equilibrium condition equating aggregate supply and demand. Determination of inventories in this way as a residual and hence as an adjustment variable between aggregate supply and demand has the drawback that it contains not only the statistical discrepancy between the income and expenditure accounts but also the estimation errors of all other equations in the model. For simulation purposes, therefore, appropriate limits based on historical experience are set on the magnitude of inventories and if the estimated values of inventories lie outside these limits, suitable adjustments are made on the supply side and the model resimulated to obtain the feed-back effects on the expenditure side and the price level. It may be worth mentioning here that the exchange rate variations which are considered to be exogenous in the above model are closely related to the domestic price level, the level of foreign assets relative to imports and the deficit on current account, as may be seen from the following equation:

$$fER = \underset{(55-66)}{0.511} \; \underset{(4.022)}{fP_{-1}} - \underset{(2.013)}{0.319 \, f} \frac{FAN_{-1}}{M_{-1}} + \underset{(1.607)}{0.201 \; f(M-X)_{-1}}$$

$$+ \; \underset{(0.632)}{2.805} \qquad R^2 = 0.65$$

The above equation points out the significant impact of the foreign exchange position and domestic price level on government decisions relating to exchange rate changes which would be useful for purposes of simulating the model for future periods.

3.2. Model of the Indian Economy 1950/51 – 1968/69 [12]

3.2.1. Endogenous variables

A = Total area under crops, index 1949–50 = 100

AF = Area under food crops, index 1949–50 = 100

ANF = Area under non-food crops, index 1949–50 = 100

AYF = Average yield per acre – food crops, index 1949–50 = 100

$AYNF$ = Average yield per acre – non-food crops, index 1949–50 = 100

BL^* = Commercial bank loans to private sector, Rs. 10 million

---

[12] The model presented here draws partly on a model of India constructed by Dr. P.K. Pani of the University of Pennsylvania, Philadelphia, U.S.A.

*BR** = Borrowings of commercial banks from the Reserve Bank, Rs. 10 million

*C** = Currency held by the public

CU = Capacity utilisation

*CPR** = Profits after tax in the corporate sector, Rs. 10 million

*D** = Demand deposits, Rs. 10 million

*DEP** = Depreciation, Rs. 10 million, current prices

*EF** = External finance of the corporate sector, Rs. 10 million, current prices

*FER** = Foreign exchange reserves, Rs. 10 million, current prices

*GSB** = Commercial banks holdings of government securities, Rs. 10 million

*GSBP** = Total holdings of government securities excluding the Reserve Bank holdings, Rs. 10 million

*GSP** = Public, other than Reserve Bank and commercial banks, holdings of government securities, Rs. 10 million

*H** = Inventory investment, Rs. 10 million, current prices

ICF = Investment in fixed assets, corporate sector, Rs. 10 million, 1960–61 prices

INCF = Investment in fixed assets, non-corporate sector, Rs. 10 million, 1960–61 prices

*L** = Money supply with the public, currency + demand deposits, Rs. 10 million

MF = Imports of food grains, million tons

*MG** = Total imports of goods, Rs. 10 million, current prices

MOF = Imports other than food, index 1958 = 100

P = Implicit GNP deflator, 1960–61 = 100

PA = Implicit deflator of income in agricultural sector, 1960–61 = 100

PAW = Wholesale prices of agricultural commodities, 1952–53 = 100

PCL = Consumer price index, 1949 = 100

PF = Wholesale prices of food articles, index 1952–53 = 100

PFG = Wholesale prices of manufactured articles, index 1952–53 = 100

PI = Price index of investment goods, 1952–53 = 100

PNA = Implicit deflator of income in non-agricultural sector, 1960–61 = 100

PNF = Wholesale price of agricultural raw materials, index 1952 –53 = 100

PW = Wholesale price index, 1952–53 = 100

PXO = Unit value index of other exports, 1958 = 100

QAF = Agricultural output – food crops, index 1949–50 = 100

QANF = Agricultural output – non-food crops, index 1949–50 = 100

RA = Commercial banks advance rate

RG = Average rate of return on government securities held by commercial banks

*RG*1 = Yield on long-term government bonds

*RS*1 = Call-money rate

*R*12 = 12-month time deposit rate

SC* = Savings of the corporate sector, Rs. 10 million, current prices

SF = Total supply of food grains, million tons

SG = Savings of the government sector, Rs. 10 million, 1960– 61 prices

SH = Savings of the household sector, Rs. 10 million, 1960– 61 prices

T = Total current receipts of the government sector, Rs. 10 million, 1960–61 prices

T* = Time deposits, Rs. 10 million

TD* = Direct taxes of central and state governments, Rs. 10 million

TI* = Indirect taxes of central and state governments, Rs. 10 million

TO* = Other current receipts of central and state governments, Rs. 10 million

TR* = Total reserves of commercial banks with the Reserve Bank, Rs. 10 million

W* = Average annual earnings per worker in factories, Rs. current prices

XEG = Exports of engineering goods, volume index, 1958 = 100

XG* = Total value of exports, Rs. 10 million, current prices

XJ = Exports of jute manufactures, volume index, 1958 = 100

XO   = Other exports, volume index, 1958 = 100
XS*   = Exports of services net, Rs. million, current prices
XT   = Exports of tea, volume index, 1958 = 100
Y   = Net national product, Rs. billion, 1960–61 prices
Y*   = Net national product, Rs. billion, current prices
YA   = Net national product in agricultural sector, Rs. billion, 1960–61 prices
YA*   = Net output in agricultural sector, Rs. billion, current prices
YF*   = Factor income paid abroad net, Rs. billion, current prices
YMC   = Net output in manufacturing-corporate sector, Rs. billion, 1960–61 prices
YMCP   = Capacity output in manufacturing-corporate sector, Rs. billion, 1960–61 prices
YMNC   = Net output in manufacturing-non-corporate sector, Rs. billion, 1960–61 prices
YMNCP= Capacity output in manufacturing-non-corporate sector, Rs. billion, 1960–61 prices
YNA   = Net output in non-agricultural sector, Rs. billion, 1960–61 prices
YNA*   = Net output in non-agricultural sector, Rs. billion, current prices
YS   = Net output of services, Rs. billion, 1960–61 prices

3.2.2. Exogenous variables

C*   = Currency with the public
F   = Foreign capital inflow, Rs. 10 million
GD*   = Government deficit on current account, Rs. 10 million
IG*   = Total investment in the government sector, Rs. 10 million
IGD*   = Government sector investment in departmental undertakings Rs. 10 million
IGO*   = Government sector investment, other than in departmental undertakings, Rs. 10 million
PM   = Unit value index of total imports, 1958 = 100

PMF   = Unit value index of food imports, 1958 = 100
PMOF = Unit value index of other imports, 1958 = 100
PXEG = Unit value index of exports of engineering goods, 1958
            = 100
PXJ   = Unit value index of exports of jute manufactures, 1958
            = 100
PXT   = Unit value index of exports of tea, 1958 = 100
R   = Rainfall, expressed as percentage of normal
RB   = Reserve Bank discount rate
RDT   = Average rate of direct taxes, expressed as a percentage of
            national income
RIT1   = Average rate of other indirect taxes, expressed as a per-
            centage of national income
RIT2   = Average rate of customs duties, expressed as a percentage
            of the value of imports + exports
t   = Time trend

3.2.3. Predetermined variables

$$KCG_{-1} = \sum_{0}^{t-1} (ICF_t + IGO_t)$$

$$KGD_{-1} = \sum_{0}^{t-1} IGD_t$$

$$KNC_{-1} = \sum_{0}^{t-1} INCF_t$$

3.2.4. Estimated equations

I.   Production

1. AF

$$AF = 0.2094 \frac{PF}{PNF} + 0.7452\ AF_{-1} + 10.7215$$
$$\quad\ (3.0013) \qquad\qquad (9.4307) \qquad\qquad (1.1306)$$

$$\bar{R}^2 = 0.876 \quad s = 2.24 \quad \text{Mean} = 114.32$$

$$DW = 2.19$$

2. A $\quad = \quad 0.1353 \dfrac{PAW}{P} + 0.6237 \; A_{-1} + 30.3224$
$\qquad\qquad\quad$ (1.4763) $\qquad\quad$ (4.5889) $\qquad\quad$ (3.2033)

$\qquad\qquad \bar{R}^2 = 0.868 \quad s = 2.20 \quad \text{Mean} = 119.35 \quad DW = 2.43$

3. AYF $\quad = \quad 0.3057 \; R + 1.5589 \; t + 63.6661$
$\qquad\qquad\quad$ (2.6349) $\qquad$ (5.6137) $\qquad$ (5.1118)

$\qquad\qquad \bar{R}^2 = 0.663 \quad s = 6.07 \quad \text{Mean} = 110.84 \quad DW = 1.91$

4. $AYNF$ $\quad = \quad 0.0863 \; R + 1.1014 \; t + 79.5221$
$\qquad\qquad\quad$ (1.1223) $\qquad$ (5.9810) $\qquad$ (9.6284)

$\qquad\qquad \bar{R}^2 = 0.666 \quad s = 4.02 \quad \text{Mean} = 99.79 \quad DW = 2.43$

5. $YMCP$ $\quad = \quad 0.0008 \; KCG_{-1} + 7.5884$
$\qquad\qquad\quad$ (26.7592) $\qquad\qquad$ (29.3794)

$\qquad\qquad \bar{R}^2 = 0.976 \quad s = 0.68 \quad \text{Mean} = 13.00 \quad DW = 0.47$

6. $YMNCP$ $\quad = \quad 0.0009 \; KNC_{-1} + 12.6484$
$\qquad\qquad\quad$ (7.8836) $\qquad\qquad$ (12.9596)

$\qquad\qquad \bar{R}^2 = 0.782 \quad s = 2.10 \quad \text{Mean} = 19.28 \quad DW = 0.40$

7. CU $\quad = \quad 0.3116 \; YA_{-1} + 0.0547 \; MOF -$
$\qquad\qquad\quad$ (3.1848) $\qquad\qquad$ (3.0655)

$\qquad\qquad - 0.0005 \; KCG_{-1} + 0.6270 \; CU_{-1} + 8.3706$
$\qquad\qquad\quad$ (4.3227) $\qquad\qquad$ (8.4929) $\qquad\qquad$ (1.4686)

$\qquad\qquad \bar{R}^2 = 0.920 \quad s = 1.43 \quad \text{Mean} = 85.27 \quad DW = 1.74$

8. YA $\quad = \quad 0.2579 \; QAF + 0.1230 \; QANF + 14.3570$
$\qquad\qquad\quad$ (28.8242) $\qquad\qquad$ (16.2037) $\qquad\qquad$ (24.1649)

$\qquad\qquad \bar{R}^2 = 0.997 \quad s = 0.34 \quad \text{Mean} = 64.34 \quad DW = 1.21$

9. YS $\quad = \quad 0.0044 \; KGD_{-1} + 0.1388 \; Y + 12.0855$
$\qquad\qquad\quad$ (10.7388) $\qquad\qquad$ (4.8951) $\qquad$ (4.2210)

$\qquad\qquad \bar{R}^2 = 0.996 \quad s = 0.59 \quad \text{Mean} = 39.38 \quad DW = 1.15$

II. Savings and investment

10. SH = 14.3940 YD + 4.0726 $\dfrac{PNA}{PA}$ + 0.3414 SH_{-1} −
 (2.9550)   (1.4705)   (1.5685)

 − 1485.7220
  (2.0572)

 $\bar{R}^2 = 0.814$ $s = 130.95$ Mean $= 921.84$ $DW = 2.09$

11. SG = 0.0588 T + 0.5666 SG_{-1} + 7.8322
  (1.2355)   (2.3610)   (0.1645)

 $\bar{R}^2 = 0.703$ $s = 70.76$ Mean $= 239.48$ $DW = 1.21$

12. SC^* = 0.2775 CPR^* + 0.3060 SC^*_{-1} + 2.6423
  (2.0738)   (1.2631)   (0.1638)

 $\bar{R}^2 = 0.552$ $s = 26.27$ Mean $= 70.94$ $DW = 1.61$

13. ICF = 7.1421 YNA + 0.2957 $\dfrac{EF^*}{P}$ − 218.5516
  (8.6587)   (2.4868)   (4.9593)

 $\bar{R}^2 = 0.914$ $s = 45.35$ Mean $= 314.50$ $DW = 2.49$

14. H^* = 2.0095 Y^* − 93.8160
  (3.1240)   (0.8772)

 $\bar{R}^2 = 0.340$ $s = 165.49$ Mean $= 217.28$

 $DW = 1.48$

15. DEP^* = 2.7972 KGP_{-1} + 367.1398
  (25.5252)   (16.8522)

 $\bar{R}^2 = 0.974$ $s = 56.32$ Mean $= 808.06$ $DW = 0.87$

III. Prices and wages

16. PF = − 1.6603 SF_{-1} − 2.3970 SF_{-2} +
  (3.3022)   (4.6669)

 + 2.5829 YNA + 6.2492 $\dfrac{L^*}{Y}$ + 92.2586
  (4.1720)   (4.8152)   (3.1736)

 $\bar{R}^2 = 0.970$ $s = 8.35$ Mean $= 136.28$ $DW = 1.42$

17. PNF $= -10.5152 \dfrac{QANF_{-1}}{YMC + YMNC} + 6.8493 \dfrac{L^*}{Y} +$
        (1.7084)   (9.3805)

    $+ 33.3296$
      (0.7094)

    $\bar{R}^2 = 0.957$ $s = 9.22$ Mean $= 114.65$ $DW = 1.37$

18. PFG $= 0.3100\ PNF + 0.4623\ CU + 0.4538\ PFG_{-1}$
        (6.4347)   (2.3869)   (3.8672)

    16.0645
    (0.7430)

    $\bar{R}^2 = 0.980$ $s = 3.06$ Mean $= 123.24$

19. W^* $= 6.5895\ PCL + 17.8942\ YMC + 339.6005$
        (8.8529)   (2.3016)   (7.5853)

    $\bar{R}^2 = 0.976$ $s = 48.02$ Mean $= 1444.41$

    $DW = 1.97$

20. PW $= 0.5317\ PF + 0.1550\ PNF +$
        (82.3556)   (14.6248)

    $+ 0.3298\ PFG - 1.8836$
       (16.6117)   (1.6710)

    $\bar{R}^2 = 0.999$ $s = 0.31$ Mean $= 133.64$ $DW = 1.80$

21. P $= 0.6544\ PW + 28.6471$
        (20.3456)   (6.4074)

    $\bar{R}^2 = 0.962$ $s = 5.07$ Mean $= 116.10$ $DW = 0.43$

22. PCL $= 0.5931\ PF + 0.4473\ PFG + 0.8756$
        (14.6622)   (4.9886)   (0.1459)

    $\bar{R}^2 = 0.996$ $s = 2.23$ Mean $= 136.82$ $DW = 1.85$

23. PAW $= 0.6138\ PF + 0.2870\ PNF + 9.7543$
        (11.2693)   (4.8732)   (3.9722)

    $\bar{R}^2 = 0.995$ $s = 2.74$ Mean $= 134.91$ $DW = 1.52$

24. PA $\quad = \quad 0.9695\ PAW - 12.8402$
$\qquad\qquad\quad (38.9110)\qquad\quad (3.6550)$

$\qquad\qquad \bar{R}^2 = 0.989\ \ s = 4.21\ \ \text{Mean} = 117.95\ \ DW = 1.50$

25. PNA $\quad = \quad 0.4993\ P + 58.6261$
$\qquad\qquad\quad (9.3084)\qquad (9.1944)$

$\qquad\qquad \bar{R}^2 = 0.842\ \ s = 5.63\ \ \text{Mean} = 116.60\ \ DW = 0.40$

26. PXO $\quad = \quad 0.5627\ PW + 0.2084\ PXO_{-1} + 14.7770$
$\qquad\qquad\quad (3.9866)\qquad\ (1.0530)\qquad\qquad (0.9829)$

$\qquad\qquad \bar{R}^2 = 0.743\ \ s = 15.00\ \ \text{Mean} = 112.06\ \ DW = 1.81$

27. CPR^* $\quad = \quad 2.0561\ YNA^* + 9.9064$
$\qquad\qquad\quad (5.7749)\qquad\qquad (0.3359)$

$\qquad\qquad \bar{R}^2 = 0.655\ \ s = 42.71\ \ \text{Mean} = 170.02$

$\qquad\qquad DW = 0.49$

IV. Government and monetary sectors

28. TD^* $\quad = \quad 139.3652\ RDT + 6.5171\ YNA^* - 443.5920$
$\qquad\qquad\quad (13.8947)\qquad\ (33.3515)\qquad\quad (16.9952)$

$\qquad\qquad \bar{R}^2 = 0.993\ \ s = 19.69\ \ \text{Mean} = 488.11$

$\qquad\qquad DW = 1.44$

29. TI^* $\quad = \quad 277.2230\ RIT1 + 101.0271\ RIT2 +$
$\qquad\qquad\quad (14.1141)\qquad\quad (13.2151)$

$\qquad\qquad + \quad 6.9731\ Y^* + 0.0018\ MG^* +$
$\qquad\qquad\quad (14.1949)\qquad (2.5629)$

$\qquad\qquad + \quad 0.0042\ XG^* - 1285.9594$
$\qquad\qquad\quad (3.4415)\qquad\quad (30.9176)$

$\qquad\qquad \bar{R}^2 = 0.999\ \ s = 24.98\ \ \text{Mean} = 1306.5$

$\qquad\qquad DW = 2.11$

30. TO^* $\quad = \quad$ 2.1327 $Y^* -$ 49.3945
$\qquad\qquad$ (9.4004) $\qquad\quad$ (1.3094)

$\qquad\qquad \bar{R}^2 = 0.837 \quad s = 58.37 \quad$ Mean $= 280.78 \quad DW = 1.24$

31. $GSBP^*$ $\quad = \quad$ 0.4592 $GD^* +$ $\quad$ 0.9228 $GSBP^*_{-1} +$
$\qquad\qquad$ (1.8030) $\qquad\qquad\qquad$ (11.2898)

$\qquad\qquad +$ 149.0526
$\qquad\qquad\quad$ (1.2544)

$\qquad\qquad \bar{R}^2 = 0.961 \quad s = 103.21 \quad$ Mean $= 1827.90$

$\qquad\qquad DW = 2.12$

32. $C^* - C^*_{-1}$ $\quad = \quad$ 0.4189 $GD^* +$ 58.3337
$\qquad\qquad$ (3.4748) $\qquad\qquad$ (2.1234)

$\qquad\qquad \bar{R}^2 = 0.394 \quad s = 78.84 \quad$ Mean $= 1284.20$

$\qquad\qquad DW = 1.50$

33a. $\ln\left(\dfrac{L^*}{P}\right)$ $\quad = \quad$ 0.7605 $\ln Y -$ $\quad$ 0.2749 $\ln RG1 +$
$\qquad\qquad$ (2.4510) $\qquad\qquad$ (1.0619)

$\qquad\qquad +$ 0.5563 $\ln\left(\dfrac{L^*}{P}\right)_{-1} -$ 1.8225
$\qquad\qquad\;$ (2.4561) $\qquad\qquad\qquad$ (2.1683)

$\qquad\qquad \bar{R}^2 = 0.926 \quad s = 0.06 \quad$ Mean $= 3.27 \quad DW = 1.44$

33b. $\ln\left(\dfrac{L^*}{P}\right)$ $\quad = \quad$ 0.5901 $\ln Y -$ $\quad$ 0.2738 $\ln RSH +$
$\qquad\qquad$ (2.3200) $\qquad\qquad$ (2.1497)

$\qquad\qquad +$ 0.5143 $\ln\left(\dfrac{L^*}{P}\right)_{-1} +$ 1.5240
$\qquad\qquad\;$ (2.2232) $\qquad\qquad\qquad$ (2.5660)

$\qquad\qquad \bar{R}^2 = 0.940 \quad s = 0.05$

34. T^* $\quad = \quad$ 6.6866 $YNA^* +$ 238.9561 $R12 -$
$\qquad\qquad$ (3.3637) $\qquad\qquad\quad$ (3.7669)

$\qquad\qquad -$ 361.6561 $RG1 +$ 0.6936 $T^*_{-1} +$ 551.4968
$\qquad\qquad\quad$ (3.3497) $\qquad\qquad$ (7.2643) $\qquad\qquad$ (2.2411)

$$\bar{R}^2 = 0.991 \quad s = 60.79 \quad \text{Mean} = 1051.75$$

$$DW = 1.70$$

35. $BR*$ $\quad = 111.4452 \ RG - 34.4719 \ RB + 0.0133 \ BL* -$
$\qquad\qquad (2.6603) \qquad\quad (1.7628) \qquad\quad (0.9142)$

$\qquad\quad - 158.1568$
$\qquad\qquad (1.9180)$

$$\bar{R}^2 = 0.597 \quad s = 22.87 \quad \text{Mean} = 76.17 \quad DW = 1.93$$

36. $LB*$ $\quad = \ 27.4926 \ YNA* + \ 1.0119 \ ICF* -$
$\qquad\qquad (15.6396) \qquad\qquad (5.3134)$

$\qquad\quad - 107.0176 \ RA - 275.7971$
$\qquad\qquad (3.5273) \qquad\qquad (2.0368)$

$$\bar{R}^2 = 0.995 \quad s = 59.48 \quad \text{Mean} = 1490.19$$

$$DW = 1.93$$

37. $TR*$ $\quad = \ 0.0458 \ D* + \ 0.0641 \ T* - 10.2119 \ RS1 +$
$\qquad\qquad (3.7564) \qquad\ (6.2744) \qquad\quad (4.0417)$

$\qquad\quad + 55.2665$
$\qquad\qquad (8.2240)$

$$\bar{R}^2 = 0.981 \quad s = 7.85 \quad \text{Mean} = 133.53 \quad DW = 2.51$$

38. RA $\quad = \ 0.9464 \ RB + \ 0.0004 \ BL* + \ 2.1967$
$\qquad\qquad (3.6646) \qquad\quad (1.6744) \qquad\qquad (2.7770)$

$$\bar{R}^2 = 0.884 \quad s = 0.42 \quad \text{Mean} = 6.84 \quad DW = 1.67$$

39. $RS1$ $\quad = \ - 0.5545 \ \dfrac{TR}{DT} + \ 1.1703 \ RB - 0.0004 \ L* +$
$\qquad\qquad (3.7179) \qquad\quad (4.1416) \qquad\quad (2.0826)$

$\qquad\quad + 3.9185$
$\qquad\qquad (2.3436)$

$$\bar{R}^2 = 0.874 \quad s = 0.40 \quad \text{Mean} = 3.59 \quad DW = 1.60$$

40. $RG1$ $= - \; 0.0287 \; \dfrac{GSBP^*}{YNA^*} + \;\; 0.4892 \;\; R12 + \;\; 3.2042$
                $\quad\;\; (2.3020) \qquad\qquad\;\; (16.6095) \qquad\;\; (8.5422)$

$\qquad\qquad\qquad \bar{R}^2 = 0.958 \;\; s = 0.13 \;\; \text{Mean} = 4.34 \;\; DW = 2.22$

41. EF^* $= \;\; 0.4131 \;\; \Delta(L^* + T^*) + 113.9088$
                $\quad\;\; (3.7000) \qquad\qquad\qquad\quad (2.4392)$

$\qquad\qquad\qquad \bar{R}^2 = 0.42 \;\; s = 117.82 \;\; \text{Mean} = 252.83$

$\qquad\qquad\qquad DW = 1.42$

42. $R12$ $= \;\; 0.2565 \;\; RS1 + \;\; 0.7614 \;\; R12_{-1} + \; 0.1457$
                $\quad\;\; (2.1722) \qquad\;\; (7.2624) \qquad\qquad\; (0.5670)$

$\qquad\qquad\qquad \bar{R}^2 = 0.93 \;\; s = 0.321 \;\; \text{Mean} = 3.78 \;\; DW = 2.54$

43. RG $= \;\;\;\; 0.5636 \;\; RG1 + \;\; 0.7950$
                $\quad\;\; (11.1006) \qquad\;\; (3.5686)$

$\qquad\qquad\qquad \bar{R}^2 = 0.87 \;\; s = 0.141 \;\; \text{Mean} = 3.24 \;\; DW = 2.36$

V.   External trade

44. MF $= - \; 0.0780 \;\; QAF + \; 0.1476 \;\; YNA \; -$
                $\quad\;\; (2.8178) \qquad\quad (4.1140)$

$\qquad\qquad\quad\; - \; 0.0639 \; \dfrac{PMF}{PW} + \; 9.5570$
$\qquad\qquad\qquad (1.8449) \qquad\quad (2.4873)$

$\qquad\qquad\qquad \bar{R}^2 = 0.76 \;\; s = 1.256 \;\; \text{Mean} = 4.36 \;\; DW = 1.06$

45. MOF $= \;\; 2.0025 \;\; YNA - \;\; 0.0056 \;\; PMOF +$
                $\quad\;\; (2.9223) \qquad\qquad (2.6260)$

$\qquad\qquad\quad\; + \; 0.1964 \; (\dfrac{FR}{PM})_{-1} + 30.9055$
$\qquad\qquad\qquad (3.2129) \qquad\qquad\; (0.7088)$

$\qquad\qquad\qquad \bar{R}^2 = 0.38 \;\; s = 16.426 \;\; \text{Mean} = 141.54$

$\qquad\qquad\qquad DW = 1.92$

46. XT $\quad = XT_{65-69} (1.01)^t$

47. XJ $\quad = XJ_{65-69} (1.01)^t$

48. XEG $\quad = -5.8362 \ (PXEG \cdot ER) + 747.5702$
$\qquad\qquad$ (5.0302) $\qquad\qquad\qquad$ (6.2897)

$\qquad\qquad \bar{R}^2 = 0.68 \quad s = 98.554 \quad \text{Mean} = 167.08$

$\qquad\qquad DW = 1.44$

49. XO $\quad = 0.5651 \ EW - 0.1565 \ (PXO \cdot ER) + 49.6852$
$\qquad\qquad$ (6.9935) $\qquad$ (0.8667) $\qquad\qquad$ (3.8346)

$\qquad\qquad \bar{R}^2 = 0.84 \quad s = 6.417 \quad \text{Mean} = 83.91 \quad DW = 1.72$

50. $\ln XS^*$ $\quad = 0.0625 \ t - 0.2612$
$\qquad\qquad$ (7.3186) $\qquad$ (2.7466)

$\qquad\qquad \bar{R}^2 = 0.76 \quad s = 0.172 \quad \text{Mean} = 1.51 \quad DW = 1.18$

51. YF^* $\quad = 0.0536 \ CDF_{-1} - 0.0588$
$\qquad\qquad$ (21.4033) $\qquad\qquad$ (1.1732)

$\qquad\qquad \bar{R}^2 = 0.96 \quad s = 0.146 \quad \text{Mean} = 0.70 \quad DW = 1.02$

VI. Definitions and identities

52. ANF $\quad = A - AF$

53. QAF $\quad = AYF \cdot AF$

54. $QANF$ $\quad = AYNF \cdot ANF$

55. YMC $\quad = CU \cdot YMCP$

56. $YMNC$ $\quad = CU \cdot YMNCP$

57. YNA $\quad = YMC + YMNC + YS$

58. YNA^* $\quad = PNA \cdot YNA$

59. YA^* $\quad = PA \cdot YA$

60. Y^* $\quad = YA^* + YNA^*$

61. $Y \quad = YA + YNA$

62. $Y^* \quad = pY$

63. $MG^* \quad = PMF \cdot MF + PMOF \cdot MOF$

64. $XG^* \quad = PXT \cdot XT + PXJ \cdot XJ + PXEG \cdot XEG + PXO \cdot XO$

65. $SF \quad = 0.88\ QAF + MF$

66. $L^* \quad = C^* + D^*$

67. $D^* + T^* \quad = EL^* + GSB$[13]

68. $GSP \quad = GSBP - GSB$

69. $T \quad = \dfrac{(TD^* + TI^* + TO^*)}{P}$

70. $p(SH+SG) + SC^* + DEP^* + YF^* = p_I(ICF+INCF+IG) + H^* + XG^* - MG^* + XS^*$

71. $\cdot F^* \quad = MG^* - XG^* - XS^* + FER^* - FER^*_{-1}$

3.2.5. Supply equations

Eqs. (1) to (9) relate to the supply of output which is disaggregated into three broad sectors: agriculture, manufacturing and a residuary sector consisting mainly of services. In explaining the supply of agricultural output, acreage under crops and yield per acre have been considered separately. Since the rate of growth of food supply has been one of the crucial constraints in the development of the economy, a division of agricultural output into food and non-food sectors is made in order to study the substitution in the acreage decisions. Total area under crops is related to the relative price level of agricultural output and makes allowance for a lag in response due to possible rigidities. Though the *t*-ratio of the price effect is not highly significant it points in the expected direction.

[13] This is an approximation since other miscellaneous assets and liabilities which are usually very small are ignored.

However, in making use of this equation for long-term or medium-term forecasting purposes, a ceiling may have to be imposed. The reason is that the possibilities of bringing additional areas under cultivation are severely limited and any increase in acreage will have to be in the form of land improvement. The equation for the acreage under food crops shows a significant price substitution between food and non-food crops.

The yields per acre under food crops are related to an index of rainfall, expressed as a percentage of normal rainfall, and a trend factor. In the absence of data on capital expenditures such as irrigation, research on improved seeds etc., the trend factor is used as a "catch-all" proxy. The short-term and long-term elasticities of acreage under food crops with respect to the ratio of food to non-food prices are 0.21 and 0.80 respectively. The effect of rainfall, elasticity 0.31, on food output per acre is much higher than on non-food output – elasticity 0.10. The highly significant upward trends in the yield per acre under both food and non-food crops are noteworthy. This analysis of supply does not distinguish between production and marketed surplus, although it is the latter that is of vital importance to the growing urban population. Analysis of the impact of price expectations and of the increasing ability in holding stocks at the farm level on marketed surplus would be an improvement in the model.

Manufacturing production is explained by eqs. (5) to (7). Capacity output in the corporate and non-corporate manufacturing sectors are related to cumulative investment in the respective sectors and capacity utilisation, the available measure for which covers both sectors, is related to agricultural output lagged one year which reflects both pressure of demand and also the constraint imposed by the supply of raw materials, supply of non-food imports, cumulative investment and capacity utilisation lagged one year. Variations in capacity utilisation are well explained by this equation indicating thereby that the supplies of domestic raw materials and non-food imports are major constraining factors on manufacturing production.

3.2.6. Domestic demand equations

Consumer expenditure may be analyzed either from the consumption side or from the savings side. The data on savings in India, estimated on the basis of the net-worth approach, are considered fairly reliable and a sectoral breakdown is also available. Eqs. (10) to (12) relate to household, government and corporate savings respectively. Household savings are related to disposable income, the terms of trade between non-agricultural and agricultural sectors, expressed as a ratio of the national income deflators of the two sectors and lagged savings. The terms of trade effect is considered to be important in the Indian context for two reasons; first, for a given level of income a movement in the terms of trade in favour of the agricultural sector would cause a redistribution of income from the urban to the rural sector and to the extent that small and medium farmers share in the rise of agricultural prices, savings would be reduced, since their propensity to save is likely to be lower. [14] Second, to the extent that a change in the terms of trade reflects a scarcity of the supply of food relative to other consumption goods, savings will be adversely affected since food is the most important item of consumption. From eq. (10) it will be seen that the short-run propensity to save is of the order of 14% whilst the long-run propensity is about 22%. The effect of the terms of trade is not highly significant, but is of the expected sign with an elasticity of 0.47.

Government savings are related to tax revenue and corporate savings are related to corporate profits. The equation for the corporate sector provides a reasonably good "fit" with the long-run marginal propensity to save of the order of 40%. The relationship between government savings and tax revenue is not quite satisfactory, and the savings propensity is not stable in the sub-period. In any case, the average ratio should be taken as a policy parameter for simulation purposes.

As regards investment expenditure, three sectors are distin-

[14] Raj, K.N., 'The Marginal Rate of Saving in the Indian Economy', *Oxford Economic Papers*, February 1962.

guished: government, corporate and the rest, which covers both unincorporated enterprises and households. Government investment is taken as exogenous. Corporate investment is determined by the level of non-agricultural income and by the availability of real external finance. As pointed out by Eshag [15], dependence on external finance is likely to be much greater in the developing countries as compared to the industrially advanced countries. The reason is the small size of the corporate business relative to the substantially rich field of profitable investment opportunities. The level of income serves as a proxy both for investment opportunities and profits. Both these factors are found to be highly significant in explaining investment in fixed assets by the corporate sector (eq. (13)). For the non-corporate private sector, access to the capital markets is more limited and consequently dependence on internal finance will be much greater. Moreover, investment under this category includes direct investment in construction by the household sector. For these reasons, non-corporate investment is determined as a residue implying thereby that the savings and investment decisions are one and the same for this sector. Data on inventories are considered to be extremely unreliable. A simple relationship between inventories and national income, both in current prices, is postulated in eq. (14). Depreciation is related to cumulative investment (eq. (15)).

3.2.7. Price equations

Analysis of the price formation has been carried out by distinguishing three basic groups of commodities; food and non-food groups in the agricultural sector (eqs. (16) and (17)) and manufactured goods in the non-agricultural sector (eqs. (18) and (19)). In the agricultural sector prices of non-food articles are determined by excess demand and a liquidity variable expressed as the ratio of cash balances (currency plus deposits) with the public to total real output. The time lags in the impact of supply on prices of both

[15] Eshag, E., 'The Relative Efficiency of Monetary Policy', *Economic Journal*, June 1971.

food and non-food articles may be partly due to the annual nature of the crops and the differences in the crop year (July-June) and the financial year (April-March) and partly due to the rigidities in adjustment. The inclusion of the ratio of cash balances to output as a separate variable in the explanation of agricultural prices reflects the pressure on the general price level arising on the monetary side. The bulk of the increase in the money held by the public sector is due to deficit financing. The introduction of the ratio $L*/Y$ as a separate explanatory variable enables a direct analysis of the impact of deficit financing on the price level.

Prices of manufactured goods are determined by raw material costs and as may be seen from eq. (18) the mark-up varies directly with capacity utilisation. Due to non-availability of data on the share of wages in manufacturing output, wage costs were not taken into account. Data on average wage rates are, however, available and wage rates are determined as a function of the consumer price index and the level of manufacturing output. All the other price equations are formulated in terms of the prices of the three basic groups of commodities referred to above.

3.2.8. Government and monetary sectors

In the Government sector current revenues are disaggregated into three components: direct taxes, indirect taxes and other miscellaneous revenue (eqs. (29) to (32)). Direct taxes are related to the average tax rate and income in the non-agricultural sector while indirect taxes are related to average rates of excise and customs duties, total income at current prices and current values of imports and exports. Miscellaneous revenues are related to total income. Eqs. (31) and (32) determine the financing of the overall deficit of the Government by domestic borrowing and by money creation respectively. Currency creating activity is identified with the Government sector in this case but this may not be appropriate for countries where the Central banks have some measures of autonomy.

The monetary sector has been considered in some detail. Eqs. (33a) and (33b) are two alternative demand equations for real cash balances expressed in terms of real income and interest rates; the yield on long-term Government securities is used in eq. (33a) and the yield on corporate equities is used as an alternative in eq. (33b). The interest elasticity is of the order of 0.3 whichever interest rate is used. The demand for time deposits is determined by non-agricultural income at current prices, the 12-month fixed deposit rate and the yield on long-term government securities taken as a competing asset (eq. (34)). The remaining eqs. (35) to (42) relate to the behaviour of commercial banks and the determination of interest rates. Given the legal reserve ratios, variations in the supply of demand and time deposits can be expressed in terms of variations in the excess and borrowed reserves which the commercial banks wish to hold. Accordingly, borrowings from the Reserve Bank are related to the discount rate, the level of demand for loans from the private sector and the average yield which the banks earn on Government securities held by them (eq. (35)). Total reserves held are determined by the level of demand and time deposits and the short-term rate of interest (eq. (37)). The rate which the commercial banks set on their loans to the private sector is determined by the discount rate and by the level of demand while the short-term rate of interest is determined by the bank rate and the supply of cash balances (eqs. (38) and (39)). Eq. (40) shows that the yield on Government securities is determined by the ratio of supply, which is considered exogenous, to the demand as a proxy for which income in the non-agricultural sector is used. The availability of external finance to the corporate sector is related to total liquidity measured by the sum of currency, demand and time deposits. The remaining two equations relate to the rate of 12-month fixed deposits and the average yield on Government securities held by commercial banks which are determined by the levels of other interest rates. It may be noted that this system of equations explaining the organised monetary and banking sectors bears a close resemblance to its counterparts in the advanced economies. However, one major difference appears to be that the impact of these sectors on the real sector is through the control of the total volume and sectoral allocation of liquid assets rather than through the interest rate mechanism.

3.2.9. External trade

Imports are disaggregated into two broad groups; food and non-food imports, the latter consisting almost entirely of raw materials and capital goods and only a small amount of consumer goods. Food imports are determined by domestic food output, real income of the non-agricultural sector and real prices of food imports. Non-food imports are determined by non-agricultural income and import prices. In addition to these two variables, the level of foreign exchange reserves, deflated by the import price index, is taken as an additional factor to reflect Government policy constraints. All the regression coefficients in the equation for non-food imports are highly significant and are of the expected sign, but the total variation explained is only of the order of 39%.

Tea and jute manufactures are the two main traditional exports. Exports of tea were virtually stagnant, while the fortunes of jute manufactures fluctuated widely, depending upon the competition from synthetics and the new uses found for it. World consumption was almost stagnant during most of the 1960's and in addition the domestic jute industry was faced with the problem of cost competitiveness. The export prospects for jute manufactures seem to be quite uncertain. In view of these considerations, simple time trends were assumed for tea and jute manufactures. Other exports, particularly non-traditional items like engineering goods performed very well. Engineering goods, however, had to face competition from the industrially advanced countries and the elasticity with respect to the relative price level is as high as -3.5 (eq. (48)). A number of incentives were given to exports of engineering goods which enabled the exporters to sell them at prices substantially lower than domestic prices. [16] Exports other than engineering goods are related to world exports and the relative price level of these exports. The elasticity with respect to world trade is 0.6 while the price effect is not found to be significant.

On the services account, India has a surplus in services other

[16] Patel, R.H., 'Exports of Engineering Goods, Problems and Prospects', *Reserve Bank of India Bulletin*, October 1970.

than factor services, with a significant upward bend (eq. (50)). Net factor income payments are related to the cumulative import surplus (eq. (51)) which indicates a rate of return on a marginal unit of capital inflow of 5.3%. An analysis of this relationship during sub-periods gives the following results:

Period	Equation	$\bar{R}^2$
1951–67	$YF^* = 0.0536\ CDF_{-1} - 0.0588$	0.97
1955–67	$YF^* = 0.0577\ CDF_{-1} - 0.1684$	0.98
1960–67	$YF^* = 0.0628\ CDF_{-1} - 0.3279$	0.97
1963–67	$YF^* = 0.0696\ CDF_{-1} - 0.5788$	0.94

It will be seen from these equations that there has been a significant hardening of terms in the 1960's as compared to the 1950's.

3.3. Model of the Nigerian Economy 1955–1966

3.3.1. Endogenous variables

GDP	= Gross domestic product at factor cost
GDPM	= Monetary value added
VAG	= Value added by the agricultural sector
VAGS	= Subsistence agriculture
VAGM	= Net output of the monetised agricultural sector
VMN	= Value added in the mining sector
VI	= Value added in the manufacturing, construction, transportation and gas and electricity sectors
VS	= Value added in the service sector
VG	= Value added in the public sector
CPS	= Private subsistence consumption
CPM	= Private monetary consumption
CG	= Public consumption
I	= Total fixed capital formation
IP	= Private investment in the petroleum sector
INP	= Private investment excluding the petroleum sector

MG	= Imports of goods
MS	= Non-factor services
MGP	= Imports going into the petroleum sector
MGR	= Imports of goods other than those going into the petroleum sector
MF	= Imports of foodstuffs
MR	= Imports of raw materials
MIC	= Imports of capital and manufactured consumer goods net of capital goods destined for the petroleum sector
X	= Exports of goods and services
XS	= Non-factor service receipts
XMN	= Exports from the mining sector
XAG	= Agricultural exports
FP	= Net factor income payments
TG	= Net foreign capital inflow
R	= Total government revenue
TD	= Direct taxes
TM	= Import taxes
TE	= Excise taxes
TO	= Total public revenue from the petroleum sector
TRG	= Government transfers to the domestic private sector
TIND	= Indirect taxes net of subsidies
YD	= Disposable income

3.3.2. Exogenous variables

IG	= Government investment
MP	= Imports of fuels
TPF	= Foreign transfers to Nigerian citizens
NTFN	= Transfer payments to the rest of the world
TX	= Export taxes
NTR	= Non-tax government revenue
PX	= Implicit price index of exports, 1962 = 100
PM	= Implicit price index of imports, 1962 = 100
t	= Time trend
SUB	= Subsidies

3.3.3. Estimated equations

I. Production

1. $VR = 289.914 + 0.231 \sum_{t=0}^{t-1} (INP + IG)_t$
   $\quad\quad\;\; (27.583) \quad (18.325)$

   $\bar{R}^2 = 0.97 \quad s = 17.37 \quad \text{Mean} = 456.89 \quad DW = 1.97$

2. $VG = 37.135 + 0.034 \sum_{t=0}^{t-1} IG_t$
   $\quad\quad\;\; (10.919) \quad (5.223)$

   $\bar{R}^2 = 0.72 \quad s = 4.97 \quad \text{Mean} = 53.40 \quad DW = 0.57$

3. $VS = 26.394 + 0.345 \, (GDPM - VS)$
   $\quad\quad\;\; (1.350) \quad (8.281)$

   $\bar{R}^2 = 0.87 \quad s = 3.59 \quad \text{Mean } 213.32 \quad DW = 1.65$

4. $VMN = VMN_{t-n} \, (1.24)^n$

5. $VAGS = VAGS_{t-n} \, (1.015)^n$

6. $VAGM = VAGM_{t-n} \, (1.057)^n$

II. Consumption and investment

7. $CPM = 47.20 + 0.665 \, YD$
   $\quad\quad\;\;\; (2.158) \quad (23.737)$

   $\bar{R}^2 = 0.98 \quad s = 20.07 \quad \text{Mean} = 547.92 \quad DW = 1.44$

8. $CG = 43.120 + 0.273 \, R$
   $\quad\quad\; (14.350) \quad (13.035)$

   $\bar{R}^2 = 0.85 \quad s = 15.14 \quad \text{Mean} = 80.44 \quad DW = 1.32$

9. $\ln IP = 1.300 + 0.537 \, \ln VMN$
   $\quad\quad\quad (3.720) \quad (4.970)$

   $\bar{R}^2 = 0.68 \quad s = 0.29 \quad \text{Mean} = 2.99 \quad DW = 1.34$

10. INP $= -81.708 + 0.300\,GDPM -$
              $(2.482) \quad (3.805)$

$$-\; 0.078 \sum_{t=0}^{t-1} (INP + IG)_t$$
     (2.321)

$$\bar{R}^2 = 0.82 \quad s = 10.96 \quad \text{Mean} = 74.60 \quad DW = 2.14$$

III. External trade

11. MGR $= 72.268 + 0.061\,(GDP - VMN) +$
            $(4.228) \quad (1.365)$

$$+\; 0.351\;\; X\frac{PX}{PM}$$
    (2.000)

$$\bar{R}^2 = 0.78 \quad s = 13.25 \quad \text{Mean} = 180.70 \quad DW = 1.29$$

12. R $= -\; 2.187 + \;\; 0.025\,(VI + VMN)$
         $(4.195) \quad (10.879)$

$$\bar{R}^2 = 0.91 \quad s = 0.53 \quad \text{Mean} = 3.23 \quad DW = 1.82$$

13. MIC $= 57.932 + 0.085\;CPM + 0.345\;(INP + IG)$
         $(4.011) \quad (1.700) \quad\quad (1.650)$

$$\bar{R}^2 = 0.80 \quad s = 11.57 \quad \text{Mean} = 152.37 \quad DW = 1.24$$

14. MGP $= \;\; 2.166 + 0.141\;\; VMN$
         $(1.815) \quad (6.199)$

$$\bar{R}^2 = 0.82 \quad s = 2.29 \quad \text{Mean} = 7.84 \quad DW = 2.50$$

15. MS $= -16.4 \quad\;\; + 0.592\;GDPM$
         $(2.448) \quad (6.755)$

$$\bar{R}^2 = 0.80 \quad s = 6.00 \quad \text{Mean} = 27.39 \quad DW = 1.50$$

16. XMN $= -\; 6.743 + \;\; 0.920\;\; VMN$
         $(3.676) \quad (26.361)$

$$\bar{R}^2 = 0.98 \quad s = 3.52 \quad \text{Mean} = 30.36 \quad DW = 2.01$$

17. XS $\quad = \quad 1.899 \; + \; 0.087 \; t$
$\qquad\qquad (28.912) \quad (9.741)$

$\qquad\qquad \bar{R}^2 = 0.89 \quad s = 0.10 \quad \text{Mean} = 2.46 \quad DW = 1.73$

18. $\ln FP$ $\quad = \; - \; 22.89 \; + \; 4.618 \; \ln(VMN + VI)$
$\qquad\qquad (10.343) \quad (11.225)$

$\qquad\qquad \bar{R}^2 = 0.92 \quad s = 0.39 \quad \text{Mean} = 1.91 \quad DW = 1.67$

IV. Government sector

19. TD $\quad = \quad 8.91 \; + \; 0.022 \; GDPM$
$\qquad\qquad (4.799) \quad (10.601)$

$\qquad\qquad \bar{R}^2 = 0.93 \quad s = 1.12 \quad \text{Mean} = 26.57 \quad DW = 1.27$

20. TM $\quad = \; - \; 10.823 \; + \; 0.317 \; MG$
$\qquad\qquad (0.435) \quad (2.728)$

$\qquad\qquad \bar{R}^2 = 0.44 \quad s = 8.78 \quad \text{Mean} = 56.57 \quad DW = 0.83$

21. TE $\quad = \; - \; 23.977 \; + \; 0.061 \; CPM$
$\qquad\qquad (2.041) \quad (3.157)$

$\qquad\qquad \bar{R}^2 = 0.53 \quad s = 6.94 \quad \text{Mean} = 12.41 \quad DW = 0.64$

22. TO $\quad = \quad 1.116 \; + \; 0.241 \; VMN$
$\qquad\qquad (0.884) \quad (8.302)$

$\qquad\qquad \bar{R}^2 = 0.89 \quad s = 2.71 \quad \text{Mean} = 26.57 \quad DW = 1.68$

23. TRG $\quad = \; - \; 7.394 \; + \; 0.052 \; GDPM$
$\qquad\qquad (1.317) \quad (7.694)$

$\qquad\qquad \bar{R}^2 = 0.88 \quad s = 3.59 \quad \text{Mean} = 34.79 \quad DW = 1.31$

V. Definitions and identities

24. GDP $\quad = \; CPS + CPM + CG + XMN + XAG + XS + I -$
$\qquad\qquad - \; MG - MS - TIND$

25. $TG \quad = MG + MS - XMN - XAG - XS + FP - TFP +$
$\quad\quad\quad\quad + TFW$

26. $YD \quad = GDPM - TD + TRG + TFP$

27. $GDP \quad = VAG + VMN + VI + VS + VG$

28. $VI \quad = VR - VS - VG$

29. $VAG \quad = VAGM + VAGS$

30. $GDPM \quad = GDP - VAGS$

31. $CPS \quad = VAGS$

32. $I \quad = IP + INP + IG$

33. $MF \quad = MGR - MR - MP - MIC$

34. $MG \quad = MGP + MGR$

35. $R \quad = NTR + TM + TE + TO + TX + TD$

36. $TIND \quad = TM + TE + TX - SUB$

37. $X \quad = XMN + XAG + XS$

3.3.4. Discussion of the equations

The main problem in building an econometric model for Nigeria is the lack of reliable and adequate data over a length of time. Until recently there was no organisation for the collection of economic data on a systematic and continuing basis. The first attempt at estimating national income accounts over a period of years was made by Okigbo [17], who compiled the accounts for the period 1950–1957. Subsequently, the Federal Statistical Office (FSO) of Nigeria initiated the collection of relevant economic data on a regular basis. Okigbo's estimates of the national accounts for the

---

[17] Okigbo, P.N.C., *Nigerian National Accounts, 1950–57*, Government Printer, Enugu, 1962.

period 1950–57 and those of the Federal Statistical Office for the subsequent years are not strictly comparable and the data for the early 1950's are considered particularly unreliable. The decision was therefore made to use Okigbo's data for the 1955–1957 period and the official data of the FSO for the period 1958 to 1966. As a result of the paucity of data the scope of the model is rather limited and is confined to the real side of the economy.

In formulating the model for the Nigerian economy, it is desirable to consider the subsistence or non-monetised part separately since the flows between this sector and the rest of the economy are small. An estimate of this sector's output for the year 1960 showed that it accounted for 20% of total agricultural output. Output of this part of the agricultural sector is assumed to grow at the same rate as the rural population which seems to be a reasonable assumption for short-term and medium-term purposes.

3.3.5. Production and domestic demand equations

The supply of output is disaggregated into five sectors: agricultural, mining, manufacturing, government services and non-government services. As regards the agricultural sector, there is practically no information on acreage and inputs such as fertilizers, etc. Thus, trend growth rates are assumed for the supply of output from this sector, and within the sector, subsistence and monetary output are considered separately. As mentioned earlier, the subsistence growth rate is assumed to be the same as that of the rural population, while the monetary sector is assumed to grow at the historical rate of 5.7% per year. In the mining sector, consisting mainly of petroleum, output expansion which was interrupted during the 1967–1970 civil war period, is expected to be 15.0% per year.

Total value added in the non-primary sector including both manufacturing output and services is related to cumulative investment in the private non-petroleum government sectors. Non-government services are explained by the level of monetary income while public services are related to cumulative investment in the government sector. Manufacturing output is then obtained as the difference between total value added in the non-primary sector and the value of services.

In the analysis of consumption demand, private and government consumption are considered separately. Within the private sector consumption in the subsistence sector is assumed to be equal to its output while for the monetised sector consumption is determined by private disposable income. Public consumption expenditures are related to the current revenue of that sector. Investment in the petroleum sector is related to the level of its output. In other words, it is assumed that for the near future the level of demand is the main factor affecting capital expenditures in the sector. Investment in the non-petroleum sector is explained by the level of its own output and cumulative non-petroleum investment. Finally, government investment expenditures are taken to be exogenous.

3.3.6. External sectors

Total imports for the non-petroleum sectors of the economy are explained by the level of domestic activity in the non-agricultural sector and the purchasing power of exports (PPE), the latter being taken as a proxy for restrictions on imports. The estimated elasticity of non-petroleum imports with respect to domestic activity is considerably less than one, 0.54, while with respect to PPE it is around 0.63. The next step was to estimate import functions by commodity groups. In accordance with the LINK classification, imports are divided into four groups: foodstuffs (SITC 0 + 1), raw materials (2 + 4), fuel (3) and manufactured goods (5−9). The last group is further subdivided into imports for the petroleum and non-petroleum sectors. Fuel imports are exogenously determined because of their replacement by domestic production. Foodstuffs, on the other hand, are estimated as a residual. Imports for the petroleum sector are explained by the level of activity in that sector. Manufactured imports, including both capital and consumer goods, for the non-petroleum sectors (*MIC*) are explained by monetary consumption and non-petroleum investment. The elasticity of *MIC* with respect to *CMP* is 0.55, while with respect to non-petroleum investment is 0.64 and with respect to the industrial sector (*VI*) is 0.59. The relatively low elasticities, in particular with respect to investment and value added in the industrial sector, most probably reflect the non-homogeneous nature of *MIC*. However, when imports of capital goods are considered separately, their elasticity with respect to investment is 1.00. On the other hand, the low elasticity of *MIC* with respect to private monetary consumption is the result of increasing import substitution in consumer goods. Imports of raw materials (*MR*) are explained by industrial activity, and the elasticity of *MR* with respect to industrial value added is close to 1.5.

Exports are divided into mining (primarily petroleum) and agricultural products. Exports originating in the petroleum sector are explained by the level of the output of that sector. Since Nigeria's agricultural exports are fairly diversified, and in each case account for a small proportion of the world market, they are assumed to be supply determined, after making allowance for domestic absorption. However, domestic demand for monetised agricultural output and in particular for the exportable commodities is very limited.

Net factor income payments are explained by the level of output in the mining and industrial sectors combined. All of the foreign capital is invested either in the mining sector (the largest share) or in the industrial sector and the economic activity of these two sectors would partly explain the net factor income flow. The logarithmic form of the relationship was preferred because of the recent acceleration of factor income payments associated with oil operations which is reflected in the high estimated elasticity of 4.6.

A number of government sector tax functions are estimated in order to close the model. The interesting feature is that direct taxes and total revenue from oil operations have elasticities of less than 1.00, with respect to monetary *GDP* (0.65) and mining output (0.83). On the other hand, the import tax and excise tax elasticities with respect to imports of goods and monetary private consumption are 1.40 and 1.30 respectively.

4. Developing countries in Project LINK

Since individual country models for a sufficiently large number of developing countries are not yet completed, a short-cut method was adopted for the purpose of "Mini-LINK" simulations. Some reduced-form equations for imports and exports were estimated for these countries, which were grouped into eleven regions on the basis of geographical contiguity and taking into account any special trade and payments arrangements. For each of these regions the following eight equations were estimated:

(a) Four import equations, one for each of the LINK commodity groups [18], relating imports in 1963 U.S. dollars of the concerned commodities to the total exports of the concerned regions, and to a trend variable in some cases.

(b) Four export equations, one for each commodity group, relating exports of the concerned commodities by the concerned regions to the world exports of the same commodity group.

The short method was considered adequate for purposes of the "Mini-LINK" but for the "Maxi-LINK", however, these reduced form equations are obviously not sufficient since the price effects are not taken into account. The "Maxi-LINK", as it is envisaged at present, requires essentially two things for each individual country or region. First, equations explaining the quantum of imports are required for each country or region. These equations should be capable of reflecting (a) the direct effect of import prices on the volume of imports and (b) the indirect effect of the volume of world trade, via its impact on the country's exports and the consequent effects on the domestic activity level. Second, equations explaining export prices are required. Both these requirements of the "Maxi-LINK" could be met only if complete models at the country level are available. Since the completion of the work on

---

[18] The commodity groups are the following:
(1) Food, beverages and tobacco, SITC 0 + 1.
(2) Raw materials, SITC 2 + 4.
(3) Fuels, SITC 3.
(4) Manufactures, SITC 5 to 9.

the construction of these macro models for a larger number of individual developing countries is still a long way off, an intermediate step is proposed which consists of dividing the entire developing world into four broad geographical regions and constructing simple models for each of these regions so as to meet the minimal requirements of the "Maxi-LINK". For this purpose, the developing countries will be divided into four regions: (i) Latin America, (ii) Africa excluding Libya, (iii) West Asia plus Libya and (iv) South and East Asia.

4.1. General structure of the regional models

Taking into account the data limitations, the following system of equations is proposed for describing the developing economies at the highly aggregative regional levels. It is hoped that this system will bring out the essential features which distinguish the developing countries from the industrialised ones. For empirical estimation, some departures from this general system will be made in order to take into account regional characteristics.

4.1.1. Model specification [19]

Y_a	= Output in the agricultural sector
Y_{na}	= Output in the non-agricultural sector
YD	= Gross domestic product
Y_{na}^p	= Capacity output in the non-agricultural sector
C	= Consumption expenditure
IF	= Investment in fixed assets
IS	= Inventory investment
X	= Exports
M	= Imports
YF	= Net factor income payments in constant dollars
YF^*	= Net factor income payments in current dollars
YN	= Gross national product

[19] All variables other than prices are measured in U.S. dollars in constant prices except those marked with an asterisk, which are in current prices.

K	= Cumulative investment in fixed assets
CDF^*	= Cumulative external deficit in current prices
R^*	= Foreign exchange reserves
p_a	= Index of agricultural prices in domestic currency
p_{na}	= Index of non-agricultural prices in domestic currency
p	= GDP deflator in domestic currency
p_m	= Import unit value index in dollars
p_{xd}	= Export unit value index in domestic currency
p_x	= Export unit value index in dollars
TW	= Index of world trade
p_w	= Unit value index of world exports in dollars
F^*	= Net foreign capital inflow
L	= Index of cash balances with the public
Z	= Index of exchange rates expressed as dollars per unit of domestic currency
t	= Time trend
N	= Population

I.   Supply of outputs

1. $Y_a \quad = a_0 + a_1 t$

2. $Y_{ha}^p \quad = b_0 + b_1 K_{-1}$

3a. $\dfrac{Y_{na}}{Y_{na}^p} \quad = c_0 + c_1 M + c_2 Y_a$

II.   Demand for output

3b. $Y_{na} \quad = d_0 + d_1 C + d_2 I + d_3 X$

4. $\dfrac{C}{N} \quad = e_0 + e_1 \dfrac{YN}{N} + e_2 \left(\dfrac{C}{N}\right)_{-1}$

5. $IF \quad = f_0 + f_1 YD + f_2 YD_{-1}$

6. $X \quad = g_0 + g_1 TW + g_2 \dfrac{p_x}{p_w}$

7. $M \quad = h_0 + h_1 YD + h_2 \dfrac{R}{p_m}_{-1} + h_3 \dfrac{p_m}{p \cdot Z}$

III. Price equations

8. $p_a \quad = k_0 + k_1 Y_a + k_2 Y_{a-1} + k_3 Y_{na}$

9a. $p_{na} \quad = l_0 + l_1 \dfrac{Y_{na}}{Y_{na}^p} + l_2 \dfrac{L}{YD} + l_3 p_a + l_4 p_m$

9b. $\dot{p}_{na} \quad = m_0 + m_1 Y_{na} + m_2 Y_{na-1} + m_3 \dfrac{L}{YD}$

10. $p \quad = n_0 + n_1 p_a + n_2 p_{na}$

11. $p_{xd} \quad = r_0 + r_1 p + r_2 X + r_3 p_{xd-1}$

IV. Others

12. $YF^* \quad = a_0 + a_1 CDF^*_{-1} + a_2 X p_x$

13. $K \quad = \displaystyle\sum_1^t I_t$

14. $CDF^* \quad = \displaystyle\sum_1^t (M p_m + YF^* - X p_x)$

15. $YF \quad = \dfrac{YF^*}{p_m}$

16. $YD \quad = Y_a + Y_{na}$

17. $YN \quad = YD - YF$

18. $IS \qquad = YD + M - C - I - X$

19. $R^* \qquad = R^*_{-1} + F^* + Xp_x - Mp_m - YF^*$

20. $p_x \qquad = p_{xd}Z$

Endogenous variables (20)

Y_a, Y_{na}^p, Y_{na}, YD, YF^*, YF, YN, K, C, IF, IS, X,

M, R^*, CDF^*, p_a, p_{na}, p, p_{xd}, p_x

Exogenous variables (7)

TW, p_m, F^*, L, t, Z, p_w, N

4.1.2. Features of the model

The basic features of the simple model set forth above are the following. On the supply side, two sectors are distinguished. As regards the agricultural sector, the supply is considered to be exogenous and for projection purposes a simple trend equation is used. The concept of potential or capacity output does not seem to be meaningful for this sector. At the individual country level the supply side could be further refined by relating acreage to prices and other factors and yield per acre to the relevant inputs and to exogenous factors such as rainfall. In many countries, the variations in output resulting from exogenous factors seem to be far more important in the short-run. Treating the supply of agricultural output as exogenous for the short-run projections and using the trend equation for medium-term projections are fairly reasonable assumptions regarding this sector.

For the output originating in the non-agricultural sector, a distinction is made between capacity and actual output as is usually done for the industrialised countries. Capacity output can be measured in the Wharton tradition. However, in obtaining a measure of the degree of capacity utilisation by this method at the regional level it would be more appropriate to build up the measure from individual countries. The determinants of the degree of capacity utilisation might be different as between the developed market economies and the developing countries. In the former, effective demand is the principal determinant of the actual level of output and hence the degree of capacity utilisation. This may not be the case for many of the developing countries where constraints from the supply of imported capital goods and raw materials play a dominant role. Eq. 3(a) is formulated to reflect these factors while the alternative 3(b) may be used where the demand side is considered to determine the actual level of output.

Eqs. (4) to (7) are the customary equations explaining the variables consumption, investment in fixed assets, exports and imports on the expenditure side of the national accounts. Two basic features which distinguish this explanation of the expenditure side from that usually adopted for the developed countries may be mentioned; one is that the level of the foreign exchange reserves available imposes a restraint on the import demand and the other is inventories are determined as a residue. This procedure may not be unreasonable in respect of the developing economies which are characterised by disequilibrium between supply and demand provided that the inventories thus determined have an impact on prices or output in the subsequent periods. Even so the procedure has a serious drawback, in that the inventories thus estimated would not only include the statistical discrepancy between the income and expenditure sides of the national accounts but also the estimation errors in all the other equations of the model. In order to overcome this difficulty, it is proposed to set limits on the level of inventories on the basis of the historical relationship between inventories and output and in case the estimated inventories fall outside these limits to make suitable adjustments in the constant terms of the equations for consumption and investment expenditures.

Turning to price equations, agricultural prices are determined by the exogenous supply and urban demand. Eq. 9(a) explains the formulation of the non-agricultural price level in terms of cost, for which the price of agricultural products is taken as a proxy, the degree of capacity utilisation and relative liquidity. This formulation corresponds to the assumption (eq. 3(b) discussed earlier) that the output in this sector is demand determined. On the other hand, if output is restrained by supply bottlenecks, non-agricultural prices are determined (eq. 9(b)) in the same way as the agricultural price level. Eq. (10) is simply a statistical equation showing that the *GDP* deflator is a weighted average of the agricultural and non-agricultural prices. The export price index, eq. (11), is related to the domestic price level and the level of external demand. Eq. (13) expresses factor income payments as a function of the cumulative deficit on current account which as a proxy for outstanding debt determines the interest component and exports which explain the dividends component. Eqs. (13) to (20) are self-explanatory and need no comment.

The above is the general structure of the models which are presently being developed to be used until such time as they are replaced by more comprehensive models for at least the major individual countries in each region. In this connection, a commodity breakdown much thinner than the one presently used in Project LINK may be required, and for this purpose research is underway on the possibility of developing commodity submodels operating on the periphery of the LINK framework.

7. A MODEL OF WORLD TRADE

G.B. TAPLIN

1. Introduction

This chapter reports on some calculations using a model of world trade built in the Research Department of the International Monetary Fund. The model, called the Expanded World Trade Model (EWTM), is designed for short-term forecasting of trade flows and for analysing economic policies. It has been built to employ relatively few exogenous variables to forecast the imports and exports of each country in the model, and at the same time to incorporate the feedback of a country's exports on its own imports. Therefore, the model yields a level of imports, exports and economic activity for each country which is consistent with those variables in other countries. While the model gives trade balances of the developed countries, it also throws some light on the trade prospects of the developing world considered as a whole.

The present version of the model treats the world as divided into 27 countries and regions: each of the 25 developed countries [1], the CMEA countries [2] and the rest of the world (RW). Although work on the geographical disaggregation of the RW

---

[1] The 25 developed countries are: Australia, Austria, Belgium-Luxembourg, Canada, Denmark, Finland, France, Federal Republic of Germany, Greece, Iceland, Ireland, Italy, Japan, Netherlands, New Zealand, Norway, Portugal, South Africa, Spain, Sweden, Switzerland, Turkey, United Kingdom, United States and Yugoslavia.

[2] Member countries of the Council of Mutual Economic Assistance (Albania, Bulgaria, Czechoslovakia, Eastern Germany, Hungary, Mongolia, Poland, Rumania and the Union of Soviet Socialist Republics), mainland China, and other countries politically and economically associated with these two areas, including North Korea and North Vietnam.

group is underway, it has been necessary to group the less developed countries together at this stage of the work. Data on prices, incomes and other needed variables for geographically defined regions of the developing world are not generally available. Trade data for the individual less developed countries disaggregated by commodity and by origin and destination are available on data tapes at the United Nations, but to prepare these data in a form usable in the EWTM would have required more manpower than was available. It was also desirable to harmonise as much as possible the work on the EWTM with the Fund's work for Project LINK. Project LINK decided to work with four commodity groupings − SITC 0 + 1, SITC 2 + 4, SITC 3 and SITC 5–9, and the Fund staff agreed to prepare the corresponding trade matrices. UNCTAD, having access to the detailed trade data for the less developed countries collected by the United Nations, undertook to provide to Project LINK the import and export functions for the less developed countries. [3]

The global imports (i.e., imports from all other countries and regions taken together) of each of the developed countries are determined by an import function reflecting the dependence of imports on economic activity, relative prices and other relevant variables. Since no internal price information is available for the CMEA region, that region's imports are determined by its economic activity and exports. RW's imports are a function of current and past foreign exchange receipts. Each country's and region's exports are obtained by distributing the forecast imports by an export shares matrix. Insofar as an export forecast based on other countries' imports may differ from the export level assumed in determining the economic activity variable used in its own import function, a new import forecast is calculated reflecting the export forecast derived from the model. A programme for solving a set of simultaneous nonlinear equations is used to obtain, by iteration, a consistent set of imports and exports.

Export shares matrices lie at the centre of the system, as they do in the Project LINK system. In fact, the matrices used in the

---

[3] These results are reported in ch. 6.

calculations reported in this chapter are the same matrices employed in the "Maxi-LINK" exercise, described in ch. 13. In the "Maxi-LINK" exercise, a country's imports are determined by a multi-equation model whereas here they are determined by a single equation.

Two versions of the EWTM are presented here. One version treats total merchandise trade flows and will hereafter be called the "total trade model", while the other divides imports and exports into the four Project LINK commodity groupings and will be identified as the "commodity trade model". Thus, the latter version has four import demand functions for each country, and four export shares matrices; total imports and exports are the sums of the respective commodity flows. Details of each of the component blocks of the model are presented in the next section. Sect. 3 describes some of the simulations undertaken, comparing the model based on total flows to the one on commodity flows. The importance of errors in the various components is also discussed. Also, there is a forecast for 1970 using the total trade model. The final section indicates directions for future work.

2. Description of the model

The model based on total trade flows consists of 84 equations. There are 27 equations each for imports, exports and the trade balance:

$$M_i = f_i(X_i, Z_i) \tag{1}$$

$$X_i = \sum_{j=1}^{27} a_{ij}(M_j/\delta_j) \tag{2}$$

$$B_i = X_i - M_i .\ {}^{4} \tag{3}$$

---

[4] In a linear system $M_i = c_i X_i + Z_i$. By transforming the vector of c_i's into a diagonal matrix C and representing the vector of f.o.b.-c.i.f. adjustment factors $1/\delta_j$ by Δ, the model written in matrix notation becomes:

In addition there are three world trade identities:

$$M_{28} = \sum_{i=1}^{27} M_i \tag{4}$$

$$X_{28} = \sum_{i=1}^{27} X_i \tag{5}$$

$$B_{28} = X_{28} - M_{28} .^{5,6} \tag{6}$$

Therefore,

$$B_{28} = \sum_{i=1}^{27} B_i$$

where

$$i,j \begin{cases} 1, ..., 25 & = \text{the individual developed countries} \\ 26 & = \text{CMEA countries} \\ 27 & = \text{RW, the developing countries grouped together} \\ 28 & = \text{Total World} \end{cases}$$

$$M = CX + Z \tag{1'}$$
$$X = A\Delta M \tag{2'}$$
$$B = X - M. \tag{3'}$$

It follows that the solution to this system is:

$$M = (I - CA\Delta)^{-1}Z \tag{1''}$$
$$X = A\Delta(I - CA\Delta)^{-1}Z \tag{2''}$$
$$B = (A\Delta - I)(I - CA\Delta)^{-1}Z. \tag{3''}$$

The identity matrix is denoted by I and, the superscript -1 signifies the operation of matrix inversion.

[5] This equation gives the difference between total world imports and exports. If all trade flows were measured either f.o.b. or c.i.f., B_{28} would be equal to zero.

[6] The disaggregated model is essentially the same. There are four import equations:

$$M_j^k = f_j^k(X_j, Z_j)$$

four export equations:

$$X_i^k = \Sigma a_{ij}^k(M_j^k/\delta_j^k)$$

and identities $M_j = \Sigma M_j^k$ and $X_i = \Sigma X_i^k$, where k is the commodity identification.

M_i = Total imports of region i, c.i.f. [7], in current prices and expressed in U.S. dollars.

X_i = Total exports of region i, f.o.b., in current prices and expressed in U.S. dollars.

B_i = Merchandise trade balance of region i.

Z_i = Explanatory factors other than exports, and assumed independent of exports, determining the imports of country i.

δ_j = The f.o.b.-c.i.f. adjustment factor (discussed below).

a_{ij} = $X_{ij}/\Sigma_i X_{ij}$; the share of country i in the total of all countries' exports to market j.

With this formulation, exports and trade balances can be obtained from a set of import forecasts (M_j), and knowledge of the market shares (a_{ij}) and the f.o.b.-c.i.f. adjustment factors (δ_j). Each of these components is discussed in turn.

2.1. Import equations

Merchandise imports of any country consist of the purchases of a wide range of foreign goods including an assortment of raw materials and semi-processed goods that are subsequently transformed in domestic production and for which there may not be domestic substitutes; machinery and equipment for the replacement or expansion of productive facilities; and a variety of consumer goods, which are often sold without substantial alteration. Any classification of imports is quite arbitrary, however, since many imported products serve more than one function.

In order to analyse and forecast imports, equations are needed which incorporate the various economic forces determining each type of import. For consumer goods imports, for example, such a specification would be based on demand theory and would give the relationship between overall consumer demand, demand for particular goods and imports of consumer goods. Imports of raw materials and semi-processed goods would be related to the techni-

---

[7] The imports of the United States, Canada and Australia are recorded f.o.b.

cal needs of production and the availability of similar supplies from domestic sources. Investment decisions based on the cost and expected return of the investment would have to be reflected in the equations explaining imports of machinery and equipment. This complex system entails a full-scale, detailed, fully specified model, and this of course is one of the purposes of Project LINK.

Lacking such models, an alternative might be to use reduced form equations relating imports to the exogenous variables of the complete, multi-equation system, rather than estimating the structural equations by simultaneous equation maximum likelihood estimating procedures. The number of exogenous variables in the reduced form, however, might be larger than that which could be handled satisfactorily in single equation estimation. A similar problem is often encountered in the context of two-stage least squares, when the number of exogenous variables in the system exceeds the number of observations of the dependent variables, thereby exhausting the degrees of freedom. In the two-stage least squares case, either a few selected exogenous variables are used in any particular equation, or some method such as principal components is employed to combine the influence of the exogenous variables. The gain from using the reduced form approach with a few explanatory variables is that the system is much smaller, can be more easily estimated and interpreted, and is feasible for a small group of workers. The import equations can be estimated without knowing their structural form, which is necessary in two-stage least squares, and without knowing the precise structural form of the other parts of the complete system. In addition, imports can then be forecast with the use of a few variables, rather than relying on the completely specified system. However, knowledge of the intricacies of imports given by the structural equations is lost, as are some of the superior statistical properties of two-stage least squares and maximum likelihood estimators.

Theoretical, as well as practical, considerations led to the following import equation specification for most countries in the model. [8]

[8] For a detailed discussion of theoretical aspects for specifying import functions, see chapter 8.

$$M/P_M = a_0 WAE^{a_1} P^{a_2} \qquad (7)$$

where M = Import value

P_M = Import unit value index

WAE = $0.5\ AE_t + 0.5\ AE_{t-1}$; average of autonomous expenditure

AE = $G + I + X$; autonomous expenditure in constant prices defined as the sum of government expenditure, gross fixed capital formation and exports of goods and services

P = Domestic price index divided by import unit value index

a_1 = Elasticity with respect to WAE

a_2 = Elasticity with respect to relative prices (P)

While Gross National Product is typically the economic activity variable used in import functions, these equations are based on autonomous expenditure (AE). This is, in principle, more appealing than GNP as the activity variable, particularly in a reduced form system. First, the calculation of GNP in the national income accounting identity incorporates imports, and thus GNP is an endogenous variable in a multi-equation system and is simultaneously determined with imports. The simultaneity characteristic is not present when autonomous expenditure is the activity variable, however, and equations with autonomous expenditure can be estimated directly. Second, within the context of a simple income-expenditure model, income is usually defined as the sum of consumption, investment, government expenditure and exports of goods and services, less imports of goods and services. Consumption is a function of income and imports are a function of either income or consumption, or both. Investment, government expenditure and exports are often considered as autonomous. In such a system, total imports of goods and services as a function of investment, government expenditure and exports would be a reduced form equation.

If commodity groupings of imports are considered in such a framework, consumer goods imports would be related to overall consumption in the structural equation and the reduced form mechanism, with these imports as a function of the three exogenous factors, could be interpreted as a shorthand representation of the chain of causality leading from increases in the autonomous variables to increases in income and, therefore, in consumption and finally in imports. Raw material imports could be related in a reduced form equation to the same exogenous variables, but this would implicitly represent the chain from demand to output and from output to input requirements. For machinery and equipment imports, the relationship would be quite straightforward and would represent in part the import content of investment, when related to investment only, but when related to the other autonomous variables the relationship would reflect once more an economic chain of events. Since these are indirect relationships, and since the precise structure is usually unknown, there is little a priori feeling as to the size of the coefficients or of the implicit elasticities of imports with respect to the activity variables. Of course, if it is argued that these factors are not exogenous, then one would have to fall back on those variables which would be considered as exogenous in the system.

Practical considerations as well lead to the use of import equations based on autonomous expenditure. In the EWTM, increases in demand for imports lead to increases in demand for exports of the supplying countries. Increases in demand for a country's exports also lead to increases in that country's demand for imports, through the income generation process described above. In earlier discussions of the model [9], the import equations were presented as functions of GNP, relative prices and other variables unique to one country or another. That formulation was justly criticised for not providing a feedback mechanism of exports on imports [10], although it could be argued that a country's policy goal might be to maintain a given level of GNP regardless of the level of imports

[9] See, for example, Rhomberg, R.R. and G.B. Taplin, 'A Disaggregated Short-Term World Trade Model', presented at the *European Meeting of the Econometric Society*, Amsterdam, 1968.
[10] Particular thanks are due to Professor B. Hickman for his suggestions on this question.

and exports. Estimating separate parameters for exports and other activity variables is often unsatisfactory, because of multicollinearity and other statistical problems. The use of autonomous expenditure as the activity variable in the import equation, a variable which incorporates exports of goods and services and from which merchandise exports can be algebraically separated for the model solution, is designed to handle that problem. *WAE*, the simple average of the current and previous year's autonomous expenditure is used to capture the income generation process.

Prices play a role in import demand determination. As imports become cheaper relative to domestically produced goods, ceteris paribus, imports substitute for domestic goods. Accordingly, prices are usually present in the structural equations, often in the form of a price ratio consisting of a domestic price measure and an import price measure. Such a price ratio has been used in the equations here, although the variable is not, strictly speaking, exogenous.

In principle, domestic prices are determined by the cost of the various inputs; often these inputs consist of imported materials. Thus, domestic prices are partly determined by import prices. At the same time, imports often act as a safety valve, dampening potential domestic price increases. This is particularly important in excess demand situations and in countries with large external sectors. Furthermore, whereas import prices may in many situations be exogenous to an individual country, they are not in the context of total world demand. Thus, changes in import demand in any one country may influence, albeit in many cases very little, export prices in the supplying countries. Thus the role of prices, both domestic and foreign, is very complicated and there appears to be no simple means for representing the various roles played by prices.

The ideal solution would be the joint estimation of all export supply functions and import demand functions for each country, but this would certainly exceed current data availability. Another possibility might be to incorporate import prices as an explanatory variable in the price equations used in larger models. In the context of the EWTM, perhaps price functions could be specified and estimated, and this would represent a further step in endogeneising the model. A weighted average of export prices or domestic prices of the supplying countries in place of import prices may also be attempted. Lacking complete information on the structure for prices, while at the same time wanting to incorporate prices in some form, and not expecting the bias to be too large in most instances, the traditional approach is followed at this stage. Nevertheless, these conceptual difficulties are reflected in the price elasticity estimates presented in table 2 below.

Other variables unique to one country or another were tried. For example, the rate of unemployment and changes in inventories were used as explanatory variables to reflect cyclical and excess demand factors. It is often argued that the import component of inventories is higher than in other sectors of the economy and that inventories have certain counter cyclical aspects, and thus that inventory investment has a different impact on imports than do other types of investment, However, inventories have in certain instances the same safety valve characteristics in situations of excess domestic demand as imports. Thus, it is not clear whether inventories should be considered as exogenous or jointly dependent in the import equation. What was seen while estimating the equations, however, was that the change in inventories was often an important explanatory variable, and in several cases its inclusion led to prices having higher and more significant coefficients. Nevertheless, the use of this variable in forecasting exercises is difficult. Unemployment rates are often used to reflect excess demand conditions, especially in cases where measured prices do not adequately portray implicit price factors. For certain countries, that variable was tried and the statistical results accepted. GNP rather than autonomous expenditure was used for New Zealand, since none of the estimates using AE or WAE were satisfactory. Previous period exports was the explanatory variable in the equations for Turkey.

For the CMEA group, imports were made a function of the index of Gross Domestic Product and the value of exports to the total world. Although the movements of imports and exports are reflected in the index, it was assumed that the index would have moved in the same fashion if imports and exports had been excluded.

For the RW group, imports were made to depend on gross foreign exchange earnings – defined in this context as exports plus the net balance of invisibles including the net inflow of private and official capital and transfers – in the current year and in the preceding year. [11] Therefore, these imports depend partly on current exports, and can be estimated by the model, partly on gross foreign exchange receipts of the preceding year, which would probably be known at the time a forecast is made.

Import elasticities obtained from the regressions and used in the simulations are presented in tables 1 and 2. Table 1 gives elasticities with respect to the economic activity variable, which in most instances was *WAE*. Table 2 gives the elasticities with respect to relative prices. The elasticity esimates are obtained by ordinary least-squares regressions on annual observations, usually from 1953 or 1954 to 1969 or 1970. All trade flows are measured in U.S. dollars; autonomous expenditure data at constant prices were converted to U.S. dollars at 1963 exchange rates. Price indices are also on a U.S. dollar basis. [12] It should be borne in mind that the commodity import functions were estimated independently of the total import functions. Normally, the elasticity for total imports would be the weighted average of the commodity elasticities. However, the estimated activity elasticities for total imports for the Netherlands, Sweden and Greece are inconsistent with this principle, as are many of the price elasticities. Further work on the import functions will be directed toward correcting this problem.

2.2. Export shares matrices

Shares matrices are central to obtaining export forecasts from import forecasts. If the shares matrices for the forecast period were known, the reliability of the forecasts would be greatly enhanced.

[11] See Rhomberg, R.R. 'Transmission of Business Fluctuations from Developed to Developing Countries', *IMF Staff Papers*, March 1968.
[12] Details on data sources, variables and equations are available from the author upon request.

G.B. Taplin

Table 1
Elasticity of imports with respect to economic activity [a]

Country	Total imports	Imports by commodity			
		SITC 0+1	SITC 2+4	SITC 3	SITC 5–9
1. United States	1.81 *	0.65 *	0.31 *	1.36 *	2.50 *
2. Canada	1.18 *	0.72 *	0.23	0.63 *	1.42 *
3. Japan	1.12 *	1.82 *	0.71 *	1.84 *	1.77 *
4. Belgium-Luxembourg	1.27 *	1.19 *	0.73 *	0.98 *	1.65
5. France	1.30 *	0.61 *	0.46 *	0.98 *	1.89
6. Germany	1.35 *	0.82 *	0.64 *	1.68 *	1.50 *
7. Italy	1.26 *	1.82 *	0.97 *	1.04 *	1.66 *
8. Netherlands	1.27 *	1.11 *	0.50 *	0.90 *	1.25 *
9. Austria	1.04 *	0.60 *	0.54	0.97 *	1.59 *
10. Denmark	1.08 *	0.11	0.64 *	0.86 *	1.34 *
11. Norway	0.90 *	0.62 *	1.67 *	0.67 *	1.24 *
12. Sweden	1.02 *	0.80 *	0.54 *	0.93 *	0.54
13. Switzerland	1.25 *	0.72 *	0.44 *	0.93 *	1.63 *
14. U. Kingdom	1.24 *	0.32 *	0.15	1.79 *	2.61 *
15. Finland	1.02 *	0.52 *	0.47 *	1.34 *	1.26 *
16. Greece	0.80 *	0.80 *	0.57 *	0.80 *	0.65 *
17. Iceland	1.13 *	1.16 *	0.47 *	0.32 *	1.31 *
18. Ireland	0.96 *	0.41 *	0.64 *	0.62 *	1.12 *
19. Portugal	0.86 *	0.99 *	0.79 *	0.45 *	0.98 *
20. Spain	1.48 *	0.63	1.39 *	1.24 *	2.08 *
21. Turkey [b]	1.29 *	1.29 *	1.29 *	1.29 *	1.29 *
22. Yugoslavia	0.20 [c], 0.97 *[d]	0.20 [c], 0.97 *[d]	0.72 * [c], 0.54 *[d]	0.20 [c], 0.97 *[d]	0.17 [c], 1.40 *[d]
23. Australia	1.12 *	0.52 *	0.64 *	0.26 *	1.33 *
24. New Zealand	1.00 *[e]	1.00 *[e]	2.01 *[e]	0.42 *[f]	1.04 *[f]
25. South Africa	0.92 *	0.63 *	0.66 *	0.44 *	0.79 *
26. CMEA [g]	0.57 *	0.57 *	0.57 *	0.57 *	0.57 *

* Significantly different from zero at the 5% level of significance.
[a] Economic activity is measured by *WAE*. See eq. (7) in the text.
[b] Activity variable is previous period exports.
[c] With respect to $(G+I)_{t-1}$.
[d] With respect to exports.
[e] Activity variable is GNP.
[f] Activity variable is *AE*.
[g] Activity variable is the index of Gross Domestic Product.

Table 2
Elasticity of imports with respect to relative prices [a]

Country	Total imports	Imports by commodity			
		SITC 0+1	SITC 2+4	SITC 3	SITC 5−9
1. United States	1.05 *	0.86 *	0.43	1.30	3.02 *
2. Canada	1.59 *	0.43*,0.33	2.55 *	0.23	2.07 *
3. Japan	0.81	0.0	0.22, 0.69	0.43	1.42
4. Belgium-Luxembourg	0.65	0.0	0.22	2.04 *	0.44
5. France	0.39	0.30	0.13	0.54 *	1.61
6. Germany	0.14, 0.47*	0.60	0.01	0.76	0.66, 1.68*
7. Italy	1.03 *	0.11	0.59 *	0.94*, 0.22	0.92
8. Netherlands	0.02	0.10	0.81	0.01	0.88
9. Austria	0.39, 0.56*	0.0	0.47	0.0	0.53, 0.21
10. Denmark	0.85 *	1.56	0.47	1.00 *	0.96
11. Norway	1.20 *	0.43	1.12	1.36 *	0.50
12. Sweden	0.23, 0.53*	0.38 *	0.52	0.24	0.32, 0.94
13. Switzerland	1.10	0.15	0.17	2.78	1.05 *
14. U. Kingdom	0.22	0.91	0.21	0.44 *	0.66 *
15. Finland	0.50	0.09	0.99 *	0.0	0.99 *
16. Greece	1.47 *	0.33	1.66	0.33	2.37*,0.73
17. Iceland	0.06 *	0.02	0.02	0.06	0.07
18. Ireland	2.40 *	1.59 *	0.93 *	0.44	2.64 *
19. Portugal	0.40	0.30	0.24	0.31	0.0
20. Spain	1.55	0.26, 1.13	0.0	0.0	2.54
21. Turkey [b]	0.65 *	0.65 *	0.65 *	0.65 *	0.65 *
22. Yugoslavia	0.76	0.76	0.80 *	0.76	1.25 *
23. Australia	0.0	0.73 *	0.0	0.0	0.0
24. New Zealand	1.12	1.12	1.75	0.34	1.23
25. South Africa	−	1.22 *	0.06	0.78	0.40
26. CMEA	−	−	−	−	−

* Significantly different from zero at the 5% level of significance.
− means that data were not available or that concept was not applicable.
[a] Relative price is the domestic wholesale price index divided by the import unit value index. In the cases where two elasticity figures are given, the first refers to period t and the second to period $t-1$.
[b] With respect to import price (sign reversed).

The question is how best to obtain a forecast for the shares matrix itself.

Market shares (a_{ij}'s) vary, of course, because of changes in relative competitiveness which result from relative price changes and other factors, and because of exogenous changes in tastes and preferences. If these changes evolve in a systematic manner, they could be approximated by trend variables and by relative price movements. For each year and each commodity, there are 729 (27 times 27) shares. To look at each share separately poses an unmanageable problem. Shares could be looked at by exporter, by market, by commodity or by time. Pooled time-series and cross-section data are required to estimate one or two key parameters to "explain" the development of shares through time, while at the same time satisfying the constraint that, in any market, the shares must sum to one.

The problem of adjustment of shares is quite similar to the problem handled by Armington.[13] He showed that the demand function for n goods from m suppliers could be simplified (compressed), provided it was assumed that in any market: (1) preference for different products of one type of good were independent of the purchases of any other type and (2) the elasticity of substitution for any type of good was constant between suppliers. In other words, an increase in American purchases of French chemicals does not affect American preferences for German, Italian or French automobiles. At the same time the elasticity of substitution between French and German automobiles is the same as that between Italian and Japanese automobiles; it is also equal to that between domestically produced and imported automobiles. Given these two assumptions, Armington showed that the demand function of country j for the kth type of good supplied by country i (or group of countries i), $\hat{X}_{ij}^k$ is:

$$\hat{X}_{ij}^k = b_{ij}^{\sigma kj} \hat{X}_j^k (P_{ij}^k/\bar{P}_j^k)^{-\sigma kj} \tag{8}$$

[13] Armington, P.S., 'A Theory of Demand for Products Distinguished by Place of Production', *IMF Staff Papers*, March 1969.

and

$$P_{ij}^k \hat{X}_{ij}^k = a_{ij}^{\sigma kj}(\bar{P}_j^k \hat{X}_j^k)(P_{ij}^k/\bar{P}_j^k)^{1-\sigma kj} . \tag{9}$$

Here, $\hat{X}_j^k$ is the total quantity of the kth good demanded regardless of the country of supply, σ_{kj} is the elasticity of substitution for the kth in the jth market, P_{ij}^k is the import price in country j of good k supplied by country i and $\bar{P}_j^k$ is the average price level of good k in country j.

Armington divided eq. (8) by $\hat{X}_j$ and (9) by $\bar{P}_j^k \hat{X}_j^k$ to obtain an expression for market shares:

$$\frac{\hat{X}_{ij}^k}{\hat{X}_j^k} = b_{ij}^{\sigma kj}(P_{ij}^k/\bar{P}_j^k)^{-\sigma kj} \tag{10}$$

$$\frac{P_{ij}^k \hat{X}_{ij}^k}{P_j^k \hat{X}^k} = b_{ij}^{\sigma kj}(P_{ij}^k/\bar{P}_j^k)^{1-\sigma kj} . \tag{11}$$

In formulae (8)–(11), $\hat{X}_j^k$ and $\bar{P}_j^k$ are defined by a constant elasticity of substitution (CES) function. As a consequence, neither $\hat{X}_j^k$ nor $\bar{P}_j^k$ are directly observable, although the individual value flows X_{ij}^k and unit value indices P_{ij}^k are.

By making further assumptions, the Armington formulation is helpful in handling our shares matrices. First, all imports are grouped together for the total trade model, or into the four LINK groupings for the commodity trade model. The domestic demand for, and supply of, domestically produced tradable goods shall be overlooked. Second, bilateral prices are replaced by export unit-value indices of the exporting countries, thereby implicitly assuming that, for example, the price of French manufactures (SITC 5–9) exported to Italy is the same as the price of French manufactures exported to England.

Next, P_j^k in eqs. (8)–(11) was approximated by a linearly weighted average of the export unit-value indices, with the previous year's share of country i in country j being the weight for the current period. [14] Finally, constant market share elasticities were assumed rather than constant elasticities of substitution. [15]

Thus, in terms of the notation of this chapter, the market share is:

$$\frac{\hat{X}^k_{ij}}{\Sigma_i \hat{X}^k_{ij}} = a^k_{ij} = A^k_{ij}(P^k_{ij})^{-\sigma_{kj}} \qquad (12)$$

where

$$P^k_{ij} = P^k_i / \bar{P}^k_j$$

and

$$\bar{P}^k_j = \sum_m a^k_{mj,\,t-1} P^k_m \; . \qquad (13)$$

Except for the weights, all variables are for time period t. $\hat{X}^k_{ij}$ is constant-price, or "volume", export flow of commodity k from country or region i to country or region j and is obtained by dividing the export value flow by the exporting country's export unit-value index. The market share a^k_{ij} is based on volume flows, P^k_i is the export unit-value index of country i for commodity k and $\bar{P}^k_j$ is the average export unit-value index for commodity k in market j, obtained by weighting each supplying country's export unit-value index by that country's share in the previous period. The market share elasticity is σ_{kj}, and A_{ij} is a constant term.

With the introduction of appropriate dummy variables, or by transforming the variables into relative differences, market share elasticities can be calculated for each market, or each commodity. Table 3 gives some equations of market share elasticities in the world market for each of the four commodities and for total

---

[14] By specifying a weighting scheme for the price index, the weighting pattern for quantity aggregation is also specified.

[15] Professor P.J. Verdoorn has shown in private correspondence that the market share elasticity equals the elasticity of substitution only if the share is zero or the price ratio equals one.

Commodity	Coefficient of logarithm[b]				Market share elasticities[c]	
	$P_{ij,t}^k$	$P_{ij,t-1}^k$	$P_{ij,t-2}^k$	$a_{ij,t-1}^k$	Short-run	Long-run
Set A						
Total	−0.426 (0.118)				−0.426	
SITC 0+1	−0.668 (0.125)				−0.668	
SITC 2+4	−0.152 (0.158)				−0.152	
SITC 3	−0.914 (0.213)				−0.914	
SITC 5–9	−1.275 (0.176)				−1.275	
Set B						
Total	−0.433 (0.120)	0.038 (0.122)			−0.433	−0.395
SITC 0+1	−0.664 (0.125)	−0.145 (0.128)			−0.664	−0.809
SITC 2+4	−0.141 (0.156)	−0.140 (0.163)			−0.141	−0.281
SITC 3	−0.931 (0.214)	0.195 (0.225)			−0.931	−0.736
SITC 5–9	−1.273 (0.175)	0.280 (0.180)			−1.273	−0.993
Set C						
Total	−0.440 (0.126)	0.442 (0.166)	−0.318 (0.140)		−0.440	−0.316
SITC 0+1	−0.638 (0.145)	0.544 (0.172)	0.160 (0.150)		−0.638	0.066
SITC 2+4	−0.090 (0.159)	−0.016 (0.213)	−0.167 (0.196)		−0.090	−0.273
SITC 3	−0.787 (0.268)	1.104 (0.363)	−0.161 (0.300)		−0.787	0.156
SITC 5–9	−1.244 (0.184)	1.339 (0.232)	−0.382 (0.230)		−1.244	−0.287
Set D[d]						
Total	−0.316 (0.098)			0.763 (0.050)	−0.316	−1.333
SITC 0+1	−0.440 (0.122)			0.605 (0.060)	−0.440	−1.114
SITC 2+4	−0.119 (0.131)			0.606 (0.061)	−0.119	−0.302
SITC 3	−0.357 (0.220)			0.480 (0.066)	−0.357	−0.687
SITC 5–9	−0.742 (0.159)			0.705 (0.055)	−0.742	−2.507

[a] Dependent variable in regression sets A–C is the logarithm of the volume share in Total World in period t minus the logarithm of the comparable share in period $t-1$. The logarithm of proportionate price changes for t, $t-1$ and $t-2$, are weighted by shares in $t-1$, $t-2$ and $t-3$ respectively. For set D, the dependent variable is the logarithm of the share in period t, whereas $P_{ij,t}^k$ refers to the logarithm of relative prices in period t weighted by shares in $t-1$. Maximum time span of the data is 1961–69. The set D equations are specified, by the use of dummy variables, to obtain a constant price coefficient for all exporting countries.

[b] Standard errors are given in parentheses.

[c] Elasticity of volume share with respect to relative prices. The short-run elasticity is the coefficient of $P_{ij,t}^k$. Long-run elasticity is: sets B and C, the sum of the price coefficients. For set D, the price coefficient divided by one minus the coefficient of $a_{ij,t-1}^k$.

[d] See eq. (16) in the text.

trade. [16] Set A in the table gives proportionate changes in current market shares regressed on proportionate changes in current price ratios. The elasticity for total trade in -0.43, with a t-statistic of 3.6; the elasticity is significantly different from -1, as well as from zero. By commodities, the coefficients range from -0.152 for SITC $2 + 4$ to -1.275 for manufactures. These results indicate somewhat higher price sensitivity of manufactures, and lower price sensitivity of various raw materials.

The Armington formulation is for equilibrium conditions, however. It is not known how long it takes after an initial exogenous change to reach a new equilibrium. To get at the long-run effects, three more sets of estimates are presented in table 3. In set B, the previous period price changes ($P_{ij,\,t-1}$) are used as an additional explanatory variable, whilst set C uses both $P_{ij,\,t-1}$ and $P_{ij,\,t-2}$. Neither of these sets produce encouraging results. A smooth reaction pattern does not emerge, nor do the coefficients have the small relative confidence limits that the estimates in set A have. Furthermore, many of the coefficients have positive signs, implying lower elasticities in the long-run than in the short-run.

Set D gives the results of using a Koyck-type specification. Assume that quantity Q responds to price in the following manner:

$$Q_t = b_0 P_t^{b_1} P_{t-1}^{b_1\lambda} P_{t-2}^{b_1\lambda^2} P_{t-3}^{b_1\lambda^3} . \tag{14}$$

By simple arithmetic manipulation, eq. (14) can be transformed to:

$$Q_t = b_0^{(1-\lambda)} P_t^{b_1} Q_{t-1}^{\lambda} . \tag{15}$$

Replacing Q_t by the volume share $a_{ij,t}^k$ and P_t by $P_{ij,t}^k$, eq. (15) becomes

$$a_{ij,t}^k = B_{ij}^k (P_{ij,t}^k)^{b_{jk}} (a_{ij,t-1}^k)^{c_{jk}} . \tag{16}$$

Set D shows that (b_j) ranges from -0.119 to -0.742 and that c_j

---

[16] Estimation was undertaken for each of the 27 markets. These results will be available separately.

ranges from 0.480 to 0.763. The c_j estimates yield long-run elasticities of -0.302 for SITC $2 + 4$ to -1.333 for total trade, to
-2.507 for manufactures. However, the impact elasticities are lower than the elasticities estimated in set A. In the simulations reported in sect. 3 of this chapter simple auto-regressive adjustments, market shares elasticities and Koyck-type results have been
used.

As part of this model building exercise, matrices of the dimen-
sion 27 by 27 were constructed for each year, 1961−69, for total
trade and for each of the commodity groupings. The matrices are
based on data published by the United Nations [17], the OECD [18]
and the national statistical offices. [19] The shares matrices are calculated by dividing the value of exports, f.o.b., from country i to
country j of commodity k by all countries' exports of commodity
k to country j. By definition, the shares sum to one. The 1963
matrix for total trade is given in table 4.

The export flow matrices were constructed in a three-step procedure. First, data were obtained for each country's exports to
each of the other countries, and to the CMEA group, that is X_{ij}
for $j = 1, ..., 26$. Each country's exports of ship stores, miscellaneous and special categories were grouped together in an unallocated grouping. Exports to region 27, the rest of the world, were
obtained by subtracting from total exports the exports to countries 1−26 and to the unallocated grouping. Finally, the exports to
the unallocated grouping were distributed over the 27 countries
and regions by the relative importance of each country and region
in total exports excluding unallocated. Since similar steps were
followed for each of the four LINK commodity groupings, the
sum of the commodity flow matrices did not equal the total trade
flow matrix.

The procedure was slightly more complicated for exports of the

---

[17] Primarily the World Trade Tables in the March issue of the *Monthly Bulletin of
Statistics*. Also, U.N. *Commodity Trade Statistics* for Japan, 1961−62, Finland,
1961−64, Australia, 1961−69 and New Zealand, 1961−62, 1964−69.

[18] Primarily the annual *Trade by Commodities: Series C*.

[19] National statistical sources were used for South Africa, 1961−68, and to derive
the figures for New Zealand for 1963.

Market	Export country					
	United States	Canada	Japan	Belgium [b]	France	German
1. United States	0.0000	0.2209	0.0913	0.0252	0.0255	0.0641
2. Canada	0.7047	0.0000	0.0197	0.0069	0.0083	0.0211
3. Japan	0.3248	0.0481	0.0000	0.0061	0.0078	0.0348
4. Belgium [b]	0.1123	0.0146	0.0077	0.0000	0.1479	0.2086
5. France	0.0910	0.0075	0.0038	0.0876	0.0000	0.1992
6. Germany	0.1036	0.0141	0.0099	0.0782	0.1159	0.0000
7. Italy	0.1329	0.0100	0.0111	0.0343	0.1023	0.1878
8. Netherlands	0.1384	0.0138	0.0108	0.1842	0.0448	0.2401
9. Austria	0.0308	0.0039	0.0027	0.0199	0.0480	0.4534
10. Denmark	0.0829	0.0036	0.0070	0.0332	0.0412	0.2279
11. Norway	0.0633	0.0409	0.0052	0.0262	0.0369	0.1759
12. Sweden	0.0894	0.0063	0.0098	0.0309	0.0427	0.2413
13. Switzerland	0.0990	0.0077	0.0171	0.0414	0.1494	0.3212
14. U. Kingdom	0.1031	0.0767	0.0126	0.0228	0.0324	0.0455
15. Finland	0.0541	0.0059	0.0048	0.0219	0.0439	0.1784
16. Greece	0.1283	0.0083	0.0616	0.0408	0.0779	0.1757
17. Iceland	0.1282	0.0029	0.0267	0.0303	0.0133	0.1266
18. Ireland	0.0650	0.0128	0.0125	0.0242	0.0274	0.0693
19. Portugal	0.0934	0.0091	0.0114	0.0411	0.0975	0.1698
20. Spain	0.1708	0.0103	0.0019	0.0202	0.1178	0.0135
21. Turkey	0.3386	0.0032	0.0194	0.0183	0.0504	0.1404
22. Yugoslavia	0.1744	0.0157	0.0075	0.0119	0.0449	0.1036
23. Australia	0.2121	0.0413	0.0713	0.0075	0.0138	0.0576
24. New Zealand	0.0950	0.0345	0.0532	0.0078	0.0077	0.0281
25. South Africa	0.1738	0.0321	0.0454	0.0135	0.0314	0.1055
26. CMEA	0.0103	0.0155	0.0136	0.0047	0.0160	0.0257
27. RW	0.2434	0.0155	0.0771	0.0131	0.0709	0.0640
28. Total World	0.1496	0.0422	0.0353	0.0317	0.0527	0.0954

CMEA and the RW groupings. In the UN terminology, these groups are the Centrally Planned Economies and the Developing Countries, respectively. Their export flows are given in the U.N. world trade tables, although certain export estimates are derived from imports reported by partner countries. More important for

3

y	Nether-lands	Austria	Denmark	Norway	Sweden	Swit-zerland	United Kingdom
296	0.0125	0.0031	0.0075	0.0064	0.0108	0.0136	0.0583
079	0.0049	0.0013	0.0020	0.0009	0.0046	0.0053	0.0763
075	0.0067	0.0008	0.0016	0.0007	0.0028	0.0106	0.0241
376	0.1518	0.0040	0.0042	0.0036	0.0241	0.0161	0.0571
661	0.0488	0.0038	0.0071	0.0047	0.0186	0.0260	0.0623
800	0.1124	0.0302	0.0277	0.0135	0.0392	0.0336	0.0516
000	0.0315	0.0303	0.0132	0.0049	0.0189	0.0333	0.0627
315	0.0000	0.0068	0.0070	0.0057	0.0271	0.0147	0.0784
824	0.0334	0.0000	0.0088	0.0043	0.0172	0.0517	0.0484
275	0.0479	0.0095	0.0000	0.0393	0.0162	0.0218	0.1522
181	0.0462	0.0069	0.0683	0.0000	0.2131	0.0157	0.1581
349	0.0620	0.0110	0.0639	0.0478	0.0000	0.0237	0.1521
037	0.0375	0.0268	0.0141	0.0030	0.0207	0.0000	0.0601
226	0.0394	0.0042	0.0354	0.0158	0.0352	0.0121	0.0000
208	0.0340	0.0072	0.0314	0.0170	0.1195	0.0238	0.1302
782	0.0333	0.0161	0.0097	0.0070	0.0286	0.0163	0.0941
124	0.0388	0.0014	0.0774	0.0997	0.0652	0.0065	0.1518
114	0.0302	0.0017	0.0104	0.0030	0.0156	0.0079	0.5452
444	0.0363	0.0092	0.0055	0.0088	0.0225	0.0381	0.1444
455	0.0263	0.0065	0.0087	0.0076	0.0264	0.0323	0.1025
559	0.0166	0.0106	0.0059	0.0035	0.0155	0.0135	0.0988
116	0.0153	0.0326	0.0049	0.0050	0.0139	0.0204	0.0459
168	0.0130	0.0031	0.0029	0.0034	0.0184	0.0130	0.2911
087	0.0116	0.0016	0.0018	0.0021	0.0126	0.0069	0.3871
311	0.0220	0.0060	0.0041	0.0036	0.0170	0.0180	0.3157
166	0.0048	0.0112	0.0049	0.0029	0.0077	0.0038	0.0214
285	0.0188	0.0028	0.0054	0.0033	0.0100	0.0121	0.0980
331	0.0324	0.0087	0.0122	0.0070	0.0209	0.0157	0.0745

our purposes, the geographical destinations given in those tables are not the same as those needed for the 27 by 27 trade matrices. For example, the U.N. tables give the European Economic Community as a destination, whereas the exports of CMEA and of RW to each of the EEC member countries are needed in the model.

Tabl

| Market | Exporting country | | | | | |
	Finland	Greece	Iceland	Ireland	Poland	Spain
1. United States	0.0037	0.0033	0.0009	0.0025	0.0030	0.0049
2. Canada	0.0003	0.0002	0.0001	0.0015	0.0011	0.0011
3. Japan	0.0005	0.0006	0.0000	0.0002	0.0009	0.0004
4. Belgium [b]	0.0077	0.0011	0.0000	0.0008	0.0023	0.0044
5. France	0.0070	0.0013	0.0001	0.0010	0.0026	0.0091
6. Germany	0.0119	0.0048	0.0009	0.0015	0.0027	0.0080
7. Italy	0.0051	0.0020	0.0006	0.0010	0.0025	0.0099
8. Netherlands	0.0121	0.0013	0.0006	0.0010	0.0016	0.0044
9. Austria	0.0024	0.0025	0.0000	0.0002	0.0018	0.0021
10. Denmark	0.0203	0.0005	0.0015	0.0003	0.0046	0.0047
11. Norway	0.0055	0.0009	0.0018	0.0011	0.0022	0.0073
12. Sweden	0.0184	0.0010	0.0020	0.0005	0.0039	0.0049
13. Switzerland	0.0023	0.0017	0.0001	0.0007	0.0021	0.0089
14. U. Kingdom	0.0196	0.0018	0.0015	0.0335	0.0046	0.0099
15. Finland	0.0000	0.0027	0.0027	0.0003	0.0018	0.0027
16. Greece	0.0100	0.0000	0.0008	0.0006	0.0021	0.0020
17. Iceland	0.0223	0.0001	0.0000	0.0002	0.0004	0.0032
18. Ireland	0.0144	0.0016	0.0008	0.0000	0.0017	0.0040
19. Portugal	0.0019	0.0023	0.0021	0.0007	0.0000	0.0129
20. Spain	0.0053	0.0005	0.0009	0.0013	0.0050	0.0000
21. Turkey	0.0040	0.0021	0.0000	0.0000	0.0016	0.0037
22. Yugoslavia	0.0076	0.0097	0.0000	0.0000	0.0005	0.0004
23. Australia	0.0051	0.0004	0.0000	0.0002	0.0013	0.0017
24. New Zealand	0.0019	0.0000	0.0000	0.0005	0.0009	0.0002
25. South Africa	0.0044	0.0001	0.0000	0.0003	0.0020	0.0010
26. CMEA	0.0136	0.0032	0.0009	0.0002	0.0004	0.0015
27. RW	0.0024	0.0006	0.0002	0.0005	0.0043	0.0034
28. Total World	0.0075	0.0019	0.0006	0.0035	0.0027	0.0048

Sources: see text.
[a] Defined as the value of exports from country i to country j divided by the sum of the value of all countries' exports to country j.
[b] Includes Luxembourg.

This problem has been overcome by distributing the total exports of the Centrally Planned Economies to the EEC as reported in the U.N. tables by the relative importance that each of the member

(:inued)

ey	Yugo-slavia	Australia	New Zealand	South Africa	CMEA	RW
30	0.0028	0.0196	0.0096	0.0127	0.0056	0.3597
)1	0.0004	0.0084	0.0020	0.0030	0.0041	0.1137
)5	0.0001	0.0850	0.0077	0.0175	0.0409	0.3693
22	0.0008	0.0109	0.0046	0.0114	0.0234	0.1407
20	0.0021	0.0172	0.0069	0.0060	0.0311	0.2869
53	0.0070	0.0077	0.0029	0.0063	0.0360	0.1951
59	0.0217	0.0152	0.0039	0.0096	0.0578	0.1916
13	0.0011	0.0025	0.0023	0.0056	0.0219	0.1423
16	0.0174	0.0027	0.0000	0.0013	0.1216	0.0416
39	0.0017	0.0011	0.0009	0.0007	0.0485	0.0911
)6	0.0004	0.0042	0.0005	0.0020	0.0318	0.0669
12	0.0038	0.0023	0.0008	0.0023	0.0508	0.0922
63	0.0039	0.0006	0.0001	0.0016	0.0213	0.0489
38	0.0035	0.0412	0.0339	0.0322	0.0419	0.3146
30	0.0004	0.0006	0.0002	0.0017	0.2226	0.0683
40	0.0111	0.0037	0.0019	0.0018	0.0821	0.1041
00	0.0003	0.0018	0.0000	0.0009	0.1757	0.0241
15	0.0000	0.0074	0.0012	0.0061	0.0166	0.1080
10	0.0000	0.0039	0.0033	0.0090	0.0081	0.2129
34	0.0007	0.0054	0.0015	0.0046	0.0278	0.2217
00	0.0065	0.0234	0.0000	0.0027	0.0728	0.0917
17	0.0000	0.0137	0.0005	0.0000	0.2333	0.1250
01	0.0001	0.0000	0.0190	0.0073	0.0125	0.1869
01	0.0006	0.2159	0.0000	0.0028	0.0061	0.1123
00	0.0000	0.0111	0.0013	0.0000	0.0040	0.1567
20	0.0119	0.0168	0.0005	0.0008	0.6958	0.0935
10	0.0044	0.0131	0.0013	0.0062	0.0848	0.2146
24	0.0052	0.0182	0.0058	0.0084	0.1222	0.2056

countries has in the imports from the CMEA region as given in the OECD or national data. A similar procedure was used for CMEA and for RW exports to "other EFTA", to "other Europe" and to "Australia and New Zealand".

2.3. The f.o.b.-c.i.f. problem [20]

The export shares matrices are constructed using data reported by exporters, and these data are on an f.o.b. basis. Matrices could also be constructed using data reported by importers. However, while the majority of countries report imports c.i.f., a few countries report imports f.o.b. − namely the United States, Canada and Australia. For reasons of consistency, therefore, export flows are used.

For any historical period, the model provides an estimate of each country's total imports f.o.b. ($\Sigma_i X_{ij}$). At the same time recorded import data are either c.i.f. or f.o.b. For each of the countries and regions in the EWTM, the ratios of reported imports to the sum of all countries' exports, $M_j/\Sigma_i X_{ij} = \delta_j$, were calculated and called the "f.o.b.-c.i.f. adjustment factor". For total trade, the factors are presented in table 5. Similar ratios were calculated for each commodity and were used in the simulation of the disaggregated commodity version.

With complete matrices of export and import flows, bilateral ratios $M_{ij}/X_{ij} = \delta_{ij}$ could be calculated. If the difference between a country's reported imports and imports f.o.b. obtained from the model represented only freight and insurance charges [21], the ratio would always be greater than one. However, differences also reflect statistical discrepancies arising because of timing, uncertainties regarding origins and destinations, and differences in the reported valuation of the trade flows. Trade flows are recorded at the time the merchandise crosses the border of the reporting country. If shipments are by post, two or three months might elapse between the time the flow is reported as an export and as an import. Such discrepancies should not arise between countries

---

[20] Particular thanks are due to Professor B.G. Hickman for his suggestions on this question.

[21] These charges, to the extent that merchandise is transported by foreign carriers, appear as debit items in the balance of payments statistics of the importing countries and as credit items in the balance of payments statistics of the countries providing the transportation and insurance services. Here, however, these costs are discussed in the context of the importing countries.

Table 5
F.o.b.-c.i.f. adjustment factors for total imports [a]

Importing country	1961	1962	1963	1964	1965	1966	1967	1968	1969
1. United States [b]	0.988	1.024	1.032	1.027	1.023	1.035	1.027	1.031	1.019
2. Canada	1.008	0.979	0.960	0.983	0.997	0.980	1.035	1.026	1.024
3. Japan	1.168	1.220	1.171	1.176	1.181	1.164	1.175	1.183	1.190
4. Belgium	1.031	1.049	1.032	1.016	0.986	0.999	0.982	0.999	1.003
5. France	1.069	1.084	1.074	1.080	1.072	1.080	1.068	1.066	1.058
6. Germany	1.094	1.119	1.125	1.074	1.106	1.098	1.093	1.077	1.084
7. Italy	1.034	1.036	1.038	1.071	1.054	1.059	1.052	1.056	1.049
8. Netherlands	1.000	0.991	0.996	0.982	0.947	0.951	0.943	0.933	0.952
9. Austria	1.023	1.027	1.026	1.025	1.021	1.020	1.014	1.014	1.005
10. Denmark	1.048	1.074	1.085	1.117	1.094	1.105	1.099	1.095	1.084
11. Norway	1.056	1.072	1.085	1.079	1.071	1.069	1.062	1.092	1.092
12. Sweden	1.067	1.080	1.088	1.092	1.077	1.087	1.086	1.061	1.047
13. Switzerland	0.978	0.962	0.962	0.983	0.977	0.969	0.961	0.952	0.955
14. U. Kingdom	1.084	1.104	1.100	1.106	1.151	1.143	1.149	1.145	1.148
15. Finland	1.065	1.062	1.044	1.049	1.084	1.070	1.071	0.989	1.025
16. Greece	1.030	1.001	0.956	0.939	1.003	1.002	0.990	1.006	0.923
17. Iceland	1.011	0.992	0.976	1.069	0.977	1.038	1.062	1.107	1.080
18. Ireland	1.106	1.081	1.121	1.139	1.092	1.100	1.069	1.021	1.032
19. Portugal	1.026	1.047	1.065	1.046	1.086	1.080	1.065	1.060	1.056
20. Spain	0.892	1.008	1.048	1.050	1.073	1.107	1.079	1.069	1.099
21. Turkey	0.893	0.982	0.983	0.986	0.948	0.965	0.884	0.966	0.842
22. Yugoslavia	1.036	1.014	1.015	1.034	1.005	0.993	1.006	1.023	0.995
23. Australia [b]	1.093	1.026	1.069	1.068	1.112	1.122	1.083	1.095	1.107
24. New Zealand [c]	1.028	0.983	0.986	1.068	1.055	1.102	1.122	1.065	1.098
25. South Africa	1.043	1.035	0.959	1.000	1.024	1.005	1.051	1.021	1.001
26. CMEA	1.000	1.000	1.000	1.000	1.000	1.000	1.000	1.000	1.000
27. RW	0.983	0.963	0.977	0.974	0.935	0.985	0.975	0.978	0.974

[a] Defined as value of total imports of country *j* divided by the sum of all countries' exports to that country.
[b] Import data in national sources reported f.o.b.
[c] For 1961–62, import data are f.o.b.

having common borders but, even here, the data show some differences. The importance of each of these factors depends on the time period under consideration and the countries involved.

As seen in table 5, the adjustment factors are in most cases greater than 1. For the United States, for example, the ratios range from 1.02 to 1.035 (except for 1961), obviously reflecting timing differences and errors in statistical reporting, since the U.S. records imports on an f.o.b. basis. For Japan, reported imports run up to 20% higher than exports reported by partner countries, reflecting fairly well the considerable geographical distance between Japan and its trading partners in North America and Europe. The Netherlands is an example of a country which reports a lower level of imports than that which other countries report as exports to that country. Examination of bilateral data showed this to be the case for most of the bilateral trade flows with the Netherlands, most likely reflecting that country's role as an entrepot.

Marginal discrepancies also arise when the exporting country labels the destination of exports by continent only, rather than by the specific country. These flows appear in the data as, for example, "Europe – not specified". The existence of "special category" and "secret" exports and imports compound the problem, particularly when these flows are treated differently in statistical reports by importers and by exporters.

These types of statistical discrepancies have important effects in the model. Consistent reporting errors bias the shares a_{ij} and can cause serious errors in the estimation of exports, particularly if different countries have substantially different price or activity elasticities. The importance and magnitude of these problems can only be seen, however, when each bilateral flow is examined from both the import and export side. Such an examination is beyond the limits of this chapter. Since an f.o.b.-c.i.f. adjustment factor is needed to modify each bilateral flow, the historical factors given in table 5 were used, with the assumption that the average δ_j for any importing country applies to each bilateral export to that country.

3. Some simulations

As described in the previous section, the three key elements to the model are the import equations, the export shares matrices and the f.o.b.-c.i.f. adjustment factors. Incorrect values for one or more of these variables will lead to errors in the forecasts of exports and trade balances. Within the context of this model, a number of questions arise, such as: How important are the various components in producing errors in the model? How large are the errors, and do errors arising from one set of endogenous variables offset those arising from another? At this stage in building the model, what is the best guess for current market shares and current f.o.b.-c.i.f. adjustment factors? Does the commodity trade model forecast total exports more accurately than the total trade model does?

In general, these questions cannot be answered by looking at the components independently of the model itself. Rather, these questions are primarily statistical in nature, and can only be answered within the context of full model solutions and by comparing model solutions under alternative assumptions regarding the endogenous variables. Those calculations are described and examined in this section.

3.1. The mechanism of the calculations

For the total trade model, a solution for any year t consists of solving simultaneously the following set of 84 equations:

$$M_i = P_{mi} \cdot f_i(X_i/Px_i, Z_i, Pd_i/Pm_i) , \quad{}^{22} \qquad (1)-(27) \qquad (17)$$

$$M_T = \sum_{i=1}^{27} M_i \qquad (28) \qquad (18)$$

$$X_i = \sum_i \hat{a}_{ij} \cdot M_j / \hat{\delta}_j \qquad (29)-(55) \qquad (19)$$

$$X_T = \sum_{i=1}^{27} X_i \qquad (56) \qquad (20)$$

$$B_i = X_i - M_i \qquad (57)-(83) \qquad (21)$$

---

[22] The change in inventories is used in certain equations.

$$B_T = X_T - M_T .   (84)   (22)$$

Most of these variables are described in sect. 2. In addition,

Pd_i = Domestic price index
Pm_i = Import unit-value index
Px_i = Export unit-value index
Z_i = $WAE_{it} - X_{it}/Px_{it}.$ [23]

In eqs. (28), (56) and (84), the "T" stands for total world, and in eqs. (29)–(55), "$\wedge$" indicates forecast values for the shares matrices and adjustment factors. In this system, M_i, X_i, B_i, a_{ij} and δ_j are endogenous variables, whereas all price measures and Z_i are exogenous. The import equations for each country incorporate the elasticity estimates presented in tables 1 and 2. Eqs. (28) and (57)–(84) are definitions and are used to calculate trade balances and the level of world trade.

The structure of the commodity trade model is essentially the same, except that for each country there is an import and export equation for each commodity grouping. There is also a shares matrix and a set of adjustment factors for each commodity grouping. [24]

The model is solved by iteration using historical values of the exogenous variables in conjunction with the import equations and selected export shares and adjustment factors. In the iteration process, the selected shares and adjustment factors were unaffected by each iteration, whereas export values from an iteration were fed into the import equations in the subsequent iteration. This process continued until the differences in the values of imports and of exports from one iteration to the next were less than 0.1%. In all instances, solutions were obtained with less than 100 iterations.

---

[23] For a few equations, Z_i represented $GNP_i - X_i/Px_i + M_i/Pm_i$.

[24] In the commodity trade model, the following imports are made exogenous: Portugal, SITC 2 + 4 and SITC 3, Turkey, SITC 0 + 1 and SITC 2 + 4, Yugoslavia, SITC 0 + 1 and SITC 3, and New Zealand, SITC 0 + 1 and SITC 2 + 4.

For both models, a set of computer runs were made consisting of annual solutions for a span beginning in 1961–64 and ending in 1969. These runs consisted in using either actual imports or imports obtained by the equations, combined with various assumptions about the export shares matrices and the f.o.b.-c.i.f. adjustment factor. In certain runs, for example, previous period market shares were considered as forecast values of current period shares.

3.2. Error measures

One of the questions of interest is how errors in one variable affect errors in another. For instance, if import values and shares were known, what impact would errors in the f.o.b.-c.i.f. adjustment factors (δ_j) have on the trade forecasts? Another example would be to see if the model is affected by errors in forecasting the shares. These lead to the question of how to measure the errors themselves in each of the variables.

Since the overall goal of the model is to forecast imports and exports, one indication of error in the system would be to compare exports and imports of the model solution to respective historical values. This comparison can be represented by the square root of the weighted-squared-proportional error ($RWSPE$) [25] of imports and of exports, with the weights being the share of each country in total world exports of the particular commodity in 1963. The same weights were used to calculate $RWSPE$ for the f.o.b.-c.i.f. adjustment factors. Other measures could also be used such as root-mean-squared-proportional error, root-mean-squared error and root-weighted-squared error. The $RWSPE$ was chosen because it gives some indication of the relative size of the errors in the model.

An error measure for the market shares is not as clear-cut. An extremely large squared proportional error could substantially distort the $RWSPE$ measure itself, even when given a very small weight. Consider a case where the export shares of a previous

[25] A proportional error is defined as the difference between the actual and calculated value (the error) divided by the actual value.

period are being used as forecast values for the current period and suppose that for a particular share the forecast value is 0.0005, whereas the known current share is 0.0001. The proportionate error in this case would be -4, and when squared, 16. If all other proportionate errors are very small, that proportionate squared error of 16 for one country would lead to a rather large *RWSPE*, even if that country is given a very small weight. Very large proportionate squared errors in the share often occurred because many of these shares were very close to zero. In the case of shares, therefore, we decided to use the square root of the weighted squared errors, (*RWSE*), with 1963 market shares as weights, although this measure is not completely satisfactory, since it does not give an idea of the size of relative errors. It was used, nevertheless, to give comparative indication of how the shares perform in the model.

The goal of the simulations was twofold. First was an investigation of the impact on the model of errors arising from forecasting imports, shares and adjustment factors. Each of these was considered by itself, then with one another, and finally with all three at once. These results are presented in table 6 and 7, and discussed in sect. 3.3. The second goal was to see how various attempts to forecast shares measured up within the full model framework. These are discussed in sect. 3.4 and summarised in tables 8 and 9.

Concerning the examination of errors, a first level error was calculated for each of the three sets of key endogenous variables by solving the model for each year using the forecast value of one set of variables in conjunction with the actual values for the other two sets. For example, in the model solutions based on the import forecasting equations, actual shares and adjustment factors gave the first level error for imports. The solutions obtained by taking forecast components two at a time with the set of actual values of the other endogenous variable provide second level errors. Finally, a third level, or total forecast error, is obtained from the model solution using all three sets of forecast variables together. These error measures are presented in table 6 for the total trade model and in table 7 for the commodity trade version.

(per cent except for export shares)

Forecast variable	Errors in [b]	1964	1965	1966	1967	1968	1969	Average [c] 1964–69
First level errors								
Imports	Imports	3.76	3.57	2.52	4.74	3.25	3.14	3.50
	Exports	1.52	1.34	1.63	3.82	0.93	0.99	1.71
Export shares	Export shares	0.0140	0.0205	0.0260	0.0345	0.0372	0.0375	0.0283
	Exports	3.90	6.28	8.24	10.63	13.30	14.35	9.44
F.o.b.-c.i.f. factors	Factors	1.91	2.32	2.19	2.92	2.90	2.88	2.52
	Exports	0.41	0.73	0.70	0.89	0.91	0.96	0.77
Second level errors [d]								
Imports	Imports	5.23	5.90	9.78	10.87	8.54	12.75	8.85
	Exports	5.37	8.07	11.46	14.62	15.36	17.93	12.14
F.o.b.-c.i.f. factors	Imports	3.83	3.42	3.04	4.78	3.22	3.04	3.56
	Exports	1.62	1.75	2.62	4.12	1.34	1.31	2.13
Export shares / F.o.b.-c.i.f. factors	Exports	4.03	6.60	8.48	11.02	13.67	14.73	9.76
Third level errors [d]								
Imports	Imports	5.12	6.58	10.85	11.02	8.52	13.13	9.04
Export shares / F.o.b.-c.i.f. factors	Exports	5.34	8.86	12.49	15.13	15.73	17.90	12.58

[a] Forecast values for imports are from the import equations; for shares, the 1963 shares; and for the f.o.b.-c.i.f. adjustment factors, the 1963 values.

[b] For exports, imports and f.o.b.-c.i.f. adjustment factors, the square root of weighted-proportional-squared errors, expressed as percentages, weighted by the 1963 share of exports in total world trade. For shares, squared errors (not proportional) are weighted by the 1963 export share by market.

[c] Unweighted, across years.

[d] Since neither export shares nor adjustment factors are altered by the iterations, the errors for these variables are equal to those in the first level errors.

Table 7

Errors in total imports and total exports arising from forecast variables in the commodity trade model: 1964–69 [a]

(per cent)

Errors in		1964	1965	1966	1967	1968	1969	Average 1964–69
Forecast variable								
First level errors								
Imports	Total imports	3.64	3.17	4.11	6.33	4.50	5.33	4.51
	Total exports	1.02	1.22	2.91	3.99	0.73	2.20	2.01
Export shares	Total exports	3.81	5.24	6.37	8.68	10.55	11.91	7.76
F.o.b.-c.i.f. factors	Total exports	0.55	0.93	0.94	1.08	1.11	1.14	0.96
Second level errors								
Imports	Total imports	6.87	5.56	9.47	10.48	7.14	10.90	8.40
	Total exports	6.58	7.11	9.88	11.78	11.61	14.30	10.21
Imports	Total imports	3.67	3.17	4.83	6.54	4.56	5.32	4.68
F.o.b.-c.i.f. factors	Total exports	0.98	1.93	4.13	4.47	1.31	2.63	2.58
Export shares	Total exports	3.90	5.52	6.49	8.95	10.75	12.23	7.97
F.o.b.-c.i.f. factors								
Third level errors								
Imports	Total imports	6.95	6.39	10.91	10.58	7.26	10.36	8.72
Export shares	Total exports	6.63	7.92	11.13	12.16	11.85	14.27	10.66

[a] See footnotes to table 6. See Appendix for first level errors by commodity for imports, export shares and f.o.b.-c.i.f. factors.

Table 8

Summary of export shares used in simulations

Case	Computer algorithm	Structural equation	Implicit price elasticity [a] Short-run	Long-run
Value shares				
1	$a_{ij,t} = a_{ij,1963}$	$a_{ij,t} = a_{ij,1963}$	-1.0	-1.0
2	$a_{ij,t} = a_{ij,t-1}$	$a_{ij,t} = a_{ij,t-1}$	-1.0	n.a.
3	$a_{ij,t} = 2.0\,a_{ij,t-1} - a_{ij,t-2}$	$\Delta a_{ij,t} = \Delta a_{ij,t-1}$	n.a.	n.a.
4	$a_{ij,t} = 1.5\,a_{ij,t-1} - a_{ij,t-3}$	$\Delta a_{ij,t} = \frac{1}{2}\Delta a_{ij,t-1} + \frac{1}{2}\Delta a_{ij,t-2}$	n.a.	n.a.
Volume shares				
5 [b]	$a_{ij,t} = a_{ij,t-1}\left[1 + b_j\left(\dfrac{P_{ij,t}}{P_{ij,t-1}} - 1\right)\right]$	$a_{ij,t} = B_{ij}(P_{ij,t})^{b_j}$	b_j	n.a.
6 [b]	$a_{ij,t} = a_{ij,t-1}\left[\dfrac{P_{ij,t}}{P_{ij,t-1}}\right]^{b_j}\left[\dfrac{a_{ij,t-1}}{a_{ij,t-2}}\right]^{c_j}$	$a_{ij,t} = B_{ij}(P_{ij,t})^{b_j}(a_{ij,t-1})^{c_j}$	b_j	$\dfrac{b_j}{1-c_j}$
7 [b]	$a_{ij,t} = a_{ij,t-1}\left\{1 + b_j\left[\dfrac{P_{ij,t}}{P_{ij,t-1}} - 1\right]\right\} + c_j[a_{ij,t-1} - a_{ij,t-2}]$	$a_{ij,t} = B_{ij}(P_{ij,t})^{b_j}(a_{ij,t-1})^{c_j}$	b_j	$\dfrac{b_j}{1-c_j}$

[a] Elasticity of volume shares with respect to relative prices.
[b] For coefficients, see table 3.

210 *G.B. Taplin*

Table 9
Errors in total exports [a] arising from errors in shares matrices: 1964–69
(per cent)

	1964	1965	1966	1967	1968	1969	Average 1964–69
Total trade model							
Case no. [b]							
1	5.34	8.86	12.49	15.13	15.73	17.90	12.58
2	5.34	5.43	3.91	5.11	3.93	4.13	4.64
3	5.05	7.22	4.51	4.26	4.48	4.01	4.92
4	8.44	5.94	3.16	4.26	3.79	4.74	5.05
5	5.76	5.51	3.86	4.96	3.86	4.29	4.71
6	3.78	7.80	3.90	4.17	4.72	3.18	4.59
7	5.22	7.02	4.48	4.27	5.03	3.53	4.92
Commodity trade model							
Case no. [b]							
1	6.95	6.38	10.91	10.58	7.26	10.26	8.72
2	6.63	4.09	4.09	5.15	2.89	3.98	4.47
3	7.13	5.96	5.11	4.78	4.06	3.69	5.12
4	12.10	4.60	3.76	5.07	3.28	4.33	5.52
5	7.14	4.04	3.75	4.97	3.00	4.00	4.48
6	6.12	5.49	3.95	5.18	4.30	3.63	4.78
7	7.11	5.26	4.61	4.59	3.53	3.42	4.75

[a] Root-mean-square-weighted-proportional error.
[b] See table 8.

3.3. Results of simulations

For the total trade model, the *RWSPE* for imports ranged from 2.52% in 1966 to 4.74% in 1967, with an average of about 3.5%. The first level error in exports averaged 1.71% and ranged from a little under 1% to 3.82%. In the commodity trade model, errors in imports and exports were usually larger [26], although some interesting features emerged. In 1967, for example, errors in imports were substantially larger in the commodity trade model

[26] For purposes of presentation, only the *RWSPE* for total exports and imports are presented in table 7, although there are corresponding errors for each import and export grouping. See tables in Appendix.

than those in the total trade model, whereas errors in exports were only slightly larger in the former instance. In 1968, imports in the commodity trade model were again much larger than in the total trade model (4.50% compared to 3.25%), whereas the overall error in exports was lower in the former instance (0.73% compared to 0.93%). It is also seen that the years with the lowest errors in imports did not necessarily yield the lowest errors in exports.

To calculate the first level errors due to export shares, the 1963 observed shares were employed in conjunction with actual imports and adjustment factors for each year's solution. In this case, constant shares led to errors in exports in the total trade model ranging from 3.70% to 14.35%. In the commodity trade version, the first level errors in total exports were somewhat smaller, ranging from 3.80% to 11.90%, indicating that there were some gains from disaggregation. This was not true of the adjustment factors, however, when the 1963 factors were used for each year. In the total trade model, there was an average error between the current year and the 1963 adjustment factors of 2½%, and these errors led to an average $RWSPE$ of 0.77% in exports. Substantially larger errors were obtained for the adjustment factors on a commodity-to-commodity basis, and these yielded larger first level errors in exports in the commodity trade model than in the total trade version.

Second level errors revealed the impact of two sets of forecast variables used together. When forecast imports were used with a forecast set of one of the other endogenous variables, imports in the final iteration differed from those obtained in the first iteration to the extent that the exports calculated by the model and fed into the import determining equations differed from the level of exports assumed for the first iteration. The impact of the model solution on imports can be seen by comparing the first level errors of imports to the second level errors. Thus, for example, when import forecasts and 1963 shares were used in one run, the error in imports was increased substantially from an average of 3.5% to 8.85% in the total trade model, and 4.51% to 8.40% in the commodity trade model. The error in exports also increased, and was usually larger than the sum of the first level errors in exports due to imports and to constant shares. This was not the case of the other second level errors. When constant shares and adjustment factors were used together, the second level error in exports averaged 9.76% in the total trade model, whereas the sum of the average of the first level errors was 10.21%.

Turning to third level errors, it is seen that except for 1964 the commodity trade model yielded lower errors than the total trade version. Nor were these errors substantially different from second level errors arising from import forecasts and constant shares. It appears, therefore, that errors in the model slightly offset one another, and that although there is a loss in accuracy in forecasting imports by using the commodity trade model, the loss is more than offset by lower errors stemming from the shares.

3.4. Some aspects of shares matrices

Exports are forecast in the model by distributing forecast imports across suppliers by the use of an export shares matrix. Errors in forecasting arise from the fact that the shares matrix used in the computations tend to differ from the set of actual shares realised in the forecast period. The problem then is to find the best approximation of the actual shares in the forecast period. Seven such attempts, several of which incorporate the elasticity estimates presented in table 3, were tried, and they are compared in this section.

The forecast shares matrix must have two characteristics. First, all shares must be non-negative and not greater than one and second, the sum of shares in any market must be equal to one. The second condition can always be met by normalising the shares, that is, by dividing each calculated share by the sum of newly calculated shares. A procedure based upon normalisation is less appealing, however, than one in which the shares sum identically to one without normalisation. Furthermore, it would be more appealing to have some method for treating groups of shares rather than a method for obtaining shares on a one-by-one basis. These two conditions are satisfied by using a shares matrix of some previous period, or average of previous periods, as the forecast matrix. For example, the first of the seven cases consisted in solving the model by using the 1963 value shares matrices for every year in the simulation period. This implicitly assumes that both the short-run and long-run elasticity of volume shares with respect to relative prices is -1. A second case was to assume that the forecast share in period t was equal to the actual share in the previous period, implying a short-run elasticity of -1. This assumption for the short-run elasticity is not so far off from the estimated short-run elasticities for SITC 3 and SITC 5$-$9 presented in sect. 2.2. However, a long-run elasticity of -1 appears to be fairly wide of the mark in comparison to elasticity estimates in set D.

Forecast shares could be based on trend extrapolations of known shares, although the use of trends encounters some difficulties. One problem with trends is that they cannot be estimated on a pooled-by-market basis, since trends in individual shares would cancel each other out. Trends pooled by supplier could be estimated, as could individual trends, but in both cases the extrapolated shares could take on positive values greater than one as well as negative values, thus violating one of the requirements. If constant percentage changes are used, values greater than one could be obtained. To use trend methods then, negatively calculated shares must be set equal to zero or to some positive value, and all the non-negative shares must be normalised to sum to one. This procedure was followed in cases 3 and 4. In case 3, the following formulation was used:

$$\Delta a_{ij,t} = \Delta a_{ij,t-1} \tag{23}$$

whereas in case 4,

$$\Delta a_{ij,t} = \tfrac{1}{2}\Delta a_{ij,t-1} + \tfrac{1}{2}\Delta a_{ij,t-2}. \tag{24}$$

Under certain restricted conditions one method that fulfills the two basic conditions without normalisation is the discrete version of the elasticity definition. Considering volume shares, that definition is $\partial a_{ij}/a_{ij} = \epsilon(\partial P_{ij}/P_{ij})$, which in terms of discrete intervals becomes,

$$\frac{a_{ij,t} - a_{ij,t-1}}{a_{ij,t-1}} = \epsilon \frac{P_{ij,t} - P_{ij,t-1}}{P_{ij,t-1}} \tag{25}$$

$$\hat{a}_{ij,t} = a_{ij,t-1} \left\{ 1 + \epsilon \left(\frac{P_{ij,t}}{P_{ij,t-1}} - 1 \right) \right\} \tag{26}$$

where "^" is used to denote the forecast value. Elasticity estimates given in set A, table 3, could be used for ϵ. The price ratio P_{ij} is defined as $P_i / \sum_m w_m P_m$. Crucial to the requirement that the shares sum to one is the manner in which the weighted price index is defined. Or looking at the question from a different angle, how should the price index be constructed so that $\sum_i \hat{a}_{ij,t} = 1$?

By substituting $P_i / \sum_m w_m P_m$ for P_{ij} in expression (26),

$$\hat{a}_{ij,t} = a_{ij,t-1} \left\{ 1 + \epsilon \left\{ \frac{P_{i,t}/P_{i,t-1}}{\sum_m w_m P_{m,t} / \sum_m w_m P_{m,t-1}} - 1 \right\} \right\} . \tag{27}$$

Summing the new expression over i,

$$\sum_i \hat{a}_{ij,t} = \sum_i a_{ij,t-1} + \epsilon \sum_i \left\{ \frac{a_{ij,t-1}[P_{i,t}/P_{i,t-1}]}{\sum_m w_m P_{m,t} / \sum_m w_m P_{m,t-1}} - 1 \right\} \tag{28}$$

In order for $\sum_i \hat{a}_{ij,t}$ to be equal to 1, the expression multiplied by ϵ must sum to zero. This will be the case when

$$\frac{\sum_m w_m P_{m,t}}{\sum_m w_m P_{m,t-1}} = \sum_i a_{ij,t-1} \frac{P_{i,t}}{P_{i,t-1}} \tag{29}$$

thus defining the price index and weights. The crucial ingredients are the relative change in prices and the previous period's volume shares. This became case 5 in the simulations. [27]

---

[27] Because of rounding errors, these shares were also normalised.

Eq. (26) could have been expressed as

$$\log a_{ij,t} = B_{ij} + b_j \log P_{ij,t} \tag{30}$$

or,

$$\hat{a}_{ij,t} = \hat{B}_{ij} \cdot P_{ij,t}^{b_j} \tag{31}$$

with b_j being the estimated elasticity ϵ. The elasticity parameter could be estimated by applying least squares to the logarithmic expression (30), provided zero shares are removed. Nevertheless, zero shares occurred quite frequently in the historical data, particularly when trade was disaggregated, and must accordingly be handled. While the presence of zeros does not complicate this simple case, zeros do complicate the formulations discussed below.

As pointed out in sect. 2, eq (27) implies a simultaneous adjustment of shares for price changes; in other words, price influences are fully worked out in the same period. Price changes of earlier periods and relevant elasticities could be added to eq. (27), provided that the price changes are always weighted by the market shares of period $t-1$. Since regression sets B and C of table 3 were unsatisfactory, this approach was not incorporated in the simulations.

Lagged price effects were included in the simulations by using transformation of a Koyck-type equation. These took two forms, each of which posed its own problems. One form of the Koyck-type equation was the equation estimated in set D of table 3,

$$a_{ij,t} = B_{ij} \cdot P_{ij,t}^{b_j} \cdot a_{ij,t-1}^{c_j} . \tag{32}$$

Several problems emerge immediately with this formulation. First, there is no way of knowing whether the shares sum to one. A linear approximation of eq. (32) could be employed but in that case the sum of the shares would only approximate to one and thus the shares would have to be normalised. With the use of dummy variables, estimation of the parameters of eq. (32) is straightforward. Nevertheless, a second complication arises in employing the equation in model solutions. For estimation purposes, the equation is transformed to logarithms and any exporter that in any year had a zero share in the jth market was removed from the calculation. Yet, in prescribing an algorithm for the computer based on these parameters, a constant term is required for each exporting country. But they cannot be obtained for each and every exporting country, namely for countries that had one or more zero shares.

The constant term in eq. (32) could be removed from the computational algorithm by dividing $\hat{a}_{ij,t}$ by a similar expression for $\hat{a}_{ij,t-1}$ and setting $\hat{a}_{ij,t-1}$ equal to $a_{ij,t-1}$, thus yielding

$$\hat{a}_{ij,t} = a_{ij,t-1}[P_{ij,t}/P_{ij,t-1}]^{b_j}\left[\frac{a_{ij,t-1}}{a_{ij,t-2}}\right]^{c_j} \tag{33}$$

In this formulation, if $a_{ij,t-1} = 0$, then $a_{ij,t} = 0$. But as $a_{ij,t-2}$ approaches zero, $a_{ij,t-1}/a_{ij,t-2}$ approaches infinity. Although c_j would always be less than one, this ratio could be very large, to the extent that previous period shares reflected factors not incorporated in the price variable, and therefore could yield forecast shares greater than one. Although none of our calculations led to individual shares greater than one, large share changes did occur and the sum of shares in any market often exceeded one by a large margin.

Similar problems were confronted when trying to obtain the constant terms by solving eq. (32) by using the 1963 values of P_{ij}. In that year all price indices equal one. Thus,

$$B_{ij} = \frac{a_{ij,63}}{(a_{ij,62})^{c_j}} \tag{34}$$

provided $a_{ij,62}$ is not equal to zero. Here, too, as the denominator approaches zero, the constant term approaches infinity. It seems safe, therefore, that this type of formulation would work when shares are not subject to large fluctuations, and when shares in previous periods reflect primarily earlier price movements. In any case, shares based on eq. (32) and normalised became the sixth case in the simulations.

Another possible formulation of the Koyck-type is the discrete version of

$$\frac{\partial a_{ij,t}}{a_{ij,t}} = b_j \frac{\partial P_{ij,t}}{P_{ij,t}} + c_j \frac{\partial a_{ij,t-1}}{a_{ij,t-1}} \tag{35}$$

namely

$$\hat{a}_{ij,t} = a_{ij,t-1} \left\{ 1 + b_j \left[\frac{P_{ij,t}}{P_{ij,t-1}} - 1 \right] + c_j \left[\frac{a_{ij,t-1} - a_{ij,t-2}}{a_{ij,t-2}} \right] \right\} \tag{36}$$

or

$$\hat{a}_{ij,t} = a_{ij,t-1} \left\{ 1 + b_j \left[\frac{P_{ij,t}}{P_{ij,t-1}} - 1 \right] \right\} + a_{ij,t-1} \left\{ c_j \left[\frac{a_{ij,t-1} - a_{ij,t-2}}{a_{ij,t-2}} \right] \right\} \tag{37}$$

For eq. (37) to equal one when summed over i, both the term incorporating relative prices and proportionate changes in previous period shares must sum to zero. Looking at the terms separately, this requires that the prices must be defined in the same manner as the prices in eq. (29). The c_j term, however, will not necessarily sum to zero if $a_{ij,t-1}$ differs from $a_{ij,t-2}$. When they are not equal, one might set the $a_{ij,t-1}$ term written to the left of c_j equal to the $a_{ij,t-2}$ in the denominator and calculate as an approximation

$$\hat{a}_{ij,t} = a_{ij,t-1} \left\{ 1 + b_j \left[\frac{P_{ij,t}}{P_{ij,t-1}} - 1 \right] \right\} + c_j (a_{ij,t-1} - a_{ij,t-2}) . \tag{38}$$

In this case, however, large decreases in previous period shares could lead to negative shares, while large increases could lead to shares greater than one. In those instances, the normalisation principle would have to be followed after setting negative shares equal to zero. [28] This formulation was case 7.

---

[28] Another possible Koyck formulation would have been to assume that the 1961 and 1962 shares fully represent past price influences and to build each year's shares from the shares in 1961 and 1962 and observed price movements after 1962.

Cases 5–7 have been designed to reflect instances where shares are modified in a consistent manner for current and past price influences. The problem becomes more difficult when trying to incorporate other factors which are not fully reflected in relative prices, such as changes in preferences, changes in technology, and unique events (strikes, wars and natural disasters). Except as these factors are implicitly reflected in price changes or in changes in previous period shares, they are not considered in this paper.

In summary, then, seven types of forecast shares, along with the import equations and previous period f.o.b.-c.i.f. adjustment factors, were used in the simulations. The features of the shares are summarised in table 8; the simulation results for 1964–69 are presented in table 9.

As seen in table 9, a share forecast that led to the lowest export error in one year was not as successful in other years. Several generalisations can be made, however. Constant 1963 shares gave the poorest results in the simulations (except for 1964), with errors in the total trade model in excess of 5% in 1964 and increasing each year to 17.90% in 1969. Previous period shares (case 2) led to results that were substantial improvements over constant shares, but which were in certain instances still inferior to the other cases.

Previous period shares performed the best of the seven cases in the commodity trade model, averaging 4.47% during the six years. for the total trade version, the average was slightly higher. The simultaneous price formulation (case 5) performed almost as well as previous period shares in the disaggregated version, and a little poorer in the total trade model; in fact, in the commodity trade model it is difficult to distinguish the results of previous period shares from those of case 5. This would seem to suggest that, lacking other information, assuming a one-year elasticity of −1 is not too far from the mark, but that this only holds for period-to-period changes.

Efforts to reflect earlier, as well as current, price changes led to mixed results. In the total trade model, case 6 yielded the lowest average export errors, although in 1964 these errors were substantially larger than those produced by cases 2 and 5. In the commodity trade model both cases 6 and 7 produced poorer results than cases 2 and 5.

In summary then, the results obtained are more suggestive than decisive. They indicate that previous period shares and current price changes yield the best results, although substantial errors arising from both the shares and the import forecasts remain.

3.5. A forecast for 1970

As mentioned above, case 6 led to the best results on average for the total trade model. This shares adjustment procedure was used to obtain a 1970 shares matrix based on 1969 shares and 1970 price developments. The 1970 shares matrix, 1969 adjustment factors and 1970 values for the exogenous variables yielded a 1970 model solution. That solution provided a basis for a forecast, obtained by adding the difference between the model solutions for 1969 and 1970 to the 1969 recorded trade values; no efforts were made to adjust the data for unique factors. The forecast is presented in table 10. Total world imports calculated, as seen in table 10, by the model were $ 318.7 billion, about $ 5 billion short of recorded world imports. Exports were forecast to be $ 308.9 billion, underestimating actual exports by about $ 2.5 billion. On a country-by-country basis, substantial errors are seen. In terms of dollar values, the largest errors were for the U.S., Germany, the CMEA and the RW groupings. In most instances, however, the errors in exports were smaller than in imports. For some of the larger trading countries, the export error was less than 2.5%. In many instances, however, the errors in exports and imports were not offsetting and thus substantial errors in the trade balances were obtained.

4. Plans for future work

The Expanded World Trade Model is by no means a finished piece of work, rather it is an ongoing project with substantial potential

G.B. Taplin

Table 10

Imports and exports for 1970: model forecast [a] (billions of U.S. dollars)

	Imports			Exports			Trade balances		
	Actual	Model Solution	Error [b]	Actual	Model Solution	Error [b]	Actual	Model Solution	Error [b]
United States [a]	39.768	37.058	2.710	42.593	41.344	1.249	2.825	4.285	-1.460
Canada [c]	14.526	14.880	-0.354	16.134	14.817	1.317	1.608	-0.064	1.672
Japan	18.881	19.566	-0.685	19.318	19.553	-0.235	0.437	-0.012	0.449
Belgium	11.362	11.978	-0.616	11.595	11.876	-0.281	0.233	-0.101	0.334
France	18.923	19.633	-0.710	17.739	17.278	0.461	-1.184	-2.355	1.166
Germany	29.947	28.886	1.061	34.189	33.620	0.567	4.242	4.734	-0.492
Italy	14.939	14.295	0.644	13.188	12.913	0.275	-1.751	-1.381	-0.370
Netherlands	13.393	13.034	0.359	11.767	11.873	-0.106	-1.626	-1.160	-0.466
Austria	3.549	3.515	0.034	2.857	3.057	-0.200	-0.692	-0.458	-0.234
Denmark	4.385	4.194	0.191	3.290	3.302	-0.012	-1.095	-0.892	-0.203
Norway	3.697	3.631	0.066	2.455	2.533	-0.078	-1.242	-1.098	-0.144
Sweden	7.005	7.184	-0.179	6.782	6.696	0.086	-0.223	-0.487	0.264
Switzerland	6.551	6.166	0.385	5.137	5.439	-0.302	-1.414	-0.727	-0.687
U. Kingdom	21.724	21.493	0.231	19.351	19.390	-0.039	-2.373	-2.102	-0.271
Finland	2.637	2.505	0.132	2.306	2.585	-0.276	-0.331	0.081	-0.412
Greece	1.956	1.756	0.200	0.642	0.702	-0.060	-1.314	-1.054	-0.260
Iceland	0.157	0.142	0.015	0.147	0.163	-0.016	-0.010	0.020	-0.030
Ireland	1.569	1.632	-0.063	1.035	0.972	0.063	-0.534	-0.660	0.126
Portugal	1.556	1.403	0.153	0.946	1.059	-0.113	-0.610	-0.343	-0.267
Spain	4.747	4.861	-0.114	2.387	2.321	0.066	-2.360	-2.538	0.178
Turkey	0.920	0.863	0.057	0.588	0.607	-0.019	-0.332	-0.257	-0.075
Yugoslavia	2.874	2.680	0.194	1.679	1.790	-0.111	-1.195	-0.889	-0.306
Australia [c]	4.482	4.591	-0.109	4.772	5.083	-0.311	0.290	0.492	-0.202
New Zealand	1.245	1.177	0.068	1.201	1.432	-0.231	-0.044	0.255	-0.299
South Africa	3.922	3.336	0.586	2.153	2.030	0.123	-1.769	-1.306	-0.463
CMEA	31.220	28.724	2.496	32.990	31.280	1.710	1.770	2.556	-0.786
Rest of the World	57.700	59.488	-1.788	54.160	55.173	-1.013	-3.540	-4.316	0.776
Total World	323.635	318.667	4.968	311.400	308.891	2.509	-12.236	-9.776	-2.460

[a] "Model Forecast" is the difference between model solutions for 1969 and 1970 added to actual value in 1969. Components may

for modification and improvement. The results of the simulations point to areas where future work should be directed.

With the current structure of the model many interesting simulations can be undertaken. For example, the model can be used to examine the impact of any one country's error in import forecasts on the entire system. Also the simulations reported in this chapter employ historical values of lagged endogenous variables. Future solutions will examine the model when previous period model solutions are used for those variables.

Improvements are necessary in every part of the model. Large errors arise from both the import equations and the shares. In the import equations, variables unique to individual countries will be tested. Variables should be introduced to capture the impact of special trade factors such as the U.S.-Canadian automobile agreement. In addition, efforts to capture the effects of excess demand conditions on imports will be undertaken. More precise specification of the price term will be investigated, both for the import equations and the export shares.

Further "endogeneisation" of the model is necessary. Perhaps the next effort will be to build in stronger feedbacks of exports on imports and to replace the import and export prices, now exogenous in the model, by price functions reflecting supply factors — the lack of supply factors is perhaps the largest missing element.

Appendix

Table A

Relative errors [a] of import and export forecasts in the disaggregated model: 1961–69 (per cent)

	1961	1962	1963	1964	1965	1966	1967	1968	1969
Imports									
SITC 0+1	7.88	7.38	3.65	7.92	6.52	6.31	4.42	5.09	8.28
SITC 2+4	9.76	10.23	3.60	5.92	4.14	7.14	5.87	8.68	9.50
SITC 3	5.64	5.66	3.78	3.59	5.37	6.52	5.30	5.31	3.56
SITC 5–9	7.05	7.43	7.93	6.91	7.84	7.31	8.09	6.85	7.33
Total	4.63	4.99	4.48	3.64	3.17	4.11	6.33	4.50	5.33
(Total [b])	(4.48)	(4.14)	(4.39)	(3.76)	(3.57)	(2.52)	(4.74)	(3.26)	(3.14)

Table A (continued)

	1961	1962	1963	1964	1965	1966	1967	1968	1969
Exports									
SITC 0+1	3.03	2.99	1.23	4.34	3.34	1.78	1.13	2.34	5.99
SITC 2+4	1.40	1.80	0.70	0.86	1.28	1.49	3.02	1.95	1.62
SITC 3	2.45	2.22	1.69	1.21	3.69	5.60	4.70	2.26	2.17
SITC 5−9	2.68	3.42	4.47	2.63	2.28	4.51	5.04	1.38	1.75
Total	1.92	2.25	2.54	1.02	1.22	2.91	3.99	0.73	2.20
(Total [b])	(1.66)	(2.00)	(1.47)	(1.52)	(1.36)	(1.63)	(3.82)	(0.93)	(0.99)

[a] "Relative errors" are the root-weighted-squared-proportional errors expressed as percentages. Weights are the 1963 shares of total world trade by commodity.

[b] From the total trade model.

Table B

Relative errors [a] of f.o.b.-c.i.f. adjustment factors in the commodity trade model: 1961−69 (per cent)

	1961	1962	1963	1964	1965	1966	1967	1968	1969
Current value compared to 1963 factors for:									
SITC 0+1 [b]	5.91	5.06	n.a.	4.90	4.92	4.94	6.71	5.61	5.68
SITC 2+4	4.71	3.87	n.a.	5.26	6.39	6.73	7.68	6.29	8.25
SITC 3	4.99	4.62	n.a.	1.98	2.47	3.50	4.18	4.16	4.69
SITC 5−9	3.86	3.65	n.a.	3.93	5.17	4.81	5.22	5.59	5.32
Total [c]	2.80	1.56	n.a.	1.91	2.32	2.19	2.92	2.90	2.88
Current value compared to previous year's factors for:									
SITC 0+1 [b]		5.30	5.06	4.90	1.84	2.54	4.58	3.47	1.88
SITC 2+4		4.25	3.87	5.26	4.25	2.15	2.67	4.13	4.77
SITC 3		4.92	4.95	1.98	2.00	2.11	2.21	1.02	2.56
SITC 5−9		2.39	3.90	3.93	4.52	2.20	1.99	1.69	1.43
Total [c]		2.55	2.08	1.91	2.25	0.94	1.58	1.30	1.22

n.a. = not applicable

[a] Root-weighted-squared-proportional errors, expressed in percentages. Weights are the 1963 share of world trade by commodity.

[b] Excluding Turkey.

[c] From the total trade model.

Table C
Errors in export shares [a]: 1964–69

		1964	1965	1966	1967	1968	1969
Case [b]							
1	SITC 0+1	0.0524	0.0510	0.0598	0.0868	0.1022	0.1127
	SITC 2+4	0.0355	0.0423	0.0457	0.0595	0.0606	0.0646
	SITC 3	0.0409	0.0676	0.0745	0.0870	0.0815	0.0942
	SITC 5–9	0.0158	0.0213	0.0265	0.0375	0.0403	0.0419
	Total [c]	0.0140	0.0205	0.0260	0.0345	0.0372	0.0375
2	SITC 0+1	0.0524	0.0322	0.0309	0.0584	0.0400	0.0242
	SITC 2+4	0.0355	0.0497	0.0228	0.0245	0.0241	0.0325
	SITC 3	0.0409	0.0398	0.0312	0.0424	0.0295	0.0394
	SITC 5–9	0.0158	0.0144	0.0129	0.0187	0.0143	0.0119
	Total [c]	0.0140	0.0122	0.0109	0.0150	0.0131	0.0112
3	SITC 0+1	0.0676	0.0700	0.0499	0.0639	0.0650	0.0387
	SITC 2+4	0.0416	0.0732	0.0533	0.0350	0.0347	0.0390
	SITC 3	0.0621	0.0430	0.0509	0.0586	0.0566	0.0533
	SITC 5–9	0.0176	0.0215	0.0178	0.0198	0.0213	0.0200
	Total [c]	0.0155	0.0163	0.0152	0.0181	0.0176	0.0239
4	SITC 0+1	0.0576	0.0515	0.0380	0.0621	0.0522	0.0320
	SITC 2+4	0.0400	0.0683	0.0329	0.0277	0.0303	0.0366
	SITC 3	0.0536	0.0456	0.0452	0.0471	0.0437	0.0502
	SITC 5–9	0.0168	0.0200	0.0153	0.0193	0.0184	0.0185
	Total [c]	0.0155	0.0144	0.0124	0.0148	0.0150	0.0170
5	SITC 0+1	0.0523	0.0316	0.0307	0.0588	0.0392	0.0242
	SITC 2+4	0.0356	0.0514	0.0233	0.0246	0.0238	0.0317
	SITC 3	0.0410	0.0394	0.0313	0.0424	0.0297	0.0404
	SITC 5–9	0.0158	0.0143	0.0219	0.0188	0.0144	0.0134
	Total [c]	0.0140	0.0124	0.0108	0.0124	0.0132	0.0112
6	SITC 0+1	0.0895	0.0631	0.0373	0.0581	0.0630	0.0274
	SITC 2+4	0.0376	0.0665	0.0370	0.0280	0.0283	0.0347
	SITC 3	0.0505	0.0163	0.0399	0.0487	0.0486	0.0449
	SITC 5–9	0.0157	0.0224	0.0149	0.0175	0.0185	0.0175
	Total [c]	0.0149	0.0183	0.0180	0.0154	0.0171	0.0152
7	SITC 0+1	0.0600	0.0520	0.0419	0.0606	0.0475	0.0289
	SITC 2+4	0.0366	0.0662	0.0394	0.0300	0.0294	0.0337
	SITC 3	0.0497	0.0368	0.0365	0.0485	0.0395	0.0437
	SITC 5–9	0.0154	0.0185	0.0155	0.0181	0.0180	0.0169
	Total [c]	0.0141	0.0145	0.0132	0.0153	0.0173	0.0150

[a] Square root of weighted-squared error. Weights are 1963 shares.
[b] See text, table 8.
[c] From the total trade model.

Part III

MODELS OF TRADE CAPITAL AND SERVICES

8. COMMODITY TRADE EQUATIONS IN PROJECT LINK

G. BASEVI *

1. Introduction

The general problem of linking national econometric models into a coherent world trade model is discussed elsewhere in this volume. [1] Various solutions are proposed, all aiming at consistency between total world imports and exports. Whatever the particular solution adopted, however, the general approach that seems to impose itself on the project is a global, as opposed to a bilateral, one. In it, national or regional models are connected indirectly through the fictitious construction of a world "reservoir" to which, and from which, commodity trade (and also trade in services and capital) of each country or region flows. The bilateral flows studied for particular pairs of countries — like Canada and the U.S.A. and Japan and the U.S.A. [2] — are for the time being to be considered as an exception to the general LINK approach.

Within the world "reservoir" approach, two different types of solutions have been proposed in order to assure that total world imports are equal to total world exports. One is to reach consistency in an "ad hoc" manner, i.e. by modifying the estimates of the exogenous variables until consistency is obtained, or by allocating among countries the discrepancy between world imports and

* This chapter is based on "best" trade functions of models in Project LINK as they were known to the author up to September 1971. The analysis is based only on LINK country models for developed market economies. On the inclusion of trade functions for the less developed countries, see ch. 6.

[1] See chs. 2, 3 and 4.

[2] See chs. 11 and 12.

world exports. This solution might be called the "export function" approach because it is based on the retention of traditional
export demand functions together with import demand functions
in each national or regional model. [3] The other type of solution
makes explicit use of the consistency constraint imposed on total
world trade, by introducing directly into the national or regional
export functions the share that they represent in total world imports. This second approach might be called the "import allocation" approach, and is the one which Project LINK is currently
using.

From the point of view of the problems to be treated in this
chapter, the most important difference between these two approaches is the fact that the second one substitutes export share
equations for the traditional export demand functions. In practice,
the approach currently followed by model builders in Project
LINK is not yet consistent with a full-fledged "import allocation"
approach: they generally include as endogenous to each model the
demand for exports. From the point of view of the country or
regional models considered individually it is in fact necessary to
proceed along these lines in order to determine exports. It should,
however, be remembered that this is only a provisional solution
and that traditional export demand equations will have to be dis-
carded when simultaneous estimation and simulation of a world-
wide model becomes possible along the lines suggested in ch. 7.
Provisionally also, some LINK country models treat import prices
as exogenous, thus implying a perfectly elastic supply of imports
for each class of product to each country. This procedure is also a
practical necessity, waiting for the implementation of the complete linkage of country models as suggested in ch. 7.

Sect. 2.3 will consider problems of aggregation. For the time
being let us suppose that imports and exports are groups of homogeneous products traded with the "rest of the world" by an homogeneous community called the country or the region.

---

[3] This approach is explained in greater detail in ch. 4.

2. Commodity trade

2.1. Commodity imports

In international trade textbooks the demand for imports is traditionally considered as an excess demand resulting, under perfect competition, from the difference between total domestic demand for, and domestic supply of, the good in question. A theoretical approach to estimation would be to treat these demand and supply functions separately. This approach, however, is impractical for various reasons. Goods of domestic origin that correspond to imported goods, even supposing that they exist, are generally difficult to identify precisely. This is a problem of aggregation compounded in practice by different classification procedures underlying data collection on production, international trade and domestic absorption. Moreover, even if these problems could be solved, estimation of total demand and domestic supply would contain errors that do not necessarily cancel out when taking differences to obtain trade flows. These, especially if small relative to the total quantities demanded and domestically produced, would thus be greatly affected by estimation errors. It follows from the above that the demand for imports is a function of all those variables that determine total domestic supply and demand of the importable good. Let us analyse these two components separately.

2.1.1. Domestic demand

In theory, it is necessary to distinguish whether the importable good is a producer or consumer good. In all cases, however, price determines demand. The price relevant for demand is the one actually paid, which includes, beside transport costs, import duties and other taxes. Moreover, price is not the only element that reflects the competitiveness and availability of a good. Non-price elements, such as servicing, delivery delays, etc., may also determine demand. [4] All these "effective price" elements will affect the

---

[4] These elements are emphasised in a recent article by Gregory, R.G., 'U.S. Imports and Internal Pressure of Demand', *American Economic Review*, March 1971.

demand for the good directly, i.e., when they refer to the same
good and, indirectly, when they refer to goods that are substitutes
or complements in consumers' or producers' demand for the good
in question.

In addition to "effective price" variables, disposable income will
determine consumers' demand, while the level of production of
the activity into which the good enters as an input will determine
producers' demand for it. Thus, we can write:

$$M_c^d = M_c^d(p,t,e,s,Y_d,...) \tag{1}$$

for the consumers' demand, where p is a vector of c.i.f. import
prices of the good in question and of its substitutes and complements, t, e and s are, respectively, corresponding vectors of duties,
compensatory taxes (or subsidies) and variables quantifying non-
price elements that determine the competitiveness of the importable good relative to its substitutes and complements, and Y_d is
consumers' disposable income. Similarly, we can write:

$$M_p^d = M_p^d(p,t,e,s,A,...) \tag{2}$$

for a typical importable producer good, where A is a variable
measuring the level of production of the activity into which the
good enters as an input.

The nature of the importable good as a capital good for producers, and as a durable good for consumers, will also determine
demand through particular variables. Unfortunately, the level of
aggregation chosen in Project LINK for merchandise trade does
not allow identification of particular imports with producers' capital or consumers' durable goods. Thus this point will not be pursued here.

Demand may also reflect the desire to accumulate or decumu-
late inventories. Actual accumulation of inventories is made up of
two components, i.e. intended and unintended accumulation. If
we assume that, since unintended accumulation results from the
difference between expected sales and actual sales, demand reflects only intended accumulation of inventories, we then have:

$$M_t^d = f\left[(\Delta I)_t^*\right] = f\left[\delta\left(I_t^* - I_{t-1}\right)\right]$$

where $(\Delta I)_t^*$ is the planned accumulation of inventories from $t-1$ to t, which is assumed to be a fraction δ of the difference between desired and actual inventories.

We can then either estimate demand on the basis of the function for planned inventory accumulation, or on the basis of the difference between total and unintended inventory accumulation. The first choice would unduly complicate estimation of the import function. The second one is simpler in so far as it reduces the number of variables determining imports by getting around the need to consider variables that determine planned accumulation of inventories. The latter will then have to be estimated separately. Thus:

$$M_t^d = f\left[(\Delta I)_t^*\right] = f\left[\Delta I_t - (\Delta I)_t^u\right]$$

$$= f\left[\Delta I_t - (S_t^e - S_t)\right]$$

where S_t^e and S_t are expected and actual sales. An expectation forming function can now be substituted into this equation. For example, on the basis of geometrically declining weights, we obtain:

$$M_t^d = f\left[\Delta I_t - \lambda \sum_{i=0}^{\infty} (1-\lambda)^i S_{t-i}\right] \tag{3}$$

as an estimating function for the demand for importables due to inventory accumulation. [5] Note that ΔI_t and S_t refer, respectively, to actual changes in inventories and sales of the importable good M. Statistics on these might not be available in practice, so that special devices become necessary to get round the problem. [6]

Including in eqs. (1) and (2) the new variables that determine

---

[5] In his study, Gregory, *op. cit.*, introduces inventories into the import function as a variable which determines the "effective price".

[6] On this point see, in particular, the LINK models for the U.K. and the Netherlands.

(3), we now have for the total demand for importables:

$$M^d = M^d \ (p,t,e,s,Y,\Delta I,S,...) \tag{4}$$

where, for brevity, we do not distinguish between demand for consumers' and producers' goods so that Y represents Y_d or A and the time subscripts have been dropped.

2.1.2. Domestic supply

The producer price of the good in question is a prime variable determining the profitability of its production. This price, in principle, is equal to the c.i.f. import price plus the tariff. Moreover, the price of inputs will determine the convenience of supply. The wage level (w) and a vector of material input prices (p_i) should thus be included. To take into account the cost of capital, a vector of financial variables (r) might also be added. In addition, if technology is not assumed to be constant over the sample period, an index of productivity (π) is necessary to incorporate possible shifts in the production function. This variable might be collapsed with a variable representing labour costs, by the use of an index of unit labour costs. Finally, in a non-competitive market, special cyclical factors might affect the availability of goods without implying a change in the supply price. These factors, which are commonly referred to by variables measuring the pressure of internal demand and which we shall indicate with the variable u, interplay with some elements that are measured by s among the determinants of demand, in introducing rationing processes in markets that are not in equilibrium. [7] We then have:

$$M^s = M^s(p,t,w,p_i,r,\pi,u,...) \tag{5}$$

[7] For a specific study of these factors on the export side, see Ball, R.J., J.R. Eaton and M.D. Steuer, 'The Relationship between United Kingdom Export Performance in Manufactures and the Internal Pressure of Demand', *Economic Journal*, September 1966. Gregory's article *op. cit.* presents a thoughtful analysis of the influence of these factors on the demand for U.S. imports.

2.1.3. Import demand

Adherence to the excess demand specification would imply, from eqs. (4) and (5), an import demand function in the following variables:

$$m = M^d - M^s = m\,(p,t,e,s,u,Y,\Delta I,S,w,p_i,r,\pi)\ .\tag{6}$$

However, the consideration of the demand for imports as the excess of demand over the domestic supply is based on the assumption that importables are homogeneous goods regardless of their place of origin. If this is not the case, we can no longer consider the demand for imports as an excess demand, and we should allow for the possibility of imperfect competition in the supply of their domestic substitutes. The producers' price of the domestically produced importable good is then no longer identical with the c.i.f. and tariff-paid price of imports. An explicitly structured model should, therefore, determine the price of domestically produced importable goods from the equilibrium solution of separate demand and supply or cost functions, allowing the demand for imports to adapt to import supply, which is generally considered exogenous in country and regional models. Thus, the demand for imports and import substitutes will now be separate functions, with arguments corresponding to those presented in eq. (4) and with, in addition, in each equation the price of the closest substitute, i.e. the domestically produced good or the imports respectively. As for the domestic supply of importables, it will be a function of type (5). An alternative is to take a short-cut and consider in the model only the reduced form of the demand-supply relationship for the domestically produced goods. In other words, we could eliminate the quantity variable by expressing only the solution for the price variable, which would then be a function of all variables determining supply and demand, except the quantity variable. The analysis of such price-determining equations, however, belongs more properly to the internal sector of a national model, and is therefore not pursued here.

2.2. Commodity exports

The *demand* for the goods exported by a country or a region to
the rest of the world is the demand for imports of the rest of the
world. As such, it should be considered a function of variables
identified in a way analogous to that discussed in sect. 2.1.
Following this line, we have demands for exports that are
different according to whether exports are producers' or consumers' goods, and whether they are or are not capital (durable)
goods. Some problems arise, however, from the aggregation of
foreign countries into the category "rest of the world". These
problems will be discussed in the next section.

The *supply* of exports is, in principle, an excess supply resulting
from the (positive) difference between total domestic supply of
the exportable good and its internal demand. This assumes, in a
way symmetrical to the treatment of import demand, that exports
and domestically absorbed exportables are perfect substitutes. If
this assumption is accepted, the resulting excess supply should be
a function of variables similar to those appearing in eq. (6), whereas, if it is not, we would have to consider export supply as a pure
supply function in a way similar to eq. (5). In either case we
should allow for the possibility of non-competitive supply and
thus of price-fixing behaviour.

2.3. Aggregation

The preceding discussion has been conducted without specific
treatment of the degree of aggregation with respect to different
variables and dimensions. *Spatial* aggregation, however, was
touched upon in connection with the choice between bilateral and
world trade models. If the world trade model is chosen, particular
problems arise in the aggregation of the income or "activity" variable for the world and of the world price level, which represents an
index of the prices of the goods that are substitutes for the country's or region's exports in the world market. The world income
(or "activity") variable should be reweighted by the importance
that each contributing market has in the exports of the country,

and in any case should be purged of the country's or region's income ("activity"). However, for practical reasons [8], Project LINK has chosen real world trade as the general "activity" variable, at least provisionally. This is purged of the country's own exports in some models. [9] Similarly, for the world export variable, the index should be constructed so as to exclude from the weighting scheme the export prices of the country or region.

Aggregation over *commodities* poses special problems for trade functions. The main one, as we have already seen, is the difficulty of reaching a detail fine enough to allow identification of goods perfectly homogeneous regardless of origin of production. Given that this detail is in practice unattainable, it should be recognised that the only consistent approach is to treat, as explained above, import demand (and export supply) as pure demand (and supply) functions and not as excess demand (or supply) functions.

The degree of commodity disaggregation generally adopted in Project LINK is not very detailed. Only four commodity groups are considered: food and agricultural products (SITC $0 + 1$), raw materials (SITC $2 + 4$), fuel and lubricants (SITC 3) and manufactured products (SITC $5-9$). This has various consequences. First, excepting the group of raw materials, it is inevitable that these aggregates comprise both consumers' and producers' goods and both capital (durable) and non-capital (non-durable) goods. Secondly, commodity aggregation gives rise to well known problems due to the use of price indices, problems which are often compounded by the necessity of relying on indices of unit import or export values rather than on indices of actual prices. [10] Thirdly, other variables beside prices determine trade and they present

---

[8] Theoretical reasons may also be advocated in favour of trade, rather than income, as the world "activity" variable. See Leamer, E.E. and R.M. Stern, *Quantitative International Economics*, Allyn and Bacon, 1970.

[9] Apparently, for the time being, only in the U.S., Japanese, Canadian and Dutch models.

[10] On these problems, see Leamer and Stern, *op. cit.*, and Kravis, I.B. and R.E. Lipsey, *Price Competitiveness in World Trade*, Studies in International Economic Relations, No.6, N.B.E.R., 1971. See also Leamer, E.E., 'Empirically Weighted Price Indices for Import Demand Functions', University of Michigan Research Paper in International Economics No.30, March 1971.

problems of aggregation too. Those sometimes discussed by LINK model builders arise in connection with the domestic income or "activity" variable, which is then reconstructed by weighting its components with their particular (average) propensities to import as they result, for example, from input/output tables. [11]

Aggregation over *decision units* poses special problems for the interpretation of marginal propensities and errors of estimation. The aggregate "parameters" are, in fact, variables that depend on income distribution, while the errors become functions of the individual parameters. This suggests that variables reflecting changes in income distribution (for consumers' goods) and changes in industrial structure (for producers' goods) should be included in the function.

Aggregation over *time* raises problems of lags and seasonality which do not seem to present particular features in trade functions.

2.4. Specification of the functions

We shall consider problems of specification in the light of the discussion of sect. 2.1.3., where it was explained that, given the level of aggregation adopted in Project LINK, imports and domestically produced importables (and exports and domestically absorbed exportables) are not homogeneous goods. This implies that import and export functions are not to be considered as excess demand functions. Moreover, we shall follow LINK country models in treating the supply of imports (the import price) as exogenous and, therefore, we shall not discuss it here.

A first problem arising with respect to specification of trade functions is whether a unique structure can indeed be assumed to exist during the sample period, or whether there are likely to have been shifts in the function. A second problem is whether the function can be assumed to be homogeneous with respect to a

---

[11] On this approach, see Evans, M.K. and R.S. Preston, "A New Way of Using Input/Output in Macroeconomic Models", *Journal of the American Statistical Association,* Proceedings, 1969.

subset or even the whole set of variables that are arguments of the function. A third problem involves the specific form to be assumed for the function. A fourth question is whether, for estimation, the variables in the function should be left in absolute levels or transformed into differences or rates of change. A fifth problem arises with respect to the distribution of time lags with which some of the variables determine the function. Since this question is strictly linked with the degree of time aggregation adopted in each model and with the dynamic features of them, it will not be discussed here in a general way.

Let us consider these problems with reference to the demand for imports, the demand for exports and the supply of exports.

2.4.1. Demand for imports

If imports are consumers' goods, their function with respect to other variables may change if tastes change over time, or if some other variable that is not included in the function (reflecting, for example, the introduction of special controls, the outbreak of wars, strikes, special incidents, etc.) changes and affects the demand for imports. In this situation the best strategy would be to identify, by opportune testing, subsets of the sample period during which a stable function can be assumed and to estimate separate structures on these subsets. However, the reduction of the sample period reduces the degrees of freedom in estimation and this is a price often too high to pay. The alternative is to include, in some way, the effect of the unusual change. The technique generally followed is to use dummy variables. Time trends are also sometimes imposed on the parameters of the variables to take into account possible changes in tastes. If imports are producers' goods, their function might shift because of technological changes or for political, institutional or accidental reasons. Short of reducing the sample size to an homogeneous period, discrete changes are usually treated with dummy variables, while technological change is introduced by time trends.

The demand for imports of consumers' goods is commonly assumed to be homogeneous of degree zero in all prices and disposable money income (or consumption). The rationale behind this is the assumption of the absence of money illusion. While it might be argued that this assumption should be tested as a separate hypothesis rather than imposed a priori [12], it implies in any case that the price and income (or consumption) variables be divided by the consumers' price index. This is generally done for the income (consumption) variable, but not always done for the price of imports and of their domestic substitutes. The price indices for the latter two are usually collapsed into one variable by using their ratio. Theoretically it would be appropriate to divide them separately by the consumers' price index to allow for the possibility of substitution between importables and other goods in consumers' expenditure, even though multicollinearity might then affect the estimates of the price coefficients. Similar homogeneity assumptions are made, or could explicitly be tested, in the case of the demand for imports of producers' goods.

No theoretical support is generally provided to the choice between linear or loglinear functions in the specification of import demand. It is the general practice to let the data speak for themselves by fitting them to alternative specifications. This, however, might be a dangerous procedure to follow if estimates are obtained by ordinary least squares in a simultaneous equation system. The alternative approaches suggested in sect. 3.5 are superior on this ground, since they assume a priori and consistent forms for import and export demand functions.

Empirical considerations are also advocated in favour of functions explaining rates of change of the quantities demanded. This procedure, in fact, reduces problems of dimensionality and multicollinearity. On the other hand, it may wash out important trends and long-run phenomena and preserve only short-run components of the variables.

2.4.2. Export functions
The *demand* for exports of a country or region is a demand of the rest of the world for the imports from that country or region. As

---

[12] See Leamer and Stern, *op. cit.*

such, the discussion of its specification does not present, in theory, problems different from those already discussed.

A *supply* function of exports can be assumed to exist independent of the export demand function only under perfect competition. With imperfect competition the function should rather be specified as a description of price-fixing behaviour.

The assumption of a well defined, unique function over the sample period may not be generally valid for the supply of exports or its price-fixing counterpart. Besides the institutional, political and accidental factors already discussed, technological change seems to be the most frequent cause of shifts in these functions. To take this into account, an effort could be made to identify the type of technological change, i.e. whether it affects the productivity of all factors and material inputs in a neutral way, or whether it is biased toward one or the other of the coefficients representing the production technique underlying the supply function. No work specific to the export functions has been produced in this area, but it seems that the progress generally made at both theoretical and empirical levels in the estimation of production and supply functions could be applied to export functions too.

Export supply or export price functions are usually presented by expressing the price of exports as a function of other variables. In practice, this is often accompanied by the exclusion of the quantity variable (the export volume) from the argument of the function. This is the reflection either of assuming a perfectly elastic supply with respect to its own price, or of considering the export price function as a reduced form function. In the latter case, retaining both a demand for exports function and a hybrid export price function seems a compromise between theoretical rigour and practical expediency.

As for homogeneity, it seems a priori reasonable to assume it, or to test for it, in terms of the price of the product and all input prices. With respect to the specific form of the function efforts should be made in order to derive it from underlying production functions and profit maximising behaviour. This approach seems, at least theoretically, more satisfactory than simply letting the data choose between theoretically unsupported alternatives. On the other hand, aggregation and non-competitive behaviour might reduce the prospects of a fruitful application of such theoretical schemes.

3. International comparisons

In this part an attempt is made to classify and compare LINK country models with respect to various characteristics of their trade functions.

3.1. Equations considered

The commodity trade equations in LINK country models are re-produced in the appendix to this chapter. While all models in Project LINK implicitly or explicitly reject the textbook assumption of perfect substitutability between imports and domestically

Table 1
Equations considered in the foreign trade sector of LINK models

Countries	Import demand		Import supply		Export demand		Export supply	
	Total demand	Excess demand	Exo-genous	Endo-genous	Pure demand	Mixed form	Pure supply	Price-fixing function
U.S.A.	*		*		*			*
Japan	*		*		*			*
West Germany	*			*	*			*
U. Kingdom	*			*	*			*
Italy	*	*	*		*			*
Canada	*		*		*		*	
Nether-lands	*	*	*			*		*
Belgium	*	*	*		*		*	
Sweden	*		*		*			*
Austria		*	*		(n.a.)	(n.a.)	(n.a.)	(n.a.)
Finland	*	*	*		*		(n.a.)	(n.a.)

(n.a.) – equations not available to the author.

produced importables and between exports and domestically absorbed exportables, not all models treat import and export demand functions as pure demand functions. Moreover, not all models specify pure export supply or export price-fixing equations, but sometimes estimate mixed forms. Table 1 attempts to classify models according to these criteria.

As shown in the table, some *import demand* functions in the Italian, Dutch, Belgian, Austrian and Finnish models may be interpreted as excess demand functions, since they include variables representing either the degree of utilisation of domestic productive resources or the domestic production of the importable good. *Import supplies* are exogenous in almost all models and are implicitly assumed to be perfectly elastic. For the U.K. and West Germany the equations estimating import prices are only meant to endogenise them provisionally by linking them to world export prices and by introducing a trend, rather than to provide a truly endogenous import supply function. Some attempts in the latter direction, however, are being made in the latest version of the German model.

With respect to *export demand*, the Dutch model presents an anomaly, since it introduces variables such as domestic unit costs, unemployment and changes in domestic harvests, which would rather belong to the export supply function or to a reduced form determining the price of exports. Yet the Dutch model also contains an equation determining the export price index. [13] On the *export supply* side, most models estimate functions for the price of exports in which the quantity exported does not appear as a determining variable. The implicit assumption might be that export supply is perfectly elastic with respect to price. In most of the export price functions, foreign variables also appear among the

---

[13] In private correspondence, however, Professor Verdoorn has pointed out that the mixed export demand equation in the Dutch model performs well and is relatively free from simultaneity bias. Moreover, (a) it allows for an estimate of the price-volume elasticity of substitution that cannot be obtained from the reduced form equation, as the sub-system is overidentified, and (b) it is more elegant than the reduced form equation since it still shows the economic phenomena more clearly than the "mixed-up" picture offered by the reduced form equation.

determining variables. This suggests, as already mentioned, that export price functions be interpreted in some cases as describing price-fixing behaviour in non-competitive markets. This would then be a function of variables affecting the demand for exports.

3.2. Level of aggregation

Table 2 summarises the characteristics of the models with respect to spatial and commodity aggregation. Except for the particular bilateral links in the models for Canada and Japan, all models use

Table 2
Level of aggregation in the foreign trade sector of LINK models

Countries / Dimension of aggregation	Space		Commodities			
	World "reservoir" models	Bilateral trade models	Imports		Exports	
			4 SITC groups	Other	4 SITC groups	Other
U.S.A.	*		*			*
Japan	*	*	*	*		*
West Germany	*		*			*
U. Kingdom	*		*	*		*
Italy	*		*			*
Canada	*	*	*	*		*
Netherlands	*		*			*
Belgium	*		*			*
Sweden	*		*	*		*
Austria	*		*		(n.a.)	(n.a.)
Finland	*		(*)	*		*

(n.a.) – equations not available to the author.

the "world reservoir" approach. Thus, their compliance with the LINK four group commodity classification on the import side does not imply the same classification on the export side, since the two flows are separated by the world reservoir.

3.3. Variables

It might be useful to study the trade functions in LINK models in the light of what was said in sects. 2.1 and 2.2 on the variables that determine import and export demand and the supply of exports.

3.3.1. Import demand functions

Table 3 compares the models with respect to the type of variables included in their import demand functions. It appears that, except for the import demand for SITC 0 + 1 in Italy and Austria, and for total imports in the Netherlands, which include as an explanatory variable domestic production of importables, models do not generally rely on variables purely relating to domestic supply, although some of them also include variables that measure non-price rationing effects. The price variable appearing in these functions is generally expressed as a ratio of import prices to domestic prices, since the underlying assumption is that imports and domestically produced importables are not perfect substitutes. Relative prices, however, do not appear in the import functions of all countries. The models for the U.K. and Sweden in no case consider relative prices as affecting the demand for imports, while in the Japanese model only imports of manufactures (SITC 5–9), and in the Austrian model imports of raw materials (SITC 2 + 4) are sensitive to prices. In Germany and the U.S. imports of raw materials do not seem to be sensitive to relative prices, while in Italy and Holland imports of fuel (SITC 3) are inelastic with respect to this variable. While specific inelasticities or different degrees of elasticity for certain groups of products in different countries are certainly justifiable, it seems hard to believe that for some countries the relative price variable never appears to be important. Thus, it is probably only a reflection of provisional statistical difficulties in the collection or construction of price indices that the U.K. and Swedish models do not yet include prices in their import functions.

Variables measuring tariffs and other barriers to trade are rarely considered in import demand functions. Notable exceptions are the U.S. and Canada for their agreement on automotive vehicles,

Table 3
Variables in import demand functions of LINK models

Countries	Variables	Domestic supply	Relative prices	Tariffs and trade barriers	Internal taxes and subsidies	Non-price rationing variables	Income and activity	Inventories
U.S.A.	SITC 0 + 1		*			*	*	
	2 + 4					*	*	*
	3		*			*	*	*
	5 − 9		*	*		*	*	
Japan	SITC 0 + 1						*	
	2 + 4						*	*
	3						*	
	5 − 9		*				*	
West Germany	SITC 0 + 1		*			*	*	
	2 + 4						*	
	3		*				*	
	5 − 9		*			*	*	
U. Kingdom	SITC 0 + 1						*	
	2 + 4						*	*
	3						*	
	5 − 9			*		*	*	*
Italy	SITC 0 + 1	*	*				*	
	2 + 4		*			*	*	
	3						*	
	5 − 9		*			*	*	
Canada	SITC 0 + 1		*			*	*	
	2 + 4		*			*	*	*
	3		*				*	
	5 − 9		*	*		*	*	
Netherlands	SITC 0 + 1			*	*		*	*
	2 + 4		*				*	*
	3	*					*	*
	5 − 9		*			*	*	*
Belgium	SITC 0 + 1		*				*	
	2 + 4						*	
	3		*				*	
	5 − 9						*	
Sweden	SITC 0 + 1						*	
	2 + 4						*	*
	3						*	
	5 − 9						*	

Table 3 (continued)

Countries	Variables	Domestic supply	Relative prices	Tariffs and trade barriers	Internal taxes and subsidies	Non-price rationing variables	Income and activity	Inventories
Austria	SITC 0+1	*					*	
	2+4		*				*	*
	3							
	5−9						*	*
Finland	raw materials and producers' goods		*				*	*
	consumers' goods		*			*	*	
	investment goods						*	*
	fuels and lubricants						*	*

the U.K. for the special surcharge provision and the Netherlands for the period before and after the formation of the Common Market. In all these cases, dummy variables are used to measure the change. It seems that more work could be done in this area to improve the measure of the evolution of changes in trade barriers. Similar considerations are in order for the influence of taxes or subsidies applied to imports to compensate for equivalent internal indirect taxes or subsidies. These seem to have been considered only in one case, the imports of food and agricultural products by Holland. Yet certain excise and other taxes surely have important effects on imports. A striking example is the registration tax on automobiles in Italy, which seems to have been deliberately used in certain periods to discourage imports of foreign cars, by adjusting it in such a way as to discourage the purchase of large cars (generally imported) relative to that of small cars (typically domestically produced). Similar influences might be found for taxes on fuel products and on certain agricultural products, although price elasticities in both these cases are probably very low.

Some models include, in addition to "price" variables (relative prices, tariffs and other taxes or subsidies) non-price rationing variables. The usual way is to consider the rate of unemployment or capacity utilisation as a variable that, by affecting the availability of domestic importables without necessarily influencing their price, makes more or less attractive the import alternative. This might be very important with certain products, of which a typical example is again imports of automobiles in Italy. It is, however, necessary that model builders refine the measurement of these effects by using variables specific to the disequilibrium situation in the particular markets covered by the import classification, rather than variables generic to the whole productive sector, as is usually the case with the index of capacity utilisation. Similar influences are meant to be shown by dummy variables for strikes, either internal or at the importing ports. [14]

In all models the main determining variables are the income or "activity" variables, represented variously according to the group of imports, by domestic consumption, disposable income, industrial production, national product, etc. In only a few cases, however, does the investment components of these macro-variables appear separately to account for the capital good nature of some imported goods. These are the import function of raw materials for Austria, of manufactures for Japan and the U.K., and, of course, given the more appropriate classification, the import function of investment goods for Finland.

Inventory demand for imports is generally considered important in the case of imports of raw materials (all models except Germany, Italy and Belgium). Inventory demand also affects imports of fuels in the U.S., the Netherlands and Finland, imports of manufactured products in the U.K., the Netherlands and Austria, and imports of agricultural products in the Netherlands. The way in which inventory changes are shown to influence import demand varies from the simple inclusion of total inventory changes as explanatory variables to particular transformations of the variables

[14] See the U.S. import functions.

that determine them. Notable examples of this are the British and Dutch models.

On the question of inventory demand for imports, as well as on that related to their demand as capital or durable consumers' goods, it seems that much more work remains to be done in Project LINK. Some models, in particular Germany, Italy and Belgium, do not yet include any influence coming from inventory accumulation.

3.3.2. Export demand functions

Table 4 summarises the type of variables that appear in export demand functions of LINK country models. All models present relative prices and a foreign activity variable as the main determinants of export demand. Trade barriers are generally disregarded, except in the Japanese model for exports of textiles to the U.S., and in the Dutch model for total exports. Special dummies for dock strikes in the U.S. and the U.K. are meant to represent the queueing and general disruption effects of these events. Although, as already pointed out, export demand must logically have the same

Table 4
Variables in export demand functions of LINK models

Variables Countries	Domestic supply	Relative prices	Tariffs and trade barriers	Taxes and subsidies	Non-price rationing variables	Income and activity	Inventories
U.S.A.		*			*	*	
Japan		*	*			*	
West Germany		*				*	
U. Kingdom		*			*	*	
Italy		*				*	
Canada		*				*	
Netherlands	*	*	*			*	
Belgium		*				*	
Sweden		*				*	
Austria	functions not available to author						
Finland		*			*	*	

characteristics as import demand functions, no attempts are made
in any model to measure the special influences that the capital
good nature of exports or their accumulation for inventories must
have in their demand. This is due, of course, to the lack of statistics at the world level for variables like investment and inventories.
However, attempts could be made to construct these variables by
weighting the corresponding elements of the main importing countries to which goods are exported. This seems to be in order at
least for those models that include special bilateral trade flows.
In addition, the Dutch model includes in the export demand function variables like unit costs and changes in domestic harvests, that
belong rather to the export supply functions. Thus, as already
explained, this equation is to be considered as a mixed one.

3.3.3. Export supply functions

Table 5 summarises the models' characteristics with respect to the
variables included in export supply functions. As already pointed
out, these functions are seldom specified as describing export supply in competitive markets, since variables belonging to the demand for exports often appear in them. The only pure supply
cases seem to be those for Canada, West Germany and Belgium.

Table 5

Variables in export supply functions of LINK models

Variables Countries	Export demand elements	Relative prices	Labour costs	Produc- tivity	Prices of material inputs	Non-price rationing variables	Export quantity
U.S.A.	*	*			*		
Japan		*	*	*		*	
West Germany	*	*	*	*		*	
U. Kingdom	*	*			*		
Italy	*	*			*	*	
Canada		*	*			*	*
Netherlands	*	*	*	*	*	*	
Belgium		*	*	*	*	*	
Sweden	*	*	*	*		*	
Austria } Finland	functions not available to the author						

The Canadian functions are remarkable for they include, in two cases (for the price of chemicals and fertilizers exported to the U.S. and for the price of minerals and metals exported to the rest of the world), the export quantity variable, which naturally determines supply price unless supply is considered perfectly elastic, and yet is never, except in these Canadian cases, considered in export supply functions.

Beside the export price, which is generally presented as the dependent variable, prices of competing exports sometimes appear as explanatory variables (in the U.K., Italian, Dutch and Swedish models). Labour cost variables appear in the West German, Canadian, Belgian, Dutch and Swedish functions, together with (except for Canada) a productivity variable. Similarly, input costs elements seem to be represented by the introduction of internal price or raw material price indices in the British, Italian and Dutch functions. Cyclical variables referring to non-price rationing elements also appear in the German, Italian, Canadian and Dutch functions. The latter is also determined by weighted world imports, emphasising the interpretation of the Dutch export price function as a description of price-fixing behaviour in imperfectly competitive markets.

3.4. Specification

As discussed in sect. 2.4 many problems arise under this heading,

Table 6

Specification of functions in the foreign trade sector of LINK models

Functions	Form		Dimension of the dependent variable	
	Linear	Loglinear	Absolute values	Rates of change or differences
Import demand	US, J, UK, I, CN, N, SW, AU	WG, J, B, CN, FI	US, WG, J, UK, I, CN, B, SW, FI	N, AU
Export demand	US, UK, I, CN, N, SW, FI	WG, J, B, CN	US, WG, J, UK, I, CN, B, FI	N
Export supply	US, WG, J, UK, CN, N, B, I, SW		WG, J, UK, I, CN	US, N, B

Table 7

Elasticities of demand for imports in LINK models

Countries	SITC 0 + 1				SITC 2 + 4				SITC 3				SITC 5 − 9			
	Price		Activity		Price		Activity		Price		Activity		Price		Activity	
	S.R.	L.R.	S.R.	L.R.	S.R.	L.R.	S.R.	L.R.	S.R.	L.R.	S.R.	L.R.	S.R.	L.R.	S.R.	L.R.
U.S.A.		−0.460		0.560		−0.025		0.214	−0.068	−0.955	0.173	2.439		−0.618		1.672
Japan			0.637	1.416			1.778	0.888			0.572	1.208	−0.537	−0.692	1.066	1.373
West Germany		−0.956		1.009				0.778		−1.577		1.386		−1.677		1.592
U. Kingdom			0.208					1.455			1.567	2.654				1.780
Italy		−1.663		3.117		−0.521		1.024				2.139	−0.426	−1.130	0.793	2.103
Canada	−0.711	−0.961		0.818		−0.303		0.755		−0.811		1.112	−1.593	−2.492		1.036
Netherlands		−0.420		0.610		−0.420		1.190				0.840		−0.490		1.180
Belgium	−0.347	−1.055	0.924	1.371			1.792	1.011		−0.653	0.732	0.950			1.381	1.995
Sweden				1.690				0.550				1.320				1.180
Austria				0.258		−0.077		0.452								0.744
Finland						−0.500		0.850				1.560				

S.R. = Short-run.
L.R. = Long-run.

so that a classification of models is very difficult in this respect. We shall limit our tabulation to the choice between linear and logarithmic forms and between absolute levels or rates of change of the dependent variable (table 6). In addition, it should be noticed that in the Austrian import demand functions the dependent variable is expressed in value rather than volume terms.

3.5. *Quantitative results*

While the empirical structures estimated for the trade equations of each model are presented as an appendix to this chapter, it might be useful to present separately those features that might be comparable among them and with results obtained on the basis of other studies than those of Project LINK. For this we report in tables 7 and 8 only relative price elasticities and income or "activi-

Table 8
Elasticities of demand for exports in LINK models

puntries	Exports of commodities				Exports of commodities and services			
	Relative prices		Activity		Relative prices		Activity	
	S.R.	L.R.	S.R.	L.R.	S.R.	L.R.	S.R.	L.R.
S.A.	−0.487	−1.438	0.312	0.922	−0.189	−1.047	0.185	1.026
pan		−2.378		1.618				
est Germany		−1.682		1.327				
Kingdom	−0.400	−0.711	0.096	0.613				
ıly		−0.720		1.176				
ınada		−0.587	0.943	1.156				
etherlands		−2.390		0.850				
elgium						−2.580		1.290
veden		−1.920		1.220				
ıstria	(n.a.)	(n.a.)	(n.a.)	(n.a.)	(n.a.)	(n.a.)	(n.a.)	(n.a.)
ıland		−0.750		1.600				

R. = Short-run.
R. = Long-run.
a.) Not yet available.

ty" elasticities of import and export demand functions. [15] In the interpretation of short-run elasticities, the level of time aggregation of each model should be considered.

It is too early to draw conclusions from the comparison of the results for different countries or regions. In future work, however, it might be interesting to study and justify significant differences or similarities in estimated elasticities. In fact, a priori information based on cross-country comparisons may be formed in this way and could be systematically used to improve the estimates of the elasticities for a particular country or region. Similarly, a systematic study of the residuals from estimated trade functions may lead to the identification of important omitted variables and of changes of structures. Correlations between the residuals of estimated trade functions for different countries could also be utilised in improving their estimation.

On the other hand, systematic estimation and comparison of trade functions would be more acceptable, at least in theory, if they were based, for all countries or for a subset of comparable countries, on a theoretically founded system of consistent equations. Indeed, given the general equilibrium approach that characterises Project LINK, it seems that specification and estimation of trade functions would have to be founded on the theory of consumers' and producers' expenditure systems, which has recently begun to be applied to international trade functions. [16]

Appendix

Unless otherwise specified, variables' names refer to the variables of the country to which the equation belongs. Thus, the same

[15] Except when specified as constant, the elasticities are estimates based on sample averages. When for a country the commodity classification used is more detailed than the standard four SITC groups for imports and the total commodity trade for exports that have been adopted as the rule in Project LINK, elasticities have been aggregated on the basis of appropriately weighted means.

[16] On this too the article by Gregory, *op. cit.* is a valuable contribution. For a good survey of this promising field, see the recent work by Berner, R., 'Specifying Import Demand Functions', Institut des Sciences Economiques, Discussion Paper No. 7109, Louvain, October 1971.

name (e.g. *M*01, *GNP*, etc.) applies to different variables as they change from country to country. For the sake of standardisation, the same name has been used whenever the economic variables to which it refers are sufficiently close economic concepts (e.g. *P* indicates either the GNP or the GDP price deflator, or an unspecified "general price level"). Differences in units of account are not considered. All relative prices are to be considered adjusted for exchange rates, when relevant.

Changes in absolute levels (first differences) are indicated by Δ; rates of changes are indicated by DOT (...). The numbers in parenthesis below the regression coefficients indicate the ratios between the coefficients and their standard errors. $\bar{R}^2$ indicates the coefficient of determination adjusted for degrees of freedom. *DW* indicates the Durbin-Watson statistic. r_1 and r_2 indicate first and second order autocorrelation coefficients.

Commodity trade functions in country models of project LINK

1. Import Demand Functions

1.1. *United States of America*

$M01$
$$= \underset{(6.56)}{3.757} + \underset{(9.3)}{0.005}\ YD_{-1} - \underset{(4.84)}{1.93}\ (PM01/PD01) +$$

$$+ \underset{(2.8)}{0.78}\ DKW - \underset{(5.45)}{0.737}\ DOCK$$

$$\bar{R}^2 = 0.84 \quad DW = 1.85$$

$M24$
$$= \underset{(21.74)}{2.198} + \underset{(4.84)}{0.003}\ VI + \underset{(4.48)}{0.031}\ IINA + \underset{(4.78)}{0.935}\ DKW -$$

$$- \underset{(0.94)}{0.089}\ DOCK$$

$$\bar{R}^2 = 0.54 \quad DW = 1.75$$

$M3$ $= 0.013 + 0.002\,VI - 0.125\,(PM3/PD3) -$
 (0.05) (1.56) (0.44)

 $- 0.145 DOCK + 0.934\,\frac{1}{4}\sum_{i=1}^{4}M3_{-i}$
 (2.17) (14.02)

 $\bar{R}^2 = 0.96 \quad DW = 1.63$

$M59$ $= -1.426 + 0.029\,GNP + 0.064\,GNP \cdot DACU -$
 (0.47) (10.95) (9.53)

 $- 5.869\,(PM59/PD59) - 38.691\,DACU -$
 (3.09) (8.49)

 $- 1.937\,DOCK$
 (6.18)

 $\bar{R}^2 = 0.99 \quad DW = 1.82 \quad r_1 = 0.269 \quad r_2 = 0.269$

1.2. Japan

$M01$ $= -60.8 - 0.381\,Q3 - 0.435\,Q4 + 0.053\,C +$
 (2.59) (4.29) (3.45) (3.88)

 $+ 0.55\,M01_{-1}$
 (4.66)

 $\bar{R}^2 = 0.97 \quad DW = 2.36$

$M24$ $= 313.987 + 0.568\,Q2 - 0.305\,Q4 + 3.744\,PROD +$
 (2.61) (4.08) (1.81) (4.23)

 $+ 8.779\,\Delta PROD - 2.819\,(KINA_{-1}/PROD) +$
 (2.9) (2.05)

 $+ 0.403\,M24_{-1}$
 (3.2)

 $\bar{R}^2 = 0.98 \quad DW = 1.59$

$M3$ $= -64.6 - 0.127\,Q3 + 0.184\,Q4 + 2.525\,PROD +$
 (4.04) (2.22) (2.69) (4.24)

 $+ 0.526\,M3_{-1}$
 (4.35)

 $\bar{R}^2 = 0.99 \quad DW = 2.44$

$$M59 \quad = -721.1 \quad + \quad 0.109\, Q2 - \quad 0.386\, Q3 - \quad 1.003\, Q4 +$$
$$\qquad\qquad (4.48) \quad (0.78) \qquad (2.76) \qquad (3.53)$$

$$+ \quad 0.238\, IFP + \quad 0.042\, (GNP - IFP)$$
$$(3.57) \qquad\quad (2.53)$$

$$+ \, 536.8 \quad (P/PM59) + \quad 0.224\, M59_{-1}$$
$$(4.79) \qquad\qquad\qquad (1.89)$$

$$\bar{R}^2 = 0.98 \quad DW = 1.85$$

1.3. West Germany

$$\log M01 = \quad \log 0.051 + \quad 1.009 \log YD + \quad 0.956 \log (PD01/PM01) +$$
$$\qquad\qquad\qquad\qquad (5.66) \qquad\qquad\quad (2.24)$$

$$+ \quad 1.34 \quad \log RHO_{-1}$$
$$(1.96)$$

$$\bar{R}^2 = 0.98 \quad DW = 3.12$$

$$\log M24 = \quad \log 0.274 + \quad 0.778 \log PROD$$
$$\qquad\qquad\qquad\qquad (10.56)$$

$$\bar{R}^2 = 0.96 \quad DW = 1.93$$

$$\log M3 \quad = \quad \log 0.009 + \quad 1.386 \log PROD + \quad 1.577 \log (PD3/PM3)_{-1}$$
$$\qquad\qquad\qquad\qquad (2.55) \qquad\qquad\qquad (2.16)$$

$$\bar{R}^2 = 0.98 \quad DW = 0.60$$

$$\log M59 = \quad \log 0.003 + \quad 1.592 \log ((GNP + GNP_{-1})/2) +$$
$$\qquad\qquad\qquad\qquad (3.08)$$

$$+ \quad 1.677 \cdot$$
$$(2.77)$$

$$\log ((P/PM58 + P_{-1}/PM58_{-1})/2) + \quad 1.702 \log PROD$$
$$\qquad\qquad\qquad\qquad\qquad\qquad\qquad (2.42)$$

$$\bar{R}^2 = 0.99 \quad DW = 1.54$$

1.4. *United Kingdom*

$M01 \quad = 342.0 \quad + 1.6\,Q1 - 3.1\,Q2 - 20.8\,Q3$
$\qquad\quad (13.15) \quad (0.27) \quad (0.52) \quad (3.47)$

$$+ \; 0.0155 \cdot \lambda \sum_{i=0}^{t-1} (1-\lambda)^i \, (YD/PC)_{t-i}$$
$\quad\; (3.37)$

$\bar{R}^2 = 0.39 \quad DW = 1.80$

$M24 \quad = -550.0 \; - \; 1.6\,Q1 - \; 1.5\,Q2 + \; 3.1\,Q3 +$
$\qquad\qquad (4.3) \quad (0.42) \quad\; (0.39) \quad\; (0.82)$

$+ \, 33.7 \, TIME + \; 3.47 \, PROD +$
$\;\; (3.74) \qquad\quad (5.42)$

$$+ \; 0.177 \sum_{1}^{t-2} PROD - \; 0.216 \sum_{1}^{t-2} M24$$
$\;\; (3.76) \qquad\qquad\qquad (4.14)$

$\bar{R}^2 = 0.72 \quad DW = 1.80$

$M3 \qquad = -158.8 \quad + 13.7\,Q1 + \; 2.2\,Q2 - \; 4.5\,Q3 +$
$\qquad\qquad\;\; (4.25) \quad\; (3.34) \quad\; (0.48) \quad\; (1.07)$

$+ \; 0.036 \, GDP + \; 0.409 \, M3_{-1}$
$\;\; (4.47) \qquad\quad\; (3.06)$

$\bar{R}^2 = 0.95 \quad DW = 2.30$

$M59SF = 813.7 \quad + 13.4\,Q1 + \; 9.1\,Q2 + \; 1.2\,Q3 -$
$\qquad\qquad (2.48) \quad\; (2.98) \quad\; (1.94) \quad\; (0.26)$

$73.5 \quad TIME + \; 4.31 \quad PROD$
$(3.43) \qquad\qquad (5.07)$

$$- \; 0.345 \sum_{1}^{t-2} M59SF + \; 1.54 \sum_{1}^{t-2} PROD -$$
$\;\; (3.29) \qquad\qquad\qquad\quad (3.35)$

$$- \; 5.84 \sum_{1}^{t-2} DT1$$
$\;\; (2.92)$

$\bar{R}^2 = 0.96 \quad DW = 1.20$

$$M59MC = -63.8 + 5.4 Q1 + 8.4 Q2 - 2.0 Q3 +$$
$$(4.73) \quad (2.16) \quad (3.36) \quad (0.8)$$

$$+ 1.7 TIME + 0.096 (IFP + IFG) - 8.8 DT1 -$$
$$(5.67) \quad\quad (4.26) \quad\quad\quad (2.15)$$

$$- 10.4 DT2$$
$$(1.93)$$

$$\bar{R}^2 = 0.98 \quad DW = 1.40$$

$$M59MM = -70.9 + 3.6 Q1 + 3.7 Q2 + 0.4 Q3 +$$
$$(1.61) \quad (2.4) \quad\quad (2.64) \quad (0.27)$$

$$+ 0.015 (YD/PC) + 13.17 (PROD/PRODT) +$$
$$(2.68) \quad\quad\quad (4.51)$$

$$0.576 M59MM_{-1} - 12.8 DT1 - 0.3 DT2 +$$
$$(3.89) \quad\quad\quad (2.17) \quad\quad (0.08)$$

$$+ 5.1 DT1_{-1} + 0.1 DT2_{-1}$$
$$(0.94) \quad\quad (0.03)$$

$$\bar{R}^2 = 0.97 \quad DW = 1.80$$

1.5. *Italy*

$$M01 = 2.813 - 0.222 Q1 - 0.178 Q2 - 0.309 Q3 -$$
$$(2.76) \quad (2.15) \quad\quad (1.54) \quad\quad (3.12)$$

$$- 0.368 VA_{-1} + 0.129 (C + CG)$$
$$(2.83) \quad\quad\quad (10.47)$$

$$- 0.598 (PM01/PD01)$$
$$(3.91)$$

$$\bar{R}^2 = 0.92 \quad DW = 2.08 \quad r_1 = 0.45$$

$$M24 = 0.15 Q1 + 0.177 Q2 - 0.117 Q3 + 0.158 VI +$$
$$(1.67) \quad (1.77) \quad\quad (1.89) \quad\quad (11.94)$$

$$+ 0.228 RHO - 0.366 (PM24/PD24)$$
$$(3.18) \quad\quad\quad (4.61)$$

$$\bar{R}^2 = 0.94 \quad DW = 1.69 \quad r_1 = 0.54$$

$$M3 \quad = -2.722 - 0.168\,Q1 - 0.21\;Q2 - 0.221\,Q3 +$$
$$\quad\quad (12.84) \quad (2.0) \quad\quad (2.38) \quad\quad (2.69)$$

$$\quad + \quad 0.069\,GNP$$
$$\quad\quad (27.03)$$

$$\bar{R}^2 = 0.96 \quad DW = 2.16 \quad r_1 = 0.20$$

$$M59 \quad = - \; 0.713 - 0.062\,Q2 + 0.007\,GNP + 0.082\,RHO -$$
$$\quad\quad (5.40) \quad (4.02) \quad\quad (7.24) \quad\quad (6.95)$$

$$\quad - \; 0.049\,(PM59/PD59) + 0.623\,M59_{-1}$$
$$\quad\quad (3.67) \quad\quad\quad\quad\quad (6.5)$$

$$\bar{R}^2 = 0.97 \quad DW = 2.05$$

1.6. *Canada*

$$\log M01U = \;\; 3.475 + \;\; 0.74 \;\; \log(CND + CS)$$
$$\quad\quad (7.93) \quad (5.33)$$

$$\quad - \;\; 0.885 \log(PM01U/PD01) -$$
$$\quad\quad (2.99)$$

$$\quad - \;\; 0.437 \log(PM01U/PD01)_{-1}$$
$$\quad\quad (1.59)$$

$$\bar{R}^2 = 0.95 \quad DW = 2.31 \quad r_1 = 0.47$$

$$\log M01W = \;\; 4.028 + \;\; 0.905 \log(CND + CS) -$$
$$\quad\quad (40.3) \quad\quad (29.5)$$

$$\quad - \;\; 0.516 \log(PM01W/PD01)$$
$$\quad\quad (18.8)$$

$$\quad - \;\; 0.04 \log(PM01W/PD01)_{-1}$$
$$\quad\quad (1.5)$$

$$\bar{R}^2 = 0.99 \quad DW = 2.21 \quad r_1 = 0.59$$

$$\log M24U = -3.355 + \;\; 0.783 \log VI + \;\; 1.491 \log RHO$$
$$\quad\quad (13.9) \quad\quad (10.2) \quad\quad\quad (2.36)$$

$$\bar{R}^2 = 0.91 \quad DW = 1.93 \quad r_1 = 0.49$$

$\log M24W$ $= - 4.019 + 0.692 \log VI + 2.484 \log RHO -$
$\qquad$ (5.63)$\quad$(3.42)$\qquad\qquad$(3.7)

$\qquad\qquad - 0.983 \log (PM24W/PD24)$
$\qquad\qquad$ (8.46)

$\qquad\qquad \bar{R}^2 = 0.99 \quad DW = 2.00$

$\log M3U$ $= - 8.452 + 1.881 \log VI - 0.974 \log (PM3U/PD3)$
$\qquad$ (7.06)$\quad$(5.37)$\qquad\qquad$(1.03)

$\qquad\qquad \bar{R}^2 = 0.91 \quad DW = 1.48$

$\log M3W$ $= - 3.173 + 0.632 \log VI - 0.71 \log (PM3W/PD3)$
$\qquad$ (6.0)$\quad$(4.2)$\qquad\qquad$(4.45)

$\qquad\qquad \bar{R}^2 = 0.99 \quad DW = 2.05 \quad r_1 = 0.64$

$\log M59NAU$ $= - 1.913 + 0.877 \log VI + 1.7 \log RHO -$
$\qquad$ (7.13)$\quad$(10.6)$\qquad\qquad$(4.14)

$\qquad\qquad - 2.135 \log (PM59NAU/PD59) -$
$\qquad\qquad$ (3.27)

$\qquad\qquad - 1.096 \log (PM59NAU/PD59)_{-1}$
$\qquad\qquad$ (2.03)

$\qquad\qquad \bar{R}^2 = 0.98 \quad DW = 2.13 \quad r_1 = 0.21$

$\log M59NAW$ $= -5.258 + 1.539 \log VI$
$\qquad$ (22.4)$\quad$(22.4)

$\qquad\qquad - 1.059 \log (PM59NAW/PD59)$
$\qquad\qquad$ (4.49)

$\qquad\qquad \bar{R}^2 = 0.98 \quad DW = 1.62 \quad r_1 = 0.22$

$M59APU$ $= - 1.996 + 0.021 VI + 1.938 RHO$
$\qquad$ (7.61)$\quad$(12.56)$\qquad$(7.29)

$\qquad\qquad + 1.945 DACU$
$\qquad\qquad$ (41.4)

$\qquad\qquad \bar{R}^2 = 0.99 \quad DW = 1.87$

$$\log M59APW = -10.278 + 2.466 \log VI$$
$$(8.02) \quad (6.43)$$

$$-11.637 \log (PM59APW/PXAPU)$$
$$(4.52)$$

$$\bar{R}^2 = 0.86 \quad DW = 1.61 \quad r_1 = 0.30$$

1.7. Netherlands

$$DOT(M01) = 5.49 + 0.61 \ DOT(C) + 2.52 \ \Delta(IIP/(GNP\text{-}IIP\text{-}SER))$$
$$(2.17) \qquad\qquad (5.26)$$

$$-0.27 (DOT(M01) - 0.61 DOT(C))_{-1} -$$

$$-0.42 \ (DOT(PM01) - DOT(PC)_{-\frac{1}{2}}) - 2.49 \ DCM$$
$$(2.38) \qquad\qquad\qquad\qquad (1.64)$$

$$\bar{R}^2 = 0.89 \quad DW = 2.30$$

$$DOT(M24) = 1.88 + 1.19 DOT(GNP - IIP - SER) -$$
$$(4.0)$$

$$-4.78 \ (IIP/(GNP - IIP - SER))_{-1} + 1.1 DOT(P) -$$
$$(6.67) \qquad\qquad\qquad\qquad\qquad (2.86)$$

$$-0.17 \ (DOT(M24)_{-1} - DOT(GNP - IIP - SER)_{-1})$$
$$(1.54)$$

$$\bar{R}^2 = 0.92 \quad DW = 2.45$$

$$DOT(M3) = -5.81 + 0.84 \ DOT(GNP - IIP - SER) +$$
$$(2.32)$$

$$+0.31 \ DOT(X3) + 0.19 \ RHO_{-1} +$$
$$(3.45) \qquad\qquad (1.92)$$

$$+0.6 \ DOT(GNP - IIP - SER)_{-1} + 0.14 \ \Delta DOT(PM3)$$
$$(1.33) \qquad\qquad\qquad\qquad (1.25)$$

$$-0.07 (DOT(M3) - 0.84 DOT(GNP - IIP - SER) -$$

$$-0.31 DOT(X3))_{-1}$$

$$\bar{R}^2 = 0.83 \quad DW = 2.81$$

$$\text{DOT}(M59) = 1.664 + \underset{(3.12)}{1.18} \ \text{DOT}(GNP - IIP - SER) - \underset{(3.85)}{7.51} \ \Delta UR +$$

$$+ \underset{(5.88)}{1.18} \ \Delta \text{DOT}(P) - \underset{(1.56)}{0.49} \ (\text{DOT}(PM59) - \text{DOT}(PC)_{-\frac{1}{2}}) -$$

$$- 0.19 \ (\text{DOT}(M59) - 1.18 \ \text{DOT}(GNP - IIP - SER))_{-1}$$

$$\bar{R}^2 = 0.96 \quad DW = 2.37$$

1.8. *Belgium*

$$\log M01 \ = -0.009 + \underset{(19.29)}{1.371} \log GDP - \underset{(2.07)}{1.055} \log (PM01/PD01)$$

$$\bar{R}^2 = 0.98 \quad DW = 2.14$$

$$\log M24 \ = -0.014 + \underset{(8.31)}{1.011} \log VI$$

$$\bar{R}^2 = 0.87 \quad DW = 1.56$$

$$\log M3 \ = -0.046 + 0.95 \log VI3 - 0.653 \log (PM3/PD3)$$

$$\bar{R}^2 = 0.99 \quad DW = 1.78$$

$$\log M59 \ = 0.033 + 1.995 \log C$$

$$\bar{R}^2 = 0.99 \quad DW = 2.39$$

1.9. *Sweden*

$$M01 \quad = 1830.79 + \underset{(18.69)}{0.327} \ CF_{-\frac{1}{4}}$$

$$\bar{R}^2 = 0.99 \quad DW = 1.73$$

$$M24C \ = 345.21 + \underset{(2.3)}{0.012} \ CND_{-\frac{1}{4}}$$

$$\bar{R}^2 = 0.61 \quad DW = 2.69$$

$$M24NC \ = 244.9 + \underset{(9.89)}{2.574} \ VI^+ + \underset{(5.23)}{0.125} \ IIM^+$$

$$\bar{R}^2 = 0.97 \quad DW = 2.60$$

$M3$ $\qquad = 1404.76 + \quad 0.308\,CND_{-\frac{1}{4}}$
$$\qquad\qquad\qquad (16.21)$$

$$\bar{R}^2 = 0.98 \quad DW = 2.07$$

$M59C$ $\qquad = -794.55 + \quad 0.095\,(CND - CF)_{-\frac{1}{4}}$
$$\qquad\qquad\qquad (13.53)$$

$$\bar{R}^2 = 0.98 \quad DW = 1.44$$

$M59CD$ $\qquad = -508.09 + \quad 0.118\,CD$
$$\qquad\qquad\qquad (3.22)$$

$$\bar{R}^2 = 0.95 \quad DW = 2.60$$

$M59IB$ $\qquad = -87.68 + \quad 0.029\,IB$
$$\qquad\qquad\qquad (6.92)$$

$$\bar{R}^2 = 0.92 \quad DW = 1.14$$

$M59II$ $\qquad = -465.4 + \quad 19.755\,PROD + \quad 0.08 \quad IIM^{+}$
$$\qquad\qquad\qquad (25.07) \qquad\qquad\qquad (0.79)$$

$$\bar{R}^2 = 0.99 \quad DW = 2.39$$

$M59ISB$ $\qquad = 2.25 + \quad 0.013\,IB$
$$\qquad\qquad\qquad (4.12)$$

$$\bar{R}^2 = 0.81 \quad DW = 1.23$$

$M59ISO$ $\qquad = 190.15 + \quad 4.492\,VI^{+} + \quad 0.591\,IIME$
$$\qquad\qquad\qquad (10.69) \qquad\qquad (6.9)$$

$$\bar{R}^2 = 0.98 \quad DW = 1.28$$

$M59EM$ $\qquad = -470.35 + \quad 0.33 \quad IFP$
$$\qquad\qquad\qquad (11.19)$$

$$\bar{R}^2 = 0.97 \quad DW = 1.34$$

$M59EB$ $\qquad = -131.24 + \quad 0.028\,IB$
$$\qquad\qquad\qquad (8.28)$$

$$\bar{R}^2 = 0.94 \quad DW = 1.27$$

$M59EO$ $\qquad = 80.39 + \quad 10.931\,VI^{+} + \quad 0.386\,IIME$
$$\qquad\qquad\qquad (13.89) \qquad\qquad (2.64)$$

$$\bar{R}^2 = 0.98 \quad DW = 1.44$$

$M59EC$ $\quad = 109.23 + \underset{(5.88)}{0.191\,CD_{-\frac{1}{4}}} + \underset{(1.7)}{1.017\,IIAU}$

$\qquad\qquad \bar{R}^2 = 0.92 \quad DW = 1.35$

$M59TI$ $\quad = -472.19 + \underset{(9.97)}{11.704\,VTI}$

$\qquad\qquad \bar{R}^2 = 0.96 \quad DW = 1.94$

$M59TO$ $\quad = -69.65 + \underset{(9.22)}{1.332\,VI^+}$

$\qquad\qquad \bar{R}^2 = 0.95 \quad DW = 2.36$

$M59TC$ $\quad = -1887.79 + \underset{(10.1)}{0.205\,(CND - CF)_{-\frac{1}{4}}}$

$\qquad\qquad \bar{R}^2 = 0.96 \quad DW = 0.61$

1.10. *Austria*

$\mathrm{DOT}(M01\cdot PM01) = \underset{(4.54)}{0.129\,(\mathrm{DOT}(C\cdot PC))^2} - \underset{(4.54)}{0.969\,\mathrm{DOT}(AR)_{-\frac{1}{2}}}$

$\qquad\qquad \bar{R}^2 = 0.67 \quad DW = 2.31$

$\mathrm{DOT}(M24\cdot PM24) = \underset{(4.76)}{0.226\,(\mathrm{DOT}(GNP - IIP - SER))^2} +$

$\qquad\quad + \underset{(2.44)}{0.427\,\Delta\mathrm{DOT}\,(IF\cdot PIF)}$

$\qquad\quad + \underset{(2.56)}{4.511\,IIP/(GNP - IIP - SER)_{-1}} +$

$\qquad\quad + \underset{(2.56)}{0.923\,(\mathrm{DOT}(PMG) - \mathrm{DOT}(P)_{-\frac{1}{2}})}$

$\qquad\qquad \bar{R}^2 = 0.89 \quad DW = 2.25$

$\mathrm{DOT}(M59\cdot PM59) = \underset{(25.0)}{0.372\,(\mathrm{DOT}(GNP - IIP - SER))^2} +$

$\qquad\quad + \underset{(3.03)}{1.82\,IIP/(GNP - IIP - SER)_{-1}}$

$\qquad\qquad \bar{R}^2 = 0.94 \quad DW = 1.89$

1.11. *Finland*

$$\log MR = 0.08 + \underset{(18.33)}{0.88} \log PROD + \underset{(4.62)}{0.6} \log (PROD/PROD_{-4}) -$$

$$- \underset{(4.2)}{0.50} \log (PMR/PDR)_{-1}$$

$$\bar{R}^2 = 0.99 \quad DW = 1.62$$

$$\log MK = 0.19 + \underset{(28.17)}{1.69} \log (YW/PC) - \underset{(5.54)}{0.87} \log (PMK/PDK) +$$

$$+ \underset{(3.75)}{0.03} \log RHO - \underset{(3.08)}{0.04} DCR$$

$$\bar{R}^2 = 0.99 \quad DW = 1.85$$

$$\log MA = -0.44 + \underset{(19.37)}{0.93} \log SALA$$

$$\bar{R}^2 = 0.94 \quad DW = 1.30$$

$$\log MI = 0.69 + \underset{(4.77)}{0.62} IB_{-2} + \underset{(4.33)}{2.66} \log (PROD/PROD_{-4})$$

$$\bar{R}^2 = 0.73 \quad DW = 1.40$$

$$\log M3 = -1.97 + \underset{(9.4)}{1.56} \log PROD_{-1} + \underset{(2.42)}{0.39} \log (KI3/KI3_{-1})$$

$$+ \underset{(0.22)}{0.051} \log TIME$$

$$\bar{R}^2 = 0.94 \quad DW = 1.55$$

2. Export demand functions

2.1. *United States of America*

$$XG = -13.184 + \underset{(2.22)}{0.087} \underset{(5.56)}{(WXG - XG)_{-1}} + \underset{(1.07)}{0.142} GFA +$$

$$+ \underset{(2.75)}{13.81} PWX/PXG - \underset{(9.51)}{2.824} DOCK + \underset{(1.59)}{1.026} DSUE +$$

$$+ \quad 0.526 \, \tfrac{1}{4} \sum_{i=1}^{4} XG_{-i}$$
$$(4.6)$$

$$\bar{R}^2 = 0.96 \quad DW = 1.93 \quad r_1 = 0.6025 \quad r_2 = 0.6031$$

2.2. Japan

$$\log XMCU = -4.013 - \underset{(6.09)}{0.002 \, Q1} + \underset{(1.74)}{0.001 \, Q2} + \underset{(1.15)}{0.001 \, Q3} +$$

$$+ \quad \underset{(2.11)}{0.902 \log CDU} - \underset{(1.29)}{0.361 \log (PXMC/PUMC)} +$$

$$+ \quad \underset{(7.15)}{0.732 \log XMCU_{-1}}$$

$$\bar{R}^2 = 0.99 \quad DW = 2.19$$

$$\log XMEU = -15.635 - \underset{(1.62)}{0.001 \, Q1} + \underset{(2.05)}{0.001 \, Q2} + \underset{(0.86)}{0.001 \, Q3} +$$

$$+ \quad \underset{(2.61)}{1.39 \, \log VIU} - \underset{(3.57)}{1.545 \log (PXME/PUIS)} +$$

$$+ \quad \underset{(4.92)}{0.599 \log XMEU_{-1}}$$

$$\bar{R}^2 = 0.98 \quad DW = 1.19$$

$$\log XTEU = -20.374 - \underset{(4.42)}{0.002 \, Q1} + \underset{(0.39)}{0.0002 \, Q2} + \underset{(2.32)}{0.001 \, Q3} +$$

$$+ \quad \underset{(10.98)}{3.18 \, \log CNDU} - \underset{(4.28)}{2.887 \log (PXTE/PUTE)} -$$

$$- \quad \underset{(3.07)}{0.594 \log} \left(\sum_{i=1}^{4} XTEU_{-i} / \sum_{i=1}^{2} SALTEU_{-i} \right)$$

$$\bar{R}^2 = 0.86 \quad DW = 0.99$$

$$\log XOU = -2.266 - \underset{(6.0)}{0.002 \, Q1} + \underset{(2.2)}{0.001 \, Q2} + \underset{(2.2)}{0.001 \, Q3} +$$

$$+ \quad \underset{(2.8)}{0.862 \log CNDU} + \underset{(4.02)}{0.584 \log XOU_{-1}}$$

$$\bar{R}^2 = 0.89 \quad DW = 1.62$$

$$\log XGW = -\ 4.846 +\ 0.001\ Q3 +\ 0.001\ Q4 +$$
$$(3.41)\quad (5.41)\qquad (4.31)$$

$$+\quad 1.71\ \log WXG -\ 1.238 \log (PXGW/PWX)$$
$$(15.13)\qquad\qquad (3.17)$$

$$\bar{R}^2 = 0.98\quad DW = 1.24$$

2.3. West Germany

$$\log XG\quad =\ \log 0.015 +\quad 1.327 \log WXG_{-1} +\ 1.682 \log (PWX58/PX$$
$$(17.81)\qquad\qquad\qquad (1.76)$$

$$+\ 1.753 \log RHO$$
$$(2.24)$$

$$\bar{R}^2 = 0.99\quad DW = 1.55$$

2.4. United Kingdom

$$XG\quad =\ 722.1\quad +\ 0.69\ WXG - 459.2\quad (PXGS/PWX)_{-3} +$$
$$(3.76)\quad (1.09)\qquad\qquad (2.58)$$

$$+\ 0.438\ XG_{-1} + 168.4\ DOCK + 190.7\ DOCK_{-1}$$
$$(3.63)\qquad\quad (5.33)\qquad\qquad (4.77)$$

$$\bar{R}^2 = 0.98\quad DW = 1.70$$

2.5. Italy

$$XG\quad =\ 597.71\ -\ 26.51\ Q1 - 50.26\ Q2 - 47.66\quad Q3 +$$
$$(1.37)\quad (1.63)\qquad (2.67)\qquad (2.97)$$

$$+\ 77.2\ WXG - 44.29\ (PXG/PWX)$$
$$(10.65)\qquad (1.89)$$

$$\bar{R}^2 = 0.99\quad DW = 1.82\quad r_1 = 0.80$$

2.6. Canada

$$\log XFW =\ -1.646 +\ 0.754 \log PRODW -\ 1.395 \log (PXFW/PUF)$$
$$(51.7)\quad (6.83)\qquad\qquad\qquad (1.43)$$

$$\bar{R}^2 = 0.79\quad DW = 1.44$$

$$\log XPU = \begin{array}{cc} 0.215 + & 0.684 \log PRODU - & 0.254 \log(PXPU/PUP) \\ (31.5) & (20.2) & (2.87) \end{array}$$

$$\bar{R}^2 = 0.99 \quad DW = 2.33$$

$$\log XPK = \begin{array}{cc} -2.853 + & 0.983 \log PRODK - & 1.079 \log(PXPK/PKP) \\ (7.68) & (3.04) & (3.0) \end{array}$$

$$\bar{R}^2 = 0.90 \quad DW = 1.66$$

$$XPW = \begin{array}{cc} -0.024 + & 0.052 \, PRODW + & 0.959 \, XPW_{-1} \\ (1.17) & (1.03) & (4.47) \end{array}$$

$$\bar{R}^2 = 0.95 \quad DW = 2.06$$

$$\log XMU = \begin{array}{cc} 0.034 + & 1.182 \log PRODU - & 1.13 \, \log(PXMU/PUM) \\ (0.92) & (8.24) & (1.14) \end{array}$$

$$\bar{R}^2 = 0.94 \quad DW = 1.67 \quad r_1 = 0.43$$

$$\log XMK = \begin{array}{cc} -1.347 + & 1.021 \log PRODK - & 0.294 \log(PXMK/PKM) \\ (5.70) & (6.52) & (1.24) \end{array}$$

$$\bar{R}^2 = 0.78 \quad DW = 1.76$$

$$\log XMW = \begin{array}{cc} -0.857 + & 1.235 \log PRODW - & 0.774 \log(PXMW/PUM) \\ (18.8) & (12.0) & (1.5) \end{array}$$

$$\bar{R}^2 = 0.93 \quad DW = 1.55$$

$$XCU = \begin{array}{cc} -0.086 + & 0.141 \, PRODU + & 0.464 \, XCU_{-1} \\ (4.62) & (4.39) & (2.87) \end{array}$$

$$\bar{R}^2 = 0.98 \quad DW = 2.28$$

$$XCK = \begin{array}{cc} -0.034 + & 0.07 \, PRODK \\ (3.96) & (7.87) \end{array}$$

$$\bar{R}^2 = 0.81 \quad DW = 1.64$$

$$XCW = \begin{array}{cc} 0.032 + & 0.039 \, PRODW + & 2.92 \, XCW_{-1} \\ (3.36) & (2.12) & (1.19) \end{array}$$

$$\bar{R}^2 = 0.83 \quad DW = 1.86$$

$$XIU \quad = -1.01 + \quad 1.399\,PRODU$$
$$\qquad\qquad (11.7) \quad (18.7)$$

$$\bar{R}^2 = 0.96 \quad DW = 1.78$$

$$XIK \quad = - \;\; 0.081 + \;\; 0.196\,PRODK - \;\; 0.15 \;\; (PXIK/PKI)$$
$$\qquad\qquad (1.6) \qquad (8.52) \qquad\qquad (1.58)$$

$$\bar{R}^2 = 0.97 \quad DW = 1.45$$

$$\log XIW \quad = -1.378 + \;\; 0.978 \log PRODW - \;\; 3.814\,(PXIW/PUI)$$
$$\qquad\qquad\; (17.1) \qquad (7.36) \qquad\qquad\qquad (3.14)$$

$$\bar{R}^2 = 0.83 \quad DW = 1.58$$

$$XAPU \quad = - \;\; 0.253 + \;\; 0.274\,PRODU + \;\; 2.855\,DACU$$
$$\qquad\qquad (4.82) \quad (5.52) \qquad\qquad (56.1)$$

$$\bar{R}^2 = 0.99 \quad DW = 2.01$$

2.7. Netherlands

$$\mathrm{DOT}(XG) = 1.12 + \;\; 0.85 \;\; \mathrm{DOT}(WMG^+) - \;\; 2.39\,(\mathrm{DOT}(PXG) -$$
$$\qquad\qquad\qquad (4.17) \qquad\qquad\qquad (2.0)$$

$$\qquad - \mathrm{DOT}(PXCG))_{-\frac{1}{2}}$$

$$\qquad - \;\; 0.98 \;\; (\mathrm{DOT}(UC1) - \mathrm{DOT}(PXG))_{-\frac{3}{4}} +$$
$$\qquad\quad (1.89)$$

$$\qquad + \;\; 3.87 \;\; \Delta UR_{-\frac{1}{2}} + \;\; 0.92 \;\; \Delta(A/C)_{-1} +$$
$$\qquad\quad (0.96) \qquad\qquad (2.17)$$

$$\qquad + \;\; 0.39 \;\; \mathrm{DOT}(LIB)$$
$$\qquad\quad (1.09)$$

$$\bar{R}^2 = 0.90 \quad DW = 2.28$$

2.8. Belgium

$$\log XGS \quad = -0.098 + 1.29 \log TIME - 2.58 \log (PXGS/PWX)$$

$$\qquad\qquad \text{transformed from} \log TIME - 2 \log (PXGS/PWX) =$$

$$\qquad = \;\; 0.076 + \;\; 0.775 \log XGS$$
$$\qquad\quad (0.07) \quad (4.84)$$
$$\qquad \bar{R}^2 = 0.62 \quad DW = 1.26 \quad r_1 = 0.72$$

2.9. *Sweden*

$$XG = 38811 + \underset{(10.8)}{0.134} \, WXG - \underset{(1.92)}{413.6} \, (PXG/PWX)$$

$$\bar{R}^2 = 0.99 \quad DW = 1.18$$

2.10. *Finland*

$$XG = 79.36 + \underset{(9.63)}{2.6} \, PRODO^+ + \underset{(1.60)}{2.21} \, UR -$$

$$- \underset{(2.75)}{0.604} \, PRODU - \underset{(5.56)}{0.89} \, PXG/PXCG$$

$$\bar{R}^2 = 0.99 \quad DW = 1.96$$

3. Export price functions

3.1. *United States of America*

$$(PX - PX_{-4})/PX_{-4} = -0.0124 + 0.2414 \, (ULC_{-1} - ULC_{-5})/ULC_{-5} +$$

$$+ 0.156 \, (RHO - RHO_{-4})/RHO_{-4}$$

$$+ 0.002 \, (\sum_{i=1}^{4} RHO_{-i}/4)$$

$$\bar{R}^2 = 0.36 \quad DW = 1.80$$

3.2. *Japan*

$$PXMC = -0.616 + \underset{(2.1)}{0.66} \, PI + \underset{(10.6)}{0.955} \, PXMC_{-1}$$

$$\bar{R}^2 = 0.78 \quad DW = 2.22$$

$$PXME = -0.06 - \underset{(1.4)}{0.0001} \, Q2 - \underset{(1.6)}{0.0002} \, Q3 - \underset{(1.7)}{0.0002} \, Q4 +$$

$$+ \; 0.201 \, PI - \underset{(2.3)}{0.114} \sum_{i=4}^{5} IFP_{-i} / \sum_{i=6}^{7} IFP_{-i} +$$

$$+ \; 0.99 \, PXME_{-1}$$
$$(14.4)$$

$\bar{R}^2 = 0.91 \quad DW = 1.55$

$$PXTE \; = \; -0.16 + \underset{(5.2)}{0.0005 \, Q2} + \underset{(6.0)}{0.0005 \, Q3} + \underset{(2.1)}{0.357 \, PI} +$$

$$+ \; 0.777 \, PXTE_{-1}$$
$$(7.3)$$

$\bar{R}^2 = 0.86 \quad DW = 1.69$

$$PXOU \; = \; 0.994 - \underset{(2.73)}{0.0003 \, Q2} - \underset{(1.65)}{0.0002 \, Q3} - \underset{(3.46)}{0.0004 \, Q4} +$$

$$+ \; \underset{(1.42)}{0.001 \, YW} - \underset{(2.58)}{0.105} \sum_{i=4}^{5} IFP_{-i} / \sum_{i=6}^{7} IFP_{-i}$$

$\bar{R}^2 = 0.80 \quad DW = 0.72$

$$PXGW \; = \; \underset{(1.11)}{0.144} + \underset{(1.61)}{0.0001 \, Q_2} + \underset{(1.58)}{0.0001 \, Q3} + \underset{(1.42)}{0.169 \, PI} -$$

$$- \; \underset{(1.56)}{0.222 \, IFP} + \underset{(6.32)}{0.715 \, PXGW_{-1}}$$

$\bar{R}^2 = 0.84 \quad DW = 2.08$

3.3. West Germany

$$PXG \; = \; \underset{(2.62)}{0.265} + \underset{(6.71)}{0.308 \, PM58} + \underset{(7.62)}{0.537 \, ULC} + \underset{(3.24)}{0.226 \, RHO_{-1}}$$

$\bar{R}^2 = 0.95 \quad DW = 2.42$

3.4. United Kingdom

$$PXGS \; = \; \underset{(2.79)}{0.243} - \underset{(0.79)}{0.003 \, Q1} - \underset{(1.32)}{0.005 \, Q2} + \underset{(0.09)}{0.0003 \, Q3} +$$

$$+ \; \underset{(2.74)}{0.326 \, PWX} + \underset{(11.27)}{0.436 \, P} + 0.084 \, DDEV$$

$\bar{R}^2 = 0.99 \quad DW = 1.50$

3.5. *Italy*

$$PXG/PWX \quad = \quad 0.121 + 0.008\,PI - 0.002\,RHO - 0.001\,TIME$$
$$ (2.79) \quad (1.71) \qquad (1.27) \qquad\quad (2.78)$$

$$\bar{R}^2 = 0.93 \quad DW = 1.39 \quad r_1 = 0.75$$

3.6. *Canada*

$$PXFU \qquad = \quad 0.603 + \quad 0.223\,WRNA$$
$$ (23.2) \quad\;\; (17.4)$$

$$\bar{R}^2 = 0.96 \quad DW = 1.82$$

$$PXFK \qquad = \quad 0.137 + \;\; 0.375\,PXFU + \;\; 0.492\,PXFK_{-1}$$
$$ (1.3) \quad\;\; (3.31) \qquad\quad (2.75)$$

$$\bar{R}^2 = 0.89 \quad DW = 1.88$$

$$PXFW \qquad = \quad 0.364 + \quad 0.628\,PXFU$$
$$ (7.07) \quad\;\; (12.8)$$

$$\bar{R}^2 = 0.92 \quad DW = 1.63$$

$$PXPU \qquad = \quad 0.493 + \; 0.193\,WRNA + \; 0.378\,RHO +$$
$$ (1.22) \quad (3.89) \qquad\quad\; (3.06)$$
$$ + \; 0.017\,TIME + \; 0.403\,PXPU_{-1}$$
$$ (3.33) \qquad\qquad (1.33)$$

$$\bar{R}^2 = 0.87 \quad DW = 1.95$$

$$PXPK \qquad = \; - \; 0.378 + \; 0.649\,RHO + \; 0.753\,PXPK_{-1}$$
$$ (1.24) \quad\;\; (2.03) \qquad\quad (8.05)$$

$$\bar{R}^2 = 0.85 \quad DW = 1.75$$

$$PXPW \qquad = \; - \; 0.207 + \; 0.408\,RHO + \; 0.248\,PXPU +$$
$$ (1.29) \quad\;\; (3.8) \qquad\quad (2.8)$$
$$ + \; 0.566\,PXPW_{-1}$$
$$ (4.51)$$

$$\bar{R}^2 = 0.82 \quad DW = 2.10$$

$PXMU$

$$= - \ 0.221 + \ 0.099 \, WRNA + \ 0.751 \, RHO +$$
$$ \ (0.89) \quad (1.98) \ (2.68)$$

$$+ \ 0.321 \, PUM$$
$$ \ (1.5)$$

$$\bar{R}^2 = 0.93 \quad DW = 1.46$$

$PXMK$

$$= - \ 1.287 + \ 0.955 \, RHO + \ 0.98 \ PXMU +$$
$$ \ (3.39) \quad (2.37) \ (3.25)$$

$$+ \ 0.392 \, PXMK_{-1}$$
$$ \ (1.9)$$

$$\bar{R}^2 = 0.94 \quad DW = 1.42$$

$PXMW$

$$= - \ 1.919 + \ 2.276 \, RHO + \ 0.628 \, PXMW_{-1} +$$
$$ \ (6.01) \quad (6.76) \ (5.69)$$

$$0.263 \, XMW$$
$$(3.59)$$

$$\bar{R}^2 = 0.94 \quad DW = 2.03$$

$PXCU$

$$= \ 0.196 + \ 0.784 \, PXCU_{-1} + \ 0.205 \, XCU$$
$$ \ (1.37) \quad (5.42) \phantom{PXCU_{-1} +} \ (4.01)$$

$$\bar{R}^2 = 0.87 \quad DW = 2.10$$

$PXCK$

$$= - \ 0.756 + \ 0.272 \, RHO + \ 0.389 \, PXCU +$$
$$ \ (2.41) \quad (1.96) \ (2.46)$$

$$+ \ 1.092 \, PXCK_{-1}$$
$$ \ (8.1)$$

$$\bar{R}^2 = 0.83 \quad DW = 2.04$$

$PXCW$

$$= - \ 0.562 + \ 0.215 \, RHO + \ 0.344 \, PXCU +$$
$$ \ (2.18) \quad (1.61) \ (2.28)$$

$$+ \ 0.999 \, PXCW_{-1}$$
$$ \ (9.11)$$

$$\bar{R}^2 = 0.85 \quad DW = 2.47$$

$$PXIU = -0.066 + 0.523\,PVI + 0.55\,PXIU_{-1}$$
$$\qquad\qquad (1.74) \quad (3.4) \qquad\quad (3.57)$$

$$\bar{R}^2 = 0.98 \quad DW = 1.78$$

$$PXIK = 0.288 + 0.368\,PXIU + 0.306\,PXIK_{-1}$$
$$\qquad\qquad (2.04) \quad (2.37) \qquad\quad (1.45)$$

$$\bar{R}^2 = 0.96 \quad DW = 1.26$$

$$PXIW = 0.505\,PXIU + 0.914\,PXIK_{-1} - 0.011\,TIME$$
$$\qquad\qquad (2.78) \qquad\quad (7.66) \qquad\quad (2.49)$$

$$\bar{R}^2 = 0.95 \quad DW = 1.56$$

3.7. Netherlands

$$\mathrm{DOT}(PXG) = -1.24 + 0.75\,\mathrm{DOT}(UC2) + 0.37\,\mathrm{DOT}(PXCG)_{-\frac{1}{4}} +$$
$$\qquad\qquad\qquad\qquad (11.11) \qquad\qquad (5.26)$$

$$+ 0.06\,\Delta\mathrm{DOT}(WMG^+) - 1.63\,\Delta UR -$$
$$\quad (2.27) \qquad\qquad\qquad (3.23)$$

$$- 0.18\,(A/C)_{-1/12} + 2.06\,DPW$$
$$\quad (3.23) \qquad\qquad (4.55)$$

$$\bar{R}^2 = 0.98 \quad DW = 2.91$$

3.8. Belgium

$$PXG/PXG_{-1} = -0.616 + 0.234\,WR/WR_{-1} + 0.813\,PMG/PMG_{-1} +$$
$$\qquad\qquad\qquad (1.68) \quad (1.15) \qquad\qquad (3.2)$$

$$+ 0.335\,((VI/K)/(VI/K)_{-1})$$
$$\quad (2.26)$$

$$\bar{R}^2 = 0.72 \quad DW = 1.81$$

3.9. Sweden

$$PXG = -37.6 + 1.25\,PWX + 0.145\,(\mathrm{DOT}(YW)/\mathrm{DOT}(PROD))_{-1} +$$
$$\qquad\qquad\qquad (5.0) \qquad\quad (1.93)$$

$$+ 0.024\,VSD$$
$$\quad (2.02)$$

$$\bar{R}^2 = 0.99 \quad DW = 1.24$$

Variable definitions

A	= Volume of domestic harvests
AR	= Index of domestic harvests
C	= Total private consumption expenditure; at constant prices
CD	= Private expenditure on consumers' durable goods; at constant prices
CDU	= Private expenditure on consumers' durable goods in the U.S.; at constant prices
CF	= Consumption expenditures on food; at constant prices
CG	= Government consumption expenditure; at constant prices
CND	= Private expenditure on consumers' non durable goods; at constant prices
CNDU	= Private expenditure on consumers' non durable goods in the U.S.; at constant prices
CS	= Private expenditure on services; at constant prices
DACU	= Dummy variable for the automobile trade agreement between the United States and Canada
DCM	= Dummy variable for the Common Market reduction of intra-trade barriers
DCR	= Dummy variable for credit restriction
DDEV	= Dummy variable for the 1967 pound sterling devaluation
DKW	= Dummy variable for the effect of the Korean War
DOCK	= Dummy variable for dock strikes
DPW	= Dummy variable for the pre-war period
DSUE	= Dummy variable for the effect of the interruption of the Suez Canal
*DT*1	= Dummy variable for the effect of surcharge on imports in the United Kingdom
*DT*2	= Dummy variable for the introduction and removal of surcharge on imports in the United Kingdom
GDP	= Gross domestic product; at constant prices
GFA	= U.S. government foreign aid

GNP	=	Gross national product; at constant prices
K	=	Fixed capital equipment (in the industrial sector)
KINA	=	Stock of inventories in the non-agricultural sector
KI3	=	Inventories of fuels and lubricants
IB	=	Investment in building and construction, excluding roads and maintenance; at constant prices
IF	=	Total fixed investment; at constant prices
IFG	=	Fixed investment in the public sector; at constant prices
IFP	=	Fixed investment in the private sector; at constant prices
IHP	=	Housing investment in the private sector; at constant prices
IIAU	=	Inventory investment in new cars
IIM *	=	Inventory investment in raw materials; at constant prices; weighted by import content
IIME	=	Inventory investment of raw materials in the engineering industry; at constant prices
IINA	=	Non-agricultural inventory investment; at constant prices
IIP	=	Inventory investment in the private sector; at constant prices
LIB	=	Liberalisation and import restrictions in countries importing from the Netherlands
MA	=	Imports of passenger cars; at constant prices
MK	=	Imports of finished consumers' goods; at constant prices
MI	=	Imports of investment goods; at constant prices
MR	=	Imports of raw materials and producers' goods; at constant prices
M01 *M01U* *M01W*	=	Imports of commodities under SITC $0 + 1$, total, from the U.S. and from the rest of the world; at constant prices
M24	=	Imports of commodities under SITC $2 + 4$; at constant prices
M24C	=	Imports of consumers' goods in SITC $2 + 4$; at constant prices

M24NC	=	Imports of non consumers' goods in SITC 2 + 4; at constant prices
M24U *M24W*	=	Imports of commodities under SITC 2 + 4 from the U.S. and from the rest of the world; at constant prices
M3 *M3U* *M3W*	=	Imports of commodities under SITC 3 total, from the U.S. and from the rest of the world; at constant prices
M59	=	Imports of commodities under SITC 5–9; at constant prices
M59 APU *M59 APW*	=	Imports of motor vehicles and parts from the U.S., from the rest of the world; at constant prices
M59C	=	Imports of consumers' goods within SITC 5–9; at constant prices
M59CD	=	Imports of durable consumption goods within SITC 5–9, excluding engineering and textile products; at constant prices ·
M59EB	=	Imports of engineering products for the building sector; at constant prices
M59EC	=	Imports of engineering products for direct consumption; at constant prices
M59EM	=	Imports of engineering products for machine investments; at constant prices
M59EO	=	Imports of other engineering products; at constant prices
M59IB	=	Imports of input materials, within 5–9, for the building sector, excluding iron and steel, and engineering products; at constant prices
M59II	=	Imports of input materials, within SITC 5–9, for the industry, excluding iron and steel, and engineering products; at constant prices
M59ISB	=	Imports of iron and steel products for the building sector; at constant prices
M59ISO	=	Other imports of iron and steel products; at constant prices
M59MC	=	Imports of machinery; at constant prices
M59MM	=	Imports of miscellaneous manufactures; at constant prices

$M59\,NAU$ } = Imports of SITC 5–9, motor vehicles and parts ex-
$M59NAW$ cluded, from the U.S. and from the rest of the
world; at constant prices

$M59SF$ = Imports of semi-finished manufactures; at constant
prices

$M59TC$ = Imports of footwear, textiles, skin and leather for
direct consumption; at constant prices

$M59TI$ = Imports of textiles and leather as inputs for textile
and clothing industry; at constant prices

$M59TO$ = Imports of textiles and leather as inputs to other
industries; at constant prices

P = General (GNP) price index (deflator)

PC = Price deflator for total consumption

PDK = Domestic price index of finished consumers' goods

PDR = Domestic price index of raw materials and producers' goods

$PD01$
$PD24$ = Domestic price index of goods competitive with im-
$PD3$ port categories SITC $0 + 1$, $2 + 4$, 3 and 5–9
$PD59$

PI = Wholesale (industrial) price index

PIF = Deflator for IF

PKI = U.K. retail price index of miscellaneous goods

PKM = U.K. = Whlesale price index of metals and minerals
used in mechanical engineering industry

PKP = U.K. Wholesale price index of metals and minerals
used in the paper industry

PMG = Implicit price deflator (or unit value index) for
total imports of commodities

PMK = Import price index for MK

PMR = Import price index for MR

$PM01$
$PM01U$ = Import price index (unit value index) for $M01$,
$PM01W$ $M01U$ and $M01W$

$PM24$
$PM24U$ = Import price index (unit value index) for $M24$,
$PM24W$ $M24U$ and $M24W$

$PM3$
$PM3U$ } = Import price index (unit value index) for $M3, M3U$
$PM3W$ and $M3W$

$PM59$ = Import price index (unit value index) for $M59$
$(PM58)$ $(M58)$

$PM59APW$ = Import price index (unit value index) for $M59$ APW

$PM59NAU$ } = Import price index (unit value index) for $M59$ NAU
$PM59NAW$ and $M59$ NAW

$PROD$ = Index of industrial production

$PRODK$ = Index of industrial production in the U.K.

$PRODO^*$ = Index of industrial production in the OECD coun-
                 tries, weighted by their shares in exports

$PRODT$ = Trend value of $PROD$

$PRODU$ = Index of industrial production in the U.S.

$PRODW$ = Index of industrial production in the world

PUF = U.S. wholesale price index of farm products

PUI = U.S. wholesale price index of industrial commodi-
                 ties

$PUIS$ = U.S. price index of iron and steel

PUM = U.S. wholesale price index of metals and metal
                 products

$PUMC$ = U.S. price index of all machinery

PUP = U.S. wholesale price index of pulp, paper and allied
                 products

$PUTE$ = U.S. price index of textiles

PVI = Price deflator for VI

PWX = Index of world export unit values

$PWX58$ = Index of world export unit values for SITC $5-8$

$PXAPU$ = Export price index (unit value index) for $XAPU$

$PXCG$ = Price index of competing exports

$PXCK$
$PXCU$ } = Export price index (unit value index) for XCK,
$PXCW$ XCU and XCW

$PXFK$
$PXFU$ } = Export price index (unit value index) for XFK,
$PXFW$ XFU and XFW

PXG = Implicit price deflator (or unit value index) for
                 total exports of commodities

PXGS	= Implicit price deflator (or unit value index) for total exports of commodities and services
PXGW	= Export price index (unit value index) for *XGW*
PXIK *PXIU* *PXIW*	= Export price index (unit value index) for *XIK, XIU* and *XIW*
PXMC	= Export price index (unit value index) for *XMC*
PXME	= Export price index (unit value index) for *XME*
PXMK *PXMU* *PXMW*	= Export price index (unit value index) for *XMK, XMU* and XMW
PXOU	= Export price index (unit value index) for *XOU*
PXPK *PXPU* *PXPW*	= Export price index (unit value index) for *XPK, XPU* and *XPW*
PXTE	= Export price index (unit value index) for *XTE*
Q_i	= Dummy variables for quarters of the year
RHO	= Rate of utilisation of productive capacity
SALA	= Internal sales (registrations) of automobiles
SALTEU	= Sales of textile manufactures in the U.S.
SER	= Net invisible transactions with the foreign sector
TIME	= Increasing sequence for time
UCI	= Domestic unit costs
UC2	= Domestic costs: weighted average of import prices, raw materials and wages less labour productivity
ULC	= Unit labour cost
UR	= Rate of unemployment
VA	= Output (value added) in the agricultural sector; at constant prices
VI	= Output (value added) in the industrial sector; at constant prices
VI^+	= Output (value added) in the relevant industrial sector; at constant prices; weighted by relevant import content
VIU	= VI in the U.S.
VI3	= Value added in oil refining, coke and gas industry; at constant prices

VSD	= Shortage of labour (vacancies) multiplied by special dummy variable
VTI	= Output (value added) in the textile industry
WMG [+]	= World imports of commodities, weighted by Dutch export content
WR	= Wage rate
WRNA	= Wage rate in the non agricultural sector
WXG	= World exports of commodities, seasonally adjusted; at constant prices
XAPU	= Exports of automobiles and parts to the U.S.; at constant prices
XCK *XCU* *XCW*	= Exports of chemicals and fertilizers to the U.K., to the U.S. and to the rest of the world; at constant prices
XFK *XFU* *XFW*	= Exports of farm and fish products to the U.K., to the U.S. and to the rest of the world; at constant prices
XG	= Total exports of commodities; at constant prices
XGW	= Exports of commodities to the rest of the world; at constant prices
XIK *XIU* *XIW*	= Exports of other manufactured goods to the U.K., to the U.S. and to the rest of the world; at constant prices
XMC *XMCU*	= Exports of machinery, total and to the U.S.; at constant prices
XME *XMEU*	= Exports of metals and metal products, total and to the U.S.; at constant prices
XMK *XMU* *XMW*	= Exports of minerals and metals to the U.K., to the U.S. and to the rest of the world; at constant prices
XOU	= Exports of other commodities to the U.S.; at constant prices
XPK *XPU* *XPW*	= Exports of forest products to the U.K., to the U.S. and to the rest of the world; at constant prices
XTE *XTEU*	= Exports of textiles, total and to the U.S.; at constant prices

$X3$	= Exports of commodities under SITC 3; at constant prices
YD	= Disposable income; at constant prices
YW	= Total wage income; at current prices

9. INTERNATIONAL CAPITAL MOVEMENTS: THEORY AND ESTIMATION *

A. AMANO

1. Introduction

Contrasted to the widespread application of econometric techniques in the study of international trade flows, similar studies in international capital movements are not so extensive.[1] Even the theory of international capital movements has not yet been well organised so as to provide a basis for systematic econometric research. Perhaps the most important reason for this is that the estimation of the current account balance is essential for aggregate income determination, whereas capital accounts do not have similar importance in macro-econometric models. Moreover, the usual macro-economic models centre around the concept of flow equilibrium, whereas the equilibrium concept appropriate for the capi-

* The computational work of this study has been done by Messrs. Kazuo Koizumi, Takayuki Matsumoto and Nobuhiko Kosuge of the Institute of Economic Research, Economic Planning Agency. The author wishes to express his deep gratitude for their helpful co-operation.

[1] The post-war developments in the present field were stimulated by the pathbreaking studies of Bell, Kenen and Cohen. See, Bell, P., "Private Capital Movements and the U.S. Balance of Payments Position", in U.S. Congress Joint Economic Committee, *Factors Affecting the U.S. Balance of Payments,* U.S. Government Printing Office 1962; Kenen, P., "Short-term Capital Movements and the U.S. Balance of Payments", and Cohen, B., "A Survey of Capital Movements and Findings Regarding Their Interest Sensitivity", both in U.S. Congress Joint Economic Committee, *Hearings on the United States Balance of Payments, Part 1*, U.S. Government Printing Office, 1963. For the succeeding literature, see the references quoted in Leamer, E.E. and R.M. Stern, *Quantitative International Economics,* Allyn and Bacon, 1970, which gives a neat survey on various problems of the theory and measurement of international capital movements.

tal account relationships is one of stock equilibrium. The recent development of the theory of portfolio selection and its application to aggregative economics must, therefore, be incorporated into empirical studies when one is concerned with international capital movements.

In Project LINK the situation is a little better. Extensive research on this subject is now being conducted by the Canadian group, especially on the capital account equations of the Canadian model, and on the bilateral linkage of the Canadian and United States economies which involves capital account transactions.[2] Some preliminary studies on capital accounts have also been done for the Belgian and Japanese country models. However, in view of the recent rapid growth of international financial markets and the consequent liaison of the national economies through international capital movements, it is of great importance to consolidate the country models with the capital flow equations. This, in turn, will necessitate an amplification of the domestic financial sector of each country model as well. Furthermore, in order to implement a full-scale linkage of national models including international capital transactions, it seems indispensable to construct a separate model to deal with the Euro-dollar market.

The scope of the present paper, however, is rather limited. It simply attempts to put in order some basic problems of formulating and estimating international capital movements. Sect. 2 of this paper is concerned with the question of providing a suitable theoretical framework for the specification of capital account relationships. We then apply the results of sect. 2 to Japanese data in order to show how they can serve our purposes. Sect. 3 presents the implications of our statistical estimation, and sect. 4 summarises the estimated equations.

---

[2] See ch. 12 in this volume and Helliwell, J.F. and T. Maxwell, "Short-term Capital Flows and the Foreign Exchange Market", mimeographed, August 1970.

2. Models of international capital movements and foreign exchange rates

2.1. Short-term capital movements

2.1.1. Interest arbitrage

A standard theory of international short-term capital movements is the so-called "interest parity theory" or the theory of international interest arbitrage. It explains how a certain volume of funds can be allocated among different international financial centres so as to maximise profits without incurring exchange risks. There are, however, a number of alternative formulations of this theory depending on the behavioural assumptions concerning risk and liquidity which, in turn, lead to different functional specifications in estimating short-term capital flows. We shall, therefore, first review a few typical versions of the theory of pure interest arbitrage before taking into account such factors as speculation and trade financing.

Model 1

The simplest version of the interest arbitrage theory may be formulated as follows. Suppose that a representative institution attempts to invest its funds amounting to w (expressed in local currency) for a short period of time, say three months. Let there be only two investment opportunities, purchases of domestic and foreign short-term securities bearing the interest rates i_d and i_f, respectively. The representative institution is assumed to maximise its (concave) utility function

$$u = u(y, w_d, w_f) \tag{1}$$

subject to the constraints

$$y = (1 + i_d)w_d + (1 + i_f)(1 + m)w_f \tag{2}$$

$$w = w_d + w_f \tag{3}$$

where y represents the total volume of funds after the investment period, w_d the amount invested at home, w_f the amount invested abroad and m the forward margin, i.e., the excess of the forward price of foreign exchange over its spot price expressed as a percentage of the spot price.

The utility function contains w_d and w_f besides y, because short-term securities are considered to serve as the secondary reserve in the respective financial centre.[3] If we assume that i_d, i_f, m and w are given, the first-order condition for a maximum is given by

$$i_d + l_d = i_f + (1 + i_f)m + l_f \tag{4}$$

where

$$l_d = (\partial u / \partial w_d)/(\partial u / \partial y), \; l_f = (\partial u / \partial w_f)/(\partial u / \partial y) \tag{5}$$

represent the marginal convenience yield at home and abroad, respectively. Solving eqs. (2)–(4), among other things for w_f, we obtain

$$w_f = w_f(i_d, \; i_f + (1 + i_f)m, \; w) . \tag{6}$$

It can be shown that the function w_f has the following properties:

$$\frac{\partial w_f}{\partial i_d} = -\frac{1}{\Delta_1} [1 + (\frac{\partial l_d}{\partial y} - \frac{\partial l_f}{\partial y}) w_d]$$

$$\frac{\partial w_f}{\partial (i_f + (1 + i_f)m)} = \frac{1}{\Delta_1} [1 - (\frac{\partial l_d}{\partial y} - \frac{\partial l_f}{\partial y}) w_f] \tag{7}$$

$$\frac{\partial w_f}{\partial w} = -\frac{1}{\Delta_1} [(\frac{\partial l_d}{\partial w_d} - \frac{\partial l_f}{\partial w_d}) + (1 + i_d)(\frac{\partial l_d}{\partial y} - \frac{\partial l_f}{\partial y})]$$

---

[3] See Tsiang, S.C., "The Theory of Forward Exchange and the Effects of Government Intervention on the Forward Exchange Market", *IMF Staff Papers*, April 1959.

where

$$\Delta_1 = -(\frac{\partial l_d}{\partial w_d} - \frac{\partial l_f}{\partial w_d}) + (\frac{\partial l_d}{\partial w_f} - \frac{\partial l_f}{\partial w_f}) - (l_d - l_f)(\frac{\partial l_d}{\partial y} - \frac{\partial l_f}{\partial y}) > 0 \qquad (8)$$

by the second-order condition for a maximum.

If we further assume, as a first approximation, that $\partial l_d / \partial y \doteqdot \partial l_f / \partial y$, that is, the response of the marginal convenience yield with respect to the total volume of funds is approximately equal in each financial centre, then eq. (6) may be simplified to

$$w_f = \tilde{w}_f (i_d - i_f - (1 + i_f)m, \, w) \qquad (9)$$

where

$$\partial \tilde{w}_f / \partial (i_d - i_f - (1 + i_f)m) < 0, \, \partial \tilde{w}_f / \partial w > 0. \qquad (10)$$

In other words, the equilibrium amount of funds invested abroad is a decreasing function of the covered interest differential (domestic minus foreign) and an increasing function of total investible funds.

Model 2

The second formulation of the interest arbitrage theory is based upon a simplified theory of portfolio selection.[4] Even though we may be allowed to assume that risks involved in short-term securities are negligibly small in local markets, investment in foreign short-term securities is subject to another type of risk. Exchange controls may be imposed by the foreign authorities to prevent the remittance of invested funds; the foreign securities will have to be sold before maturity either to finance domestic activities or to switch funds to other investment opportunities, which will incur exchange risks not covered by the original swap transaction, and so on. Then, the foreign rate of return, $i_f + (1 + i_f)m$ in eq. (2), must be regarded as a stochastic variable. We shall therefore

---

[4] See, for example, Grubel, H.G., *Forward Exchange, Speculation and the International Flow of Capital*, Stanford University Press, 1966.

re-write (2) as

$$y = (1 + i_d)w_d + \{(1 + i_f)(1 + m) + \epsilon\} w_f \tag{11}$$

where it is assumed that ϵ is normally distributed with mean zero and variance σ^2.

Let μ_y and σ_y^2 be the mean and variance of y, respectively:

$$\mu_y = (1 + i_d)w_d + (1 + i_f)(1 + m)w_f \tag{12}$$

$$\sigma_y^2 = \sigma^2 w_f^2 . \tag{13}$$

Assuming away the convenience yield for simplicity, we write the utility function (1) as

$$u = u(y); \quad u' > 0, u'' < 0 . \tag{14}$$

Hence, the expected utility is given by

$$E[u(y)] = \int_{-\infty}^{\infty} u(y)f(y; \mu_y, \sigma_y) \, dy \tag{15}$$

where f is the probability density function of y. Define

$$z = \epsilon/\sigma; \quad E(z) = 0, E(z^2) = 1. \tag{16}$$

Then, from eqs. (11)–(13) we have

$$y = \mu_y + \sigma_y z . \tag{17}$$

Substituting (17) into (15), we may write the expected utility function as

$$v(\mu_y, \sigma_y) = \int_{-\infty}^{\infty} u(\mu_y + \sigma_y z)f(z; 0, 1) \, dz \tag{18}$$

where

$$v_\mu = \partial v/\partial \mu_y = \int_{-\infty}^{\infty} u'(\mu_y + \sigma_y z) f(z) \, dz > 0 \tag{19a}$$

$$v_\sigma = \partial v/\partial\sigma_y = \int_{-\infty}^{\infty} u'(\mu_y + \sigma_y z)\, zf(z)\, \mathrm{d}z < 0. \qquad (19\mathrm{b})$$

Maximising (18) subject to eqs. (3), (12) and (13) we have

$$i_d = i_f + (1 + i_f)\, m + \sigma v_\sigma / v_\mu. \qquad (20)$$

The last term on the right-hand side of this expression represents (a negative of) the marginal risk premium, which we shall denote by

$$\rho(\mu_y, \sigma_y, \sigma) = -\sigma v_\sigma / \bar{v}_\mu. \qquad (21)$$

Thus, in equilibrium the foreign rate of return must be sufficiently higher than the domestic rate of return to cover this risk premium. In the normal circumstances, however, this factor will be rather small and remain fairly stable.[5]

Solving eqs. (3), (12), (13) and (20) for w_f as before, we obtain

$$w_f = w_f(i_d,\ i_f + (1 + i_f)m,\ \sigma,\ w) \qquad (22)$$

where

$$\frac{\partial w_f}{\partial i_d} = -\frac{1}{\Delta_2}\left(1 + \frac{\partial\rho}{\partial\mu_y}\, w_d\right)$$

$$\frac{\partial w_f}{\partial(i_f + (1 + i_f)\, m)} = \frac{1}{\Delta_2}\left(1 - \frac{\partial\rho}{\partial\mu_y}\, w_f\right)$$

$$\frac{\partial w_f}{\partial\sigma} = -\frac{1}{\Delta_2}\left(\frac{\rho}{\sigma} + \frac{\partial\rho}{\partial\sigma_y}\, w_f\right)$$

$$\frac{\partial w_f}{\partial w} = -\frac{1}{\Delta_2}(1 + i_d)\, \frac{\partial\rho}{\partial\mu_y}$$

(23)

[5] See Branson, W.H., "The Minimum Covered Interest Differential Needed for International Arbitrage Activity", *Journal of Political Economy*, November 1969.

and

$$\Delta_2 = \rho \frac{\partial \rho}{\partial \mu_y} + \sigma \frac{\partial \rho}{\partial \sigma_y} > 0 \tag{24}$$

by the second-order condition for a maximum. Now the signs of these expressions depend on those of $\partial \rho / \partial \mu_y$ and $\partial \rho / \partial \sigma_y$. Normally, the expected marginal utility of money (v_μ) will not decline sharply as μ_y rises, while the expected marginal disutility of risk ($-v_\sigma$) will increase rather rapidly as σ_y increases. Therefore, we may expect that $\partial \rho / \partial \mu_y < 0$ and $\partial \rho / \partial \sigma_y > 0$, and hence

$$\partial w_f / \partial \left(i_f + (1 + i_f)m \right) > 0$$

$$\partial w_f / \partial \sigma < 0 \tag{25}$$

$$\partial w_f / \partial w > 0 .$$

Moreover, it should be noted that

$$\frac{\partial w_f}{\partial \left(i_f + (1 + i_f) m \right)} + \frac{\partial w_f}{\partial i_d} = - \frac{1}{\Delta_2} \frac{\partial \rho}{\partial \mu_y} w \tag{26}$$

which will normally be positive. That is, the effects of changes in foreign and domestic rates of return are not symmetric. This is so, because it is only the substitution term which is symmetric ($1/\Delta_2$ in eq. (23)), while the expression (23) contains income terms as well ($-(1/\Delta_2) (\partial \rho / \partial \mu_y) w_d$ and $-(1/\Delta_2) (\partial \rho / \partial \mu_y) w_f$). Here the substitution term represents the effect of a change in the rate of return upon the "demand" for foreign investment when the utility level is held constant, whereas the income effect represents the effect of utility re-compensation as in the theory of consumer's demand. [6] Therefore, if we assume that the substitution effect

---

[6] Replace (3) by

(i) $v(\mu_y, \sigma_y) = \bar{v}$

and solve (i), (12), (13) and (20) for w_f to obtain

(ii) $w_f = \tilde{w}_f(i_d, i_f + (1 + i_f)m, \sigma, \bar{v})$.

dominates the income effect in the first expression of (23), then we will also have

$$\partial w_f/\partial i_d < 0 . \tag{27}$$

So far we have ignored the risks involved in the purchase of securities in the local market. However, it is not difficult to extend the above model to cover this type of risk. We shall not enter into the details, but only mention that we will then obtain

$$w_f = w_f(i_d, i_f + (1+i_f)m, \sigma_d, \sigma_f, w) \tag{28}$$

where σ_d^2 and σ_f^2 are the variances of short-term rates of return at home and abroad, respectively. As before, we may normally expect that

$$\partial w_f/\partial i_d < 0, \ \partial w_f/\partial (i_f + (1+i_f)m) > 0$$
$$\partial w_f/\partial \sigma_d > 0, \ \partial w_f/\partial \sigma_f < 0, \ \partial w_f/\partial w > 0 . \tag{29}$$

Model 3
The final version of the international interest arbitrage theory which we wish to review here extends the foregoing model by introducing an additional complication, i.e., the existence of a domestic riskless asset bearing no interest, say cash. [7]

Let y_0 be the amount of total investible funds initially held, c the amount to be held in cash and w the amount to be invested in

Then we have, for example,

(iii) $\partial \tilde{w}_f/\partial i_d = -1/\Delta_2, \ \partial \tilde{w}_f/\partial \bar{v} = -(1/\Delta_2)(1/v_\mu)(\partial \rho/\partial \mu_y) .$

Hence

(iv) $\dfrac{\partial w_f}{\partial i_d} = \dfrac{\partial \tilde{w}_f}{\partial i_d}\bigg|_{\bar{v}} + \dfrac{\partial \tilde{w}_f}{\partial \bar{v}} \dfrac{\partial v}{\partial \mu_y} \dfrac{\partial \mu_y}{\partial i_d} = \dfrac{1}{\Delta_2} - \dfrac{1}{\Delta_2} \dfrac{\partial \rho}{\partial \mu_y} w_d .$

And similarly for $\partial w_f/\partial (i_f + (1+i_f)m)$.

[7] The model to be developed below is essentially the same as that of Miller and Whitman, who applied their model to the estimation of long-term capital flows. See Miller, N.C. and M.v.N. Whitman, "A Mean-Variance Analysis of United States Long-term Portfolio Foreign Investment", *Quarterly Journal of Economics*, May 1970.

risky assets. Then,

$$y_0 = c + w \tag{30}$$

$$w = w_d + w_f . \tag{31}$$

After the investment period, the total amount of funds will become

$$y = c + (1 + i_d + \epsilon_d) w_d + \{(1 + i_f)(1 + m) + \epsilon_f\} w_f \tag{32}$$

where ϵ_d and ϵ_f are normally distributed random variables with mean zero, variance σ_d^2 and σ_f^2, respectively, and covariance $r\sigma_d\sigma_f$.

Now define

$$x_d = w_d/w, \ x_f = w_f/w \tag{33}$$

$$x = \epsilon_d x_d + \epsilon_f x_f, \ (E(x) = 0) \tag{34}$$

$$\sigma_x^2 = E(x^2) = \sigma_d^2 x_d^2 + \sigma_f^2 x_f^2 + 2r\sigma_d\sigma_f x_d x_f \tag{35}$$

$$i = i_d x_d + \{i_f + (1 + i_f)m\} x_f \tag{36}$$

$$\mu_y = E(y) = c + (1 + i)w \tag{37}$$

$$\sigma_y^2 = E[(y - \mu_y)^2] = \sigma_x^2 w^2 . \tag{38}$$

A representative institution is assumed to maximise expected utility

$$E[u(y)] = \int_{-\infty}^{\infty} u(y)f(y; \mu_y, \sigma_y) \, \mathrm{d}y . \tag{39}$$

Since

$$y = \mu_y + xw , \tag{40}$$

by defining $z = x/\sigma_x$ we may again write the expected utility function as eq. (18). The present problem can, therefore, be summarised as follows:

Maximise

$$E[u(y)] = v(\mu_y, \sigma_y) \tag{41}$$

subject to the constraints

$$c + w = y_0$$

$$\mu_y = c + (1+i)w$$

$$\sigma_y = \sigma_x w$$

$$x_d + x_f = 1 \tag{42}$$

$$\sigma_x^2 = \sigma_d^2 x_d^2 + \sigma_f^2 x_f^2 + 2r\sigma_d\sigma_f x_d x_f$$

$$i = i_d x_d + \{i_f + (1+i_f)m\}x_f.$$

The first-order conditions are then shown to be

$$i = -\sigma_x v_\sigma / v_\mu \tag{43}$$

and

$$i_d - \{i_f + (1+i_f)m\} = -\frac{\sigma_x v_\sigma}{v_\mu} \frac{\sigma_d^2 x_d^2 + r\sigma_d\sigma_f x_f - \sigma_f^2 x_f - r\sigma_d\sigma_f x_d}{\sigma_x^2}. \tag{44}$$

The first condition, (43), implies that in equilibrium the marginal rate of return on the risky portfolio, i, is equated to the overall marginal risk premium, $-\sigma_x v_\sigma / v_\mu$, while the second condition, (44), requires that the difference between the rate of return and the marginal risk premium of the respective risky asset be equal.

Noting that $x_d + x_f = 1$, we may solve eqs. (43) and (44) for x_f to obtain

$$x_f = \frac{(1+R)\sigma_d^2 - r\sigma_d\sigma_f}{\{(1+R)\sigma_d^2 - r\sigma_d\sigma_f\} + \{\sigma_f^2 - (1+R)r\sigma_d\sigma_f\}} \tag{45}$$

where $R = \{i_f + (1+i_f)m - i_d\}/i_d$. Since $1+R > 0$, it follows that $0 < x_f < 1$ when $r \leqslant 0$. If $r > 0$, however, it is necessary for x_f to lie between zero and unity such that

$$(1+R)/r > \sigma_f/\sigma_d > (1+R)r. \qquad (46)$$

This condition will normally be satisfied unless r is close to unity, because as we have explained earlier σ_f is considered to be larger than σ_d. We shall henceforth assume that inequalities (46) hold. Then, eq. (45) may be re-written as

$$w_f = w_f(R, \sigma_d, \sigma_f, w) \qquad (47)$$

where

$$\frac{\partial w_f}{\partial R} = \frac{w}{\Delta_3}(1 - r^2) > 0$$

$$\frac{\partial w_f}{\partial \sigma_d} = \frac{w}{\Delta_3}[(\frac{1+R}{r}\sigma_d - \sigma_f)r\sigma_f^2 + \{\sigma_f - (1+R)r\sigma_d\}(1+R)\sigma_d\sigma_f] > 0$$

$$\frac{\partial w_f}{\partial \sigma_f} = -\frac{w}{\Delta_3}[(\frac{1+R}{r}\sigma_d - \sigma_f)(\sigma_f - r\sigma_d)r\sigma_d \qquad (48)$$

$$+ \{\sigma_f - (1+R)r\sigma_d\}(1+R)\sigma_d^2] < 0$$

$$\frac{\partial w_f}{\partial w} = x_f > 0$$

$$\Delta_3 = [\{(1+R)\sigma_d^2 - r\sigma_d\sigma_f\} + \{\sigma_f^2 - (1+R)r\sigma_d\sigma_f\}]^2 > 0.$$

Although the above expression is not a final solution in the sense that every endogenous variable is expressed in terms of exogenous variables alone, it is useful in the actual estimation procedure. Ordinarily, the domestic and foreign rates of return are highly correlated so that it is difficult to estimate their separate effects on capital flows. The covered or uncovered interest differential is, therefore, often used to avoid the problem of multicollinearity. This procedure, however, does not conform to our previous conclusion that the effects of domestic and foreign rates of return are likely to be asymmetric (see eq. (26)). The above specification can avoid both of these difficulties.

2.1.2. Speculation and trade financing

So far we have only been concerned with pure interest arbitrage unrelated to speculative activity. Speculation in the foreign exchange market does not directly lead to international capital movements in so far as it is concentrated in the forward exchange market. It affects the short-term capital flows only indirectly through its effects on the forward margin. However, speculators may sometimes speculate on the spot market. It has been shown by many writers that speculation in the spot exchanges, say a spot sale of foreign exchange, is more profitable than the corresponding forward sale when the arbitrage margin is favourable to the speculator's home country. [8] Such an uncovered spot sale is essentially a combination of a speculative forward sale and an inward arbitrage activity which involves a spot sale and a simultaneous forward purchase. Thus, if a speculator's expectation concerning the future spot rate is revised downward with current interest rates and the forward margin remaining unchanged, the speculator's spot sale of foreign exchange will be increased. The behaviour of such a speculator-arbitrager may be formulated by slightly modifying Model 2.

Model 4

Consider an investor who does not cover his foreign investment by a simultaneous forward transaction. Denoting the ratio of the mean value of the expected future spot rate to its current value by e, we re-write (11) as

$$y = (1+i_d)w_d + (1+i_f)(e+\epsilon_r)w_f \qquad (49)$$

where ϵ_r is a normally distributed random variable with mean zero and variance σ_r^2. (For simplicity of exposition we disregard the risk element other than the uncertainty concerning the future spot rate.) Hence (12) and (13) must be replaced by

$$\mu_y = (1+i_d)w_d + (1+i_f)ew_f \qquad (50)$$

[8] See, for example, Spraos, J., "Speculation, Arbitrage and Sterling", *Economic Journal,* March 1959, and Tsiang, *op. cit.*

$$\sigma_y = (1 + i_f) \sigma_r w_f .$$ (51)

Other parts of the model remain unchanged.

The utility maximisation condition (20) should now read

$$\frac{1 + i_d}{1 + i_f} - e + \rho = 0$$ (52)

where

$$\rho(\mu_y, \sigma_y, \sigma_r) = - \sigma_r v_\sigma / v_\mu$$ (53)

and the amount of funds to be invested abroad is determined by

$$w_f = w_f(i_d, i_f, e, \sigma_r, w) ,$$ (54)

the w_f function having the following properties:

$$\frac{\partial w_f}{\partial i_d} = - \frac{1}{\Delta_4} \left[\frac{1}{1 + i_f} + \frac{\partial \rho}{\partial \mu_y} w_d \right]$$

$$\frac{\partial w_f}{\partial i_f} = \frac{1}{\Delta_4} \left[\frac{1 + i_d}{(1 + i_f)^2} - \frac{\partial \rho}{\partial \mu_y} e w_f - \frac{\partial \rho}{\partial \sigma_y} \sigma_r w_f \right]$$

$$\frac{\partial w_f}{\partial e} = \frac{1}{\Delta_4} \left[1 - \frac{\partial \rho}{\partial \mu_y} (1 + i_f) w_f \right]$$ (55)

$$\frac{\partial w_f}{\partial \sigma_r} = - \frac{1}{\Delta_4} \left[\frac{\partial \rho}{\partial \sigma_r} + \frac{\partial \rho}{\partial \sigma_y} (1 + i_f) w_f \right]$$

$$\frac{\partial w_f}{\partial w} = - \frac{1}{\Delta_4} (1 + i_d) \frac{\partial \rho}{\partial \mu_y}$$

where

$$\Delta_4 = (1 + i_f) \left(\rho \frac{\partial \rho}{\partial \mu_y} + \sigma_r \frac{\partial \rho}{\partial \sigma_y} \right) > 0$$ (56)

by the second-order condition for a maximum. As in Model 2, we may normally expect that

$$\partial w_f / \partial i_d < 0, \quad \partial w_f / \partial i_f > 0, \quad \partial w_f / \partial e > 0$$

$$\partial w_f / \partial \sigma_r < 0, \quad \partial w_f / \partial w > 0. \qquad (57)$$

Finally, the international capital movements associated with the financing of international trade can easily be incorporated into the previous framework. For instance, if a home country exporter, who expects to be paid in foreign currency in three months' time, always covers the exchange risk, he is acting as a pure interest arbitrager. Or, if he does not cover the exchange risk, he is acting as an arbitrager-speculator. Similar arguments apply to a home country importer who must pay in foreign currency in three months' time.

2.1.3. The speed of adjustment

The w_f functions thus far derived explain the equilibrium or desired stock of funds to be invested in the foreign country. Or, alternatively, if we consider a borrower who attempts to maximise his (expected) utility function involving the total cost of borrowing, then these functions determine the equilibrium outstanding debt in foreign currency. The rate of international capital flow per unit of time is, therefore, given by the first difference of $w_f(t)$, where t denotes time. Take eq. (47) for example. In a linear form, we may write

$$\Delta w_f(t) = a_0 + a_1 \Delta R(t) + a_2 \Delta \sigma_d(t) + a_3 \Delta \sigma_f(t) + a_4 \Delta w(t) \qquad (58a)$$

or

$$w_f(t) = a_0 + a_1 \Delta R(t) + a_2 \Delta \sigma_d(t) + a_3 \Delta \sigma_f(t) + a_4 \Delta w(t) +$$

$$+ w_f(t-1) \qquad (58b)$$

where the a_i's denote the partial derivatives of the w_f function and $\Delta x(t) = x(t) - x(t-1)$.

The above specification, however, can be used in the actual estimation only when it is clear that the speed of adjustment is sufficiently large relative to the unit period of observation. When there exists some time lag before the desired portfolio is attained, the w_f functions cannot be directly estimated. Assuming then a partial adjustment process with an adjustment coefficient λ $(0 < \lambda < 1)$, we have

$$\Delta w_f(t) = \lambda \left[a_0 + a_1 R(t) + a_2 \sigma_d(t) + a_3 \sigma_f(t) + a_4 w(t) - \right.$$
$$\left. - w_f(t-1) \right] \tag{59a}$$

or

$$w_f(t) = b_0 + b_1 R(t) + b_2 \sigma_d(t) + b_3 \sigma_f(t) + b_4 w(t) +$$
$$+ (1 - \lambda) w_f(t-1) \tag{59b}$$

where $b_i = \lambda a_i$.

2.2. Long-term capital movements

International long-term capital accounts of any country have far more diverse elements than the short-term capital accounts. Direct investment, investment in long-term bonds and stocks (both outstanding and newly issued) and long-term bank loans associated or unassociated with foreign trade are among others, each of which are governed by different economic factors. The portfolio selection approach we have reviewed in the previous section will find a useful application to some of the long-term investments, although an appropriate choice of explanatory variables will be less obvious. The rate of return variable should reflect not only the current yield but also the expected rate of capital appreciation or depreciation; uncertainty will play a much larger role, so that the risk variable must be carefully selected; capital markets may be more imperfect; and so on.

Explanatory variables often selected, other than the long-term interest rate, are the rate of change, or the rate of growth, of activity variables such as national income, the index of production, private fixed investment, corporate profits, exports and imports to approximate long-run profitability, and the deviation from trend of these variables to represent the risk factor of an aggregate portfolio (an upward deviation implying a decrease in risk). An important institutional change that might have affected most country's international capital position was the U.S. foreign investment restraint programme. Since there has been a number of revisions of this programme, and their impact may not be uniform through time, some special consideration must be given to separate their effects.

As regards direct investment, however, the situation is less hopeful. Theoretical studies concerning the determinants of direct investment have just begun to emerge, but there still remains a gap between them and their application to macro-econometric models. For the meantime, we must content ourselves with some ad hoc specifications.

2.3. Foreign exchange rates

An econometric study of foreign exchange markets is almost indispensable when one is concerned with a system involving the capital accounts sector of the balance of payments, because the spot and forward exchange rates are almost certain to appear as endogenous variables (especially in the short-term capital accounts).

Our model of foreign exchange markets to be presented here is based on the theory of forward exchange which indicates the simultaneous determination of spot and forward exchange rates.

Let us first consider the forward exchange market. The standard argument in the theory of forward exchange suggests that every transaction in forward exchange can be functionally classified into three categories: interest arbitrage, commercial covering and speculation. [9] Let $E_a(t)$, $E_c(t)$ and $E_s(t)$ be the excess demand for forward exchange arising from the above three activities, respectively, at time t, and $V(t)$ be the excess supply of forward exchange by the monetary authorities at time t. Then, the equilibrium condition in the forward market is given by

$$E_a(t) + E_c(t) + E_s(t) = V(t) .$$ (60)

---

[9] Spraos and Tsiang, *op. cit.*

Now, the three excess demand functions may be written as

$$E_a(t) = E_a[\Delta m(t), \Delta i_d(t) - \Delta i_f(t), \Delta w(t)]$$

$$E_c(t) = E_c[r_f(t), \alpha(t)] \tag{61}$$

$$E_s(t) = E_s[r_s^e(t), r_f(t), \sigma_r(t)]$$

where m is the forward margin, i_d is the domestic short-term interest rate, i_f is the foreign short-term interest rate, w is the availability of arbitrage funds, r_f is the forward exchange rate, r_s^e is the mean value of the expected future spot exchange rate, α represents factors affecting the basic balance of payments deficit that manifest themselves in the forward exchange market and σ_r is the standard deviation of the expected future spot rate.

From the definition of $m(t)$, we have

$$\Delta m(t) = \frac{r_f(t)}{r_s(t)} - \frac{r_f(t-1)}{r_s(t-1)} \tag{62}$$

where r_s is the spot exchange rate. No detailed arguments will be needed to show that the above excess demand functions have the following properties:

$$\partial E_a/\partial(\Delta m(t)) < 0, \quad \partial E_a/\partial(\Delta i_d(t)) > 0, \quad \partial E_a/\partial\Delta w \gtrless 0$$

$$\partial E_c/\partial r_f(t) \leqslant 0, \quad \partial E_c/\partial\alpha(t) > 0 \tag{63a}$$

$$\partial E_s/\partial r_s^e(t) > 0, \quad \partial E_s/\partial r_f(t) < 0$$

and

$$\partial E_s/\partial\sigma_r(t) \gtrless 0 \quad \text{as} \quad r_s^e(t) \lessgtr r_f(t). \tag{63b}$$

The sign of $\partial E_a/\partial\Delta w$ is uncertain, because a change in w affects both demand and supply in the same direction. And under the fixed exchange rate system, E_c may be considered as independent of the forward rate.

Substituting (61) and (62) into (60), linearising the resulting equation, and solving it for $r_f(t)$, we then have

$$r_f(t) = a_0 + a_1 [\Delta i_d(t) - \Delta i_f(t)] + a_2 \Delta w(t) + a_3 \alpha(t) \div$$
$$+ a_4 r_s e(t) + a_5 \sigma_r(t) + a_6 r_f(t-1) + a_7 r_s(t) + a_8 r_s(t-1) + a_9 V(t)$$

$$a_1, a_3, a_4, a_6, a_7 > 0; \quad a_8, a_9 < 0; \quad a_2, a_5 \gtreqless 0 \qquad (64)$$

which gives an equation for the forward rate.

Turning to the spot market, let us define $E_b(t)$ as the excess demand for spot exchange arising from the basic balance of payments deficit that appears in the spot market. It is assumed that $E_b(t)$ is determined by

$$E_b(t) = E_b[r_s(t), \beta(t)]; \quad \partial E_b / \partial r_s(t) \leqslant 0, \quad \partial E_b / \partial \beta(t) > 0 \qquad (65)$$

where $\beta(t)$ represents the factors affecting the basic balance of payments deficit that always require immediate payment. Also define $G(t)$ as the net supply of spot exchange by the monetary authorities, and T as the maturity period of forward contracts. Since the forward contracts made at T periods ahead appear in the current spot market, the equilibrium condition of the spot market is given by

$$E_b(t) + E_a(t-T) + E_c(t-T) + E_s(t-T) = E_a(t) + G(t) +$$
$$+ E_s(t-T) + V(t-T). \qquad (66)$$

In view of (60), the above equation can be simplified to

$$E_b(t) - E_a(t) - E_s(t-T) = G(t). \qquad (67)$$

Substituting (61), (62) and (65) into (67) and solving the linearised equation for $r_s(t)$, we obtain

$$r_s(t) = b_0 + b_1 [\Delta i_d(t) - \Delta i_f(t)] + b_2 \Delta w(t) + b_3 \beta(t) +$$
$$+ b_4 r_s^e(t-T) + b_5 \sigma_r(t-T) + b_6 r_s(t-1) + b_7 r_f(t) +$$
$$+ b_8 r_f(t-1) + b_9 G(t) \qquad (68)$$

$$b_3, b_6, b_7 > 0; \quad b_1, b_4, b_8, b_9 < 0; \quad b_2, b_5 \gtreqless 0$$

which gives an equation for the spot rate.

3. General comments on the estimated equations

Based on our foregoing discussion we have estimated structural equations for the Japanese international capital accounts as well as the reduced form equations for the yen-U.S. dollar exchange rate. The statistical results obtained by the method of ordinary least squares are summarised in the following section. Needless to say, these equations are of a tentative nature and must be re-estimated by some method of structural estimation when the entire model is constructed. Because of space limitation, we shall only comment on the general characteristics of our statistical results.

3.1. Short-term capital accounts

In the official publication of the Japanese balance of payments statistics, short-term capital transactions are entered in two places: one above the line, and the other below the line. The latter involves the short-term capital transactions by the authorised private foreign exchange banks, while the former contains those by the private non-banking sector. Separate data on net changes in assets and liabilities are given for the banking sector, but only net balance figures are available for the non-banking sector. We have, therefore, estimated four equations: three for the above categories and one for the total private sector.

In general each equation is estimated according to two different types of specification as given by eqs. (58) and (59). In the latter specification, two alternative interest rate variables are tried: one is the ordinary interest differential and the other the interest differential divided by the domestic interest rate (see Model 3).

All the estimated equations give fairly satisfactory results. Both the difference type and the stock adjustment type of specification exhibit almost comparable performance, although the former does slightly better (in terms of the standard error of estimate) in the banking-sector asset equations whereas the latter is preferred in the other equations. In the stock adjustment type of specification, however, the normalised interest differential appears to give uniformly better results than the simple differential (see eqs. (4.2), (4.3), (4.7), (4.8), (4.9) and (4.10)).

Our statistical results suggest that the size of our foreign trade and the international interest differential are the two major determinants of Japanese short-term capital transactions. Trade variables are highly significant in every equation, and similarly for the interest differential variables except for one equation, the banking-sector asset equation. The last exception is not surprising, however, since in order to stimulate our exports the Bank of Japan has supplied credit to the foreign exchange banks against the purchase of export usance bills at a relatively low interest rate (4–5% p.a.) until quite recently. Thus, a large part of our exports have been financed by the domestic banks (or indirectly by the Bank of Japan) irrespective of the level of foreign interest rates. [10]

Another important factor is the policy adopted by the monetary authorities to regulate short-term capital flows. In view of the rapid increase in the official foreign exchange reserves since the middle of 1968, the Bank of Japan has relaxed its control over the foreign exchange banks' exchange position and encouraged the so-called "yen-shift", which means a shift of borrowings from foreign to domestic sources. This has been attained by three steps. First, the exchange control position was relaxed in April 1969, second, in September 1969 the authorities began a buying operation, specifically with the foreign exchange banks, to supply them the domestic currency funds with which the banks bought foreign exchange from the Foreign Exchange Fund to repay their foreign short-term debts, and finally, in June 1970 (a period not included in our sample) the Bank of Japan started to supply credit to support the import usance at terms equal to, or more favourable than, the U.S. BA rate.

The effects of such a series of institutional changes are dealt with by introducing a dummy variable to the constant term as well as to the coefficient of the interest differential variable. It can be seen from our results that our international short-term liabilities have been reduced substantially, and that the interest sensitivity of short-term capital flows has been considerably increased.

---

[10] In the past several months, however, the picture has become quite different because of the steep decline in U.S. interest rates.

Other events, such as the U.S. foreign investment restraint pro-gramme and devaluation of the pound sterling in 1967, have also had some significant effects.

3.2. Long-term capital accounts

In the Japanese balance-of-payments tables, long-term capital transactions are divided into the following items:

Long-term Capital

Assets		Liabilities	
A.1	Direct Investment*	L.1	Direct Investment*
A.2	Trade Credits*	L.2	Trade Credits*
A.3	Loans*	L.3	Loans*
A.4	Securities	L.4	Securities*
A.5	Others	L.5	External Bonds*
		L.6	Others

Among these items A.4 is negligibly small due to exchange con-trols; A.5 consists largely of governmental transactions such as subscriptions and contributions to international organisations; and L.6 consists mainly of repayments on GARIOA and EROA loans. We therefore fitted equations to the remaining eight items (those carrying an asterisk in the above table), the sum of L.4 and L.5 being explained by one equation.

We first tried to estimate the following type of equation with a suitable choice of explanatory variables for each item. For the long-term asset transactions, for example, we fitted

$$K = a_0 + a_1 \sum_i w_i^1 (i_d - i_f)_{-i} + a_2 \sum_i w_i^2 (Y_d/Y_f)_{-i} +$$

$$+ a_3 \sum_i w_i^3 (y_d)_{-i} + a_4 \sum_i w_i^4 (y_f)_{-i} + a_5 W + a_6 K_{-1} \qquad (69)$$

$$a_1, a_2, a_3 < 0; \quad a_4, a_5 > 0; \quad 0 < a_6 < 1$$

where K signifies outstanding long-term assets, i_d, i_f are domestic and foreign long-term interest rates, Y_d, Y_f are domestic and foreign activity variables, y_d, y_f are the deviation from trend of the domestic and foreign activity variables and W is a proxy for the wealth variable.

We used the long-term yields on industrial and governmental bonds for the i's, the indices of industrial production for the Y's and the domestic fixed capital stock or the outstanding long-term borrowing of major business enterprises for W. This attempt, however, did not succeed. The equations reported in the following section are consequently nothing but a collection of ad hoc specifications. It is apparent that much more work is needed, but a general impression of the author is that a good knowledge of institutional arrangements and government policies is particularly important in this field.

3.3. Foreign exchange rates

We decided to estimate the exchange rate equations from monthly data, because we expected that they would provide more accurate information on lag structures. In applying the specification described in sect. 2.3, we assume that the expected future spot rate is determined by

$$r_s^e(t) = r_s^e(r_s(t), X^e(t), M^e(t), \text{qualitative variables}) \qquad (70)$$

where $X^e(t)$ and $M^e(t)$ represent the value of exports and imports in the future expected at time t, respectively. The sign of $\partial r_s^e / \partial r_s(t)$ depends on the elasticity of expectations, and

$$\partial r_s^e / \partial X^e(t) < 0, \quad \partial r_s^e / \partial M^e(t) > 0. \qquad (71)$$

The data on export letters of credit received were used for $X^e(t)$ and those on the value of imports licensed for $M^e(t)$. Both of these pieces of data are supposed to indicate fairly well the actual value of exports and imports two or three months later, and the exchange dealers would certainly take them into consideration.

The estimated results are fairly satisfactory, except that the interest differential variable is not statistically significant in the forward rate equation.

4. Estimated equations

This section summarises our statistical results concerning the Japanese short-term capital accounts, long-term capital accounts and foreign exchange rates. All equations have been estimated by the ordinary least squares method. In some equations the Almon technique of estimating the distributed lag weights is applied.

The sample period generally covers the years 1961 through 1969 and the first quarter of 1970, but it varies from one equation to another due to data availability. Capital account equations are estimated from quarterly data, while exchange rate equations are estimated from monthly data.

In the following equations t-values are shown in parentheses (or below the distributed lag weights in the case of Almon-lag estimation), R^2 denotes the coefficient of determination adjusted for degrees of freedom, s the standard error of estimate and DW the Durbin-Watson statistic. The variable names are listed in sect. 4.4 in alphabetical order together with the data source.

The following operators will be used in the presentation below:

$(x)_{-i}$:   variable x lagged i periods

DFT(x): deviation from trend of the variable x, i.e., DFT(x) = $x - \hat{x}$, where $\hat{x}$ = antilog $(a_0 + a_1 Q1 + a_2 Q2 + a_3 Q3 + a_4 t)$. The Q's denote seasonal dummy variables, and t the time period.

4.1.   Short-term capital accounts

4.1.1. Private banking sector

Liabilities

(4.1a) $FSBL$ = 139.7 + 0.9236 $((MB + MF + MIS) -$
                          (8.38)

$- (MB + MF + MIS)_{-2}) +$

$+ 29.578 ((RCU - RED - FXM) -$
            (3.72)

$$- (RCU - RED - FXM)_{-2}) -$$

$$- 60.402 \, (FXS - FXS_{-1}) - 176.6 \quad DYS -$$
$$\quad (3.49) \qquad\qquad\qquad (3.78)$$

$$- 203.2 \quad DVRP + 101.9 \quad DDVP - 69.2 \quad Q1 -$$
$$\quad (5.98) \qquad\qquad (2.44) \qquad\qquad (2.06)$$

$$- 78.6 \quad Q2 - 152.7 \quad Q3$$
$$\quad (1.87) \qquad\quad (4.22)$$

$$\bar{R}^2 = 0.814 \quad s = 69.2 \quad DW = 2.13 \,(1961.\text{I}-1970.\text{I})$$

(4.1b) $KSBL$ = $124.5 + 0.9312 \,((MB + MF + MIS) -$
$$\qquad\qquad\qquad (8.14)$$

$$- (MB + MF + MIS)_{-2}) +$$

$$+ 30.33 \,((RCU - RED - FXM) -$$
$$\quad (3.61)$$

$$- (RCU - RED - FXM)_{-2}) -$$

$$- 59.699 \,(FXS - FXS_{-1}) - 183.1 \quad DYS -$$
$$\quad (3.37) \qquad\qquad\qquad (3.57)$$

$$- 212.1 \quad DVRP + 99.4 \quad DDVP - 69.3 \quad Q1 -$$
$$\quad (4.84) \qquad\qquad (2.31) \qquad\qquad (2.03)$$

$$- 79.8 \quad Q2 - 153.6 \quad Q3 + \quad 1.0065 \; KSBL_{-1}$$
$$\quad (1.86) \qquad\quad (4.16) \qquad\quad (51.73)$$

$$\bar{R}^2 = 0.995 \quad s = 70.4 \quad DW = 2.16 \,(1961.\text{I}-1970.\text{I})$$

(4.2a) $FSBL$ = $-763.9 + 0.9246 \,(MB + MF + MIS) +$
$$\qquad\qquad\qquad (9.15)$$

$$+ 43.357 \,(RCU - RED) +$$
$$\quad (5.56)$$

$$+ 46.061 \,(RCU - RED) \cdot DYS -$$
$$\quad (2.85)$$

$$- 55.7 \quad \sum_{i=0}^{t} DVRP_i - 66.9 \ Q2 -$$
$$(5.93) \qquad\qquad (2.3)$$

$$- 86.9 \quad Q3 - \quad 0.2761 \ KSBL_{-1}$$
$$(2.85) \qquad (8.9)$$

$$\bar{R}^2 = 0.813 \quad s = 70.3 \quad DW = 1.25$$
$$(1961.I - 1969.IV)$$

(4.2b) $KSBL = -763.9 + 0.9246 \ (MB + MF + MIS) +$
$$(9.15)$$

$$+ 43.357 \ (RCU - RED) +$$
$$(5.56)$$

$$+ 46.061 \ (RCU - RED) \cdot DYS -$$
$$(2.85)$$

$$- 55.7 \quad \sum_{i=0}^{t} DVRP_i - 66.9 \ Q2 -$$
$$(5.93) \qquad\qquad (2.3)$$

$$- 86.9 \quad Q3 + \quad 0.7239 \ KSBL_{-1}$$
$$(2.85) \qquad (23.33)$$

$$\bar{R}^2 = 0.995 \quad s = 70.3 \quad DW = 1.25$$
$$(1961.I - 1969.IV)$$

(4.3a) $FSBL = -794.6 + 0.9007 \ (MB + MF + MIS) +$
$$(10.39)$$

$$+ 415.504 \ (RCU - RED)/RCU +$$
$$(6.94)$$

$$+ 264.101 \ ((RCU - RED)/RCU) \cdot DYS -$$
$$(2.38)$$

$$- 55.3 \quad \sum_{i=0}^{t} DVRP_i - 70.1 \quad Q2 -$$
$$(6.71) \qquad\qquad (2.75)$$

$$- 91.7 \quad Q3 - \quad 0.2522 \ KSBL_{-1}$$
$$(3.46) \qquad (9.37)$$

$$\bar{R}^2 = 0.858 \quad s = 61.3 \quad DW = 1.41$$
$$(1961.I - 1969.IV)$$

(4.3b) $KSBL$ = $-794.6 +$ $0.9007 (MB + MF + MIS) +$
(10.39)

$+ 415.504 (RCU - RED)/RCU +$
(6.94)

$+ 264.101 ((RCU - RED)/RCU) \cdot DYS -$
(2.38)

$- 55.3 \sum_{i=0}^{t} DVRP_i - 70.1 \ Q2 -$
$(6.71) \qquad\qquad (2.75)$

$- 91.7 \ Q3 + \ 0.7478 \ KSBL_{-1}$
$(3.46) \qquad (27.77)$

$\bar{R}^2 = 0.994 \ s = 61.3 \ DW = 1.41$
$(1961.I-1969.IV)$

Assets

(4.4a) $FSBA$ = $106.3 + 0.4185 ((XB + XF + XIS) -$
(6.98)

$- (XB + XF + XIS)_{-1}) + 273.5 \ DYS -$
(5.55)

$- 128.2 \ Q2 - 59.5 \ Q3$
$(3.57) \qquad (1.80)$

$\bar{R}^2 = 0.785 \ s = 74.9 \ DW = 1.75$
$(1961.I-1969.IV)$

(4.4b) $KSBA$ = $83.3 + 0.4133 ((XB + XF + XIS) -$
(6.79)

$- (XB + XF + XIS)_{-1}) + 251.1 \ DYS -$
(4.30)

$- 123.6 \ Q2 - 56.9 \ Q3 +$
$(3.36) \qquad (1.70)$

$$+ \quad 1.0109 \, KSBA_{-1}$$
$$(67.71)$$

$$\bar{R}^2 = 0.996 \quad s = 75.4 \quad DW = 1.77$$
$$(1961.I-1969.IV)$$

$$(4.5a) \quad FSBA \quad = \; -368.7 + \; 0.3487 \, (XB + XF + XIS) +$$
$$(6.18)$$

$$+ \; 0.0972 \, LBC - \; 0.4121 \, KSBA_{-1}$$
$$(3.94) \qquad (7.05)$$

$$\bar{R}^2 = 0.760 \quad s = 79.3 \quad DW = 1.57$$
$$(1961.I-1969.IV)$$

$$(4.5b) \quad KSBA \quad = \; -368.7 + \; 0.3487 \, (XB + XF + XIS) +$$
$$(6.18)$$

$$+ \; 0.0972 \, LBC + \; 0.5879 \, KSBA_{-1}$$
$$(3.94) \qquad (10.06)$$

$$\bar{R}^2 = 0.995 \quad s = 79.3 \quad DW = 1.57$$
$$(1961.I-1969.IV)$$

4.1.2. Private non-banking sector

Net liabilities

$$(4.6a) \quad FSNN \quad = \; -3.2 + \; 0.0552 \, ((XB + XF + XIS) -$$
$$(2.38)$$

$$- (XB + XF - XIS)_{-2}) +$$

$$+ \; 0.1419 \, ((MB + MF + MIS) -$$
$$(3.06)$$

$$- (MB + MF + MIS)_{-2}) +$$

$$+ \; 0.5511 \, (MCOC - MCOC_{-2}) +$$

$$+ \; 46.365 \, ((RAL - RMUD) -$$
$$(3.32)$$

$$- (RAL - RMUD)_{-2}) + 133.9 \quad DMU +$$
$$(3.42)$$

$$+ 51.3 \quad DDVP$$
$$(2.72)$$

$$\bar{R}^2 = 0.594 \quad s = 37.8 \quad DW = 1.90$$
$$(1961.\text{I}-1969.\text{IV})$$

(4.6b) $KSNN$ = $174.2 + 0.1484 ((XB + XF + XIS) -$
$$(2.41)$$

$$- (XB + XF + XIS)_{-2}) +$$

$$+ 0.4879 ((MB + MF + MIS) -$$
$$(4.22)$$

$$- (MB + MF + MIS)_{-2}) +$$

$$+ 2.0893 (MCOC - MCOC_{-2}) +$$
$$(3.60)$$

$$+ 157.457 ((RAL - RMUD) -$$
$$(4.17)$$

$$- (RAL - RMUD)_{-2}) + 199.2 \quad DMU +$$
$$(1.02)$$

$$+ 79.6 \quad DDVP + 0.9411 \, KSNN_{-1}$$
$$(1.53) \qquad (45.39)$$

$$\bar{R}^2 = 0.991 \quad s = 94.0 \quad DW = 1.58$$
$$(1961.\text{I}-1969.\text{IV})$$

(4.7a) $FSNN$ = $-423.3 + 0.1878 (MB + MF + MIS) +$
$$(4.02)$$

$$+ 0.6689 \, MCOC + 59.523 (RAL - RMUD) +$$
$$(2.12) \qquad (4.91)$$

$$+ 138.7 \quad DMU + 26.5 \quad Q3 - 0.2602 \, KSNN_{-1}$$
$$(3.93) \qquad (1.75) \qquad (4.26)$$

$$\bar{R}^2 = 0.667 \quad s = 34.2 \quad DW = 1.78$$
$$(1961.\text{I}-1969.\text{IV})$$

(4.7b) $KSNN$ = $-423.3 + 0.1878 (MB + MF + MIS) +$
$\qquad$ (4.02)

$\qquad + 0.6689\, MCOC + 59.523\, (RAL - RMUD) +$
$\qquad$ (2.12) $\qquad\qquad$ (4.91)

$\qquad + 138.7\quad DMU + 26.5\quad Q3 + \quad 0.7398\, KSNN_{-1}$
$\qquad$ (3.93) $\qquad\quad$ (1.75) $\qquad$ (12.11)

$\bar{R}^2 = 0.991 \quad s = 34.2 \quad DW = 1.78$
$(1961.\mathrm{I} - 1969.\mathrm{IV})$

(4.8a) $FSNN$ = $-407.9 + 0.1914 (MB + MF + MIS) +$
$\qquad$ (4.01)

$\qquad + 0.5946\, MCOC +$
$\qquad$ (1.88)

$\qquad + 441.083\, (RAL - RMUD)/RAL +$
$\qquad$ (4.76)

$\qquad + 134.5\quad DMU + 24.7\quad Q3 - \quad 0.2551\, KSNN_{-1}$
$\qquad$ (3.76) $\qquad\quad$ (1.61) $\qquad$ (4.12)

$\bar{R}^2 = 0.658 \quad s = 34.7 \quad DW = 1.75$
$(1961.\mathrm{I} - 1969.\mathrm{IV})$

(4.8b) $KSNN$ = $-407.9 + 0.1914 (MB + MF + MIS) +$
$\qquad$ (4.01)

$\qquad + 0.5946\, MCOC +$
$\qquad$ (1.88)

$\qquad + 441.083\, (RAL - RMUD)/RAL +$
$\qquad$ (4.76)

$\qquad + 134.5\quad DMU + 24.7\quad Q3 + \quad 0.7449\, KSNN_{-1}$
$\qquad$ (3.76) $\qquad\quad$ (1.61) $\qquad$ (12.03)

$\bar{R}^2 = 0.991 \quad s = 34.7 \quad DW = 1.75$
$(1961.\mathrm{I} - 1969.\mathrm{IV})$

4.1.3. Private sector total

Net liabilities

(4.9a) $FSBL - FSBA + FSNN =$

$$= 75.5 - \underset{(6.29)}{0.3807} ((XB + XF + XIS) -$$

$$- (XB + XF + XIS)_{-1}) +$$

$$+ \underset{(5.16)}{0.6253} ((MB + MF + MIS) -$$

$$- (MB + MF + MIS)_{-2}) +$$

$$+ \underset{(4.39)}{46.87} ((RCU - RED) - (RCU - RED)_{-2}) +$$

$$+ \underset{(1.99)}{44.376} ((RCU - RED) -$$

$$- (RCU - RED)_{-2}) \cdot DYS - \underset{(3.20)}{200.8} \ DYS -$$

$$- \underset{(3.36)}{129.9} \ DVRP + \underset{(2.10)}{112.4} \ DDVP - \underset{(3.17)}{111.1} \ Q3$$

$$\bar{R}^2 = 0.872 \quad s = 86.9 \quad DW = 2.26 \ (1961.1 - 1970.1)$$

(4.9b) $KSBL - KSBA + KSNN =$

$$= 133.5 - \underset{(5.98)}{0.3673} ((XB + XF + XIS) -$$

$$- (XB + XF + XIS)_{-1}) +$$

$$+ \underset{(4.59)}{0.5819} ((MB + MF + MIS) -$$

$$- (MB + MF + MIS)_{-2}) +$$

$$+ \underset{(3.99)}{43.834} ((RCU - RED) - (RCU - RED)_{-2}) +$$

$$+ \ 42.557 \ ((RCU - RED) -$$
$$(1.91)$$

$$- (RCU - RED)_{-2}) \cdot DYS - 212.3 \ DYS -$$
$$(3.35)$$

$$- \ 114.9 \ DVRP + 130.5 \ DDVP - 110.3 \ Q3 +$$
$$(2.82) \qquad\qquad (2.34) \qquad\qquad (3.16)$$

$$+ \quad 0.9565 \ (KSBL - KSBA + KSNN)_{-1}$$
$$(24.58)$$

$$\bar{R}^2 = 0.964 \quad s = 86.5 \quad DW = 2.26 \ (1961.\mathrm{I}{-}1970.\mathrm{I})$$

(4.10a) $FSBL - FSBA + FSNN -$

$$= - \ 676.9 - \ 0.5389 \ (XB + XF + XIS) +$$
$$(7.26)$$

$$+ \quad 0.7130 \ (MB + MF + MIS) +$$
$$(9.1)$$

$$+ \ 29.014 \ (RCU - RED) +$$
$$(2.49)$$

$$+ \ 181.044 \ (RCU - RED) \cdot DYS + \ 0.1671 \ LBC -$$
$$(6.28) \qquad\qquad\qquad (4.31)$$

$$- \ 61.9 \ \sum_{i=0}^{t} \ DRYC_i -$$
$$(3.01)$$

$$- \ 0.3827 \ (KSBL - KSBA + KSNN)_{-1}$$
$$(7.49)$$

$$\bar{R}^2 = 0.874 \quad s = 85.7 \quad DW = 1.66$$
$$(1961.\mathrm{I}{-}1969.\mathrm{IV})$$

(4.10b) $KSBL - KSBA + KSNN =$

$$= - \ 676.9 - \ 0.5389 \ (XB + XF + XIS) +$$
$$(7.26)$$

$+$ $\quad$ 0.7130 $(MB + MF + MIS)$ +
(9.10)

$+$ $\quad$ 29.014 $(RCU - RED)$ +
(2.49)

$+$ $\quad$ 181.044 $(RCU - RED) \cdot DYS$ +
(6.28)

$+$ $\quad$ 0.1671 LBC + 61.9 $\quad \sum\limits_{i=0}^{t} DRYC_i$ +
$\quad$ (4.31) $\qquad$ (3.01)

$+$ $\quad$ 0.6173 $(KSBL - KSBA + KSNN)_{-1}$
(12.08)

$\bar{R}^2 = 0.966$ $\quad s = 85.7$ $\quad DW = 1.66$
(1961.I–1969.IV)

(4.11a) $FSBL - FSBA + FSNN =$

$=$ $-$ 682.3 $-$ $\quad$ 0.3696 $(XB + XF + XIS)$ +
$\qquad\qquad$ (4.08)

$+$ $\quad$ 0.6223 $(MB + MF + MIS)$ +
(8.04)

$+$ $\quad$ 359.331 $(RCU - RED)/RCU$ +
(3.43)

$+$ $\quad$ 1002.147 $((RCU - RED)/RCU) \cdot DYS$ +
(4.62)

$+$ $\quad$ 0.1202 LBC $-$ 72.6 $\quad \sum\limits_{i=0}^{t} DRYC_i$ +
$\quad$ (3.24) $\qquad\quad$ (3.64)

$+$ 96.7 $\quad Q1 - 0.3402 (KSBL - KSBA + KSNN)_{-1}$
$\quad$ (2.44) $\qquad$ (7.46)

$\bar{R}^2 = 0.894$ $\quad s = 78.7$ $\quad DW = 1.94$
(1961.I–1969.IV)

(4.11b) $KSBL - KSBA + KSNN=$

$$= -682.3 - \underset{(4.08)}{0.3696} (XB + \overline{XF} + XIS) +$$

$$+ \underset{(8.04)}{0.6223} (MB + MF + MIS) +$$

$$+ \underset{(3.43)}{359.331} (RCU - RED)/RCU +$$

$$+ \underset{(4.62)}{1002.147} ((RCU - RED)/RED) \cdot DYS +$$

$$+ \underset{(3.24)}{0.1202} LBC - \underset{(3.64)}{72.6} \sum_{i=0}^{t} DRYC_i +$$

$$+ \underset{(2.44)}{96.7} \; Q1 + \underset{(14.47)}{0.6598} (KSBL - KSBA + KSNN)_{-1}$$

$$\bar{R}^2 = 0.971 \quad s = 78.7 \quad DW = 1.94$$
$$(1961.\text{I}-1969.\text{IV})$$

4.2. Long-term capital accounts

4.2.1. Direct investment

Liabilities

$$(4.12) \; KLDL \; = \; 16.6 - 387.741 \sum_{i=3}^{8} w_i \; \text{DFT}(PRODA)_{-i} +$$

$$+ \underset{(3.43)}{22.1} \; DLR - \underset{(4.44)}{30.2} \; DLRR + \underset{(121.07)}{0.9941} KLDL_{-1}$$

i	3	4	5	6	7	8
w_i	0.065	0.127	0.180	0.214	0.221	0.193
	(1.3)	(2.1)	(3.4)	(4.2)	(3.3)	(2.5)

$$\bar{R}^2 = 0.999 \quad s = 6.2 \quad DW = 2.02 \, (1961.\text{I}-1970.\text{I})$$

Assets

$$(4.13) \; KLDA \; = \; -180.9 - \underset{(2.25)}{89.604} \; \text{DFT} \, (XA3C) + \underset{(5.72)}{0.0013} \; KP +$$

$$+ 62.7 \sum_{i=0}^{t} DLDF_i - 8.8 \ Q1 - 7.5 \ Q2 -$$
$$\text{(6.49)} \qquad\qquad \text{(1.62)} \qquad \text{(1.38)}$$

$$- 11.5 \ Q3 - 0.3916 \, KLDA_{-1}$$
$$\text{(2.11)} \qquad \text{(3.63)}$$

$$\bar{R}^2 = 0.999 \quad s = 11.1 \quad DW = 1.65 \, (1961.\text{I}-1970.\text{I})$$

4.2.2. Long-term trade credits

Liabilities

(4.14) $KLTL$ = $19.4 - 0.5228 \ TIME \cdot DITL - 19.3 \ DDTL +$
$\qquad\qquad\qquad\quad \text{(4.96)} \qquad\qquad\qquad \text{(3.92)}$

$$+ \quad 0.9361 \, KLTL_{-1}$$
$$\text{(30.68)}$$

$$\bar{R}^2 = 0.981 \quad s = 7.7 \quad DW = 1.21 \, (1961.\text{I}-1970.\text{I})$$

Assets

(4.15) $FLTAD = -8.8 + 0.4909 \ (XMYC + XSHC)$
$\qquad\qquad\qquad\qquad \text{(33.14)}$

$$\bar{R}^2 = 0.967 \quad s = 18.3 \quad DW = 1.68 \, (1960.\text{IV}-1970.\text{I})$$

(4.16) $FLTAC = 17.2 + 1.0454 \sum\limits_{i=7}^{24} w_i \, FLTAD_{-i} - 7.7 \ Q2$
$\qquad\qquad\qquad\qquad\qquad\qquad\qquad\qquad\qquad\quad \text{(1.82)}$

i	7	8	9	10	11	12
w_i	0.005	0.012	0.019	0.028	0.037	0.046
	(0.6)	(0.8)	(1.1)	(1.5)	(2.1)	(3.2)

i	13	14	15	16	17	18
w_i	0.055	0.063	0.071	0.077	0.082	0.085
	(5.3)	(11.5)	(25.1)	(10.5)	(6.3)	(4.7)

i	19	20	21	22	23	24
w_i	0.085	0.083	0.079	0.071	0.059	0.044
	(3.8)	(3.2)	(2.9)	(2.6)	(2.4)	(2.2)

$$\bar{R}^2 = 0.950 \quad s = 10.9 \quad DW = 1.82 \,(1961.I–1970.I)$$

4.2.3. Long-term loans

Liabilities

$$(4.17) \quad KLLL = 76.7 + 459.94 \sum_{i=1}^{6} w_i^1 \, \text{DFT}(PROD)_{-i} -$$

$$- 3551.9 \sum_{i=1}^{8} w_i^2 \, \text{DFT}(PRODA)_{-i} +$$

$$+ \; 0.9810 \, KLLL_{-1}$$
$$(63.24)$$

i	1	2	3	4	5	6
w_i^1	0.080	0.144	0.189	0.210	0.206	0.171
	(0.9)	(1.3)	(2.2)	(3.3)	(2.3)	(1.5)

i	1	2	3	4	5	6
w_i^2	0.069	0.118	0.148	0.160	0.158	0.144
	(4.1)	(5.2)	(6.9)	(8.1)	(6.6)	(4.5)

i	7	8
w_i^2	0.118	0.085
	(3.1)	(2.3)

$$\bar{R}^2 = 0.997 \quad s = 28.5 \quad DW = 2.34 \,(1961.I–1970.I)$$

Assets

$$(4.18) \quad \text{LOG}\,(KLLA/GNP \cdot PGNP) =$$

$$= 1.8559 + 2.5276 \sum_{i=0}^{8} w_i \text{LOG}(KLTA/GNP \cdot$$

$$PGNP)_{-i} + 0.3397 \, \text{LOG} \, (\tfrac{1}{2} \sum_{i=2}^{3}$$
$$(3.12)$$

$$(GFXN/GNP \cdot PGNP)_{-i}) + 0.2574 \, Q1 +$$
$$(11.74)$$

$$+ \quad 0.2639 \, Q2 + \quad 0.2445 \, Q3$$
$$(11.13) \qquad\quad (10.56)$$

i	0	1	2	3	4	5
w_i	0.082	0.134	0.159	0.163	0.150	0.126
	(7.4)	(8.3)	(9.8)	(12.5)	(18.0)	(21.6)

i	6	7	8
w_i	0.095	0.062	0.032
	(10.8)	(5.0)	(2.4)

$$\bar{R}^2 = 0.995 \quad s = 0.0416 \quad DW = 1.62 \, (1962.\text{IV}-1970.\text{I})$$

4.2.4. Security investment and external bonds

Liabilities

(4.19) $KLSL + KLBL =$

$$= 593.0 + 3065.8 \sum_{i=6}^{16} w_i^1 \, \text{DFT} \, (PROD)_{-i} -$$

$$- 26969.2 \sum_{i=6}^{16} w_i^2 \, \text{DFT} \, (PRODA)_{-i} +$$

$$+ 494.707 \sum_{i=0}^{18} w_i^3 \, (DFIR)_{-i} +$$

$$+ \quad 0.3357 \, (KLSL + KLBL)_{-1}$$
$$(1.87)$$

i	6	7	8	9	10	11
w_i^1	0.064	0.107	0.132	0.142	0.138	0.126
	(3.8)	(3.7)	(3.6)	(3.4)	(3.2)	(2.9)

i	12	13	14	15	16
w_i^1	0.016	0.082	0.057	0.033	0.014
	(2.6)	(2.1)	(1.7)	(1.1)	(0.6)

i	6	7	8	9	10	11
w_i^2	0.050	0.086	0.110	0.123	0.127	0.123
	(4.9)	(4.8)	(4.6)	(4.4)	(4.2)	(3.9)

i	12	13	14	15	16
w_i^2	0.112	0.097	0.079	0.058	0.037
	(3.6)	(3.3)	(3.0)	(2.6)	(2.3)

i	0	1	2	3	4
w_i^3	-0.049	-0.080	-0.096	-0.098	-0.089
	(3.6)	(3.6)	(3.6)	(3.5)	(3.4)

i	5	6	7	8	9
w_i^3	-0.071	-0.045	-0.013	0.022	0.059
	(3.2)	(2.7)	(1.2)	(2.0)	(3.4)

i	10	11	12	13	14
w_i^3	0.095	0.129	0.158	0.182	0.196
	(3.7)	(3.8)	(3.8)	(3.9)	(3.9)

i	15	16	17	18
w_i^3	0.201	0.193	0.171	0.133
	(3.8)	(3.8)	(3.8)	(3.8)

$\bar{R}^2 = 0.996$ $s = 28.9$ $DW = 2.66 \, (1963.1-1970.1$

4.3. Foreign exchange rates

4.3.1. Forward exchange rate

$$(4.20)\ FXF = 14.25 - 0.0012 \sum_{i=0}^{3} w_i^1\ (XLC)_{-i} +$$

$$+ 0.0008 \sum_{i=0}^{3} w_i^2\ (MLS)_{-i} + \underset{(10.39)}{0.4403\ FXS} -$$

$$\underset{(6.07)}{- 0.3164\ FXS_{-1}} + \underset{(18.62)}{0.8373\ FXF_{-1}}$$

i	0	1	2	3
w_i^1	0.300	0.352	0.252	0.096
	(1.0)	(1.8)	(1.7)	(0.2)

i	0	1	2	3
w_i^2	0.251	0.321	0.270	0.159
	(1.5)	(2.3)	(2.2)	(0.7)

$\bar{R}^2 = 0.982$ $s = 0.22$ $DW = 1.61$
(Jan. 1961–Mar. 1970)

4.3.2. Spot exchange rate

$$(4.21)\ FXS = 26.32 - 0.0021 \sum_{i=1}^{4} w_i^1\ (XC)_{-i} +$$

$$+ 0.0022 \sum_{i=1}^{4} w_i^2\ (MC)_{-i} -$$

$$- 0.5631 \sum_{i=4}^{10} w_i^3\ ((RCO - RBA) -$$

$$- (RCO - RBA)_{-1})_{-i} + \underset{(9.51)}{1.0811\ FXF} -$$

$$- \ 0.8755 \ FXF_{-1} \ - \ 0.23 \ DWB \ +$$
$$\quad (6.96) \qquad\qquad (1.95)$$

$$+ \quad 0.7209 \ FXS_{-1}$$
$$\quad (11.36)$$

i	1	2	3	4
w_i^1	0.113	0.233	0.319	0.335
	(0.9)	(2.0)	(3.0)	(2.0)

i	1	2	3	4
w_i^2	0.084	0.214	0.330	0.335
	(0.4)	(1.3)	(2.6)	(1.3)

i	4	5	6	7	8
w_i^3	0.066	0.118	0.156	0.178	0.182
	(1.4)	(1.8)	(2.5)	(3.2)	(3.2)

i	9	10
w_i^3	0.168	0.133
	(2.5)	(2.0)

$\bar{R}^2 = 0.953 \quad s = 0.35 \quad DW = 1.59$
(Jan. 1961–Mar. 1970)

4.4. List of variables and sources of data

The following abbreviations will be used for data sources.

BPM   Foreign Department, The Bank of Japan, *Balance of Payments Monthly.*

BTW   Bank of Tokyo, *Tohgin Shuho* (Bank of Tokyo Weekly).

ESA   Statistical Department, The Bank of Japan, *Economic Statistics Annual.*

ESM   Ditto, *Economic Statistics Monthly.*

FESA Ditto, *Gaikoku Keizai Tokei Nempo* (Foreign Economic Statistics Annual).

FESQ Ditto, *Gaikoku Keizai Tokei Kiho* (Foreign Economic Statistics Quarterly).

IFS International Monetary Fund, *International Financial Statistics.*

MEI OECD, *Main Economic Indicators.*

SRTJ Customs Department, Ministry of Finance, *The Summary Report: Trade of Japan.*

BLC Long-term borrowings outstanding by major business enterprises; 100 million yen; *ESA, ESM.*

DDTL Dummy variable to adjust the lack of appropriate data for *FLTL*; 1 for the quarters 1961.I to 1962.I and 0 otherwise.

DDVP Dummy variable representing the lack of confidence in the value of the pound sterling before and after the devaluation in 1967; 1 for the quarters 1967.II–1968.II and 0 otherwise.

DFIR Dummy variable representing the U.S. policy to restrain foreign investment; 1 for the quarters 1963.III to date and 0 otherwise.

DITL Dummy variable representing the effect of the U.S. interest equalisation tax upon trade credit from abroad; 1 for the quarters 1965.I to date and 0 otherwise.

DLDF Dummy variable representing the relaxation of exchange controls on direct investment abroad in 1968; 1 for the quarter 1968.IV and 0 otherwise.

DLR Dummy variable representing the liberalisation of remittances of principals and interests of stock investment by foreigners; 1 for the quarter 1963.II and 0 otherwise.

DLRR Dummy variable representing the relaxation of inter-regional regulation of direct investment in the U.S. foreign investment restraint programme; 1 for the quarter 1969.II and 0 otherwise.

DMU   Dummy variable to accommodate the re-classification of some items of import usance from the banking to the non-banking accounts; 1 for the quarter 1964.I and 0 otherwise.

DRYC   Dummy variable representing the regulation of foreign exchange banks' exchange position by the Bank of Japan to control the short-term capital inflow; 1 for the quarters 1968.I to date and 0 otherwise.

DVRP   Dummy variable representing the voluntary restraint programme by the U.S. Federal Reserve System to curb U.S. foreign investment, applicable to short-term capital flows, 1 for the quarters 1965.II–1967.IV, 1.5 for 1968.I–1969.I, 1 for 1969.II to date and 0 otherwise.

DWB   Dummy variable representing expectations of the widening of support points from 0.5 to 0.75% of the parity, which was effected in April 1963; 1 for the months May 1961–March 1963 and 0 otherwise.

DYS   Dummy variable representing the policy of the Bank of Japan to encourage the "yen-shift", i.e. a substitution of domestic debt for foreign borrowings by the foreign exchange banks; 1 for the quarters 1969.II to date and 0 otherwise.

FLDA   Net increase in foreign long-term assets, direct investment, million dollars; *BPM.*

FLDL   Net increase in foreign long-term liabilities, direct investment; million dollars; *BPM.*

FLLA   Net increase in foreign long-term assets, loans; million dollars; *BPM.*

FLLL   Net increase in foreign long-term liabilities, loans; million dollars; *BPM.*

FLSL   Net increase in foreign long-term liabilities, security investment; million dollars; *BPM.*

FLTA   Net increase in foreign long-term assets, trade credit; million dollars; = *FLTAD* − *FLTAC.*

FLTAC   Decrease in foreign long-term assets, trade credit collected; million dollars; *BPM.*

FLTAD Increase in foreign long-term assets, trade credit granted; million dollars; *BPM*.

FLTL Net increase in foreign long-term liabilities, trade credit; million dollars; *BPM*.

FSBA Net increase in foreign short-term assets, banking sector; million dollars; *BPM*.

FSBL Net increase in foreign short-term liabilities, banking sector; million dollars; *BPM*.

FSNN Net increase in foreign short-term net liabilities, non-banking sector; million dollars; *BPM*.

FXF Forward exchange rate, U.S. dollar, 3 months; yen per U.S. dollar; *BTW*.

FXM Forward margin, U.S. dollar; % p.a.; = $((FXF - FXS)/FXS) \cdot (365/90) \cdot 100$.

FXS Spot exchange rate, U.S. dollar, T.T. selling; yen per U.S. dollar; *BTW*.

GFXG Official gold and foreign exchange reserves including the gold tranche position and the SDR allocation; million dollars; *ESA, ESM,* and *IFS*.

GFXN The same as above but excluding the gold tranche position and the SDR allocation.

GNP Gross national product at constant prices; billion yen; Economic Planning Agency, Government of Japan, *Annual Report on National Income Statistics,* 1970.

KLBL Foreign long-term liabilities outstanding, external bond; million dollars; = $FLBL + KLBL_{-1}$, *KLBL* (end of 1962) = 327.

KLDA Foreign long-term assets outstanding, direct investment; million dollars; = $FLDA + KLDA_{-1}$, *KLDA* (end of 1962) = 395.

KLDL Foreign long-term liabilities outstanding, direct investment; million dollars; = $FLDL + KLDL_{-1}$, *KLDL* (end of 1962) = 274.

KLLA Foreign long-term assets outstanding, loans; million dollars; = $FLLA + KLLA_{-1}$, *KLLA* (end of 1962) = 64.

KLLL Foreign long-term liabilities outstanding, loans; million dollars; = $FLLL + KLLL_{-1}$, *KLLL* (end of 1962) = 1,144.

KLSL   Foreign long-term liabilities oustanding, security investment; million dollars; $= FLSL + KLSL_{-1}$, *KLSL* (end of 1962) = 156.

KLTA   Foreign long-term assets outstanding, trade credit; million dollars; $= FLTA + KLTA_{-1}$, *KLTA* (end of 1962) = 633.

KLTL   Foreign long-term liabilities outstanding, trade credit; million dollars; $= FLTL + KLTL_{-1}$, *KLTL* (end of 1962) = 37.

KP   Gross capital stock of the private sector; 100 million yen; Division of National Income Statistics, Economic Planning Agency.

LBC   Outstanding loans by city banks (excluding loans to small businesses); 100 million yen; *ESA, ESM.*

MB   Value of commodity imports, balance of payments basis; million dollars; *BPM.*

MC   Value of commodity imports, customs clearance basis; million dollars; *SRTJ.*

MCOC   Value of imports of crude oil, customs clearance basis; million dollars; *SRTJ.*

MF   Payments of freight; million dollars; *BPM.*

MIS   Payments of insurance on international shipments; million dollars; *BPM.*

MLS   Value of imports licensed; million dollars; *ESA, ESM.*

PGNP   GNP deflator; Economic Planning Agency, Government of Japan, *Annual Report on National Income Statistics, 1970.*

PROD   Index of industrial production; 1963 average = 100; *MEI.*

PRODA   Index of industrial production, simple average of five countries (U.S., U.K., Germany, France and Netherlands); 1963 average = 100; *MEI.*

Q1, Q2, Q3   Quarterly dummy variables; 1 for each quarter and 0 otherwise.

RAL   Average interest rate on loans of all banks; % p.a.; *ESA, ESM.*

RBA   U.S. bankers' acceptance rate, 90 days, adjusted; = (BA rate + 1.5) · 10/9; % p.a.; *FESA*.
RCO   Call rate, Tokyo, over month; % p.a.; *ESA, ESM*.
RCU   Call rate, Tokyo, unconditional; % p.a.; *ESA, ESM*.
RED   Euro-dollar deposit rate, London, 3 months, adjusted; = (Euro-dollar rate) · 10/9; % p.a.; Einzig, P., *The Euro-Dollar System* and *Financial Times*.
RMUD   Import usance rate, U.S. dollar; % p.a.; Research Department, The Bank of Japan, *Chosa Geppo* (Monthly Bulletin).
TIME   Time trend; = 1.0 + $(TIME)_{-1}$, $TIME$ (1961.I) = 1.0.
XA3C   Average of the value of commodity exports (customs clearance basis) to three regions (U.S., South-East Asia and Central and South America); million dollars; *BPM*.
XB   Value of commodity exports, balance of payments basis; million dollars; *BPM*.
XC   Value of commodity exports, customs clearance basis; million dollars; *SRTJ*.
XF   Receipts of freight; million dollars; *BPM*.
XIS   Receipts of insurance of international shipments; million dollars; *BPM*.
XLC   Export letters of credit received; million dollars; *ESA, ESM*.
XMYC   Value of exports of non-electric machinery, customs clearance basis; million dollars; *SRTJ*.
XSHC   Value of exports of ships, customs clearance basis; million dollars; *SRTJ*.

10. THE INVISIBLE COMPONENTS OF THE CURRENT ACCOUNT OF THE BALANCE OF INTERNATIONAL PAYMENTS*

J.A. SAWYER

1. Introduction

To explain the subject matter of this chapter it may be helpful to summarise the components of a country's balance on current account of its international payments. Current receipts are derived from (i) the sale of merchandise exports, (ii) the provision of services to non-residents and (iii) transfers from non-residents. Current payments are derived from (i) the purchase of merchandise imports, (ii) the provision of services by non-residents and (iii) transfers to non-residents. The net value of the first two components of receipts and payments (i.e., goods and services) is the net balance of transactions in goods and services with non-residents by a country and is a component of its gross national product. The last two components, services and transfers, are commonly referred to as "invisible" components of a country's balance of payments and are the subject of this chapter. Three categories of services are distinguished: (a) transportation and travel services, (b) investment income and (c) other. Transfer payments include migrants' funds, personal remittances, government transfer payments and withholding taxes on interest and dividends paid to non-residents. [1] Professor Basevi's chapter deals with merchandise

* I would like to thank Mr. Glen Henderson for assistance in examining the individual country models and writing the equations for invisibles in a standardised notation.

[1] Some useful discussions of classification problems are contained in Lederer, W., 'Measuring the Balance of Payments', in Joint Economic Committee of the Congress of the United States, *Factors Affecting the United States Balance of Payments*, U.S. Government Printing Office, 1962 and Woolley, H.B., *Measuring Transactions Between World Areas*, National Bureau of Economic Research, 1965.

Table 1
Balance of payments: current account
(millions of U.S. dollars)

	1956	1957	1958	1959	1960	1961	1962	1963	1964	1965
Belgium-Luxembourg										
Trade Balance	94	−46	90	−48	14	−40	0	−80	22	117
Services	151	222	265	78	20	70	68	−12	20	12
Transfers	20	24	20	42	8	14	16	−12	12	20
Current Account Balance	265	200	375	72	42	44	84	−104	54	149
Canada										
Exports-Imports f.o.b.	−758	−603	−186	−443	−148	166	164	465	652	94
Services	−616	−800	−883	−1,001	−959	−986	−894	−894	−971	−1,070
Transfers	−48	−74	−105	−134	−140	−122	−81	−87	−84	−81
Current Account Balance	−1,422	−1,477	−1,174	−1,578	−1,247	−942	−811	−516	−403	−1,057
Germany										
Trade Balance c.i.f.	698	980	1,168	1,224	1,273	1,624	746	1,406	1,338	221
Services	658	860	736	570	670	212	19	98	21	−274
Transfers	−287	−441	−452	−779	−814	−1,110	−1,289	−1,247	−1,245	−1,488
Current Account Balance	1,069	1,399	1,452	1,015	1,129	726	−524	257	114	−1,541
Italy										
Trade Balance f.o.b.	−732	−769	−373	−133	−633	−556	−880	−1,808	−568	666
Services	461	600	670	703	750	792	867	861	1,002	1,232
Transfers	176	203	267	185	200	272	290	290	262	351
Current Account Balance	−95	34	564	755	317	508	277	−657	696	2,249

Trade Balance f.o.b.	-125	-395	376	365	271	-558	402	-166	375	1,901
Services	66	-191	87	24	-103	-383	-420	-568	-783	-884
Transfers	25	-34	-198	-29	-25	-42	-31	-45	-72	-86
Current Account Balance	-34	-620	265	360	143	-983	-49	-779	-480	931
Netherlands										
Trade Balance f.o.b.	-496	-461	32	19	-116	-347	-279	-443	-719	-500
Services	311	315	382	464	227	555	454	518	533	538
Transfers	-12	-14	1	-16	4	-19	-34	44	14	n.a.
Current Account Balance	-197	-160	415	467	115	189	141	119	172	—
Sweden										
Trade Balance c.i.f.	-268	-298	-275	-194	-329	-174	-183	-182	-169	-402
Services	245	283	231	206	255	231	216	193	200	156
Transfers	-8	-13	-7	-11	-11	-10	-20	-28	-45	-42
Current Account Balance	-31	-28	-51	1	-75	47	13	-17	-14	-288
United Kingdom										
Trade Balance f.o.b.	147	-79	86	-321	-1,132	-418	-275	-219	-1,505	-738
Services	605	884	1,029	917	629	694	864	923	886	542
Transfers	-171	-197	-188	-220	-267	-315	-330	-407	-525	-581
Current Account Balance	581	608	927	376	-770	-39	259	297	-1,144	-777
United States										
Trade Balance f.o.b.	4,575	6,099	3,312	985	4,757	5,444	4,417	5,079	6,676	4,788
Services	2,180	2,471	2,029	1,867	2,023	2,756	3,140	3,097	3,901	4,206
Transfers	-5,211	-5,186	-5,496	-5,153	-5,096	-5,165	-5,103	-5,063	-4,852	-4,831
Current Account Balance	1,544	3,384	-155	-2,301	1,684	3,035	2,454	3,113	5,725	4,163

Source: International Monetary Fund, *International Financial Statistics*, Supplement to 1966/67 issues, Washington 1967.

trade. Table 1 presents data on the net contribution of goods, services and transfers to the current account balance of the countries whose models are surveyed below so that the source of variations of each of these components in this balance can be seen.

2. General specification of equations for imports and exports of services

There are two approaches to developing equations which will explain imports and exports of services. The first is to apply general demand theory, as has been done in the paper by Driehuis [2], while the second is to follow a heuristic approach in which each account is examined in turn and related to plausible explanatory factors on an *ad hoc* basis without any general specification of equations, as has been done by Duffy and Renton. [3]

If the demand theory approach is followed, the quantity demanded by a country of a service (or of a good) would be a function of a budget constraint and the opportunity cost of the service. The budget constraint may take the form of an income variable, such as gross national product. The opportunity cost is reflected by relative prices. Where the quality of a service provided by non-residents is identical to that of a domestically produced service, a demand function will exist for the total quantity demanded and factors such as location and timeliness of the provision of the service will determine the relative market shares of imported and domestically produced services. An additional factor may be a budget constraint on the consumption of imported services operating through the availability of foreign exchange. Export receipts may serve as a measure of exchange availability. Where product differentiation exists, separate demand functions

[2] Driehuis, W., 'Experiments in Explaining and Forecasting the Invisible Trade of the Netherlands', *Bulletin of the Oxford University Institute of Economics and Statistics*, November 1969.

[3] Duffy, M.H. and G.A. Renton, 'Forecasting U.K. Transactions on Invisibles Account', *Bulletin of the Oxford University Institute of Economics and Statistics*, August 1970.

for imported and domestically produced services will be appropriate. In either case, the quantity of imported services will also be a function of a pressure of demand variable. Thus, a capacity measure or a utilisation rate may enter the function to indicate a diversion of demand from domestic to foreign sources as domestic capacity limits are approached.

Where the quantity demanded by a single country of a service supplied by non-residents is small relative to the total supply of the service, that country may be able to buy all it desires at the going world price. Thus, on the assumption that its demand does not affect the world price, the price of the service in foreign currency may be exogenous in that country's model.

Exports of services by a country may be viewed as a function of the factors that determine a country's share of the total world demand for a service. They are, therefore, simply the other side of the demand for imported services and in a complete system of country models can be determined by a "shares matrix" approach once the total quantity of imported services is determined. A country's share will depend on factors such as relative prices, utilisation rates and restrictions on the availability of the services to non-residents. An example of the latter may be the limited issue of visas by a country to tourists. Where a model is to be solved independently of other country models, a shares matrix approach is not feasible unless total world demand for imported services can be established or taken as exogenously determined. An alternative approach is to develop separate functions for a country's exports of services to each of the several regions or countries which are her markets.

Export supply price functions also need to be specified. If services supplied by various countries are perfect substitutes, a price will be established on the world market and a small country may be able to sell all it can produce of the service at the world price while it will not be able to sell any of the service at a higher price. There will be no reason to sell at a lower price. Thus the country is a price taker. Receipts will, of course, vary with changes in quantity sold and with changes in foreign exchange rates. Where product differentiation exists, a country may quote a supply price that is constant over a range of quantities supplied, but in this case the quantity demanded of its services on world markets will vary with the price it quotes. The supply price will be a function of domestic cost factors, particularly unit labour costs, utilisation rates and world prices of competing services. If quantity supplied enters explicitly into the supply price function, then we have a conventional supply function which has been normalised on price as the dependent variable.

Do these general principles of the demand for an imported service and its export supply price apply to the three categories of services we have distinguished above? In a very general way, the answer must be yes. But it must be qualified by the special characteristics of some of the service components and by data problems which limit disaggregation.

The development of separate demand functions for the various categories of services requires that volume (constant dollar) estimates be available. Since balance of international payments statistics are presented, as is natural, only in nominal (current) dollars, official estimates usually only exist if they are published as part of the national income statistics. In most countries only total services are available in constant dollars. If the model builder develops his own deflators, he encounters two problems: (a) the constant dollar components will not add to the published total so that a statistical discrepancy item becomes necessary and its value must be forecast, and (b) the deflators must be explained by equations in the model. Because of these problems, most countries which have disaggregated services in their models have done so in nominal dollars. A single equation is used to forecast a deflator which is then used to produce the forecast of total services in constant dollars. This approach of disaggregating in current and deflating the aggregate of services is followed by Canada (in both the TRACE and RDX2 models), Japan (in the Kyoto model) and the United Kingdom (the LBS model). Italy distinguishes two types of exports of services (transportation and other) in current dollars and deflates the aggregate. The United States (Wharton model) disaggregates imports of transportation and travel expenditures in constant dollars. All other models have single equations for total service imports and exports in constant dollars (except for Belgium where no disaggregation of exports into goods and services is made). The Netherlands, in implementing the demand theory approach of Driehuis' paper, confines its application to an aggregative equation.

For the five quarterly models surveyed (Canada's RDX2, the Italian model, the Japanese Kyoto model, the U.K. LBS model and the U.S. Wharton model), all but the U.S. model use dummy variables in the equation to capture the seasonal pattern where a seasonal pattern was found to exist. The U.S. model uses seasonally adjusted data.

In selecting the mathematical form of the equations, a choice is implicitly made between the hypothesis that price and income elasticities of demand are constant and the alternative that they are not. In the former case exponential functions are used (i.e., after linearisation variables are expressed as percentage rates of change or linear in logarithms); in the latter the functions are usually linear in the arithmetic values of the variables (i.e., constant "slopes"). For those models that develop structural equations for the demand for services (rather than making them simply a function of the demand for goods), only the Netherlands adopts the constant elasticity approach specifying the variables as percentage rates of change. [4]

3. Aggregate equations

The aggregate service equations used by Belgium (service imports), Germany, Italy (service imports), the Netherlands, Sweden and the U.S.A. (service exports) are given below. The equations are written in accordance with rules for a standard notation system adopted for Project LINK. All variables are in capital letters for ease of translation of variable names into FORTRAN. Expenditure and

---

[4] Rhomberg, R.R. and L. Boissonneault, 'Effects of Income and Price Changes on the U.S. Balance of Payments', *IMF Staff Papers*, March 1964, also use constant slopes in their study of income and price elasticities.

output items are understood to be measured in real terms (constant dollars). Income and financial variables are understood to be measured in nominal terms (current dollars). Where expenditure or output items are in nominal terms, the letter V is added at the end of the variable name. Mathematical operators are used in the usual way; LOG is understood to be natural logarithms and EXP (X) is the exponential function of X. A $\cdot$ indicates multiplication and $**$ indicates a variable is raised to the power following the $**$. The rate of change in a variable is designated as DOT (X) and is equal to $\Delta X/X_{-1}$ where $\Delta X = X - X_{-1}$.

Where it is necessary to designate the country or region to which a variable refers the country code is suffixed to the variable name. WT refers to world totals; WO refers to the rest of the world excluding the designated country to which a variable refers; US is the United States of America. Where no country suffix appears, the variable is for the country to which the equation applies.

In the equations reported below the values in parentheses under the coefficient values are t-values; s means the standard deviation of regression (standard error of estimate); R means the correlation coefficient; R^2 means the coefficient of determination adjusted for degrees of freedom; DW means the Durbin-Watson statistic; TSLS means two-stage least squares. Equations written in exponential forms were in fact estimated after a logarithmic transformation of the variables.

The variable definitions are:

C = Consumption expenditures.
$DSTAT$ = Dummy variable relating to change in statistical recording.
$DSTR$ = Dummy variable for dock strike.
$DSUEZ$ = Dummy variable for Suez.
MG = Imports of goods (merchandise).
MS = Imports of services.
MSO = Imports of services other than transportation and transfers abroad.
$PGNPNS$ = Price of total expenditure (gross national product less inventory changes and invisibles).
PMG = Price of imports of goods.

PMS	= Price of imports of services.
PXG	= Price of exports of goods (merchandise).
PXS	= Price of exports of services.
*Q*1	= Seasonal dummy variable for 1st quarter.
*Q*2	= Seasonal dummy variable for 2nd quarter.
*Q*3	= Seasonal dummy variable for 3rd quarter.
RHO	= Rate of capacity utilisation.
TGNM	= Total government, non-military, foreign assistance.
X	= Total exports.
XG	= Exports of goods (merchandise).
XS	= Exports of services.
XSF	= Exports of services: freight and shipping.

Belgium (index, 1953 = 100)

$$MSV = EXP\,(0.022)\cdot MGV_{**} \quad 0.729$$
$$(3.14) \qquad\qquad (19.0)$$

$$\bar{R}^2 = 0.960 \quad DW = 1.38$$

Germany (billions of 1962 Deutsche marks)

$$XS = 0.704\,XG_{**} \quad 0.749$$
$$\phantom{XS = 0.704\,XG_{**}}(20.2) \qquad\qquad\qquad \text{(TSLS)}$$

$$R = 0.998 \quad DW = 0.491$$

$$MS = 0.101\,MG_{**} \quad 1.242$$
$$\phantom{MS = 0.101\,MG_{**}}(7.96) \qquad\qquad\qquad \text{(TSLS)}$$

$$R = 0.984 \quad DW = 0.931$$

Italy (millions of lire)

$$MSOV = -16.082 + 0.304\,MGV + 2.909\,Q2 +$$
$$(7.053) \quad (17.352) \qquad (3.614)$$

$$+ 3.263\,Q3$$
$$(3.991)$$

$$\bar{R}^2 = 0.954 \quad s = 2.31 \quad DW = 2.21$$

Netherlands (percentage rate of change)[5]

$DOT(XS) =$ 0.55 + 0.78 DOT $(XSWT)$ +
                          (5.78)

        + 0.26 [DOT $(XSWT)$ − DOT $(XSWT)_{-1}$]
          (3.95)

        − 0.36 {[DOT (PXS) − DOT $(PXSWT)$] −
          (5.65)

        − [DOT $(PXS)_{-1}$ − DOT $(PXSWT)_{-1}$]}+

        + 4.16 DOT $(1 - RHO)$
          (3.19)

        $\bar{R}^2 = 0.91$ $DW = 1.58$

$DOT(MS) =$ 6.26 + 0.51 DOT (XSF) + 1.35 [DOT (C) −
              (5.26)   (6.54)

        − DOT $(C)_{-1}$] + 0.41 [DOT (XG) −
                    (2.61)

        − DOT $(XG)_{-1}$] −

        − 0.20 [DOT (PMS) − DOT $(PGNPNS)$] −
          (2.49)

        − [DOT $(PMS)_{-1}$ − DOT $(PGNPNS)_{-1}$] −

        − 7.27 DOT $(1 - RHO)$ − 5.74 $DSTAT$
        (5.62)   (2.16)

        $\bar{R}^2 = 0.90$ $DW = 2.63$

---

[5] These equations were originally written in an exponential form which, after linearisation, yielded equations in which the variables are formulated as percentage rates of change. The World Total (WT) designation in these equations refers to competing countries as defined by Driehuis, *op. cit.*, whereas the term DOT $(1 - RHO)$ in the equations refers to the first difference of a logarithmic transformation of the percentage rate of unemployment.

Sweden (millions of 1959 krona)

$$XS = 1456 + \underset{(3.02)}{0.0123} \, WTXG$$

$$R = 0.98 \quad DW = 1.27$$

$$MS = 716.3 + \underset{(8.58)}{0.0982} \, (C + X) - \underset{(0.26)}{1.044} \frac{PM}{PMWT}$$

$$R = 0.98 \quad DW = 1.61$$

United States (billions of 1958 dollars)[6]

$$X = - \underset{(0.7567)}{5.5531} + \underset{(3.129)}{0.0535} \, XGWO_{-1} +$$

$$+ \underset{(1.179)}{0.1919} \, TGNM +$$

$$+ \underset{(0.9102)}{5.6858} \frac{PGXWO}{PXG} - \underset{(5.2934)}{2.9977} \, DSTR +$$

$$+ \underset{(0.9027)}{0.7191} \, DSUEZ +$$

$$+ \underset{(9.5899)}{0.8194} \, \tfrac{1}{4} \sum_{i=0}^{3} X_{t-1-i} + u$$

$$\bar{R}^2 = 0.98 \quad s = 1.38$$

$u = 0.63 \, u_{-1} + e$ where u and e are error (disturbance) terms

$$\bar{R}^2 = 0.99 \quad s = 1.087 \quad DW = 1.60$$

$$XG = - \underset{(1.6312)}{9.6334} + \underset{(4.6989)}{0.0624} \, XGWO_{-1} +$$

---

[6] Exports and imports of services in the U.S. (Wharton) model are determined residually by subtracting total merchandise exports or imports from total exports or imports.

$$+ \; 0.1376 \; TGNM + 10.1372 \frac{PXGWO}{PXG} -$$
$$\quad (0.9941) \qquad\qquad (2.0327)$$

$$- \; 2.8216 \; DSTR + \; 0.8404 \; DSUEZ +$$
$$\quad (9.1677) \qquad\qquad (1.2633)$$

$$+ \; 0.6616 \, \tfrac{1}{4} \sum_{i \, = \, 0}^{3} \; XG_{t-1-i} + u$$
$$\quad (6.3215)$$

$\bar{R}^2 = 0.97 \quad s = 1.14$

$u \;\; = 0.60 \, u_{-1} + e \;\;$ where $\;\; u$ and e are error

(disturbance) terms

$\bar{R}^2 = 0.98 \quad s = 0.911 \quad DW = 1.76$

4. Disaggregated equations

Some countries disaggregate total services into various components:

4.1. Transportation and travel services

Transportation costs, as well as insurance, may be included in the value of merchandise imports and exports if trade values are recorded on a cost, insurance and freight (c.i.f.) basis. In this case transportation services will refer only to expenditures associated with moving people and with goods which do not enter into trade. If, on the other hand, trade is recorded on a free on board (f.o.b.) point of shipment basis, transportation costs associated with merchandise trade will be included in services along with other transportation expenditures. (Insurance, in this case, may be included in the "other service" category). Of the nine countries which have econometric models in Project LINK, four present merchandise imports on a c.i.f. basis while five (Belgium, Canada, Sweden, United Kingdom and U.S.A.) record them on an f.o.b. basis. For merchandise exports only Canada, Italy and Japan use an f.o.b.

basis. Where merchandise imports and exports are both recorded on an f.o.b. basis, a large component of transportation services relates directly to merchandise trade and is explained by the factors explaining trade. Hence transportation services imported or exported will be a function of the level of merchandise trade. Duffy and Renton [7] found that trade value indices performed better in their equations than trade volume indices. For the U.K. they found that the cost of freight is probably measured reasonably accurately by liner rates in the case of exports, and by some average of tramp and liner rates in the case of imports.

Transportation services not related to trade relate to the movement of people. Travel and other expenditures by tourists are a component of consumption expenditure and should be explained in the same way as any other component of aggregate consumption. Hence, they will be a function of total consumption expenditures or of income and the ratio of domestic to foreign prices. If transportation prices for international travel decline relative to domestic travel, the volume of international travel will increase and, therefore, service exports and imports will be affected. Business travel expenditures will vary with business conditions and may be a function of gross national product and, for annual models at least, a cyclical indicator such as unemployment or a utilisation ratio.

The disaggregated equations relating to freight and shipping and travel for Canada (both TRACE and RDX2 models [8]), Italy (exports), Japan, U.K. and U.S.A.(imports) are as follows:

The variable definitions are:

C = Consumption expenditure.

$CNDS$ = Consumption expenditures on non-durables and services.

CS = Consumption expenditures on services.

CSD = Inputed consumption expenditure on services from stock of autos and other durables.

---

[7] Duffy and Renton, *op. cit.*

[8] For a complete report on RDX2 see Helliwell, J.F., H.T. Shapiro, G.R. Sparks, I.A. Stewart, F.W. Gorbet and D.R. Stephenson, 'The Structure of RDX2', Bank of Canada Staff Research Studies, No.7, 1971.

DAUTO   = Dummy variable: Canada-U.S. Auto Agreement.
DCDSF   = Consumer durables seasonal adjustment factor.
DD   = Dummy variable: changes in duty-free allowances.
DDOCK   = Dummy variable: U.K. Dock Strike.
*DEX*67   = Dummy variable: Expo '67.
DEXCR   = Dummy variable: Foreign Exchange Restrictions.
DMECR   = Dummy variable: Middle East Crisis.
DSEA   = Dummy variable: St. Lawrence Seaway Opening.
DSSTK   = Dummy variable: Seamen's Strike.
FXSUK   = Price of U.K. pound (spot rate) in local currency.
FXSUS   = Price of U.S. dollar (spot rate) in local currency.

$$JNW(X) \;=\; \sum_{i=0}^{n-1} \alpha^i X_{t-i}$$

$$JV(X) \;=\; \sum_{i=0}^{7} \alpha X_{t-i}$$

$$JW(X) \;=\; \sum_{i=0}^{3} \alpha X_{t-i}$$

M   = Total imports.
MG   = Imports of goods.
MGA   = Imports of food and beverages.
MGB   = Imports of crude materials.
MGC   = Imports of energy fuels.
MGD   = Miscellaneous imports, including aircraft and parts.
MGE   = Imports of manufactures (excluding autos and aircraft).
MGM   = Imports of motor vehicles and parts.
MGNT   = Merchandise imports excluding transportation equipment.
MGO   = Other merchandise imports.
MSA   = Imports of services: civil aviation.
MSF   = Imports of services: freight and shipping.
MSOT   = Imports of services: other transportation.

MST	= Imports of services: tourist travel.
N	= Population.
NNI	= Total non-institutional population, 14 years of age and over.
PC	= Price of consumption expenditure.
PCNDS	= Price of consumption expenditure on non-durables and services.
PCS	= Price of consumer services.
PCSD	= Price of imputed durable services.
PGNP	= Price of gross national product.
PMGA	= Price of imports of food and beverages.
PMGB	= Price of imports of crude materials.
PMGC	= Price of imports of energy fuels.
PMGD	= Price of miscellaneous imports including aircraft and parts.
PMGE	= Price of imports of manufactures excluding autos and parts.
PMGM	= Price of imports of motor vehicles and parts.
PMGN	= Price of merchandise imports excluding autos and parts.
PMGO	= Price of other merchandise imports.
PROD	= Aggregate production.
PTL	= Tramp liner rate index.
PX	= Price of total exports.
PXGA	= Price of exports of aircraft and uranium.
PXGO	= Price of other merchandise exports.
PXGW	= Price of exports of wheat.
Q1	= Seasonal dummy variable for 1st quarter.
Q2	= Seasonal dummy variable for 2nd quarter.
Q3	= Seasonal dummy variable for 3rd quarter.
RPCDF	= Ratio of domestic to foreign consumption prices.
RXWT	= Ratio of exports to world trade.
SHIP	= Number of cargo ships.
TIME	= Time trend.
TRIND	= Trade level index.
X	= Total exports.
XG	= Exports of merchandise.

XGA = Exports of aircraft and uranium.
XGO = Other merchandise exports.
XGW = Exports of wheat.
XSA = Exports of services: civil aviation.
XSF = Exports of services: freight and shipping.
$XSOT$ = Service exports of other transportation.
XST = Service exports of tourist travel.
YPD = Personal disposable income.

Canada: TRACE model (billions of current dollars)

$$XSFV = 0.1148 + 0.0904\,XSTV + 0.0544\,XGV$$
$$\ (6.12)\quad (1.30)\qquad\qquad (7.79)$$

$$\bar{R}^2 = 0.978\quad s = 0.027\quad DW = 0.85$$

$$XSTV = 0.0619 + 0.0028 \cdot (CNDSUS \cdot PCNDUS \cdot FXSUS)$$
$$\ (0.20)\quad (6.33)$$

$$-\ 0.379\,PCNDS + 0.4244\,DEX67$$
$$\ (0.86)\qquad\qquad (14.98)$$

$$\bar{R}^2 = 0.992\quad s = 0.025\quad DW = 0.98$$

$$MSFV = 0.0701 + 0.3395\,MSTV + 0.0467\,MGV$$
$$\ (2.17)\quad (2.13)\qquad\qquad (4.51)$$

$$\bar{R}^2 = 0.972\quad s = 0.03\quad DW = 1.24$$

$$MSTV = 0.3753 + 0.0382\,CNDSV -$$
$$\ (2.63)\quad (8.29)$$

$$-\ 0.5786\,PCNDSUS \cdot FXSUS - 0.0635\,DEX67$$
$$\ (2.56)\qquad\qquad\qquad (1.83)$$

$$\bar{R}^2 = 0.973\quad s = 0.03\quad DW = 1.79$$

Canada: RDX2 model (millions of current dollars)[9]

$$XSFUSV^{10} = 5.0845 - 0.0762\,Q1\,[Z] - 0.0089\,Q2\,[Z] +$$
$$\phantom{XSFUSV^{10} =}\ (1.29)\quad (5.76)\qquad\qquad (0.62)$$

---

[9] In RDX2 the seasonal dummies are defined as the difference between the designated quarter and the fourth quarter.

$$+ \ 0.0799 \ Q3 \ [Z] + \ \ 0.0678 \ XGUSV -$$
$$(6.48) \qquad\qquad (11.90)$$

$$- \ 0.005 \ DAUTO \cdot XGUSV -$$
$$(5.73)$$

$$- \ 0.0025 \ DSEA \cdot XGUSV$$
$$(1.16)$$

$$\bar{R}^2 = 0.971 \quad s = 3.97 \quad DW = 1.39$$

where $Z = (XSFUS)_{-1}$

$$\frac{X\dot{S}TUSV}{NUS} = - \ 0.6359 - \ \ 0.9962 \ Q1 \ [Z] -$$
$$\qquad\qquad (1.73) \qquad (22.51)$$

$$- \ 0.2366 \ Q2 \ [Z] + \ \ 1.4314 \ Q3 \ [Z] +$$
$$(4.53) \qquad\qquad (46.55)$$

$$+ \ JV(FXSUS) + JV \ \{[CUS/DCDSF \cdot NUS]$$
$$FXSUS\} + \ 0.3878 \ DEX67$$
$$\qquad\qquad (7.47)$$

$$\bar{R}^2 = 0.985 \quad s = 0.078 \quad DW = 2.33$$

where $Z = (XSTUSV/NUS)_{-1}$

$$XSFWOV = \ 3.7224 - \ \ 0.0253 \ Q1 \ [Z] +$$
$$\qquad\quad (1.0) \qquad\quad (0.94)$$

$$+ \ 0.0172 \ Q2 \ [Z] + \ 0.0006 \ Q3 \ [Z] +$$
$$(0.58) \qquad\qquad (0.03)$$

$$+ \ 0.0739 \ XGMOV + \ 0.0264 \ (XGWOV)_{-1} -$$
$$(5.56) \qquad\qquad (2.34)$$

$$- \ 0.0118 \ DSEA \cdot XGWOV$$
$$(2.58)$$

$$\bar{R}^2 = 0.930 \quad s = 5.42 \quad DW = 0.69$$

[10] Note that in these equations the country of destination, *US* or *WO* (rest of world), appears as a suffix to the variable name, but prior to the final suffix *V* which denotes nominal values.

where $Z = (XSFWOV)_{-1}$ and $XGWOV =$

$(XGWWO)(PXGWWO) + (XGAWO)(PXGAWO) +$

$+ (XGOWO)(PX)$

$XSTWOV = - \quad 6.2606 - \quad 0.8311\ Q1\ [Z] +$
$\qquad\qquad (4.39) \qquad (11.31)$

$\qquad + \quad 0.4427\ Q2\ [Z] + \quad 0.6278\ Q3\ [Z] +$
$\qquad (5.17) \qquad\qquad\quad (14.34)$

$\qquad + JV[FXSUS(0.001\ WOMUSCA)],\ ^{11} +$

$\qquad + 16.764\ DEX67$
$\qquad\quad (7.24)$

$\bar{R}^2 = 0.937 \quad s = 3.48 \quad DW = 2.08$

where $Z = (XSTWOV)_{-1}$

$MSFUSV = 42.552 - \quad 0.1866\ Q1\ [Z] +$
$\qquad\qquad (2.76) \quad (18.98)$

$\qquad + \quad 0.0063\ Q2\ [Z] + 0.126\ Q3\ [Z] +$
$\qquad (0.36) \qquad\qquad (6.8)$

$\qquad + \quad 0.5979\ MGUSV + 0.0098\ (MGUSV)_{-1} -$
$\qquad (6.55) \qquad\qquad (1.18)$

$\qquad - \quad 0.0043\ DAUTO{\cdot}MGUS + JW\ (FXSUS)$
$\qquad (5.73)$

$\bar{R}^2 = 0.979 \quad s = 3.84 \quad DW = 1.40$

where $Z = (MSFUSV)_{-1}$ and $MGUSV =$

$(MGAUS)(PMAUS) + (MGCUS)(PMCUS) +$

$+ (MGBUS)(PMGBUS) + (MGEUS)(PGEUS) +$

$+ (MGMUS)(PMGMUS) + (MGDUS)(PMGDUS)$

---

[11] *WOMUSCA* refers to total world imports excluding those to the United States and Canada.

$$\frac{MSTUSV}{NNI} = 15.554 - \underset{(5.25)}{0.1863} Q1 [Z] + \underset{(7.25)}{0.12} Q2 [Z] +$$

$$+ \underset{(14.94)}{0.2842} Q3 [Z] + \underset{(8.84)}{0.0378}$$

$$(PCS{\cdot}CS + PCSD{\cdot}CSD)/NNI -$$

$$- \underset{(2.67)}{0.9882} (DDUS + DDWO) + JW(FXSUS)$$

$$\bar{R}^2 = 0.896 \quad s = 0.86 \quad DW = 1.82$$

where $Z = (MSTUSV/NNI)_{-1}$

$$MSFWOV = -41.67 + \underset{(2.87)}{0.0565} Q1 [Z] - \underset{(3.41)}{0.0349} Q2 [Z] -$$

$$- \underset{(0.59)}{0.0081} Q3 [Z] + \underset{(14.62)}{0.082} MGWOV +$$

$$+ \underset{(6.35)}{9.4116} DSEA + JW(FXSUS)$$

$$\bar{R}^2 = 0.963 \quad s = 3.6 \quad DW = 0.998$$

where $Z = (MSFWOV)_{-1}$ and $MGWOV =$

$$MGNTWO{\cdot}PMGNWO + MGMWO{\cdot}PMGMWO +$$
$$+ MGOWO{\cdot}PMGOWO$$

$$\frac{MSTWOV}{NNI} = -3.3385 - \underset{(2.62)}{0.3456} Q1 [Z] - \underset{(12.42)}{0.0835} Q2 [Z] +$$

$$+ \underset{(24.51)}{0.5818} Q3 [Z] + \underset{(9.14)}{0.0175}$$

$$(PCS{\cdot}CS + PCSD{\cdot}CSD)/NNI - \underset{(2.65)}{0.6401} DEX67 +$$

$$+ \underset{(2.23)}{0.3584} (DDUS + DDWO) + JW(FXSUS)$$

$$\bar{R}^2 = 0.952 \quad s = 0.37 \quad DW = 1.92$$

where $Z = (MSTWOV/NNI)_{-1}$

Italy (millions of lire)

$$XSFV = -1.634 + 0.049\,TRINDWT +$$
$$(2.896) \quad (10.902)$$

$$+ 2.371\,RXWT + 0.29\,Q2 + 0.502\,Q3$$
$$(3.358) \qquad\quad (2.13) \qquad (3.921)$$

$$\bar{R}^2 = 0.946 \quad s = 0.354 \quad DW = 1.76$$

Japan (billions of yen)

$$XSFV = 12.065 + 0.3403\frac{SHIP}{SHIPWT} \cdot XGV +$$
$$(37.8) \qquad (72.4)$$

$$+ 0.0094\,Q3$$
$$(2.19)$$

$$\bar{R}^2 = 0.992 \quad s = 1.228 \quad DW = 1.743$$

$$XSOTV = -14.001 + 0.0225.(XGV + MGV) +$$
$$(4.54) \qquad (2.50)$$

$$+ 10.875\,PTLWT$$
$$(2.49)$$

$$\bar{R}^2 = 0.973 \quad s = 2.17 \quad DW = 0.83$$

$$MSOTV = -1.707 + 0.02955.(XGV + MGV) +$$
$$(0.51) \qquad (30.8)$$

$$+ 9.5019\,PTLWT$$
$$(2.01)$$

$$\bar{R}^2 = 0.981 \quad s = 2.344 \quad DW = 1.363$$

United Kingdom (millions of pounds sterling)

$$XSFV = 59.514 + 67.6843\frac{XWT.PXWT}{FXSUK} +$$
$$(4.64) \quad (2.57)$$

$$+ \ 1.9652 \ TIME, \ {}^{12} \ - \ 19.694 \ DSSTK$$
$$(3.24) \qquad\qquad (2.8)$$

$$\bar{R}^2 = 0.914 \quad s = 9.54 \quad DW = 0.77$$

$$XSAV \ = \ - \ 18.674 + \ 0.0416 \ XGV + \ 0.1783 \ XSTV +$$
$$(5.64) \quad (6.82) \qquad\quad (1.99)$$

$$+ \ 10.5137 \ DDOCK$$
$$(4.11)$$

$$\bar{R}^2 = 0.978 \quad s = 2.175 \quad DW = 1.496$$

$$XSTV \ = \ 327.091 \ - \ 384.666 \ [0.1 \ JNW(0.9 \ RPCDF)], \ {}^{13} +$$
$$(8.82) \qquad (11.3)$$

$$+ \quad 0.9906 \ PRODWO$$
$$(20.9)$$

$$\bar{R}^2 = 0.998 \quad s = 2.865 \quad DW = 1.406$$

$$MSFV \ = \quad 65.171 + \quad 0.0921 \ MGV - \quad 9.0947 \ DSSTK +$$
$$(13.0) \qquad (27.1) \qquad\qquad (1.78)$$

$$+ \ 21.7208 \ DMECR$$
$$(4.31)$$

$$\bar{R}^2 = 0.963 \quad s = 4.95 \quad DW = 1.33$$

$$MSAV \ = \ - \ 38.794 + \quad 0.0425 \ MGV + \ 0.2772 \ MSTV +$$
$$(9.3) \qquad (14.7) \qquad\qquad (3.33)$$

$$+ \quad 4.2751 \ DDOCK$$
$$(1.41)$$

$$\bar{R}^2 = 0.955 \quad s = 2.935 \quad DW = 0.991$$

$$MSTV \ = \quad 7.102 + \quad 0.0129 \ YPD - \quad 13.1927 \ DEXCR$$
$$(1.5) \qquad (16.1) \qquad\qquad (10.1)$$

$$\bar{R}^2 = 0.908 \quad s = 2.886 \quad DW = 1.683$$

---

[12] $\Delta TIME = 1$ with origin at 55 : 1.

[13] Countries included are Belgium, France, Ireland, Italy, Netherlands, Canada and U.S.A.

United States (billions of 1958 dollars)

$$MSF = -1.23 + 0.0245\,(MG + XG) -$$
$$(5.22) \quad (6.9655)$$

$$- 0.0765 \frac{PTLNO}{PGNP},\ ^{14} + u$$
$$(1.3573)$$

$\bar{R}^2 = 0.74 \quad s = 0.29$

$u = 0.94\,u_{-1} + e$ where u and e are error (disturbance) terms

$\bar{R}^2 = 0.98 \quad s = 0.082 \quad DW = 2.66$

$$MST = -0.8518 + 0.0072\,(YPD)_{-1} -$$
$$(1.292) \quad (17.3066)$$

$$- 0.0125 \frac{PCWO}{PC},\ ^{15} + u$$
$$(0.017)$$

$\bar{R}^2 = 0.95 \quad s = 0.14$

$u = 0.48\,u_{-1} + e$ where u and e are error (disturbance) terms

$\bar{R}^2 = 0.96 \quad s = 0.123 \quad DW = 2.02$

4.2. Investment income

Investment income paid abroad, usually in the form of interest and dividends, is part of the return on capital owned by non-residents which is used in the production of goods and services in a country. Hence, it is part of the adjustment in moving from domestic product to national product. It is also, of course, a component of a country's balance of international payments. (Labour income paid to workers who live in one country and work in another should also be given similar treatment to investment income but is usually insignificant in amount).

[14] Norwegian freight rates.
[15] Countries visited by U.S. residents.

Investment income, in contrast to the other service components, is an income item rather than an expenditure on a service. It represents the share of non-residents in the investment income component of a country's national income. One would expect dividends paid abroad to be a function of total dividends paid by business firms in a country and the proportion of its industry which is foreign owned. Interest paid abroad would be related to the proportion of foreign indebtedness, the term to maturity of the debt and the relevant interest rate for that term. Thus, higher interest rates will increase the amount of interest paid abroad on new indebtedness, and tend to partially offset the positive effect on a country's balance of payments of higher domestic interest rates.

The models for Canada (TRACE and RDX2), Japan, U.K. and U.S. (imports) have disaggregated equations for investment income as follows:

The variable definitions are:

CCAB　　= Capital consumption allowances of businesses.
CP　　　= Private claims including retained earnings.
DDEVL　= Dummy variable for U.K. devaluation of the pound.
DXDIV　= Dummy variable.
ECTY　　= Direct taxes of corporations and government business enterprises.
FCBN　　= Trade on outstanding corporate bonds, net sales abroad.
FDILUS　= Direct investment in Canada from U.S.
FDILWO = Direct investment in Canada from other foreign countries.
FDISUSV= U.S. direct investment in Canada, including retained earnings, revalued as shown below, where

$$FDISUSV = \frac{PKB}{(PKB)_{-1}} [(FDISUSV)_{-1}] + FDILUS + SUS.$$

FDPIWOV=Other countries direct and portfolio investment in shares and bonds of Canadian companies, at replacement value, where

$$FDPIWOV = \frac{PKB}{(PKB)_{-1}} \ [(FDPIWOV)_{-1}] + FDILWO +$$

$$+ \ FLCBL + SCWO.$$

FGBN = Trade on outstanding government bonds, net sales abroad.

FLCBL = Sales of Canadian corporate bonds and shares in other countries. Gross new issues, less retirements, plus net trade in outstanding bonds and shares.

FLSLUS = U.S. portfolio holdings of Canadian shares, revalued as shown below, where

$$FLSLUS = [\frac{PKB}{(PKB)_{-1}} + \frac{SRC}{KVB}] \ (FLSLUS)_{-1}.$$

FXSUS = Foreign exchange rate – "per U.S. dollar".

GFX   = Foreign exchange (and gold) reserves.

$$JNA(X) = \frac{1}{n} \sum_{i=0}^{n-1} X_{t-i}$$

$$JNS(X) = \sum_{i=0}^{n-1} X_{t-i}$$

KBV   = Market value of end-of-quarter stock of total business fixed capital and inventories.

KDIL = Value of stock of foreign direct investment.

KFB   = Net stock of business fixed assets and inventories valued at replacement cost.

KHNW = Household net wealth.

KIB   = Stock of non-farm business inventories.

KLA   = Long-term assets abroad.

KLL   = Long-term liabilities abroad.

KME   = Stock of machinery and equipment.

KNRC = Stock of non-residential construction.

KPME = Stock of private, non-farm machinery and equipment.

KPNRC = Stock of private, non-farm, non-residential construction.

KSIL	= Stock of domestic, interest-bearing liabilities.
MG	= Imports of goods and services.
PKB	$= \dfrac{(PKIB)(KIB) + (PNRC)(KNRC) + (PME)(KME)}{KIB + KNRC + KME}$
PKIB	= Price of the non-farm business inventory stock.
PME	= Price deflator for business investment in machinery and equipment.
PNRC	= Price deflator for business investment in non-residential construction.
PPE	= Price of investment in plant and equipment.
PROD	= Aggregate production.
*Q*1	= Seasonal dummy variable for 1st quarter.
*Q*2	= Seasonal dummy variable for 2nd quarter.
*Q*3	= Seasonal dummy variable for 3rd quarter.
*Q*4	= Seasonal dummy variable for 4th quarter.
RCBL	= Long-term interest rate on corporate bonds.
RGBL	= Long-term interest rate on government bonds.
SCBTA	= Corporate profits before tax, adjusted for inventory valuation.
SCGBT	= Corporate profits before tax.
SCL	= Domestic corporate bonds owned abroad.
SCN	= Gross new issues of corporate bonds.
SCR	= Retained corporate profits.
SCUS	= Canadian retained earnings of U.S. residents.
SCWO	= Canadian retained earnings of residents of other countries.
SGCL	= Domestic government bonds owned abroad.
SGL	= Government of Canada, provincial and municipal bonds, direct and guaranteed, held by residents of other foreign countries.
SGLN	= New issues of Federal Government bonds.
SGPN	= Gross new issues of provincial and municipal bonds.
TIMEB	= Dummy variable for post-war shift.
YCD	= Corporate dividend payments.
YCDL	= Dividends paid abroad.
YCTP	= Gross trading profits.

YI   = Interest income.
YIDA   = Interest and dividends (profits) received from abroad.
YIDL   = Interest and dividends (profits) paid abroad.
YIL   = Interest paid abroad.

Canada: TRACE model (billions of dollars)

$$YIDA = -\ 0.0603 + \ 0.025\ YCDUS$$
$$\quad\quad\quad (2.44)\quad\ (15.78)$$

$$\bar{R}^2 = 0.943\quad s = 0.028\quad DW = 1.77\ .$$

$$YIDL = \ 0.176 + 0.0332\ RGBL + 0.2088\ YCD +$$
$$\quad\quad\ (2.11)\quad (2.12)\quad\quad\quad (1.84)$$

$$+\ 0.0215\ YCD{\cdot}TIMEB$$
$$(5.01)$$

$$\bar{R}^2 = 0.994\quad s = 0.035\quad DW = 1.29$$

Canada: RDX2 model (millions of dollars)

$$YIDAUS/[(YIUS + YCDUS)FXSUS]$$

$$=\ \ 0.9983\ Q1\ [Z] +\ \ 0.9837\ Q2\ [Z] +$$
$$(18.11)\quad\quad\quad\quad (17.75)$$

$$+\ \ 0.983\ Q3\ [Z] +\ \ 1.3116\ Q4\ [Z]$$
$$\ (17.66)\quad\quad\quad\ (23.68)$$

$$\bar{R}^2 = 0.267\quad s = 0.244\quad DW = 1.09$$

where $Z = 1{,}000\ CPUS/[FXSUS(1{,}000{,}000$
$$KHNWUS) + CPUS]$$

$$YCDLUS = \ 0.0378\ [Z] -\ 0.0043\ Q1\ [Z] -$$
$$(5.49)\quad\quad\quad (2.29)$$

$$-\ 0.005\ Q3\ [Z] +\ 0.2432\ (YCDLUS)_{-1}$$
$$(2.6)\quad\quad\quad\ (1.68)$$

$$\bar{R}^2 = 0.853\quad s = 16.33\quad DW = 1.82$$

where

$$Z = J4S \left[\frac{FLSLUS + FDISUSV}{KFB} (SCGBT + CCAB - \right.$$

$$\left. - ECTY)\right]$$

$YIDLWO =$ $0.1924 \, [Z] + \, 0.0303 \, Q1 \, [Z] -$
(45.8)   (4.08)

   $- \, 0.0341 \, Q2 \, [Z] - \, 0.0104 \, Q3 \, [Z]$
   (4.67)   (1.43)

$\bar{R}^2 = 0.596 \quad s = 5.38 \quad DW = 1.28$

where

$Z = [0.241 \, J2OA \, (0.01 \, RGBL) + 0.013]$

$[FDPIWOV + \text{SGL}]$

$YIDAWO =$ $0.2844 \, [Z] - \, 0.0831 \, Q1 \, [Z] - \, 0.0016 \, Q2 \, [Z] -$
(20.48)   (3.39)   (0.07)

   $- \, 0.0821 \, Q3 \, [Z] + 54.629 \, DXDIV$
   (3.46)   (6.72)

$\bar{R}^2 = 0.759 \quad s = 7.76 \quad DW = 2.06$

where

$Z = [0.3042 \, J2OA \, (0.01 \, RGBLUK) + 0.0378]$

$CPWO$

$YILUS \quad =$ $0.259 \, [Z] - \, 0.0286 \, Q1 \, [Z] +$
(102.20)   (6.29)

   $+ \, 0.0363 \, Q2 \, [Z] - \, 0.0355 \, Q3 \, [Z]$
   (8.2)   (8.18)

$\bar{R}^2 = 0.972 \quad s = 5.12 \quad DW = 1.14$

where

$$Z = [0.757 \, \frac{\{J2OS[(KSNUS)(0.01 \, RCBLUS/FXSUS)]\} FXSUS}{J2OS \, (KSNUS)}$$

$$+ 0.243 \, \frac{[J2OS \, (KSNUS)(0.01 \, RGBL)]}{J2OS \, (KSNUS)} \,]$$

$$[SGCLUS + SCLUS] \quad \text{and}$$

$$KSNUS = SGLNUS + SGPNUS + SCNUS +$$

$$+ \, FGBNUS + FCBNUS$$

Japan (billions of yen)

$$YIDA \quad = - \; 0.231 + \; 0.0032 \, GFX_{-1} + \; 0.0058 \, KLA_{-1} -$$
$$\quad\quad\quad (0.18) \quad (4.0) \quad\quad\quad\quad\quad (19.3)$$

$$- \; 0.0208 \, Q2 - \; 0.0083 \, Q3 - \; 0.0316 \, Q4$$
$$\quad (2.73) \quad\quad\quad (1.15) \quad\quad\quad (4.39)$$

$$\bar{R}^2 = 0.968 \quad s = 1.681 \quad DW = 1.65$$

$$YIDL \quad = - \; 13.786 + \; 0.0338 \, MGV + 0.0074 \, KLL_{-1}$$
$$\quad\quad\quad (11.3) \quad\quad (8.24)$$

$$\bar{R}^2 = 0.967 \quad s = 2.897 \quad DW = 1.89$$

United Kingdom (millions of pounds sterling)

$$YIDA \quad = 47.2636 + \; 1.6201 \, PRODID, ^{16} + 31.4603 \, DDEVL$$
$$\quad\quad\quad (0.98) \quad\quad (3.8) \quad\quad\quad\quad\quad\quad (2.55)$$

$$\bar{R}^2 = 0.788 \quad s = 17.515 \, DW = 1.64$$

$$YIDL \quad = - \; 114.454 + \; 0.0304 \, YCTP + \; 0.0519 \, KDIL +$$
$$\quad\quad\quad (4.58) \quad\quad (1.27) \quad\quad\quad (8.65)$$

$$+ \; 0.0175 \, KSIL$$
$$\quad (3.5)$$

$$\bar{R}^2 = 0.947 \quad s = 8.512 \quad DW = 1.36$$

---

[16] *ID* – Industrial countries, i.e., France, Germany, U.S.A., Canada, Australia, South Africa and India.

United States (billions of dollars)

$$YIDL \quad = - \quad \underset{(0.727)}{0.446} \quad + 0.2386\, RGBL_{-1} \; +$$

$$+ \quad \underset{(0.0279)}{0.0012} \quad \frac{SCBTA \cdot 10^4}{PPE\,(KPME + KPNRC)} \; +$$

$$+ \quad \underset{(3.375)}{0.5061}\, J4A\,(YIDL)_{-1} \; + u$$

$\bar{R}^2 = 0.870 \quad s = 0.379$

$u \;\; = 0.93\, u_{-1} + e$ where u and e are error (disturbance) terms

$\bar{R}^2 = 0.98 \quad s = 0.137 \quad DW = 1.13$

4.3. Other services

Other services include receipts and payments for items such as professional services, film rentals, communications, fees and royalties, international advertising expenditures and other net foreign transactions of various companies (excluding merchandise trade). These may be related to the general level of economic activity in the country and in the world.

The disaggregated equations for other services for Canada (TRACE), Italy (exports), Japan (imports) and U.K. are as follows:

The variable definitions are:

$DDEVL$ = Dummy variable for U.K. devaluation of the pound.
$FXSUK$ = Foreign exchange rate – "per U.K. pound".
GNP = Gross national product.

$$JNW(X) \quad = \sum_{i\,=\,0}^{n-1} \alpha^i X_{t-i}$$

MSO = Other service imports.
$PCNDS$ = Price of consumption expenditure on non-durables and services.
$PMSS$ = Price of sub-total of service imports.

PX	= Price of total exports.
PXSS	= Price of sub-total of service exports.
*Q*1	= Seasonal dummy variable for 1st quarter.
*Q*2	= Seasonal dummy variable for 2nd quarter.
*Q*3	= Seasonal dummy variable for 3rd quarter.
RHOBN	= Utilisation ratio for business non-agriculture.
RHOM	= Manufacturing capacity utilisation.
RXWT	= Ratio of exports to world trade.
TIME	= Time trend.
TRIND	= Trade level index.
WRBN	= Wage rate in business non-agriculture.
X	= Total exports.
XG	= Exports of goods.
XSO	= Other service exports.
XSTO	= Exports of other services and tourist travel.

Canada: TRACE model (billions of dollars)

$$XSORV = -1.0721 + 0.0185\,TIME + 0.0092\,RHOMUS$$
$$\quad\quad\quad (6.12)\quad\quad (8.15)\quad\quad\quad\quad (4.51)$$

$$\bar{R}^2 = 0.883 \quad s = 0.04 \quad DW = 1.48$$

$$MSOV = 0.0127 + 1.1136\,MSOV_{-1}$$
$$\quad\quad (0.26)\quad\quad (13.08)$$

$$\bar{R}^2 = 0.919 \quad s = 0.062 \quad DW = 2.03$$

Italy (millions of lire)

$$XSTOV = 16.74 + 0.765\,TRINDWT - 67.936\,RXWT -$$
$$\quad\quad\quad (1.44)\quad (8.679)\quad\quad\quad\quad (3.632)$$

$$- 5.81\,Q1 + 17.105\,Q3 + 0.368\,XSTOV_{-1}$$
$$(1.83)\quad\quad (5.554)\quad\quad (3.591)$$

$$\bar{R}^2 = 0.865 \quad s = 7.266 \quad DW = 1.94$$

Japan (billions of yen)

$$MSOV = -\ 1.111 + \underset{(50.5)}{0.0101}\ GNPV - \underset{(2.07)}{0.044}\ Q2 -$$
$$\underset{(0.51)}{}$$

$$-\ \underset{(1.75)}{0.0372}\ Q3 - \underset{(11.9)}{0.2569}\ Q4$$

$$\bar{R}^2 = 0.977 \quad s = 4.972 \quad DW = 2.273$$

United Kingdom (millions of pound sterling)

$$XSOV = -\ 26.53 + \underset{(16.7)}{301.1329}$$
$$\underset{(2.3)}{}$$

$$[(0.1)\,JNW\,(0.9\,\frac{XWT \cdot PXWT}{FXSUS})] + 24.817\ DDEVL$$

$$\bar{R}^2 = 0.986 \quad s = 5.281 \quad DW = 0.354$$

$$MSOV = -\ 1.079 + \underset{(12.9)}{0.0686}\ [(0.3)\,JNW\,(0.7\ XGV)] +$$
$$\underset{(0.17)}{}$$

$$+\ \underset{(4.23)}{10.8941}\ DDEVL$$

$$\bar{R}^2 = 0.973 \quad s = 3.421 \quad DW = 1.358$$

5. Transfer payments

In the models surveyed for this paper, transfer payments are either included with other services or treated as an exogenous variable or as a function of time.

6. Price equations

Because of the problems of obtaining constant dollar estimates of the components of invisibles referred to earlier, most countries which have disaggregated services in their models have done so in

current dollars. In some cases, a single equation is used to forecast
a deflator which is used to produce the forecast of total services in
constant dollars. This approach of disaggregating in current dollars
and deflating an aggregate of services is illustrated by Canada's
TRACE model. In the Canadian TRACE model, following closely
the Canadian National Accounts procedure, investment income
received from abroad is deflated by the implicit price index of
imports of goods and services and income paid abroad is deflated
by the export price index. A deflator is developed in the model for
the aggregate of the other three components of service imports
and exports. If service price deflators are not available endogenously, they may be taken as exogenous (Canada's RDX2 model),
approximated by goods and services price deflators (Japan's Kyoto
model) or eliminated by aggregating goods and services at current
prices before deflating (United Kingdom LBS model).

The price equations used as deflators for service exports or
imports by Canada (TRACE), Germany, Japan (exports,), the
Netherlands and the United Kingdom are as follows:

The variable definitions are:

DDEVL = Dummy variable for U.K. devaluation of the pound.
FXSUS = Foreign exchange rate − "per U.S. dollar".
GDP = Gross domestic product.
GDPT = Trend value of gross domestic product.
PC = Price of consumption expenditure.
PCNDS = Price of consumption expenditure on non-durables and services.
PGDP = Price of gross domestic product.
PM = Price of imports.
PMM = Price of merchandise imports.
PMS = Price of service imports.
PMSS = Price of sub-total of service imports.
PSF = Price of freight and shipping service.
PWH = Wholesale prices.
PX = Price of total exports.
PXM = Price of merchandise exports.
PXS = Price of service exports.
PXSS = Price of sub-total of service exports.

$Q1$ = Seasonal dummy variable for 1st quarter.
$Q2$ = Seasonal dummy variable for 2nd quarter.
$Q3$ = Seasonal dummy variable for 3rd quarter.
QTIME = Dummy variable for time trend.
RHO = Rate of capacity utilisation.
RHOBN = Utilisation ratio for business non-agriculture.
TIME = Time trend.
WRB = Wage rate in the private sector.
WRBN = Wage rate in business non-agriculture.
X = Total exports.

Canada: TRACE model (1961 = 1.0)

$$PXSS = -\ 0.0356 + \underset{(82.58)}{0.3517}\ WRBN + \underset{(4.46)}{0.3748}\ RHOBN$$
$$\underset{(0.42)}{}$$

$$\bar{R}^2 = 0.998 \quad s = 0.008 \quad DW = 1.25$$

$$PMSS = -\ 0.3388 + \underset{(16.33)}{1.2854}\ PCNDSUS$$
$$\underset{(4.11)}{}$$

$$\bar{R}^2 = 0.947 \quad s = 0.027 \quad DW = 1.37$$

Germany (1962 = 1.0)

$$PXM = 0.943 + \underset{(0.192)}{0.174}\ RHO{\cdot}WRB$$

$$\bar{R}^2 = 0.532 \quad DW = 0.715$$

$$PMS = 0.972 + \underset{(6.24)}{0.306}\ TIME$$

$$R = 0.975 \quad DW = 0.795$$

Japan (1957–59 = 1.0)

$$PX = \underset{(0.99)}{0.0427} + \underset{(2.72)}{0.2413}\ PWH + \underset{(7.07)}{0.7168}\ PX -$$

$$-\ \underset{(2.71)}{0.0001}\ Q2$$

$$\bar{R}^2 = 0.922 \quad s = 0.008 \quad DW = 1.273$$

Netherlands [17]

$$\text{DOT}(PXS) = -0.46 + 0.42 \ \text{DOT}(PSFWT) +$$
$$(11.0)$$

$$+ 0.52 \ \text{DOT}(PXG) + 0.23 \ \text{DOT}(PC)$$
$$(4.35) \qquad\qquad (1.41)$$

$$\bar{R}^2 = 0.99 \quad DW = 2.58$$

$$\text{DOT}(PMS) = -0.15 + 1.05 \ \text{DOT}(PMG)$$

$$\bar{R}^2 = 0.99 \quad DW = 3.02$$

United Kingdom (1963 = 1.0)

$$PMG \quad = EXP\,(-\ 0.7666 + 0.0027\,Q1 - 0.0042\,Q2 -$$
$$(2.15) \qquad (0.38) \qquad\quad (0.54)$$

$$-\ 0.0067\,Q3 - 0.0007\ TIME +$$
$$(0.89) \qquad\quad (0.47)$$

$$+\quad 0.1084\ DDEVL) \cdot XWT_{**}\,0.1632$$
$$(11.1) \qquad\qquad\qquad\qquad (1.97)$$

$$\bar{R}^2 = 0.93 \quad s = 0.017 \quad DW = 0.5$$

$$PM \quad\quad = EXP\,(-\ 0.8218 + 0.0076\,Q1 - 0.008\,Q2 -$$
$$(3.24) \qquad (1.46) \qquad\quad (1.44)$$

$$-\ 0.001\,Q3 - 0.00005\ TIME +$$
$$(0.21) \qquad\quad (0.05)$$

$$+\quad 0.0986\ DDEVL) \cdot XWT_{**}\,0.1696$$
$$(14.1) \qquad\qquad\qquad\qquad (2.87)$$

$$\bar{R}^2 = 0.969 \quad s = 0.0123 \quad DW = 1.0$$

---

[17] These equations were originally written in an exponential form which, after linearisation, yielded equations in which the variables are formulated as percentage rates of change, Driehuis, *op. cit.*

PXM $= -$ $0.1731 +$ $0.9966\ PGDP +$ $0.268\ (GDP - GDPT) -$
        (0.91)   (7.4)   (2.23)

        $-$ $0.0026\ QTIME -$ $0.0035\ Q1 -$ $0.0053\ Q2 -$
        (2.6)   (0.9)   (1.36)

        $-$ $0.0038\ Q3 +$ $0.0687\ DDEVL$
        (1.0)   (12.1)

$\bar{R}^2 = 0.99$ $s = 0.009$ $DW = 1.5$

PX $=$ $0.2512 +$ $0.842\ PGDP -$ $0.0026\ TIME -$
       (3.44)   (8.75)   (3.71)

        $-$ $0.0043\ Q1 -$ $0.0043\ Q2 -$ $0.0025\ Q3 +$
        (1.34)   (1.39)   (0.81)

        $+$ $0.0776\ DDEVL$
        (16.5)

$\bar{R}^2 = 0.99$ $s = 0.007$ $DW = 1.8$

7. Dynamic structure

The Netherlands equations have the advantage in that by using percentage rates of change the estimation of time lags is facilitated and the distinction between short-run and long-run elasticities can be made. The quarterly Canadian RDX2 model and the Wharton model also have lag structures.

Part IV

APPLICATIONS OF BILATERAL LINKAGE

11. AN ECONOMETRIC ANALYSIS OF
A BILATERAL MODEL OF INTERNATIONAL ECONOMIC
ACTIVITY: JAPAN AND U.S.A.

C. MORIGUCHI and M. TATEMOTO

1. Introduction

The purpose of this research is multi-fold. Primarily, we aim at constructing a bilateral econometric model of the two economies across the Pacific Ocean by means of linking the two nation-wide econometric models through foreign trade. Second, we construct a bilateral trade sector in which disaggregated import demand equations are specified among three "countries": Japan, U.S.A. and the rest of the world. Third, by using the linked models, we analyse the basic trend in the balance of trade between the two nations as well as the total balance of payments of each country. We shall be more concerned with a general statistical treatment of the relationship between economic growth and the balance of payments than with a partial equilibrium approach in terms of income and price-elasticity of import demand. [1] This will be made possible by the use of simulation results on nation-wide econometric models of the two countries. In simulations of econometric models the effects of income and price factors on foreign trade are measured in the most general way. We also take into account short-run elasticities of supply.

We are going to make use of existing models of each country, one being the Kyoto University (KIER) model and the other is the

---

[1] Rhomberg and Boissonneault have built a multicountry model of income determination in which the income and foreign trade of each country are jointly determined. See Rhomberg, R.R. and L. Boissonneault, 'Effects of Income and Price Changes on the U.S. Balance of Payments', *IMF Staff Papers*, March 1964.

Wharton Economic Forecasting Unit model of the University of Pennsylvania. The two models have been developed and utilised for both academic and practical purposes of economic forecasting and policy analysis, and the forecasting results of these models have been proved to be of a reasonably high quality in explaining changes in macroeconomic variables of real economies. [2] In recent years economic forecasts for six quarters have been published every quarter by the two research centres across the Pacific Ocean.

The two economies, as they are represented by econometric models, are interdependent upon each other through international trade in goods and services, and transfer payments. The KIER model has three import equations classified by commodity groups, i.e., (1) raw materials and fuels, (2) foodstuffs and (3) other (manufactures); exports are broken down into two destinations, i.e. (1) the U.S.A. and (2) the rest of the world. The Wharton EFU model has four commodity import equations with the classification based on the SITC, i.e., (1) $M01$ for SITC classes 0 and 1, (2) $M24$ for classes 2 and 4, (3) $M3$ and (4) $M59$ for the classes of manufactures 5 through to 9; on the other hand the export equation is highly aggregated, treating goods and services together.

The two economies are closely linked through commodity trade. Japanese exports to the U.S. have quadrupled in the sixties with the relative share in the U.S. import market gradually increasing from 7% to 12%. In addition, nearly a third of Japanese commodity exports are shipped to the U.S.A. and the degree of dependence on this market has been unchanged. U.S. commodity exports to Japan have increased by 2.5 times in the same period and its share in U.S. exports has increased from around 5% in the early sixties to approximately 9% in the late sixties. Total Japan-

[2] Klein, L.R. and M.K. Evans, 'The Wharton Econometric Forecasting Model', *Studies in Quantitative Economics*, No. 2, University of Pennsylvania, 1968, and Moriguchi, C., M. Tatemoto and M. Uchida, 'A Quarterly Econometric Model of Japan – New Version for International Linkage Experiments', Kyoto Institute of Economic Research Discussion Paper, No. 43, a paper read at the *Regional Meeting of Project LINK*, Honolulu, March 1971. Though it bears the new name of Kyoto University model, it has taken over some of the major characteristics of the Japan Economic Research Centre, or JERC, model with which we started this bilateral trade analysis. Our new model is an enlarged version of the JERC model.

ese imports expanded, on the other hand, by three times and the U.S. relative share in the Japanese import market has declined from 30% to 27%. This is not only because of Japan's diversification in the purchase of crude materials, for if we consider only imported manufactured goods, we will see that the U.S. share has declined from 50% in the early period to below 40% in recent years. Thus the trade balance between the two countries has swung from the original deficit of Japan to the reverse position in recent years.

2. How to link the two economies in a bilateral model

To determine Japanese imports, we have to have values of Japan's exports for which Japan needs the values of the U.S. domestic variables as well as the world export total. Similarly, to determine U.S. imports we have to know the world export total and the world export prices which determine U.S. exports, in addition to variables which indicate the U.S. macroeconomic level.

One way of linking the two econometric models is to apply the above procedure jointly. That is, exports are divided by destinations and trade between the two countries is simultaneously determined, while both countries' exports to the rest of the world are treated in the same manner before the linking is carried out. The actual solution by an iterative procedure could be shown by a flow diagram as in fig. 1. Here the world export total WT is given exogenously, whereas in reality it should be at least partially endogenously determined. [3] For a given value of world exports, the level of both economies is determined such that the control variable for iteration, XUJ, that is U.S. exports to Japan, equals MSU, Japanese imports from the U.S. as determined from the Japanese model. This is the same as an ordinary iterative procedure for solving a non-linear econometric model.

---

[3] In a world-wide linking of econometric models, the world export total is a genuine endogenous variable. What we are indicating above is a partial equilibrium analysis in the sense that we neglect interdependence between the countries in question and the rest of the world.

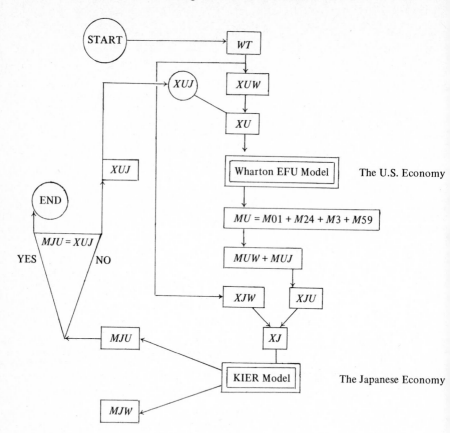

Fig. 1. Determination of bilateral trade.

However, the above procedure is not practical when the two research centres are separate and either one is not yet fully able to manipulate the two econometric models simultaneously. Neither is it absolutely necessary, when the two economies are not equal in size and one economy is heavily dependent upon another while the reverse is not the case. Economic fluctuations in the U.S. have had a strong influence upon the Japanese economy through fluctuations in foreign trade and, hence, through changes in Japan's balance of payments position. On the other hand, changes in Japanese macroeconomic activity have had no significant effect on the

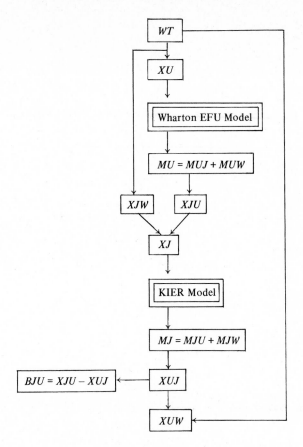

Fig. 2. Recursive determination of bilateral trade.

U.S. [4], because the degree of dependence on foreign trade is low in the U.S. and further, the importance of the Japanese market to U.S. exporters has been much lower than the importance of the U.S. market to Japanese exporters. In this case we could assume a much simpler bilateral relation as a first approximation; we assume away a channel through which Japanese imports from the U.S. contribute to income determination in the U.S. Then we can dis-

[4] Our discussion is in terms of macroeconomic activity, not in terms of particular industries.

pense with the outer loop in fig. 1 for comparing MJU and XUJ, and the entire system turns out to be bloc-recursive. The U.S. export total is determined first, and then its breakdown by region is determined by Japanese imports.

It might be useful to make a comment on the relation between our approach and the suggested alternatives to the international linkage of econometric models. Our approach is in line with the "bilateral approach" as Rhomberg has termed it. [5] The bilateral linkage requires the building of bilateral trade models for all the pairs of trading nations. If we denote country J's imports from country K by MJK, then we will have to have $N(N-1)$ import equations for any given commodity group. To determine MJK jointly, we have to simultaneously solve the related nationwide econometric models. Comparing this general procedure, our approach is specific in that we confine our interest to a particular pair of countries and that we simplify the procedure by replacing simultaneous determination by recursiveness.

3. Commodity import equations of Japan and the U.S.A. – elasticity analysis

We now describe our commodity import equations for Japan and the U.S.A. and discuss some of the problems encountered in data preparation and estimation. Throughout this paper Japan, the U.S.A. and the rest of the world are denoted by J, U and W respectively.

3.1. U.S. imports

The Wharton EFU model has four import equations (1) foods, beverages and tobacco, denoted by $M01$, (2) crude materials except mineral fuels, $M24$, (3) mineral fuels, $M3$ and (4) manufactures, $M59$. The suffixes correspond to the SITC commodity classification. Recent statistical results are shown elsewhere in this

[5] See Rhomberg, R.R., 'Possible Approaches to a Model of World Trade and Payments', *IMF Staff Papers*, March 1970.

Table 1
Price and income elasticities

U.S. Imports MU		Short-run		Long-run	
		1968-69	1958-59	1968-69	1958-59
M01	Price	−0.38	−0.51	–	–
	Income	0.60	0.50	–	–
M24	Price	0.0	0.0	–	–
	Income	0.23	0.26	–	–
M3	Price	−0.04	−0.69	−0.54	−10.32
	Income	0.14	0.27	2.13	4.00
M59	Price	−0.27	−0.84	–	–
	Income	3.12	1.98	–	–

Japanese Imports MJ		Short-run (1968)	Long-run (1968)
M01	Income	0.637	1.416
M24	Income	1.778	0.888
M3	Income	0.572	1.208
M59	Income	1.066	1.373
	Price	−0.537	−0.692

book. [6] Income and price elasticities calculated from these equations are shown in table 1. Elasticities are calculated both at the end and middle of the sample period, and they show some variation since the estimated relations are linear. As for materials and food imports, low elasticities with respect to both price and income factors are remarkable. An exception is the mineral fuels import equation in which the long-run income elasticity is high (ϵ = 2.1 to 4.0). The observation period is fairly long, 70 quarters, compared with a sample period of 35 observations for estimating *MJU* and *MUJ*. The import demand for manufactures is income-

[6] See ch. 8.

Table 2
Elasticities of bilateral trade

U.S. Imports from Japan *MUJ*		Short-run	Long-run
Machinery and equipment	Price	−0.361	−1.350
	Income	0.902	3.369
Metal products	Price	−1.545	−3.848
	Income	1.390	3.463
Textile products	Price	−2.887	—
	Income	3.180	—
Other manufactures	Price	—	—
	Income	0.862	2.074

Japanese Imports from the U.S. *MJU*			
Machinery and equipment	Price	—	—
	Income	0.503	1.258
Other manufactures	Price	—	—
	Income	2.047	0.725
Textiles and materials	Price	—	—
	Income	3.780	—
Metal ores and scrap	Price	—	—
	Income	2.864	0.538
Mineral fuels	Price	−0.690	−1.052
	Income	1.873	0.881
Foodstuffs	Price	−0.838	−1.900
	Income	—	—
Other materials	Price	—	—
	Income	0.420	1.184

elastic as is generally expected and the magnitude of the elasticity fluctuates depending on how much weight we put on the U.S.-Canada agreement on automobile production and shipments.

3.2. Japanese imports

Nearly 75% of total Japanese imports are occupied by crude materials and fuels for which it is natural to expect demand to be income-elastic, but not price-elastic, since almost all the imported materials have virtually no domestic competitors. Total imports MJ are broken down into four commodity groups, (1) foodstuffs and feed, (2) crude materials, (3) mineral fuels and (4) manufactured goods.

The materials import equations are primarily explained by income factors such as the industrial production index and inventory changes. The calculated elasticities show that the long-run income elasticities of Japan's import demand are relatively large for imports of mineral fuels and foodstuffs, reflecting a tendency for substitution of imported petroleum for domestic coal and for substitution of imported foodstuffs for domestic ones (e.g., domestic fisheries are being replaced by foreign based fisheries, and feed imported for domestic poultries, livestock and dairy industries has become economical).

As for manufacturing imports, relative prices as well as income factors show a high statistical significance as explanatory variables, although the price elasticity is low.

3.3. Japan-U.S. trade

Japan is one of many suppliers of manufactures to the U.S.A. For 1969, of the total U.S. imports of manufactures, 20% were from Japan. Imports from Japan are classified into four commodity groups: (1) machinery and equipment, (2) metal products, (3) textiles and textile products and (4) other manufactures − food, chemical, non-metal and others. Among the four commodity classes, metal products (mostly steel) and machinery have been growing rapidly and occupy large relative shares in the U.S. import market. Textile exports to the U.S. have been relatively stagnant in the sixties partly because of the voluntary control of cotton-textile exports of Japan agreed upon in 1962. The fourth class includes both the growing chemical and non-metal exports as well

as the old "light-industry" manufacture exports of Japan. At the
end of 1968, the relative shares of the four commodity groups in
the total export values to the U.S.A. were as follows:

(1) machinery and equipment   42.0% from 13.9% in 1960
(2) metal products   25.9% from 16.3% in 1960
(3) textiles   12.1% from 26.9% in 1960
(4) others   20.0% from 42.9% in 1960.

The sharp increases in the heavy-industry exports are associated
with particular commodities, such as electrical appliances, motor
vehicles and iron and steel products. Since these commodities are
strongly differentiated in the market and an increase in demand
can be expected only within the supply constraints and the diffu-
sion of information about new products, it is not sufficient to
specify an ordinary linear type of demand function in which an
income and price factor are separately treated. Since, in this type
of demand function, elasticities vary and very often decline as the
end of the sample period is approached, we simply assume an
iso-elasticity demand function.

The relative price effect is measured by the ratio of the price of
Japan's exports and the domestic price of competitive goods, and
here it may seem that the substitution effect between Japan's
exports and its competitor's (say, West Germany) exports is neglected. But this is not the case. It might be useful here to discuss
some of the problems concerning this. Let us take U.S. imports
from Japan for any commodity group, and assume that the price
elasticity of U.S. import demand with respect to the relative price
of PXJ and PDU is the same as that with respect to the relative
price of PXW and PDU, with PXW being the export price of country, or countries, W to the U.S. and PDU the domestic price level
of the commodity group in question in the U.S. Then we can write
the U.S. import equation in a separable form as follows;

$$MUJ = MUJ\,(YU,\,PMU/PDU,\,PXJ/PMU)$$
$$= MU\,(YU,\,PMU/PDU)\cdot SHUJ\,(PXJ/PMU) \qquad (1)$$

MU is total imports of the commodity group, YU is an activity variable and PMU is an import price index defined as

$$PMU = w_1 PXJ + w_3 PXW; \quad W \text{ for the rest of world} \tag{2}$$

where w_1 and w_3 are constant weights adding up to unity.

The import price elasticity η and the elasticity of substitution σ are defined as follows:

$$\eta = \frac{\partial MU}{\partial(PMU/PDU)} \cdot \frac{PMU/PDU}{MU} \tag{3}$$

$$\sigma = \frac{\partial SHUJ}{\partial(PXJ/PMU)} \cdot \frac{PXJ/PMU}{SHUJ} \tag{4}$$

From these relations we can evaluate the effect of a change in PXJ/PDU on MUJ by the following relation

$$\frac{dMUJ}{MUJ} = (\frac{w_1 PXJ}{PMU}\eta + \frac{w_3 PXW}{PMU}\sigma) \cdot \frac{dPXJ}{PXJ} \tag{5}$$

To derive the above relation we have used the following:

$$d(PXJ/PMJ) = \frac{w_3 PXW}{PMJU} dPXJ$$

and

$$\frac{dMU}{MU} = \frac{1}{MU} \cdot \frac{\partial MU}{\partial(PMU/PDU)} \cdot \frac{\partial(PMU/PDU)}{\partial PXJ} dPXJ.$$

Now it is easy to see from (5) that the effect of a change in PXJ/PDU is a weighted average of η and σ; if Japan's share in the U.S. import market of a particular commodity is small, then the whole effect will be dominated by σ. Further, if we know a priori that η is zero, that is to say the importing country has no domestic competitor, then we are still likely to estimate some price effect due to the substitution effect.

With this in mind let us turn to the estimated equations of MUJ and the table of elasticities. The remarkable result is obtained that the income elasticity of U.S. demand for Japanese commodities is very high, larger than 3.0 for machinery, metal products and textiles, and 2.0 for the remaining category.

As for machinery, the activity variable is measured by U.S. consumer durable expenditures and its high elasticity seems to explain the recent strong trend in Japan's relative share in the U.S. market for consumer durable goods. As for metals, the activity variable is GNP originating in manufacturing industries. Though voluntary control over Japanese exports of steel became effective in the late sixties, the observed income elasticity is high.

In specifying the U.S. textile import equation, we took into account the long-term voluntary control on cotton textile exports which was agreed upon in the early sixties between the U.S. and exporting countries. In addition to U.S. non-durable consumption expenditures as an activity variable, we added the "negative effect of voluntary control" in terms of the ratio of the moving sum of imports to domestic textile sales. The assumption is that exporters voluntarily control the rate of exports with constant surveillance of U.S. domestic sales.

The estimated price elasticity is high with respect to metal and textile imports (3.8 and 2.9 respectively). This result seems to explain the sharp increase in U.S. imports of steel and textiles from Japan that led to the voluntary control agreement in the sixties.

From the above estimates we can proceed to analyse the main factors that contribute to the sharp increase in Japan's share in the U.S. import market. If we could assume that the PMU/PDU elasticity of the U.S. import demand is constant with respect to any foreign country from which the U.S. purchases, then we can apply the estimated elasticity of substitution among competitors, σ, from the same table to explain the increase in Japan's share. For this purpose we estimated the linear equation $SHUJ$. However, data availability prevented us from estimating equations for other than the total. [7] Using the 1968 value for total imports from Japan ($\sigma = 2.11$), we can calculate that the increase in Japan's share should be 12.4%, since the relative price of Japan's export price to its competitors has declined by 5.9% during this period. This explains roughly half of the actual change in Japan's share which is a 23% increase (from 15.3% in 1960 to 18.8% in 1968). The remaining part might be attributed to the difference between income elasticities of U.S. import demand for Japan's exports and its competitors and, further, to the difference in supply elasticity between Japan and its competitors. The latter factor is indicated by a statistically significant estimate of the coefficient of capacity utilisation in eq. (9).

4. Multiplier analysis of Japan-U.S. trade

Here we report on some of our experimental studies on bilateral trade between the two countries, by making use of the computational results obtained from the "Mini-LINK exercise". For four different levels of assumed world export totals, the econometric models of each country and country groups, using their own export equations, were employed to calculate a full-year growth path of the economies for 1971 and 1972. This exercise was primarily aimed at deriving a consistent prediction of world trade. However, this also serves our intended study. First, following the assumption discussed in the preceding section, we input the results of the Wharton model simulations into our model, and determine the timepath of Japan's exports to the U.S. by commodity group. Given the values of world trade and the U.S. economic variables, the extended KIER model determines the level of bilateral imports and exports as well as GNP and its components. The subsector of bilateral trade equations and export price equations (export prices of the commodities to the U.S.) is solved simultaneously with the whole system.

---

[7] As for machinery and textiles, a statistical breakdown only started in 1965.

Table 3
Multiplier analysis

	1	2	3	4	5	6	7	8
U.S.A.								
1 WT	59.900	64.300	61.900	68.900	62.960 / 67.800	67.240 / 72.420	65.370 / 70.400	72.230 / 77.780
2 CD	82.700	84.900	83.600	76.900	82.080 / 82.850	85.470 / 86.690	82.720 / 84.100	83.740 / 84.560
3 CND	205.600	206.600	208.200	211.100	209.900 / 210.100	210.800 / 211.200	213.300 / 213.800	215.400 / 215.900
4 SUTEX	5.250	5.270	5.130	5.430	5.350 / 5.350	5.370 / 5.370	5.230 / 5.230	5.530 / 5.530
5 GNPMF	2.419	2.409	2.292	2.193	2.252 / 2.259	2.315 / 2.336	2.270 / 2.297	2.294 / 2.322
6 Current MGS					62.1 / 62.2 / .1	63.9 / 64.0 / .1	64.3 / 64.6 / .3	65.5 / 65.8 / .3
7 Current XGS					64.5 / 68.0 / 3.5	65.9 / 69.8 / 3.9	67.2 / 71.7 / 4.5	68.5 / 73.4 / 4.9
Japan								
1 C	6512.801	6931.566	7133.922	8124.605 / 8124.605	7439.625 / 7502.320	7836.242 / 7958.559	7917.805 / 8118.117	8840.184 / 9149.469
2 IFP	2875.200	3023.819	3593.169	3875.717	3706.949 / 3706.949	3709.953 / 3754.307	4170.270 / 4309.707	4310.332 / 4568.473
3 IIPNA	484.034	619.751	676.691	831.763	633.971 / 733.000	778.906 / 934.630	474.474 / 711.282	547.605 / 892.538

	1	2	3	4	5	6	7	8
5 XG	1331.104	1549.951	1649.886	1831.633	1462.017 1610.210	1677.679 1850.709	1801.634 1993.487	2015.014 2237.201
6 MGS	1548.172	1639.967	1780.238	1931.984	1858.311 1901.468	1920.942 1987.150	1992.220 2096.043	2112.544 2266.225
7 MG	1249.370	1323.117	1439.113	1562.256	1505.025 1538.799	1552.813 1605.890	1605.185 1690.461	1698.589 1826.650
8 GNP	12884.414	13303.645	14459.125	17242.914	14894.387 15180.500	15211.141 15671.156	15887.074 16597.016	18463.629 19509.876

Japan's exports to U.S.A.

	1	2	3	4	5	6	7	8
9 XMAC (millions of 1965 $)	338.067	382.427	395.530	355.730	270.640 272.893	316.694 322.650	329.846 339.347	323.911 333.668
10 XMT (millions of 1965 $)	421.227	501.999	495.681	439.182	386.792 388.370	435.390 441.774	424.230 434.885	402.432 415.462
11 XTEX (millions of 1965 $)	108.662	125.137	128.805	123.147	103.382 103.613	122.230 122.782	129.309 130.060	121.973 122.771
12 XOTH (millions of 1965 $)	214.365	264.119	290.426	187.745	231.444 231.634	281.056 281.651	307.520 308.522	302.742 303.926
13 PXMAC	1.413	1.446	1.488	1.543	1.587 1.587	1.628 1.629	1.677 1.677	1.739 1.739
14 PXMT	1.033	1.045	1.051	1.064	1.078 1.078	1.098 1.098	1.108 1.109	1.122 1.122
15 PXTEX	1.072	1.103	1.133	1.120	1.105 1.105	1.138 1.138	1.168 1.169	1.156 1.156
16 PXOTH	1.052	1.081	1.117	1.142	1.083 1.084	1.126 1.128	1.161 1.165	1.187 1.192
17 Current XJU (in millions of current dollars)	1255.108 1255.108	1501.631 1501.631	1579.778 1579.778	1483.589 1482.589	1211.121 1217.393	1448.957 1468.101	1531.487 1562.731	1515.182 1550.370
DIF	0.0	0.0	0.0	0.0	6.271	19.144	31.243	35.188

Table 3 (continued)

	1	2	3	4	5	6	7	8
Japan's imports from U.S.A.								
Foodstuffs	252.026	247.968	226.877	264.776	294.476	291.948	268.721	315.208
					294.476	291.948	268.721	315.208
Textile materials	36.541	23.360	22.263	48.630	37.261	21.621	16.753	35.626
					41.016	24.539	19.745	43.608
Ores	79.101	77.375	91.342	111.165	96.562	86.208	83.363	90.015
					103.848	98.370	100.897	115.666
Mineral fuels	117.083	115.802	131.401	135.695	132.974	129.830	132.579	129.127
					139.452	140.934	149.039	150.659
Other materials	282.546	276.839	312.267	347.511	363.894	340.094	366.568	390.309
					367.741	350.462	384.905	418.882
Machinery	311.659	313.520	363.273	497.478	523.089	481.396	539.156	645.695
					523.089	484.281	550.100	672.834
Other mfc	167.035	160.759	180.043	205.406	188.379	177.526	178.357	191.814
					197.078	192.264	199.563	222.075
Total	1222.893	1198.625	1315.690	1592.013	1621.785	1521.533	1583.688	1792.984
					1652.849	1578.152	1674.746	1939.003
					31.064	56.619	91.058	146.018

Table 3 shows the predicted values of bilateral trade as well as total imports and exports for two different assumptions on the movement of world trade. As for 1970, common assumptions are made in order to gauge the accuracy of prediction of the models used. The table starts with the figures of WT, and some of the related variables of the U.S. domestic economy, then total U.S. imports, U.S. imports from Japan, some of the related variables of the Japanese domestic economy and finally Japan's imports from the U.S. and the bilateral balance of trade.

The sixth row of table 3 shows a weak response of the U.S. economy to an increase in world trade — the increase of 20 billion dollars of WT brings about an increase of 4 billion dollars in U.S. exports in the following year and results in only 0.3 billion increase in imports. This can be seen by the following elasticity

$$\frac{\Delta MU}{MU} \Big/ \frac{\Delta WT}{WT} = 0.032.$$

On the other hand, Japan's exports quickly move upward due to the increase in world trade (see the fifth row of "Japan" side). This increase is mainly explained by the increase in Japanese exports to the rest of the world, but not to the U.S. Exports to the U.S. increase by only 0.092 billion dollars.

Thus, simulation results show a peculiar trend in the U.S.-Japanese trade balance, since an increase in WT is accompanied by larger increases in Japan's imports from U.S. than the increase in U.S. imports from Japan, in contrast to the actual course of development! The assumed "increase in WT" is rather ambiguous and in our model it cannot be anything but an increase in exports of the rest of the world.

However, the simulation results are useful for calculating total elasticities of individual variables of our model. As shown in table 4, we can see the direction of change in market shares in both the U.S. and Japanese import markets. The sixth and seventh rows indicate that as long as the import markets of the two economies expand at the same rate, Japan's share in the U.S. import market rises rapidly while the U.S. share in the Japanese import market

Table 4
World trade multiplier and total elasticities
(all in real terms)

1	$\Delta GNP/\Delta WT$	0.327	0.347
2	$\Delta \dot{X}/\Delta WT$	0.191	0.102
3	$\Delta M/\Delta WT$	0.083	0.051
4	$\frac{\Delta GNP}{GNP} / \frac{\Delta WT}{WT}$	0.133	0.446
5	$\frac{\Delta X}{X} / \frac{\Delta WT}{WT}$	0.865	0.153
6	$\frac{\Delta MUJ}{MUJ} / \frac{\Delta MU}{MU}$	2.12	----
7	$\frac{\Delta MJU}{MJU} / \frac{\Delta MJ}{MJ}$	----	1.103

stays constant. In other words, in order that the trade balance between the two economies stays in equilibrium, Japan's import market has to expand at a rate twice as high as that of the U.S. import market.

Appendix A. Notes on trade statistics

(1) *The Summary Report: Trade of Japan,* published by the Japan Tariff Association, is the statistical source for imports and exports by country and commodity. They are compiled on the basis of declarations submitted to the customs for clearance. Goods are classified according to "Statistical Classification of Commodities for Foreign Trade" which is based upon the United Nations' SITC.

(2) Imports are valued on a c.i.f. basis and exports are on an f.o.b. basis.

(3) Values of imports and exports are deflated by unit value indices for respective commodity groups.

(4) The most serious problem concerning prices is to find appropriate deflators for imports and exports between Japan and the U.S. They should be distinguished from those deflators for total imports and exports. For instance, Japan's imports of textile materials are mostly raw cotton, while total imports of this category include wool and other textile materials.

(5) We estimated the following series of unit value indices; Japan's exports to the U.S.

(i) Machinery; average of U.V.I. of automobiles, radios, sewing machines and televisions (with weights in proportion to 1965 export values).

(ii) Metals; average of U.V.I. of steel and metal products (with weights of 1965 export values).

(iii) Textiles; average of U.V.I. of cotton, wool, synthetic and rayon textiles and clothes (1965 weights).

(iv) Other commodities; not available.

Japan's imports from the U.S.

(i) Foodstuffs; average U.V.I. of wheat, rice and maize (with weights of 1965 import values).

(ii) Textile materials; U.V.I. of raw cotton.

(iii) Other materials; average U.V.I. of raw skin, soy bean, wood pulp and tallow (1965 weights).

(iv) Mineral fuels; average U.V.I. of coal, crude oil and petroleum products (1965 weights).

(v) Metal ores; average U.V.I. of iron ore, scrap and non-ferrous metal ore (1965 weights).

(vi) Machinery; not available.

(vii) Other mfc; not available.

(6) There is a problem concerning the relation between customs clearance data and the national income accounts. Usually this is treated by fitting a statistical relationship. In a bilateral model we cannot neglect a timelag between one country's exports and the other country's imports due to transportation. As for total goods, there are two different sets of statistics; one from Japan and the other from the U.S. Data on imports from Japan published in the Survey of Current Business match well with Japanese export data. On the other hand there are erratic differences between Japan's

data for *MJU* and the U.S. data on *XUJ*, although timelags and f.o.b.-c.i.f. valuations seem to be the main factors contributing to this difference.

Appendix B

Total U.S. imports by SITC groups

(1) Foods, beverages and tobacco

$$M01 = 3.75 + \underset{(9.3)}{0.0054} \, YPDU_{-1} -$$

$$- \underset{(4.8)}{1.926} \, (PMU01/PD01)_{-1} + \underset{(2.8)}{0.7797} \, DKW -$$

$$- \underset{(5.5)}{0.737} \, DST$$

$$\bar{R}^2 = 0.8385 \quad DW = 1.8443 \quad s = 0.2703$$

(2) Crude materials except fuels

$$M24 = 2.214 + \underset{(4.7)}{0.0031} \, GNPMFU + \underset{(4.8)}{0.0331} \, IIMFU +$$

$$+ \underset{(4.9)}{0.94} \, DKW - \underset{(1.0)}{0.0906} \, DST$$

$$\bar{R}^2 = 0.5515 \quad DW = 1.752 \quad s = 0.1875$$

(3) Mineral fuels

$$M3 = 0.0138 + \underset{(1.6)}{0.0019} \, GNPMFU - \underset{(0.4)}{0.1256} \, PMU3/$$

$$PD3 - \underset{(2.2)}{0.145} \, DST + \underset{(14.0)}{0.9332} \, \tfrac{1}{4} \sum_{1}^{4} M3$$

$$\bar{R}^2 = 0.9603 \quad DW = 1.6266 \quad s = 0.133$$

(4) Manufactures

$M59$ $= -1.409 + \ (0.0289 + \ 0.639 \, DCA)GNPU -$
$\qquad\qquad\qquad\ \ (11.1) \qquad (9.6)$

$\qquad\quad - \ 5.875 \, (PMU59/PD59) - 38.33 \, DCA -$
$\qquad\quad \ \ (3.1) \qquad\qquad\qquad\qquad (8.4)$

$\qquad\quad - \ 1.9405 \, DST$
$\qquad\quad \ \ (7.3)$

$\qquad\quad \bar{R}^2 = 0.9876 \quad DW = 1.8221 \quad s = 0.6545$

U.S. imports from Japan:

(5) $\log MUJ \ = \ - 4.013 + \ 0.0902 \log CDU -$
$\qquad\qquad\qquad\qquad\quad (2.11)$

$\qquad\quad - \ 0.3613 \log (PXJUMAC/PDMAC) +$
$\qquad\quad \ \ (1.29)$

$\qquad\quad + \ 0.7324 \log MUJ_{-1} - \ 0.246 \, Q1 +$
$\qquad\quad \ \ (7.15) \qquad\qquad\qquad (6.09)$

$\qquad\quad + \ 0.083 \, Q2 + \ 0.047 \, Q3$
$\qquad\quad \ \ (1.74) \qquad (1.15)$

$\qquad\quad \bar{R}^2 = 0.9907 \quad DW = 2.1874 \quad s = 0.083$

(6) Metals and metal products

$\log MUJ \ = \ - 15.635 + \ 1.3901 \log GNPMFU -$
$\qquad\qquad\qquad\qquad\quad (2.61)$

$\qquad\quad - \ 1.5446 \log (PXJUMET/PDI\&S) +$
$\qquad\quad \ \ (3.57)$

$\qquad\quad + \ 0.5986 \log MUJ_{-1} - \ 0.078 \, Q1 +$
$\qquad\quad \ \ (4.92) \qquad\qquad\qquad (1.62)$

$\qquad\quad + \ 0.101 \, Q2 + \ 0.04 \ \, Q3$
$\qquad\quad \ \ (2.05) \qquad (0.86)$

$\qquad\quad \bar{R}^2 = 0.9830 \quad DW = 1.1923 \quad s = 0.098$

(7)   Textiles

$$\log MUJ \; = \; -20.374 + \quad 3.1804 \log CNDU - \\ \qquad\qquad\qquad (10.98)$$

$$-\; 2.8874 \log (PXJUTEX/PDTEX) - \\ (4.28)$$

$$-\; 0.5941 \log \left(\sum_{1}^{4} MUJ_{-i} \middle/ \sum_{1}^{4} SUTEX_{-i} \right) - \\ (3.07)$$

$$-\; 0.202\, Q1 + \; 0.017\, Q2 + \; 0.113\, \dot{Q}3 \\ (4.42) \qquad\quad (0.39) \qquad\quad (2.32)$$

$$\bar{R}^2 = 0.8584 \quad DW = 0.9968 \quad s = 0.087$$

(8)   Other commodities

$$\log MUJ \; = \; -2.266 + \; 0.8619 \log CNDU + \\ \qquad\qquad\qquad (2.80)$$

$$+\; 0.5845 \log MUJ_{-1} - \; 0.207\, Q1 + \\ (4.02) \qquad\qquad\qquad\qquad (6.00)$$

$$+\; 0.11\; Q2 + \; 0.077\, Q3 \\ (2.20) \qquad\quad (2.20)$$

$$\bar{R}^2 = 0.8930 \quad DW = 1.6243 \quad s = 0.112$$

Total Japanese imports by SITC groups

(9)   Foodstuffs and feeds

$$M01 \qquad = \; -60.8 + \; 0.0531\, CFJ + \; 0.55\, (M01)_{-1} - \\ \qquad\qquad\qquad (3.88) \qquad\qquad (4.66)$$

$$-\; 38.09\, Q3 - 43.49\, Q4 \\ (4.29) \qquad\quad (3.45)$$

$$\bar{R}^2 = 0.968 \quad DW = 2.357 \quad s = 23.1$$

(10) Mineral fuels

$$M3 = -64.6 + \underset{(4.24)}{2.5255} PRODJ + \underset{(4.35)}{0.5263} (M3)_{-1} -$$

$$-\underset{(2.22)}{12.71} \; Q3 + \underset{(2.69)}{18.41} \; Q4$$

$$\bar{R}^2 = 0.994 \quad DW = 2.441 \quad s = 15.5$$

(11) Other crude materials

$$M24 = 313.99 + \underset{(4.23)}{3.7438} PRODJ +$$

$$+ \underset{(2.90)}{8.7794} \; \Delta PRODJ - \underset{(2.05)}{2.819} (KIPNAJ_{-1}/$$

$$PRODJ) + \underset{(3.20)}{0.4029} (M24)_{-1} +$$

$$+ \underset{(4.08)}{56.77} \; Q2 - \underset{(1.80)}{30.54} \; Q4$$

$$\bar{R}^2 = 0.980 \quad DW = 1.592 \quad s = 36.7$$

(12) Manufactures

$$M59 = -721.1 + \underset{(3.57)}{0.2376} IFPJ +$$

$$+ \underset{(2.53)}{0.0423} (GNPJ - IFPJ) +$$

$$+ \underset{(4.79)}{536.8} \; (PWHJ/PD59) + \underset{(0.78)}{10.88} \; Q2 -$$

$$-\underset{(2.76)}{38.62} \; Q3 - \underset{(6.28)}{100.28} \; Q4$$

$$\bar{R}^2 = 0.978 \quad DW = 1.846 \quad s = 31.9$$

Japanese imports from U.S. by seven commodity groups

(13) Foodstuffs and feeds

$$\log MJU = 1.276 + \underset{(2.47)}{0.0199\ TIME} -$$

$$- \underset{(1.62)}{0.8382}\log (PXUJFF/PFF) +$$

$$+ \underset{(3.87)}{0.5593}\log MJU_{-1} - \underset{(1.04)}{0.088}\ Q2 -$$

$$- \underset{(2.23)}{0.186}\ Q3$$

$$\bar{R}^2 = 0.863 \quad DW = 2.227 \quad s = 0.199$$

(14) Textile materials

$$\log MJU = 20.689 - \underset{(2.22)}{0.009}\ TIME - \underset{(5.14)}{3.7803}\log$$

$$(KIPNAJ_{-1}/PRODJ) + \underset{(0.62)}{0.069}\ Q1 -$$

$$- \underset{(3.48)}{0.392}\ Q2 - \underset{(5.78)}{0.65}\ Q3$$

$$\bar{R}^2 = 0.743 \quad DW = 2.13 \quad s = 0.225$$

(15) Metal ores and scraps

$$\log MJU = 12.103 + \underset{(2.35)}{0.2816}\log PRODJ - \underset{(3.95)}{2.5822}\log$$

$$(KIPNAJ_{-1}/PRODJ) +$$

$$+ \underset{(3.94)}{0.4758}\log MJU_{-1} - \underset{(1.30)}{2.458}\ DST$$

$$\bar{R}^2 = 0.671 \quad DW = 1.572 \quad s = 0.105$$

(16) Mineral fuels

$$\log MJU = 5.655 + \underset{(4.42)}{0.5779} \log PRODJ - \underset{(3.83)}{1.2947} \log$$

$$(KIPNAJ_{-1}/PRODJ) -$$

$$- \underset{(0.63)}{0.6895} \log (PXUJFU/PDFU) +$$

$$+ \underset{(2.57)}{0.3437} \log MJU_{-1} - \underset{(2.40)}{0.104} Q4$$

$$\bar{R}^2 = 0.831 \quad DW = 2.280 \quad s = 0.105$$

(17) Other materials

$$\log MJU = 0.972 + \underset{(3.89)}{0.8396} \log (PRODJ + PRODJ_{-1}) +$$

$$+ \underset{(1.66)}{0.2912} \log MJU_{-1} - \underset{(1.87)}{0.07} Q2 -$$

$$- \underset{(2.87)}{2.869} DST$$

$$\bar{R}^2 = 0.945 \quad DW = 2.021 \quad s = 0.088$$

(18) Machineries

$$\log MJU = 1.815 + \underset{(2.54)}{0.5028} \log (IFPJ) -$$

$$- \underset{(1.98)}{1.549} \log (RHOJ) + \underset{(4.11)}{0.5956} \log MJU_{-1} +$$

$$+ \underset{(0.57)}{0.045} Q1 - \underset{(1.78)}{0.137} Q2 - \underset{(1.12)}{0.087} Q3$$

$$\bar{R}^2 = 0.701 \quad DW = 2.142 \quad s = 0.156$$

(19) Other manufactures

$$\log MJU = 7.182 + \underset{(4.63)}{0.5334} \log (PRODJ + PRODJ_{-1}) -$$

$$- 1.5144 \log (KIPNAJ_{-1}/PRODJ)$$
$$(4.06)$$

$$\bar{R}^2 = 0.802 \quad DW = 1.902 \quad s = 0.107$$

(20) *Total materials share of the U.S. in Japanese import market*

$$MJU/MJ = 0.2246 - 0.800\,PUCM/PMJ -$$
$$(.8)$$

$$- 0.0012\,TIME + 0.5519\,(MJU/MJ)_{-1} +$$
$$(2.0) \qquad\qquad (3.5)$$

$$+ 0.018\,Q1 - 0.0032\,Q2 - 0.145\,Q3$$
$$(1.6) \qquad (0.3) \qquad\quad (1.3)$$

$$\bar{R}^2 = 0.673 \quad DW = 1.666 \quad s = 0.023$$

(21) *Total U.S. share in Japanese import market*

$$MJU/MJ = 0.2912 - 0.0422\,PXU/PMJ -$$
$$(2.2)$$

$$- 0.01632\,RHOU_{-1} + 0.6554\,(MJU/MJ)_{-1} +$$
$$(4.9) \qquad\qquad\qquad (3.1)$$

$$+ 0.0132\,Q1 - 0.0032\,Q2 - 0.005\,Q3$$
$$(2.0) \qquad (0.5) \qquad\quad (0.8)$$

$$\bar{R}^2 = 0.8282 \quad DW = 1.869 \quad s = 0.013$$

Variable definitions

YPD	= Personal disposable income.
GNPMF	= Gross output originating in the manufacturing sector.
GNP	= Gross national product.
CD	= Durable consumption expenditures.
CND	= Non durable consumption expenditures.
CF	= Consumption expenditures on food and drink.
PROD	= Index of manufacturing production.
IIMF	= Change in stock of manufacturing inventories.
IFP	= Private fixed investment.
KIPNA	= Stock of inventories in the non-agricultural sector.

SUTEX   = U.S. domestic textile shipments.
RHO   = Index of capacity utilisation.
PWH   = Wholesale price index.
DKW   = Dummy variable for the Korean War.
DST   = Dummy variable for U.S. dockyard strikes.
DCA   = Dummy variable for U.S.–Canada Automobile Agree-
               ment.
PM   = Import price index.
PX   = Export price index.
PD   = Price index of domestic competitive goods.
$Q1, Q2,...$= Seasonal dummy variables.
TIME   = Linear trend term, *TIME* = 1.0 for 1955.1.

Method of estimation is OLS. Figures under the estimated coefficients are *t*-values.

12. COMPREHENSIVE LINKAGE OF LARGE MODELS: CANADA AND THE UNITED STATES *

J.F. HELLIWELL, F.W. GORBET, G.R. SPARKS and I.A. STEWART

1. Introduction

The main initial thrust of Project LINK has been to use trade equations as links between existing models for countries and regions representing a large proportion of world trade and economic activity. In this chapter we describe an alternative approach, based on the comprehensive linkage of large quarterly models of Canada [1] and of the United States. [2] Although it may eventually be possible to undertake this sort of linkage on a balanced multilater-

* Financial support for the linkage project has been generously provided by grants from the I.W. Killam fund administered by the Canada Council. Our collaborators on the linkage project have included Tom Maxwell and Jillian Broadbent. The construction of the Canadian model RDX2 has been mainly supported by the Bank of Canada. Harold Shapiro was a major contributor to RDX2 and to the linkage project until pressure of other duties forced his withdrawal in mid-1970. Al Coombs developed the programming capacity to solve two large models simultaneously, and many others have contributed to the development and management of RDX2.

[1] The theory and structural equations of the Canadian Model RDX2 are presented in Helliwell, J.F., H.T. Shapiro, G.R. Sparks, I.A. Stewart, F.W. Gorbet and D.R. Stephenson, 'The Structure of RDX2', Bank of Canada Staff Research Studies, No. 7, 1971.

[2] We are using a recent version of the FRB-MIT-Penn model, now called the MPS model. The version to be used for our simulations and described in this chapter has been set out by Ando, A. and R. Rasche, 'Equations in the MIT-PENN-SSRC Econometric Model of the United States', Mimeographed, January 1971. Earlier versions of the model have been the subject of several papers, most of which are referred to by Ando, A. and F. Modigliani, 'Econometric Analysis of Stabilization Policies', *American Economic Review*, May 1969.

al basis, in the first stages we have found it necessary to employ large "other countries" categories to explain the economic links between either of the linked models and the rest of the world.

Aside from the fact that we started with a basis of experience in the construction and operation of fairly highly developed quarterly models of Canada and the United States, a Canada-U.S. bilateral linkage seemed a logical starting point for an experiment in the detailed international linkage of national econometric models. First, each country is the other's largest trading partner, and there is a highly developed set of economic links between the separate national markets for goods, labour and capital. In addition, both countries have been heavily involved in international capital flows and have compiled reasonably complete balance-of-payments statistics. Finally, from the Canadian point of view, the proximity of the two countries and the pervasiveness of the economic links between them means that it is impossible to predict the behaviour of the Canadian economy without very specific assumptions about the evolution of economic activity in the United States during the forecast period. International linkages are not so important in forecasting the much larger U.S. economy, but in some respects, e.g., international capital flows, these linkages are of very substantial policy importance.

In order to proceed with our bilateral linkage, we had to consider first what sort of questions we wished to answer with the linked models, to decide what characteristics the individual models ought to possess for these purposes, and then to do the required building or modification of models. In sect. 2 of the paper we discuss the first two issues. In sect. 3 we compare the basic structures of the two national models being linked. We describe in sect. 4 the main links between the models, and between each model and the rest of the world. We conclude, in sect. 5, with a discussion of some simulation experiments designed to make use of the comprehensive linkage mechanism linking the two economies.

2. Objectives and requirements

Our interest lies not merely in forecasting levels of trade and capital flows, but also in being able to simulate the international repercussions of policy measures adopted in one of the two linked economies. In principle we would like, as well, to be able to simulate a fully interactive system in which the repercussions of one country's policies lead to policy responses in the other country, and so on. If the dynamics of such a system could be accurately specified, it would be possible to consider the stability and other aspects of alternative policy reactions to disequilibria in domestic employment, prices and the balance of payments.

To give a specific example, it has been argued [3] that under a fixed exchange rate system it may not be possible to rely on high interest rates as a means of dealing with a balance of payments deficit, at least for any time interval extending beyond the very short term. Whether such reliance is justified depends on the dynamics of growth and adjustment in international portfolios caused by a shift in monetary policy, as well as on the effects that higher domestic interest rates eventually have on the international flows of interest and dividends. We think that any comprehensive international linkage of quarterly models should be able to answer such a question. The requirements that this imposes on the equation structure of the linked models are fairly obvious in the case of the example mentioned, but in other circumstances it is not always obvious just how much structural detail is required. The general requirements may be expressed as follows:

(1) The models ought to explain explicitly all the import trade and capital flows between the linked economies, and between each of the linked economies and the rest of the world.

(2) Since the linked models are to be used to simulate the consequences of, amongst other things, policy actions and reactions in the linked economies, it is necessary that each of the

[3] For example, by Willett, D. and F. Forte, 'Interest Rate Policy and External Balance', *Quarterly Journal of Economics*, May 1969.

models should be constructed so as to depict realistically the links between public policies and private sector decisions.

(3) To make linkage complete, the foreign activity variables and similar influences from any other linked economy must be determined within the model of the economy in which each influence originates.

(4) Finally, we find that in order to be able to explain international capital flows and other elements of the transmission mechanism accurately, it is necessary to account for the flows of funds between the major sectors of each economy so as to determine certain important portfolio balance effects and the market value of wealth.

There were no existing models that satisfied these requirements to an acceptable degree, so we found ourselves faced at the outset with a substantial job of model-building. In the course of building RDX2, the Canadian quarterly model used in the bilateral linkage, we have specified those mechanisms necessary to explain the flows of goods and capital between Canada and the United States and between Canada and the rest of the world, but for the present have not attempted to explain in any detail the links between the United States and the rest of the world. In choosing a suitable model of the U.S. domestic economy, we were anxious to obtain one that satisfied the above criteria and contained both a degree of aggregation and a financial structure reasonably compatible with those of RDX2. The MPS model appealed to us on these grounds, even though there are a number of respects in which it does not match RDX2. The most serious difference lies in the fact that RDX2 uses seasonally unadjusted data throughout. Thus, we have had to include a large number of seasonal de-adjustment factors in the linkage process in order to obtain the seasonally unadjusted equivalents of many of the variables in the U.S. model (e.g. the level of foreign exchange reserves) and portfolio determination equations (e.g., the balance sheet constraints) are not generally applicable if seasonally adjusted data are used.

3. Comparison of the two national models

RDX2 and MPS are each divided into 21 sectors. Because the sectors are defined differently in the two models, we have reclassified the equations of both models as shown in table 1. RDX2 has about twice as many estimated behavioural equations as MPS, and about the same number of technical relationships. [4] The comparison by number of equations is distorted in two ways. RDX2 contains 28 behavioural equations and 8 technical relationships explaining the quantities and prices of goods and services traded between the U.S. and Canada, and the capital account flows and liabilities between the two countries. Thus, 36 equations of RDX2 may equally well be considered part of MPS, making the two models more nearly equal in size. On the other hand, there are a number of simple definitional equations in MPS of a type that have been solved out of RDX2. The structural equations of RDX2 thus contain more complicated transformations than those of MPS, and RDX2 as a whole has a higher ratio of estimated equations to identities.

In comparing the features of the two models, we shall follow the classification used in table 1. Our comparisons will emphasise the effects of policy variables, because most of our linked simulations are designed to study the effects of policy changes in either or both of the economies.

3.1. Private aggregate demand

3.1.1. Consumption
MPS treats non-durables and services together, while RDX2 has separate equations for services and for non-durables. The services component in both models is redefined to include a synthetic series for the imputed services from durable goods owned by con-

---

[4] We have added two identities to the MPS model defining RHO2 and RHOR2, the U.S. equivalents to RHO and RHOR, the nominal and real measures of the supply price of capital. We expect to make additions to the foreign trade sector of MPS, and may add equations for capital flows between the United States and countries other than Canada.

Table 1

Comparison of the numbers of behavioural and technical equations in the RDX2 and MPS models

	RDX2		MPS	
	Behav-ioural	Tech-nical	Behav-ioural	Tech-nical
1. Private Aggregate Demand				
1.1. Consumption	4	3	2	4
1.2. Residential construction	5	0	3	7
1.3. Business investment and output	3	13	4	14
1.4. Foreign trade:				
Imports – between Canada and U.S.	9	1	1	1
– other	4	3		
Exports – between Canada and U.S.	5	1	0	0
– other	4	4	0	0
Total	34	25	10	26
2. Private Sector Employment and Wages, Prices and Income Distribution				
2.1. Employment and labour force	7	6	4	8
2.2. Wages	2	1	1	0
2.3. Prices – of trade flows between Canada and U.S.	5	0	0	0
– of other goods and services	15	3	1	19
2.4. Income distribution and related identities	3	9	4	29
Total	32	19	10	56
3. Government Sector				
3.1. Federal government taxes and transfers	14	28	6	7
3.2. Federal government wages employment and spending	4	1	0	0
3.3. Government balances and asset and liability changes	5	8	0	3
3.4. Provincial, or state, and local revenues and transfers	6	2	6	1
3.5. Provincial, or state, and local expenditures	6	2	3	4
Total	35	41	15	15
4. Financial Sector				
4.1. Financial assets of nonfinancial sector	8	3	9	4
4.2. Bank assets and interest rates	14	6	3	6
4.3. Mortgage market	2	0	10	3
4.4. Market value of shares and the cost of capital	1	6	11	2
Total	25	15	33	15

Table 1 (continued)

	RDX2		MPS	
	Behav-ioural	Tech-nical	Behav-ioural	Tech-nical
5. Foreign capital flows and the foreign exchange market				
5.1. Long-term capital:				
– between Canada and U.S.	9	6	0	0
– other	4	4	0	0
5.2. Short-term capital, and foreign exchange market	3	6	0	0
Total	16	16		
Total behavioural	142		68	
Total technical		116		112
Model totals		258		180

sumers. The MPS equation for non-durables and services makes use of a twelve-quarter lag distribution on per capita disposable personal income and a four-quarter lag on the market value of household wealth. The RDX2 equations make more direct use of the series for the supply price of capital and the market value of wealth. The consumption equations take separate account of disposable wage and nonwage incomes, asset revaluation gains and losses, the rate of return on savings and also a synthetic definition of nonwage income derived from market values of assets multiplied by their respective permanent rates of return.

In MPS, a rise in interest rates induces a fall in the market value of equities, which in turn leads to a reduction in consumption. This is the fastest and most direct effect of monetary policy in the model. In RDX2, a rise in interest rates likewise causes capital losses on outstanding bonds, but these losses enter the consumption equations as changes in the market value of bonds and shares, and not as the market value itself. There are two other direct influences of the change in interest rates. The higher interest rate is multiplied by the market value of the stock of government debt held by the private sector as part of the definition of nonwage income. As the debt matures and is refinanced at the new rate of

interest, permanent nonwage income rises. The third direct influence of the higher interest rate is a negative one, the substitution effect leading to higher savings when interest rates rise. Thus
an increase in interest rates in RDX2 has two negative effects and
one positive effect on consumption. The negative impacts are from
the substitution effect and capital losses on securities, while the
income effect is positive.

A capital stock adjustment framework is used to explain expenditure on consumer durable goods in both models. MPS has
one equation for expenditure on consumption durables, while
RDX2 has separate equations for autos and for other consumer
durables. The desired stock of consumer durables in RDX2 depends on wage and nonwage income, asset revaluation gains, population, relative prices and bank liquidity. The desired stock in MPS
is determined by total consumption, income, population, relative
prices and the corporate bond rate.

3.1.2. Residential construction
Both models explain expenditures by a lag distribution on housing
starts, and explain single (including duplexes in MPS) and multiple
starts separately. In both models, starts are explained by income
(RDX2) or consumption (MPS), the existing stocks of dwellings,
demographic variables, changes in wealth (MPS only), relative
prices (MPS only), mortgage approvals or commitments, mortgage
rates and bank liquidity (RDX2 only).

3.1.3. Business investment
The business fixed investment equations of RDX2 are jointly derived, along with the employment and hours equations, from an
explicit constant-returns Cobb–Douglas production function for
private business output using manhours, non-residential buildings,
and machinery and equipment as separate input factors, allowing
for Harrod-neutral technical progress. The desired levels of factor
employment are derived from a cost minimisation process based
upon expected output, expected prices of capital goods (at their
delivery dates), expected prices of labour services (over the life-

time of the related capital goods), tax rates and the expected supply price of capital.

The distributed lag capital stock adjustment process is derived by the difference between expected output and the output that would be forthcoming if the (vintage) capital stock were employed using the factor proportions preferred for each vintage. The predetermined production function parameters, lag weights, and some expectations weights are chosen from experiments over grids of alternative combinations. The price expectations weights are obtained from the financial sector equations for the supply price of capital.

The business investment equations of the MPS model are based on the work of Bischoff. [5] They are like the equations of RDX2 in that factor substitution is assumed to be easier ex ante than ex post, machinery and equipment are treated separately from structures, and the desired capital/output ratios depend on relative prices. The MPS model determines new orders as an intermediate stage in the investment process for equipment. Unlike RDX2, the MPS model does not use an explicit production function, so that there is no constraint forcing the demands for labour and the two types of capital to be mutually consistent with a single underlying production function. In fact, the production function implied by the producers' durable equipment equation in MPS is Cobb Douglas, while that implied by the producers' structures equation is CES with a low elasticity of substitution. In RDX2, each capital/output ratio depends on all three factor prices and the production function elasticities. In MPS, each capital/output ratio depends of the ratio of the output price to the imputed rental price for that type of capital. Thus it is difficult to compare, say, the impact of monetary policy in the two investment equations without solving the entire macro models to take proper account of the relationships between prices, wages and the rental cost of capital.

The business inventory equations in both models permit different stock/sales ratios to apply to different components of final

---

[5] Bischoff, C.W., 'The Effect of Alternative Lag Distributions', chapter 3 in: Fromm, G., ed., *Tax Incentives and Capital Spending*, Brookings Institution, 1971.

demand. The RDX2 model has an equation explaining the change in inventories by a stock adjustment model; MPS has an equation explaining the inventory stock by distributed lags on demand variables. The buffer-stock role of inventories is captured in the RDX2 equation by the difference between aggregate supply (based on the production function using current levels of factor inputs) and non-inventory final demand. The corresponding role is depicted in the MPS equation by a negative coefficient on the first difference of consumption expenditures. Financial variables do not appear directly in either equation.

3.1.4. Foreign trade

The 31 equations in the foreign trade sector of RDX2 involve disaggregation by region (U.S. and other countries) and commodity. For imports of goods we employ the 4-way SITC-based split agreed upon for Project LINK plus a separate equation for autos and parts. There is much less disaggregation for Canadian exports. For the flow of goods from Canada to the United States, for example, the only split is between "autos and parts" and "all other goods". All the equations for flows of goods are estimated in terms of constant Canadian dollars and are based on Canadian balance-of-payments statistics. In terms of goodness-of-fit, the splitting of equations for imports of goods into the United States and other countries adds considerably to the accuracy of overall explanation, while the further split by commodity class adds structural detail but no more explanatory power.

Imports and exports of services are explained in RDX2 by 13 stochastic equations estimated in current Canadian dollars. Because RDX2 contains detailed international indebtedness accounts as endogenous variables, we have been able to build considerable structural detail into our explanation of interest and dividend receipts and payments. The theoretical structure of the trade equations will be presented in more detail in sect. 4.

In MPS, there is a single foreign trade equation in which total imports of goods (excluding imports of autos and parts, which are taken as exogenous) are explained by GNP, relative prices, capacity utilisation, and variables representing the effects of major domestic strikes and of the Canadian-U.S. automotive agreement. For linked simulations, the dependent variable of this equation wili be total U.S. imports less those explained by the RDX2 equations for exports from Canada to the United States.

3.2. Private sector employment and wages, prices and income distribution

3.2.1. Employment and labour force

In RDX2, changes in business employment are based upon partial adjustment to factor demands derived from the production function, allowing for ex post as well as ex ante substitution. Changes in hours worked provide for some of the remaining variance of output, with short-term productivity changes accounting for the rest. Employment in construction, schools, and in government administration are all explained separately.

MPS has a single mechanism determining nonfarm business employment. There are separate behavioural equations for manhours per unit of output and for hours-per-man, with total employment determined as the ratio of total manhours to hours-per-man. The main equation estimated is the productivity equation using manhours per unit of output as the dependent variable. This ratio depends negatively on capacity utilisation, the current change in output, an exponential time trend and the unemployment rate. It should be noted that capacity output in MPS is defined as a weighted average of past values of actual output. The lags in the response of total manhours are thus captured mainly by capacity utilisation, for any increase in aggregate demand leads to an increase in capacity utilisation followed by subsequent movements back towards the original level. The time trend is presumably intended to reflect any technical progress and factor substitution. Hours-per-man depend positively on the change in total manhours, and lagged hours-per-man, with a lesser positive impact from the ratio of males aged 25–54 to total employment, reflecting the fact that females, on average, work fewer hours per week than do males.

There are labour force participation equations in both models. In RDX2, the labour force depends on the recent history of net immigration as well as on population, numbers in school and income. Population is made endogenous by immigration and emigration equations, as explained in sect. 4.3.

3.2.2. Wages

There are two private sector quarterly wage rate equations in RDX2, one for construction and the other for mining, manufacturing and other business. The latter wage rate applies to the bulk of private sector employment, and enters the factor demand equations derived from the production function for private sector output. There are important feed-backs from the production function to the wage rate, directly through the variable measuring the normal rate of Harrod-neutral technical progress, and indirectly through the price of business output and the unemployment rate. The equation depicts the one-quarter percentage change in the nominal wage responding to the expected rate of increase in consumer prices and any discrepancy between the lagged real wage and its determinants, which are long-term productivity and the rate of unemployment.

Only a single overall wage rate is determined in MPS. The two-quarter rate of change of compensation per hour in the nonfarm business sector is explained by the rate of unemployment, the rate of change of corporate cash flow and the rate of change of social insurance contributions. The entire wage model is formulated in first differences and its equilibrium properties are somewhat obscure.

3.2.3. Prices

The Canadian national accounts price deflators are explained on a disaggregated basis within RDX2, with the national accounts identities being used to define the aggregate indices. The Consumer Price Index is explained by a base-weighted combination of the relevant national accounts deflators. Disaggregated price explanation has permitted us to model with some precision the roles of various changes in sales tax coverage and rates as well as various

U.S. prices. U.S. prices influence Canadian final demand prices not only because of the import component of final demand, but also through their influence on the price of import-competing goods.

Although the MPS model contains a price index for each of the different components of output, only one of these, the overall deflator for private domestic nonfarm business product, is determined endogenously by the basic factors thought to affect the formation of prices. The ratios of all other prices to this deflator are determined exogenously at their historical values. The dependent variable is the log of the ratio of the aggregate price to the aggregate wage rate. It depends positively on the log of the ratio of the lagged price to the current wage, and the change in the ratio of unfilled orders to shipments of producers' durables. It depends negatively on time, the prices of imported and farm materials and a distributed lag on the log of output per manhour. The negative signs on the latter two variables are difficult to rationalise. The form of the equation implies that the short-term and long-term elasticities of the price level with respect to the wage rate are both equal to one. There is no positive influence from raw material prices, and no role is given to unit capital costs. Since all other prices are related to the aggregate price by a proportionality factor, the relative price variables will not vary under simulation, except where either numerator or denominator is in the form of a rental price variable determined partly by depreciation rates and the cost of capital.

3.2.4. Income distribution

Income distribution in RDX2 follows directly from the wage and employment equations, profits and dividends equations and various international factor payments. The corporate profits equation is derived by endogenous approximations to the value of business output at factor cost less business wage payments and exogenous series for corporate interest payments and capital consumption allowances. If these income distribution equations fail to balance the national accounts under simulation, any discrepancy between income and expenditure is added to or subtracted from personal income.

In MPS, on the other hand, any simulation residual ends up in company profits, as explained by total profits, which are in turn determined by subtracting wage payments and other, mostly exogenous, items from national income.

3.3. Government sector

3.3.1. Federal government taxes and transfers
RDX2 is considerably larger than MPS in this sector, principally because of a complex personal income tax model disaggregated by type and level of income. There are also equations for federal sales taxes, excise duties, corporation income tax accruals, interest on the government debt and a model of the unemployment insurance fund. MPS contains a smaller model of the unemployment insurance fund, and equations for personal and company income taxes and excise taxes.

3.3.2. Federal government wages, employment and spending
RDX2 has behavioural equations for federal employment, the average federal wage, current nonwage expenditure and investment in non-residential construction. In general, they depend on a mixture of demand, relative price and policy variables. The latter are rates of inflation and rates of unemployment, generally thought to trigger countercyclical fiscal policies.

In MPS, all federal government expenditure is exogenous in terms of constant dollars. The constant-dollar amounts of wage and nonwage expenditure are multiplied by the relevant wage rates and price levels respectively, to determine the current-dollar amounts. The government wage rate is assumed to move proportionately with the private wage rate, and the price of government nonwage expenditure is similarly related to the price of business output.

The linked simulations will not show any induced U.S. federal real expenditure unless we invent a policy reaction function for the purpose.

3.3.3. Government balances and asset and liability changes

Both models have identities for the income-expenditure balances of the federal government, and of state and local governments treated separately. RDX2 also has stochastic equations for corporation taxes accrued but not collected, and valuation ratios for the various maturity classes of federal government debt.

3.3.4. Provincial or state and local revenues and transfers

Both models have equations for the major income items and transfer payments at these levels of government.

3.3.5. Provincial or state and local expenditures

RDX2 has equations for provincial and municipal employment in administration, the average wage rate, the number of teachers employed, current nonwage expenditures and construction investment, with construction of schools being treated separately from other construction. MPS treats the same expenditures at a slightly higher level of aggregation, with separate equations for construction expenditure, other expenditure and total wages. The RDX2 equations embody fairly long lag distributions on demand variables, relative prices and a government income constraint variable. The MPS equations depend principally on current population, consumption and federal grants-in-aid. Thus, any induced state and local government expenditure in MPS occurs more quickly than the corresponding expenditure in RDX2.

3.4. Financial sector

3.4.1. Financial assets of nonfinancial sector

In both models the assets explained are comprised mainly of currency and liabilities of commercial banks and other financial institutions. In RDX2, demand functions for these assets plus the interest-bearing debt of the federal government are estimated jointly subject to balance sheet constraints. In the MPS model, special treatment is given to large negotiable certificates of deposits at commercial banks with supply and demand functions included to determine the rate paid and the quantity. Equations for time de-

posits other than large CDs and savings deposits in nonbank financial institutions are estimated jointly using a method similar to
that used in RDX2.

The equations for bank deposits in RDX2 include a demand
function for a type of foreign currency deposit known as swapped
deposits. These are term deposits denominated in U.S. dollars and
covered by a forward contract so that there is no foreign exchange
risk in terms of Canadian dollars. The substitutability of these
deposits with Canadian dollar deposits provides an important link
with the U.S. money market and the Euro-dollar market.

3.4.2. Bank assets and interest rates

The basic exogenous monetary policy instrument in the MPS
model is the monetary base (currency plus bank reserves net of
commercial bank borrowings from the Federal Reserve System).
The treasury bill rate is determined by the interaction of this
variable with the demand for currency, free reserves and required
reserves, the latter component being determined by the volume of
bank deposits. An equation for the demand for bank loans is
included since this variable influences the demand for free reserves
and the supply of large CDs.

This approach was rejected in the case of RDX2 primarily because of the greater influence of balance of payments considerations on monetary policy decisions in Canada. Given the importance of capital flows and the consequent need to adjust interest
rates in Canada in line with U.S. and other foreign rates, we treat
the short-term interest rate as the basic policy instrument. Monetary policy is then made endogenous through a central bank reaction function relating the short-term rate to the U.S. treasury bill
rate and other measures of policy objectives. Thus, equations for
bank deposits in RDX2 do not determine the interest rate but
rather the level of the money supply required to achieve any given
target interest rate. In addition, the volume of bank deposits and
the demand for bank loans determine the bank liquid asset ratio,
which is used as a measure of credit availability.

Both models include a number of other interest rates determined by reduced form equations reflecting the expectations theo-

ry of the term structure of interest rates, and other factors in particular security markets.

3.4.3. The mortgage market

The two models use a similar specification of the mortgage market involving a reduced form relationship for the mortgage rate and equations for the supply of funds by institutional lenders. RDX2 has equations for mortgage approvals by life insurance companies and by trust and loan companies. Four types of mortgage lenders are treated individually in the MPS model, and there are separate equations for commitments, gross mortgage flows and repayments for mutual savings banks, life insurance companies and savings and loan associations.

3.4.4. Market value of shares and the cost of capital

The share market value of the business capital stock is obtained in RDX2 from an equation explaining the difference between the long-term government interest rate and the equity earnings-yield by a relative supply variable and a distributed lag function of past changes in consumer prices. The estimated weights on this latter variable are used to generate a series for the expected rate of change of prices, which feeds into a number of other equations in the model. From this model of the share and bond markets, approximations are derived for the cost of business capital, in both real and nominal terms. The MPS model determines share prices from a regression of a dividend price ratio on the corporate bond rate, a synthetic measure of expected rate of price increases and a time trend. Because of the important role of the dividend price ratio in the dynamics of MPS, and some unsatisfactory simulation properties of the simple equation, experiments with MPS may be undertaken using alternative expressions for expected price changes.

3.5. International capital flows and the foreign exchange market

3.5.1. Long-term capital

Only RDX2 has equations in these sectors, although the equations for capital flows between the United States and Canada may equally well be considered part of MPS.

The bilateral capital flow equations, like the trade flow equations, are in general neither supply equations nor demand equations, but are quasi-reduced form relationships combining supply and demand elements. This is so because the range of measured prices and rates of return does not include separate prices for assets sold to, or held by, non-residents. There are Canadian rates of return, U.S. rates of return and the exchange rates linking the two currencies, but no independent rates of return on Canadian assets held by U.S. residents. Even though this forces the capital flow equations to include both supply and demand elements, it is possible to alter the emphasis from equation to equation. Thus, the equations for new issues of Canadian bonds sold in the U.S. are largely borrower-determined, and estimated as proportions of total borrowing requirements. The equations for trade in outstanding Canadian securities, on the other hand, depend entirely on relative rates of return and the composition of the lenders' portfolios.

In a world of growing portfolios, neither "pure stock" nor "pure flow" models of long-term capital movements are appropriate. The RDX2 equations embody combined specifications with equilibrium properties and adjustment paths that appear reasonable whatever the rate of portfolio growth. A notable feature of the capital account linkage is the determination within the model of international indebtedness accounts at both book and market values.

3.5.2. Short-term capital and the foreign exchange market

As for short-term capital flows, we have short-circuited the usual direct explanations in favour of an explicit model of the foreign exchange market, in which separate equations for the net private and official Canadian demands for foreign exchange interact to determine the price of the U.S. dollar, in terms of Canadian dollars, and the change in the Canadian official reserves of gold, U.S. dollars and convertible currencies. The forward exchange market is represented by a single equation for the price of 90-day forward exchange, while official U.S. dealings in Canadian currency are infrequent enough so that we may consider them as exogenous elements in the system. When the changes in foreign exchange reserves have been thus explained, then short-term capital flows are simply determined (given the values for trade and long-term capital flows) as a residual in the balance of payments identity. This procedure has so far only been applied to a portion of the sample period (the fixed exchange rate regime – 6301 to 6804) but it yields good estimates of the exchange rate and short-term capital flows. The highly nonlinear effect of the spot exchange rate in the equation for the official demand for foreign exchange assures that the solution values for the exchange rate will remain within the prescribed band even under simulation.

3.6. Summary of the comparison

Although the preceding paragraphs show that there are numerous important differences between the RDX2 and MPS models, the basic mechanisms of the two models appear to be fairly compatible. Only parallel simulations can reveal whether there are differences in coefficients or lag patterns that are likely to distort the linked simulations. Such judgements will be difficult to make, however, because the greater openness and smaller size of the Canadian economy ought to make the two models differ in structure and dynamic response.

Looking on the brighter side, the fairly parallel treatment of wealth, private expenditures and the cost of capital in the two models makes them more alike than any other pair of comprehensive aggregate models of separate countries.

4. Features of the linkage process

In this section we concentrate on the points of contact between the two national models, and between each model and the rest of the world. We shall deal separately with the links in goods, financial and labour markets. After a discussion of the links that have been modelled, we refer briefly to some of the links that may be important in the world, yet have not been or cannot be incorporated into the structure of the models.

4.1. Goods markets

There are a number of international links between goods markets, several of which we have tried to model. The simplest way of modelling a linkage between goods markets is to make trade flows a function of income in the purchasing country. Further, if the implied marginal propensity to import is made a function of relative prices, then the selling country occupies a less passive role in the trading process, provided that an appropriate export price equation is specified. In application this approach is not satisfactory, since the export prices actually used are merely export-weighted indices of industrial selling prices. Thus, if there is any price discrimination between domestic and foreign markets, it does not show up in the trade flow prices. Further, although these trade prices may be adjusted for freight and import duties, the size of the adjustments does not reflect the interaction of supply and demand for the traded goods. Therefore, it is not possible to regard exports as a special commodity for which a separate price is determined by the interplay of supply and demand. Equations for quantities traded must be regarded as quasi-reduced forms in which both supply and demand elements come into play. The symmetry of these equations is a feature of our approach to trade linkage.

Although we refer to the goods sold from Canada to the United States as Canadian exports, they can equally well be described as United States imports from Canada. Depending on the commodity under consideration the mix of supply and demand factors varies from equation to equation. Most of our trade flow equations depend fairly heavily on some measure of aggregate demand or output in the importing country, implying a substantial degree of complementarity between traded and domestically produced goods. The substitution of foreign for domestic goods depends on relative prices and the degree of capacity utilisation in the two economies. Where the degree of capacity utilisation enters the equation, it usually enters multiplicatively either with prices or with a weighted average of final demands in the importing country. If it enters with the final demand variable, the hypothesis is that the degree of complementarity between domestic and foreign output depends on the relative availability of the two. The basic reasoning is the same if a capacity utilisation ratio multiplies a price term — that the degree of substitution depends on pressures on capacity. In both cases the reasoning assumes that the measured prices are not market-clearing prices. To some extent this is because the measured prices do not capture the variance in the true prices due to variations in discounts, delivery charges, delivery time and so on. Most measured prices are inflexible enough that shortages and surpluses develop at current prices without causing prices to move immediately to market-clearing levels. The degree of capacity utilisation in a country may be a reasonable proxy measure for excess supply or demand pressures at current measured prices.

The discussion above is concerned with the influence of prices and capacity utilisation on trade flows. These provide the most obvious international links between goods markets, but there are further important ties to consider. Activity and prices in one country can influence final demand prices in another country in several ways. First, changes in one country's aggregate demand may lead, through changes in trade flows, to changes in the aggregate demand for output of other countries. Increases in the degree of capacity utilisation of the exporting country, brought about by the initial increase in exports and induced domestic expenditures, will influence the second country's output prices. In RDX2, these pressures are captured by variables exhibiting both the stock and flow dimensions of the relationship between aggregate demand and supply. In flow terms we use the ratio of aggregate demand UGPPA (output excluding unintended inventory changes) to "desired" output UGPPD. The latter is what the aggregate business production function would produce at average rates of employment and factor utilisation. In stock terms, we use an approximation (a twelve-quarter moving sum) to the cumulant of unintended inventory accumulation or decumulation. As long as inventory stocks are deemed by their holders to be in excess, downward pressure on prices will occur whatever the flow relation between current demand and output.

A second link between one country's output prices and another country's final demand prices arises from the import content in each final demand category. In RDX2, for example, we have attempted to obtain measures of the landed Canadian price of the import content of each expenditure category, usually based on some weighted average of relevant U.S. prices multiplied by the exchange rate.

Third, a number of domestically produced goods may be priced, other things being equal, to compete with imported or importable substitutes. Still other domestic products are sold in world markets, or are potentially saleable in such markets. The prices of these goods are naturally explained in part by foreign or world market prices.

Finally, there are a number of other international links, especially between the United States and Canada, that may lead to a strong correlation in price movements in the two economies. If Canadian and U.S. firms producing for their national markets are under common management, price changes are more likely to be made in concert than when producers of corresponding goods in the two countries are unrelated. We do not doubt that a considerable amount of international price discrimination may occur, but once the related firms have decided on the appropriate amount of the differential, any subsequent price changes are more likely to be coincident when the major firms operate in both markets. If we use U.S. price variables directly in the corresponding Canadian price equations in order to reflect some of the ill-defined organisational links, we must see to it that excessive importance is not attached to the U.S. price because of the influence of shocks (omitted variables) common to both economies. If we are careful in the choice of instrumental variables, our simultaneous equation estimation method should protect our parameter estimates from this sort of bias.

In the section above we have described the international links between goods markets as having two main aspects. First, there are trade flow equations which model the involvement of residents of each country in markets for the output of goods produced in other countries. Second, there are those aspects of the price formation mechanism which reflect the effects of the international flow of goods on price movements.

4.2. Financial markets

Financial markets, like markets for goods, are linked not only by actual flows from one country to others but also by potential flows, or common expectations, that cause prices of financial assets to move in concert.

In this section, we first describe the international ties between financial markets linked by long-term capital flows. Then we describe the linkage implied by our model of short-term capital flows and the foreign exchange market and, finally, deal with international flows of interest and dividends.

The main links we have modelled between markets for long-term assets are of the direct sort. For example, U.S. residents add to their holdings of Canadian government bonds if the relative yield of these bonds increases, or if new issues less retirements of these bonds do not increase U.S. holdings at the same rate as U.S. household wealth is growing. We describe the relevant equations as a model of "lender behaviour" because the decision to buy or sell outstanding bonds is in the hands of the lender. The equation for new issues of Canadian provincial and municipal bonds in the United States, on the other hand, is modelled as "borrower behaviour" because the choice of whether to float a new issue in New York or Toronto is made by the issuers. The decision may turn on the willingness of U.S. borrowers to acquire more Canadian bonds, so that borrowers' preferences may appear as explanatory variables. In the last analysis, bilateral allocation of the stock of any financial asset will depend on portfolio balance and growth in both countries, in addition to the relevant rates of return. Nevertheless, we have gained structural detail and accuracy by disaggregating capital flows to relate flows more closely to particular borrowers and lenders. We assure long-run global portfolio balance by having some types of capital flow depend on the combined effects of the more specific models of capital movements.

The split between "borrower models" and "lender models" is one way of dealing with the troublesome statistical problems that arise if there is ambiguity about which portfolio size is the prime determinant of a capital movement. If there is much variance in the exchange rate linking two currencies, then it matters which currency is used as the numeraire for the dependent variable. In RDX2, we have estimated most of our long-term capital flow equations in Canadian dollars, in some cases expressed as a proportion of a Canadian dollar measure of borrowing requirements. The direct investment flows from Canada to the United States are estimated as a proportion of a Canadian dollar measure of U.S. corporate cash requirements. In these cases, where a ratio is used as the dependent variable, it does not matter which currency is used as numeraire. The demand for portfolio holdings of U.S. securities, and the private and official demand equations for foreign exchange are estimated in terms of U.S. dollars. The possibility that errors that are homoscedastic if one currency is used as numeraire would be heteroscedastic if the other is used, may be more a point of principle than of practical importance. It makes no difference at all in the case of equations for imports and exports of goods, since these flows are measured in constant prices. Thus the goods flows measured in constant Canadian dollars differ only by a factor of proportionality from the U.S. constant dollar measure of the same flow.

In general, we have tried to make the capital flow equations symmetric, in the sense that they ought to take balanced account of conditions in the countries at either end of the capital flow. We have not gone far in specifying the influence of conditions in third countries on bilateral capital flows. In our application of the bilateral approach, we treat capital flows between Canada and the United States, and between Canada and other countries, as bilateral capital flows. The difficulties of obtaining sensible portfolio size and rate-of-return measures for the heterogeneous "other countries" category have restricted the detail possible in our explanation of capital flows between Canada and "other countries", and have led us to ignore third-country influences in our explanation of flows between Canada and the United States.

In financial markets, as in goods markets, the prices of assets may be linked by common expectations as well as by current flows of capital or goods. There are two main systems for pricing financial assets in RDX2. On the one hand, there are interest rate equations for four maturity classes of federal government debt and related valuation equations for the market-value/par-value ratio for each maturity class. On the other hand, we determine the market value of the business capital stock and use this series, along with price expectations, a normalised earnings stream, a long-term interest rate and a relative supply variable, to define both nominal and real rates of return representing the supply price of business capital.

The four interest rate equations are of two main types. The interest rate on the shortest maturity class (1 to 3 years) is treated as a policy variable, and is explained by variables reflecting the targets of, and some of the constraints on, monetary policy. Foreign interest rates enter because of the desire not to induce large changes in the level of foreign exchange reserves. The medium-short (3 to 5 years), medium-long (5 to 10 years) and long-term (over 10 years) interest rates are determined by distributed lags on the short-term rate, along with relative supply variables, price expectations and U.S. interest rates. The U.S. rates used are the treasury bill rate and the long-term corporation bond rate, in both cases reflecting private expectations that actual or potential capital flows cause Canadian interest rates to follow to some extent any movements in U.S. rates. The use of instrumental variables for the U.S. rates in our final estimation of these equations should help to avoid attributing excessive importance to U.S. rates due to disturbances (omitted variables) common to both economies.

The nominal supply price of capital is supposed to represent the rate of return accruing to investors in the bonds and shares of Canadian corporations. The RDX2 series is derived as a simple average of two alternative measures. One is the long-term federal government bond rate, adjusted by a constant risk premium and a variable measuring the relative supply of business capital and government bonds. The second is the sum of the current yield on the market value of the business capital stock, plus the expected rate of growth in the current dollar profits accruing to each share of the existing capital stock. U.S. interest rates influence the first component, through the channels already described. The second component is also affected by U.S. interest rates, although the chain of causation has one additional link. The market value of business capital is determined by a reduced form equation in which the Canadian long-term interest rate has a substantial net negative effect. Through this channel any increase in U.S. long or short-term interest rates is reflected in a decrease in the market value of the business capital stock and a corresponding increase in the supply price of capital.

It is possible that, despite the U.S. influences noted above, we have understated the impact of U.S. financial markets on the Canadian supply price of capital. The market value of the Canadian capital stock is measured according to a weighted average of valuation ratios of firms with shares traded on the Toronto Stock Exchange. This sample is systematically biased by excluding direct investment firms whose shares are entirely owned by a parent company. It is impossible to get appropriate valuation ratios for the part of the Canadian capital stock operated by wholly-owned subsidiaries, because the relevant numbers are lost in the consolidated accounts of the parent company. For the purpose of establishing a market value of the Canadian capital stock, it is probably appropriate to use firms with shares traded to represent all firms, but when we use the supply price of capital in business investment equations we use a combination of U.S. and Canadian supply prices of capital. The weight attached to the U.S. rate is equal to the proportion of the Canadian capital stock financed by U.S. direct investment.

The model of the foreign exchange market shows how trade and long-term capital movements give rise to changes in international short-term liabilities and net private demands for foreign exchange. The Canadian exchange authorities then respond by allowing some mix of changes in the exchange rate and the level of Canadian reserves of gold and foreign exchange. The interest rates that determine the private demand for foreign exchange include the Canadian short-term government rate, the U.S. 90-day treasury bill rate and the London 90-day Euro-dollar rate. The Euro-dollar rate takes on more importance relative to the U.S. rate as the Euro-dollar market expands, and as the Euro-dollar rate increases relative to those U.S. rates that are subject to maximum levels under Regulation Q.

The final links between the capital markets are provided by the interest and dividend flow equations that are derived from the rate of return and balance sheet variables mentioned previously. These equations provide interesting ties between the models of portfolio allocation and the current account of the balance of payments. Any induced changes in the current account balance not only affect the foreign exchange rate and the level of foreign exchange reserves, but also influence prices and goods flows through their influence on gross national expenditure.

4.3. Labour markets

Canadian labour markets are linked with those in other countries chiefly by means of migration flows and, to a lesser extent, by labour services purchased (mainly by tourists and shippers) by residents of one country from residents of another country. The RDX2 equations for immigration and emigration indicate strong ties between the job market in Canada and those in Western Europe and in the United States. The immigration rate depends strongly on recent values of the Canadian unemployment rate and of an index of relative real wages. The numerator of the real wage index is an index of Canadian real wages (lagged one quarter to allow the news to spread) and the denominator is a weighted average of real wage indices in Britain, Italy, Germany and the United States, the largest suppliers of migrants to Canada. Canadian emigration, which is mainly to the United States, depends on unemployment rates in Canada and the United States, more strongly on the latter than on the former. The substantial population flows explained by the migration equations have greater proportionate effects on the Canadian labour force than on the Canadian population, because the equation for labour force participation contains a long moving sum of net immigration with a positive coefficient. Under simulation, these labour force links will transmit labour market pressures from Europe or the United States to Canada, but not in the reverse direction. The reverse effects could not be captured without making population endogenous in the U.S. model, and designing an "other countries" model complete with migration equations.

Two service components in the balance of trade — freight and shipping and travel expenditures — represent labour services (as well as services of other factors) sold or purchased abroad. Both types of expenditure depend upon economic activity in the purchasing country, and affect capacity utilisation in the country providing the service. Neither type of expenditure was granted detailed modelling treatment, although even the simple equations used add strands to the linkage process.

4.4. Unmodelled linkages

There are a number of gaps in our picture of how economies are tied together. Brief mention will serve to remind us and others of issues to be borne in mind when considering results from our linked simulations. Natural resources provide much of the scope for international trade and much of the incentive for international direct investment, yet the production relationships implicit in our models do not provide appropriate roles for raw materials. The various national components of multinational firms may not react independently to supply and demand conditions in the ways supposed in our national models. In part this is because our models of industrial behaviour cannot take full account of technology, goodwill and security of supply as costly assets. These problems are compounded where products and markets are defined so narrowly that there are very few firms playing the game. International unions, international political parties and similar organisations may give rise to parallel movements in economic variables. Particular events, such as famines, wars, devaluations and other natural and unnatural crises have international repercussions not traced by our linkage process. Finally, in a world where news and rumours travel increasingly far and wide, there may be waves of social unrest, environmental concern, inflationary psychology and so on that affect economies in an interdependent way.

Despite all these qualifications, we think that we have modelled the most systematic and important linkages between the Canadian and the United States economies, and to a lesser extent, between Canada and the rest of the world. In the final section we shall consider the kinds of question that we can hope to answer using joint simulations of the RDX2 and MPS models.

5. Policy instruments, strategies and simulations

The results of our modelling work are the 260-odd equations comprising RDX2. The trade and long-term capital flow equations and the related trade prices linking the United States and Canada (28 stochastic equations plus several accounting relationships) are considered to be part of RDX2, although they might equally well be treated as part of the U.S. model. In addition to the U.S. variables entering these equations, there are U.S. variables from the MPS model entering other stochastic equations of RDX2. In the corresponding sectors of the MPS model there are no matching impacts representing the effects of Canadian economic activity on the U.S. economy. Only in the trade and capital flow equations is the linkage process symmetric. Even there one might argue that the influence travels mainly northward, rather than southward, because any given movement of goods or capital is ten times larger in relation to the Canadian economy than it is in relation to the U.S. economy. Beyond the trade and capital flow equations, Canadian variables do not appear in the U.S. model. This asymmetry in treatment is explained partly by the much greater size of the U.S. economy, and partly by shortage of modelling time.

If the U.S. balance of payments were not considered a constraint on the choice of U.S. policies, the structure of the linked RDX2 and MPS models would be nearly recursive, with MPS variables influencing RDX2 variables, but not vice-versa. If U.S. trade and capital flows were also small enough to ignore in the determination of U.S. final demand, then it would be possible to adopt the recursive procedure used by the Japanese group in their study of bilateral linkage between the United States and Japan. [6] Under their procedure, the U.S. model is solved to obtain time series of U.S. variables to be used as predetermined variables in alternative simulations of the Japanese model. Our Canadian-U.S. linkage experiments, on the other hand, are based on the assumption that Canadian variables can influence the U.S. balance of payments to such an extent that realistic policy simulations of RDX2 ought to take into account any induced changes in U.S. private behaviour and official policies. To take either private or official responses into account requires that the two models be solved simultaneously. Picturing official, as well as private, responses requires that the MPS model be supplemented by official reaction functions indicating how monetary and fiscal policies would be modified in the light of changes in the balance of payments.

To make full use of the simulation possibilities opened by the combined RDX2 and MPS models, some care must be taken in choosing plausible official reaction functions for inclusion in both models. For some simulations it may also be useful to introduce explicit equations for the Euro-dollar rate and similar "other countries" variables likely to be affected by the conditions underlying the simulation experiments. In the present discussion we shall consider what policies ought to be made endogenous for simulation purposes, and then outline some official strategies and simulations designed to assess the consequences of the alternative policy responses.

The great detail in the government sector of RDX2 reveals many policy instruments. The behavioural equations for government expenditure are intended to illustrate the mix of policy objectives, private sector demands and relative prices that determined government expenditures during the sample period. The revenue equations contain many statutory tax rates, exemptions and other policy variables. These policy variables are exogenous to the

---

[6] See ch. 11 in this volume.

model; hence there is no attempt to explain why they have or have not been altered. The present version of RDX2 assumes that the interest rate on short-term government securities is the main instrument through which monetary policy operates. Terminology gets confusing here because it is possible to refer to the short-term interest rate either as an "intermediate economic target" [7] or as a policy instrument under indirect control. The semantics are not as important as the underlying behavioural assumption. The RDX2 equation for the short-term interest rate is determined chiefly by policy considerations (e.g., recent rates of price increase) but the "intermediate" nature of the interest rate is also recognised by the inclusion of the rate of increase in bank loans in the reaction function of the monetary authorities to represent private sector demands for funds.

In the MPS model there are a number of policy variables, but none are themselves endogenous to the model. When designing simulations for the linked models, we must decide whether or not to suppress certain of the endogenous policy responses in RDX2. To have a fairly realistic starting point, it seems reasonable to leave all the behavioural equations as estimated, altering them only for special purposes. What MPS policy variables ought to be made the subject of reaction functions for the purposes of linked simulations? The variables most naturally falling into this class are those most often used for balance of payments purposes, since the effects of RDX2 variables on the MPS model flow through the balance of payments. History does not help much, except in a negative sense, because most of the U.S. policy responses to balance of payments difficulties have been ad hoc rules or guidelines not easily quantified or even assessed. The simplest way of achieving parallelism between the two models would be to insert a decision rule in the MPS model that raises short-term interest rates when the balance of payments deteriorates. More sophisticated versions of the rule could take account of interest-equalisation taxes and other ways of establishing different rates of interest for foreign and

---

[7] Holbrook, R. and H. Shapiro, 'The Choice of Optimal Intermediate Economic Targets', *American Economic Review*, May 1970.

domestic borrowers. At a later stage we may wish to account for induced changes in fiscal policies to produce a set of monetary and fiscal policies balanced so that U.S. employment, say, is unaffected by the balance of payments disturbances caused by Canadian events and offset to some degree by U.S. balance of payments policies.

There is no need to choose a single set of policy decision rules to be used for all simulations. Indeed, the main advantage of using two large dynamic models linked for simulation experiments is that the consequences of alternative decision rules can be assessed. It is possible to do interesting linked simulations without any endogenous policy responses in the MPS model. In these experiments, the induced changes in the U.S. balance of payments would provide a measure of the incentive for the U.S. to adopt fresh balance of payments rules or guidelines, or to alter the values of general policy instruments.

Some of the more intriguing simulation possibilities involve alterations in decision rules to assess the possible gains from international co-operation in the determination of national monetary and fiscal policies. Some crude modelling of the "other countries" group may be important in obtaining realistic answers from simulations involving differing degrees of international co-ordination of domestic economic policies. At least, simulation of the sort outlined above ought to indicate whether there are many new insights to be gained from a full balance of payments linkage of a larger number of national models.

Part V

THE OPERATION OF TOTAL LINKAGE

13. FORECASTING WORLD TRADE WITHIN PROJECT LINK

L.R. KLEIN and A. VAN PEETERSSEN

1. Introduction

The chapters by Hickman, Rhomberg and Waelbroeck that appear elsewhere in this volume, deal with the theoretical structure of model linkage. However, real world models do not always conform to the elegance of theoretical structures. In some cases data are not available for estimating the full structures set out in the theoretical models, and in other cases the data that are available, no matter how comprehensive, are not sharp enough to provide reliable estimates of all the parameters needed in the theoretical system. The smallness of samples and the inherent collinearity among observed data series often make it difficult to obtain reliable estimates of certain parameters.

Moreover, the theoretical models are often linear and sometimes static. They also tend to be uniform across countries. These characteristics contribute to the elegance. The basic philosophy of the LINK system departs from the theoretical scheme, although theory guides us in a general and important way. In LINK, we assume that each model builder knows his country's economy best, both from the viewpoint of specifying the structure of his country's model and for applying it to his country's situation. We, therefore, pool together a set of existing models for each major industrial country and groups of developing countries. [1] These existing and live models are then linked according to the procedures described

[1] They are developed by the Secretariat of the United Nations Conference on Trade and Development (UNCTAD). See ch. 6 in this volume.

by Hickman, Rhomberg and Waelbroeck or by approximate methods that try to implement their procedures as well as is practically possible.

The models used in the LINK system are those associated with the people who participate in the project and are selected so as to cover as much of the world trading area as possible. In one sense, we obtain a model of world trade through the linkage of existing national models and in another sense we have fashioned a world econometric model. The developing nations are, for some calculations, treated as a whole, and for others, treated in large geographical blocks. The blocks are:

Latin America Free Trade Association
Central America Common Market
Rest of Developing America
North Africa (except Libya)
West Africa
Central Africa
East Africa
Middle East Oil Producers and Libya
Middle East Non Oil Producers and UAR
South Asia
East Asia

At the present time, UNCTAD economists have estimated two equations by 4 SITC goods classes and total trade for each region. [2]

$$E = a + b \, (WT) + c \, TIME$$

$$M = d + e \, (E) \quad + f \, TIME \cdot$$

UNCTAD has had long experience in complete system model building for developing nations and will draw on their inventory of country models, respecifying some, aggregate them regionally and provide the LINK system with more complete models for this part of the world economy.

---

[2] In all, there are 110 equations for 11 regions. UNCTAD is defining "World Trade" in a slightly different manner than the other participants, and it has been necessary to relate the figures of World Trade – UNCTAD definition – to the figures of World Trade – LINK definition.

The Socialist Countries are seven for the purposes of LINK. They are Bulgaria, Czechoslovakia, East Germany, Hungary, Poland, Rumania and U.S.S.R. It is quite new and experimental to deal econometrically with this group of countries; therefore, tested models have not yet been systematically introduced into LINK. At this stage, the actual world trade calculations have been made only for the totality of non-Communist countries. It is expected, however, that the LINK system will eventually be enlarged to include the Socialist countries.

The Rest of the World includes countries that are not in the Communist block, are not developing countries, and are not included in the listing of industrial countries for which LINK has explicit models. These remaining countries are developed countries that are not represented now by explicit models in LINK, but they may be so represented in the future. They are

Austria	Norway	Portugal
Australia	Denmark	Turkey
New Zealand	Yugoslavia	Greece
South Africa	Switzerland	Ireland
Finland	Spain	Iceland

In some calculations, to be described below, the residual group of countries are assumed to have a given share of world trade, and in some they are assigned a composite row/column position in a world trade matrix. All together, this group of countries accounts for something less than one-fifth of all world exports or imports outside the socialist block.

France and Italy are so important in world trade that they need explicit treatment in LINK, but suitable models are not yet available.[3] Pending development of French and Italian econometric models, specially designed for the LINK system, the Central Secretariat has constructed some simple GNP-type models for these two major trading countries. They have the form

$$C_t = \alpha_0 + \alpha_1 X_t + \alpha_2 C_{t-1} + e_{1t}$$

[3] Since the time of writing, a full quarterly model for Italy has been incorporated into the latest LINK forecasts. This accounts for the inclusion of Italy in ch. 5.

$$I_t = \beta_0 + \beta_1 X_t + e_{2t}$$

$$E_t = \gamma_0 + \gamma_1 (WT)_t + \gamma_2 \left(\frac{PW}{PX}\right)_t + \gamma_3 E_{t-1} + e_{3t}$$

$$M_t = \delta_0 + \delta_1 X_t + \delta_2 (X/XC)_t + e_{4t}$$

$$P_t = \epsilon_0 + \epsilon_1 \left(\frac{X}{XC}\right)_t + \epsilon_2 (PM)_t + e_{5t}$$

$$\Delta (PX)_t = \zeta_0 + \zeta_1 \Delta P_t + \zeta_2 \Delta \left(\frac{PW}{r}\right)_t + e_{6t}$$

$$XC = \eta_0 + \eta_1 t + e_{7t}$$

$$X_t = C_t + I_t + G_t + E_t - M_t$$

C = Real domestic consumer expenditure — endogenous.
I = Real investment (including inventory change) — endogenous.
X = Real GNP — endogenous.
E = Real exports of goods and services — endogenous.
WT = Volume of world trade in constant dollars — exogenous.
P = GNP deflator — endogenous.
PW = Deflator of world trade (dollar index) — exogenous.
M = Real imports of goods and services — endogenous.
XC = Trend of capacity output, estimated as line through histori-
        cal peaks of X — endogenous.
G = Real government expenditures on goods and services — exo-
        genous.
r = Dollar exchange rate — exogenous.
PX = Export price index — endogenous.
PM = Import price index — exogenous.

Each behavioural equation is stochastic and has an additive random disturbance. From annual sample data, each equation in this simple model has been estimated for France and Italy. These simple systems give fairly good reproductions of actual economic movements and contain information on domestic performance, export and import demand. They also contain significant effects of relative prices. A team directed by G. Basevi of the University of Bologna is presently building the LINK model of Italy, and it is hoped to generate similar work for France. Eventually, the provisional LINK models of France and Italy will be replaced by the results of these new efforts.

On a provisional basis, similar small GNP-type models will be constructed for use in LINK to represent the other developed countries in the Rest of the World grouping.

2. The "Mini-LINK"

Short of developing the true world model, according to the general analysis described in the chapters by Hickman, Rhomberg and Waelbroeck, we have been able to make systems of increasing degrees of complexity which approximate some of the ideas and restrictions of a world trade system. The complete system would ultimately explain all the trade flows X_{ij}^k of the kth commodity from the ith to the jth country. If this complete system were properly constructed, there would be unique determination of all these flows, subject to statistical error, and their associated prices such that

World exports = World imports = World trade .

If each national model, however, functions in isolation from the viewpoints of specification, estimation and solution there is no guarantee that

$$\sum_i M_i = \sum_i E_i = WT. \tag{1}$$

These trade identities should hold for each separate good as well as in aggregate value.

The first LINK exercise, called "Mini-LINK", is designed to use information from separate national models in such a way that part of the identity, namely

$$\sum_i M_i = WT \tag{2}$$

is satisfied. This is a consistency condition. We shall use it in "Mini-LINK" to find an estimate of world trade that is capable of being supported by, or is consistent with, the total of the activity levels in each of the trading countries. The model of each country will imply a reduced form relationship between each of the endogenous variables, say the jth variable for the ith country, and all the predetermined variables of the ith country's model. These would be either exogenous variables or lagged values of endogenous variables. We write this equation symbolically as

$$Y_{ijt} = f_{ij} (Y_{i1,t-1}, ..., Y_{in,t-p}, X_{i1t}, ..., X_{imt}) + u_{ijt} \tag{3}$$

where the Y's are endogenous and the X's are exogenous variables. In this system there are n endogenous and m exogenous variables. Lags occur up to the pth order. The reduced form disturbances are u_{ijt}.

Generally speaking, a closed form expression for the reduced form equation cannot be derived unless the system is linear. In the Hickman and Rhomberg chapters such reduced form expressions can be derived for their linear system and are used extensively in their analyses. Instead of an explicit reduced form expression as in (3), users of econometric models, which are generally non-linear, derive numerical solutions for each time point of analysis. These are estimated values and have zero or other assigned values for the disturbance terms. The numerical solutions will be used in the same way that one would use values computed directly from reduced forms. In fact, numerical methods are so practical that even if the system is linear, numerical methods will also be used.

Among the Y_{ijt} for the ith country are its imports either in total or in sub-groups. Also, among the X_{ikt} for the ith country will be the level of world trade, at least in the LINK models, by agreement with all the model builders. For any particular value of world trade $(WT)_t^0$ at time point t and best estimates for each of the other predetermined variables, there will be a solution value for imports, M_{it}^0. The values of M_{it}^0 can be added across countries to see if they satisfy (2). In general we shall find

$$\sum_i M_{it}^0 \neq (WT)_t^0.$$

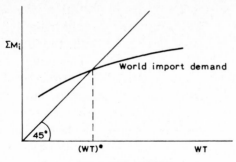

Fig. 1. "Mini-LINK".

"Mini-LINK" provides a systematic search for a value of (WT) that will generate a set of solution values for M_{it} satisfying (2). This is the logic of "Mini-LINK". Its implementation can be shown graphically.

The curve of import demand in fig. 1 is obtained by adding import demand across countries for each level of world trade and each country model's assumptions about the best inputs for predetermined variables. It is assumed in fig. 1 that only WT varies in the reduced forms and all other inputs are held constant for the working of the algorithm in period t. At the point where the curve crosses the 45° line, which is viewed as an offer curve, total imports just equal world trade. We have denoted (WT)^e as the equilibrium value of world trade satisfying (2).

To construct the diagram in an actual case, we request each model builder to solve this system 4 times, each with a different assumed level of world trade

$$(WT)^{(1)}, \quad (WT)^{(2)}, \quad (WT)^{(3)}, \quad (WT)^{(4)}$$

which are then summed

$$\sum_i M_i^{(1)}, \quad \sum_i M_i^{(2)}, \quad \sum_i M_i^{(3)}, \quad \sum_i M_i^{(4)}$$

and plotted on a graph with a 45°-line drawn in. The plotting gives total imports on the ordinate corresponding to each of the 4 abscissae values for (WT). The 4 points turn out to lie along a

Table 1

"Mini-LINK" results for the year 1971 based on forecasts available on April 24, 1971

Countries or group of countries	Ratio of goods	Rate of ex-change	Fob/cif ratio	Price index	Imports in 1970	Forecast for 1971 for four levels of World Trade – WT =				1971 Equili-brium solution	Arc elasti-city
						240.00	260.00	280.00	300.00		
1. Belgium and Luxembourg											
Bil Bfr-'63 price-goods-fob	1.000	0.020	1.000	1.000	544.87	603.75	614.26	627.34	643.36	614.29	0.26
Bil US $-'63 price-goods-fob					10.90	12.07	12.29	12.55	12.87	12.29	
2. Canada											
Bil Ca $-cur price-goods-fob	1.000	0.927	1.000	0.876	13.89	15.36	15.86	16.34	16.83	15.86	0.38
Bil US $-'63 price-goods-fob					11.48	12.48	12.88	13.27	13.66	12.88	
3. France											
Bil Fr f-'63 price-g + s-cif	0.763	0.204	0.950	1.000	110.10	116.33	118.44	120.46	122.52	118.44	0.21
Bil US $-'63 price-goods-fob					16.28	17.20	17.51	17.81	18.12	17.51	
4. Germany											
Bil DM-'63 price-g + s-cif	0.780	0.251	0.956	1.000	136.14	132.71	137.81	142.99	148.31	137.82	0.47
Bil US $-'63 price-goods-fob					25.48	24.84	25.79	26.76	27.76	25.80	
5. Italy											
Bil Lira-'63 price-g + s-cif	0.774	0.002	0.938	1.000	8919.10	9620.90	9878.60	10132.20	10384.40	9879.18	0.32
Bil US $-'63 price-goods-fob					10.36	11.18	11.48	11.77	12.06	11.48	
6. Japan											
Bil US $-'63 price-goods-fob	1.000	1.000	1.000	1.000	16.88	17.93	18.55	19.17	19.78	18.55	0.41
Bil US $-'63 price-goods-fob					16.88	17.93	18.55	19.17	19.78	18.55	
7. Netherlands											
Bil Guld-'63 price-goods-cif	1.000	0.272	0.924	1.000	44.38	45.40	47.40	49.40	51.50	47.40	0.54
Bil US $-'63 price-goods-fob					11.15	11.41	11.91	12.42	12.94	11.91	
8. Sweden											
Bil US $-'63 price-goods-fob	1.000	1.000	1.000	1.000	5.14	5.52	5.70	5.89	6.08	5.70	0.41
Bil US $-'63 price-goods-fob					5.14	5.52	5.70	5.89	6.08	5.70	

Table 1 (continued)

Countries or group of countries	Ratio of goods	Rate of exchange	Fob/cif ratio	Price index	Imports in 1970	Forecast for 1971 for four levels of World Trade – WT =				1971 Equilibrium solution	Arc elasticity
						240.00	260.00	280.00	300.00		
9. United Kingdom											
Bil US $'63 price-goods-fob	1.000	1.000	1.000	1.000	18.18	18.35	18.48	18.61	18.75	18.48	0.09
Bil US $'63 price-goods-fob					18.18	18.35	18.48	18.61	18.75	18.48	
10. United States											
Bil US $'58 price-goods-fob	1.000	1.000	1.000	0.995	33.12	34.50	34.60	34.70	34.80	34.60	0.03
Bil US $'63 price-goods-fob					32.95	34.33	34.43	34.53	34.63	34.43	
11. Latin America Free Trade Association											
Bil US $'63 price-goods-cif	1.000	1.000	0.920	1.000	8.13	7.91	8.26	8.61	8.96	8.26	0.53
Bil US $'63 price-goods-fob					7.48	7.28	7.60	7.92	8.24	7.60	
12. Central America Common Market											
Bil US $'63 price-goods-cif	1.000	1.000	0.920	1.000	1.23	1.16	1.29	1.42	1.54	1.29	1.30
Bil US $'63 price-goods-fob					1.14	1.07	1.19	1.30	1.42	1.19	
13. Rest of Developing America											
Bil US $'63 price-goods-cif	1.000	1.000	0.925	1.000	3.92	4.03	4.04	4.05	4.06	4.04	0.02
Bil US $'63 price-goods-fob					3.62	3.73	3.74	3.74	3.75	3.74	
14. North Africa minus Libya											
Bil US $'63 price-goods-cif	1.000	1.000	0.876	1.000	1.76	1.75	1.82	1.90	1.97	1.82	0.52
Bil US $'63 price-goods-fob					1.55	1.53	1.60	1.66	1.73	1.60	
15. West Africa											
Bil US $'63 price-goods-cif	1.000	1.000	0.836	1.000	2.55	2.44	2.64	2.83	3.02	2.64	0.95
Bil US $'63 price-goods-fob					2.13	2.04	2.21	2.37	2.53	2.21	
16. Central Africa											
Bil US $'63 price-goods-cif	1.000	1.000	0.972	1.000	0.68	0.70	0.70	0.70	0.70	0.70	0.0
Bil US $'63 price-goods-fob					0.67	0.68	0.68	0.68	0.68	0.68	
17. East Africa											
Bil US $'63 price-goods-cif	1.000	1.000	0.972	1.000	4.50	4.25	4.81	5.37	5.94	4.81	1.59
Bil US $'63 price-goods-fob					4.38	4.13	4.68	5.22	5.77	4.68	

Table 1 (continued)

Countries or group of countries	Ratio of goods	Rate of ex-change	Fob/cif ratio	Price index	Imports in 1970	Forecast for 1971 for four levels of World Trade – WT =				1971 Equili-brium solution	Arc elast-icity
						240.00	260.00	280.00	300.00		
18. Middle East + Libya: Oil Producers											
Bil US $-'63 price-goods-cif	1.000	1.000	0.975	1.000	3.78	3.69	4.05	4.40	4.76	4.05	1.16
Bil US $-'63 price-goods-fob					3.69	3.60	3.95	4.29	4.64	3.95	
19. Middle East + U.A.R.: Non Oil Producers											
Bil US $-'63 price-goods-cif	1.000	1.000	0.975	1.000	2.46	2.41	2.59	2.77	2.95	2.59	0.89
Bil US $-'63 price-goods-fob					2.40	2.35	2.53	2.70	2.87	2.53	
20. South Asia											
Bil US $-'63 price-goods-cif	1.000	1.000	0.915	1.000	4.84	4.71	5.00	5.29	5.57	5.00	0.73
Bil US $-'63 price-goods-fob					4.43	4.31	4.57	4.84	5.10	4.57	
21. East Asia											
Bil US $-'63 price-goods-cif	1.000	1.000	0.915	1.000	10.97	10.62	11.49	12.36	13.23	11.49	0.98
Bil US $-'63 price-goods-fob					10.04	9.72	10.51	11.31	12.10	10.52	
22. Other non-communist											
Bil US $-'63 price-goods-fob	1.000	1.000	1.000	1.000	45.08	44.09	47.77	51.44	55.11	47.77	1.00
Total World Trade – non-communist countries											
Bil US $-.63 price-goods-fob					245.40	249.84	260.03	270.25	280.61	260.05	

World Trade Equilibrium equal to 260.05 billion U.S. $ at 1963 prices, f.o.b., after 12 iterations
Increase of World Trade: 6.0 %.

For each country the upper row gives results of import functions in domestic currency, in different prices. The lower row shows these imports of goods only, in 1963 prices, in U.S. $, f.o.b.
To calculate this second row, we multiplied the first one by four coefficients:
(a) the ratio of imported goods to imported goods and services, this ratio is different from 1 when the import functions explain both goods and services;
(b) the rate of exchange: domestic currency – U.S. dollar;
(c) the correction factors fob/cif were estimated by G. Taplin (IMF), and are different from 1 when the import functions give imports c.i.f., world exports are f.o.b.;
(d) the price index transforms imports to 1963 prices;

smooth curve, almost straight, and its point of intersection with the offer curve can readily be found.

The graphical solution is quite instructive, but the whole calculation can be programmed according to an iterative procedure. A value is assumed for world trade and each country model is solved for imports. If the total import value exceeds world trade, the solution is repeated with larger values of WT (choosing them equal to the just computed value of ΣM_i) until equilibrium is reached. For this approach we need models, and computer programs for solving each, in one location – the central Secretariat of LINK.

The iteration algorithm shows clearly that the volume of trade plays a central role as an adjustment variable that achieves world equilibrium. This immediately shows a weakness of "Mini-LINK", for other variables may also serve as adjustment factors in the actual working of the world economy. The principal ones are prices. They must be built into the system. Other exogenous inputs, such as trade policies or domestic monetary and fiscal policies, may adjust to bring about an equilibrium. This has not been allowed for in "Mini-LINK". Nevertheless, this simple search for a balance in (2) is a powerful equilibrating tool and should lead us to a better solution of the world economy that gives a better estimate of world trade than the summation of uncoordinated solutions across countries.

The "Mini-LINK" calculation, either as a graphical solution or a numerical iterative solution, has been described as though it is very simple and straightforward. It does not work out that easily in practice. Before the data can be combined in the particular way indicated, many adjustments and manipulations must be made. These deal with

c.i.f./f.o.b. valuations
The price system
The currency system
The scope of imports

Each country model will be specified and estimated in its own currency system. In most cases behavioural equations of import demand will be in a constant price system. This is the way the small GNP-type models for France and Italy are formulated in the previous section.

Table 2

"Mini-LINK" results for the year 1972 based on forecasts available on April 24, 1971

Countries or group of countries	Ratio of goods	Rate of exchange	Fob/cif ratio	Price index	Imports in 1971	Forecast for 1972 for four levels of World Trade – WT =				1972 Equilibrium solution	Arc elasticity
						260.00	280.00	300.00	320.00		
1. Belgium and Luxembourg											
Bil Bfr-'63 price-goods-fob	1.000	0.020	1.000	1.000	614.29	668.78	682.39	698.55	718.70	680.05	0.32
Bil US $-'63 price-goods-fob					12.29	13.38	13.65	13.97	14.37	13.60	
2. Canada											
Bil Ca $-cur price-goods-fob	1.000	0.927	1.000	0.844	15.86	16.98	17.42	17.98	18.49	17.35	0.39
Bil US $-'63 price-goods-fob					12.88	13.28	13.63	14.07	14.47	13.57	
3. France											
Bil Fr F-'63 price-g + s-cif	0.763	0.204	0.950	1.000	118.44	126.91	128.97	131.02	133.05	128.62	0.21
Bil US $-'63 price-goods-fob					17.51	18.77	19.07	19.37	19.67	19.02	
4. Germany											
Bil DM-'63 price-g + s-cif	0.780	0.251	0.956	1.000	137.82	150.70	155.80	161.00	166.30	154.92	0.45
Bil US $-'63 price-goods-fob					25.80	28.21	29.16	30.13	31.13	29.00	
5. Italy											
Bil Lira-'63 price-g + s-cif	0.774	0.002	0.938	1.000	9879.18	10932.30	11179.70	11430.70	11676.90	11137.18	0.30
Bil US $-'63 price-goods-fob					11.48	12.70	12.99	13.28	13.56	12.94	
6. Japan											
Bil US $-'63 price-goods-fob	1.000	1.000	1.000	1.000	18.55	18.86	19.47	20.09	20.71	19.37	0.43
Bil US $-'63 price-goods-fob					18.55	18.86	19.47	20.09	20.71	19.37	
7. Netherlands											
Bil Guld-'63 price-goods-cif	1.000	0.272	0.924	1.000	47.40	47.40	49.30	51.30	53.20	48.97	0.53
Bil US $-'63 price-goods-fob					11.91	11.91	12.39	12.89	13.37	12.31	
8. Sweden											
Bil US $-'63 price-goods-fob	1.000	1.000	1.000	1.000	5.70	5.82	6.01	6.19	6.38	5.98	0.42
Bil US $-'63 price-goods-fob					5.70	5.82	6.01	6.19	6.38	5.98	

Table 2 (continued)

Countries or group of countries	Ratio of goods	Rate of exchange	Fob/cif ratio	Price index	Imports in 1971	Forecast for 1972 for four levels of World Trade − WT =				1972 Equilibrium solution	Arc elasticity
						260.00	280.00	300.00	320.00		
9. United Kingdom											
Bil US $-'63 price-goods-fob	1.000	1.000	1.000	1.000	18.48	18.96	19.09	19.22	19.35	19.07	0.09
Bil US $-'63 price-goods-fob					18.48	18.96	19.09	19.22	19.35	19.07	
10. United States											
Bil US $-'58 price-goods-fob	1.000	1.000	1.000	0.995	34.60	35.80	35.90	36.00	36.10	35.88	0.04
Bil US $-'63 price-goods-fob					34.43	35.62	35.72	35.82	35.92	35.70	
11. Latin America Free Trade Association											
Bil US $-'63 price-goods-cif	1.000	1.000	0.920	1.000	8.26	8.13	8.48	8.82	9.16	8.42	0.55
Bil US $-'63 price-goods-fob					7.60	7.48	7.80	8.11	8.43	7.75	
12. Central America Common Market											
Bil US $-'63 price-goods-cif	1.000	1.000	0.920	1.000	1.29	1.25	1.38	1.50	1.62	1.35	1.28
Bil US $-'63 price-goods-fob					1.19	1.15	1.26	1.38	1.49	1.25	
13. Rest of Developing America											
Bil US $-'63 price-goods-cif	1.000	1.000	0.925	1.000	4.04	4.16	4.16	4.17	4.18	4.16	0.03
Bil US $-'63 price-goods-fob					3.74	3.85	3.85	3.86	3.87	3.85	
14. North Africa minus Libya											
Bil US $-'63 price-goods-cif	1.000	1.000	0.876	1.000	1.82	1.82	1.90	1.97	2.05	1.88	0.54
Bil US $-'63 price-goods-fob					1.60	1.60	1.66	1.73	1.80	1.65	
15. West Africa											
Bil US $-'63 price-goods-cif	1.000	1.000	0.836	1.000	2.64	2.58	2.77	2.96	3.15	2.74	0.95
Bil US $-'63 price-goods-fob					2.21	2.16	2.32	2.48	2.64	2.29	
16. Central Africa											
Bil US $-'63 price-goods-cif	1.000	1.000	0.972	1.000	0.70	0.72	0.72	0.72	0.72	0.72	0.0
Bil US $-'63 price-goods-fob					0.68	0.70	0.70	0.70	0.70	0.70	
17. East Africa											
Bil US $-'63 price-goods-cif	1.000	1.000	0.972	1.000	4.81	4.70	5.25	5.81	6.37	5.16	1.53
Bil US $-'63 price-goods-fob					4.68	4.57	5.11	5.65	6.19	5.01	

Table 2 (continued)

Countries or group of countries	Ratio of goods	Rate of exchange	Fob/cif ratio	Price index	Imports in 1971	Forecast for 1972 for four levels of World Trade − WT =				1972 Equilibrium solution	Arc elasticity
						260.00	280.00	300.00	320.00		
18. Middle East + Libya: Oil Producers											
Bil US $-'63 price-goods-cif	1.000	1.000	0.975	1.000	4.05	4.05	4.40	4.76	5.12	4.34	1.14
Bil US $-'63 price-goods-fob					3.95	3.95	4.29	4.64	4.99	4.23	
19. Middle East + U.A.R.: Non Oil Producers											
Bil US $-'63 price-goods-cif	1.000	1.000	0.975	1.000	2.59	2.59	2.77	2.95	3.13	2.74	0.90
Bil US $-'63 price-goods-fob					2.53	2.53	2.70	2.87	3.05	2.67	
20. South Asia											
Bil US $-'63 price-goods-cif	1.000	1.000	0.915	1.000	5.00	4.96	5.24	5.52	5.81	5.19	0.75
Bil US $-'63 price-goods-fob					4.57	4.53	4.80	5.06	5.32	4.75	
21. East Asia											
Bil US $-'63 price-goods-cif	1.000	1.000	0.915	1.000	11.49	11.37	12.23	13.09	13.95	12.08	0.98
Bil US $-'63 price-goods-fob					10.52	10.41	11.19	11.08	12.76	11.06	
22. Other non-communist											
Bil US $-'63 price-goods-fob	1.000	1.000	1.000	1.000	47.77	47.77	51.44	55.11	58.79	50.81	1.00
Total World Trade − non-communist countries											
Bil US $-'63 price-goods-fob					260.05	268.19	278.31	288.61	298.95	276.57	

World Trade Equilibrium equal to 276.57 billions U.S. $ at 1963 prices, f.o.b. after 12 iterations
Increase of World Trade: 6.4 %.

Same note as for table 1.

To converge to the world trade equilibrium for 1972, we started from our equilibrium level of world trade for 1971.

The "Mini-LINK" calculation for 1971, the second year that such an exercise has been tried, is demonstrated in table 1. In this table we present each country's import calculation in the first of two rows associated with each country as the numbers are produced by the country model. These might be in local currency, although some are estimated directly in U.S. dollars; they might include services as well as goods; and they might be in c.i.f. valuation. Wherever necessary, the figures are adjusted so that they are in 1963 U.S. dollars (billions), f.o.b., goods only. These figures occur in the second row associated with each country.

For reference purposes, imports are given for 1970 together with the 1971 control solution for each country. Solution values in 1971 are given for each of 4 levels of world trade. In 1969, the

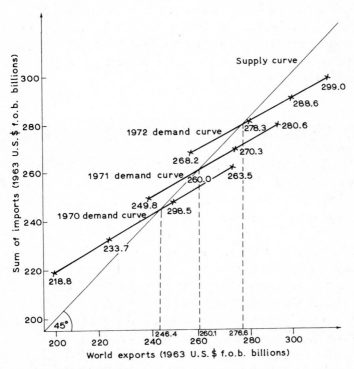

Fig. 2. Graph of the "Mini-LINK" exercises for 1970, 1971 and 1972 (based on forecasts available on April 24, 1971).

observed level of world exports was $ 225.8 (U.S.) billion and in 1970 approximately $ 245 billion. The 4 solution values requested from LINK members were at world trade levels 240, 260, 280, and 300 in 1971. As can be seen from the table, the equilibrium solution is $ 260 (U.S.) billion. This figure is reached by assuming that the residual group of countries maintain their 1970 percentage share of world trade at 240, 260, 280 or 300 in 1971. Eventually this crude assumption will be relaxed, but in the present state of LINK research it is retained.

The exercise can be repeated again for 1972. It is valuable to try to look further ahead than one year. Since many of the country models have built-in lag relationships, the 1972 solution depends on the 1971 value. We instructed each model builder to solve at 4 levels of world trade in 1972, succeeding a solution at 260 in 1971. The 4 levels for 1972 were 260, 280, 300 and 320.

The graphical results for three years, 1970–72, are presented in fig. 2. This shows a modest growth pattern in the equilibrium values in 1971 and 1972. It is considerably below the higher growth rates of earlier years.

3. The "Midi-LINK"

The basic principle of the "Mini-LINK" is that activity levels, represented by world trade, are the adjustment variables that bring about equality between world imports (computed from models) and world trade, measured as world exports and serving as an input into the models. But if there is lack of balance between world imports and world trade, there may be adjustments in other variables besides activity levels. There may be price adjustments.

Among the endogenous variables in the vector of left-hand-side variables of the national reduced form equations are prices. These include both general domestic prices, like the GNP deflator, and export prices. Import prices are exogenous in the country models and appear on the right-hand-side of the reduced forms. Apart from c.i.f.-f.o.b. differentials, the export price of a flow from country i to j (X_{ij}) should be the same as the import price of the same flow to *j*. We must, therefore, take account of this identity as well as the identity on the total flow of trade.

All country models are not equally complete in the use of price variables, either for exports or imports, but there are enough price variables in the LINK system to make a price adjustment process worthwhile. We shall assume that country *i*'s exogenous import prices move in the same proportion as in index of world export prices, from iteration to iteration, in search of equilibrium, where the world export price is formed as a weighted average of individual country export prices, endogenously generated in the solution process. The weights for the world index are the shares of world trade represented by each country's exports. We define the price index of world exports as

$$P_{wt}^{(r)} = \sum_i P_{eit}^{(r)} \cdot \frac{E_{it}^{(r)}}{(WT)_t^{(r)}} .$$ (4)

There will be such a value on each iteration corresponding to the value of $(WT)_t$ used for that iteration. Eq. (4) is written for the *r*th iteration. The change in values used for exogenous import prices assumptions in each model will then be proportional to changes in P_{wt}. The iteration equation will be

$$\frac{P_{mit}^{(r)}}{P_{mit}^{(r-1)}} = \frac{P_{wt}^{(r)}}{P_{wt}^{(r-1)}} .$$ (5)

This iteration is combined with the trade volume iteration to seek joint criteria for equilibrium — no changes in import prices from iteration to iteration and no changes in trade volume from iteration to iteration.

In order to carry out the adjustment process for "Midi-LINK", there should be an export equation for each model so that the weights can be obtained, although shares of imports could be used as well for weights. Also, there must be a capability for solving each country model for different values of import prices. Four (or so) preassigned solutions are not enough. Complete country models must be individually programmed in the LINK system and solved anew on each iteration.

In 1970, when we allowed both price and volume adjustments for world trade, we found that volume moved from 225.8 in 1969 to 244.7 in 1970 together with an increase in the world trade price index of 3.59% from 1969 to 1970.

4. The "Maxi-LINK"

The full restraint on the accounting balance in the flow of trade is not taken into account in either "Mini or Midi-LINK". World trade measured as the sum of world exports is made equal to the sum of imports from the model solution

$$\sum_i M_i = WT$$

but this restriction is imposed without regard to the behaviour of exports in individual countries or geographical blocks. WT could be measured as world imports or world exports; the figure should be the same after allowing for c.i.f./f.o.b. valuations and errors of measurement; thus we have no effective export constraint in the system.

Some, but not all, country models have export equations. Where possible, the LINK project has urged model builders to develop export equations of the form

$$E_{it} = f_i \left((WT\text{-}E_i)_t, P_{eit}/P_{wt} \right) + e_{it} . \tag{6}$$

These may be either linear or logarithmic and may have dynamic features in the form of distributed lag effects. Also, special factors like trade agreements, government grants, dock strikes, the closing of Suez and other major events are put in as quantified or "dummy" variables. There is no mechanism in the algorithm presented this far to guarantee that exports evaluated from estimated equations like (6) will satisfy

$$\sum_i M_i = \sum_i E_i = WT .$$

The LINK system is designed, in a direct sense, on the side of imports, by assuming that stable import functions can be estimated for each country or group of countries. It could have been given an export orientation, but the initial research strategy has been to concentrate on imports and determine exports from statistics of shares. This follows the theoretical treatment of Hickman and Rhomberg [4] who develop these ideas systematically in a model that falls short of estimating all trade flows between points. In the complete system that determines all X_{ij} (flows of goods from i to j) there is export determination. In a practical sense, though, we shall determine imports for each model from behavioural equations and then determine exports from imports in a way that satisfies the overall restriction.

A matrix of trade flows (X_{ij}) is transformed into a matrix of coefficients by dividing each element by total imports

$$A = (\alpha_{ij}) = (X_{ij} / \sum_i X_{ij})$$

This is the same matrix used by Hickman and Rhomberg.
The matrix equation holds for a given year

$$E_t \equiv A_t M_t \tag{7}$$

where E_t is a column vector of exports in period t, and M_t is a column vector of imports in period t.

$$E_t = \begin{pmatrix} E_{lt} \\ \vdots \\ E_{nt} \end{pmatrix}; \quad M_t = \begin{pmatrix} M_{lt} \\ \vdots \\ M_{nt} \end{pmatrix}.$$

In terms of the trade flows, we have

$$E_{it} = \sum_{j=1}^{n} X_{ijt}$$

---

[4] See chs. 2 and 3.

$$M_{jt} = \sum_{i=1}^{n} X_{ijt} \, .$$

For historical periods, we have trade matrices and have consolidated them to show the flows between the 10 industrial countries for which explicit models exist, the developing nations as one single group and the rest or the nonsocialist nations as another group. Eventually, this system will be enlarged to include the socialist nations too, either singly or as a group.

The trade and coefficient matrices have zeros on the main diagonal — they are "hollow" — for individual countries, but non-zero entries for groups of countries who trade among themselves. The consolidated trade matrices for 1968 are represented in table 3 and 4.

If the A-matrix were stable in the sense that

$$E_t = A_{t_0} M_t + e_t \tag{8}$$

where A_{t_0} is the matrix evaluated in a base period (or averaged over several periods) and e_t is a vector of random errors, then we would find, except for random error,

$$\sum_i E_{it} = \sum_i M_{it} \, .$$

This is so because (8) would have the form

$$E_{1t} = \alpha_{11}M_{1t} + \alpha_{12}M_{2t} + \dots + \alpha_{1n}M_{nt} + e_{1t}$$

$$E_{nt} = \alpha_{n1}M_{1t} + \alpha_{n2}M_{2t} + \dots + \alpha_{nn}M_{nt} + e_{nt} \tag{9}$$

and sums of both sides would yield

$$\sum_i E_{it} = M_{1t} \sum_i \alpha_{i1} + M_{2t} \sum_i \alpha_{i2} + \dots + M_{nt} \sum_i \alpha_{in} + \sum_i e_{it} . \tag{10}$$

The construction of A is such that all column sums are unity. If the errors are random, we should expect to have the trade constraint satisfied, on average.

Table 3

Constant dollar world trade matrix 1968 (millions of U.S. dollars, 1963)

	U.S.	U.K.	Japan	Netherlands	Belgium	Canada	Germany	Sweden	France	Italy	Developing countries	Other developed countries	Total exports
U.S.	0.0	1637.7	2626.6	1201.7	684.1	7122.9	1478.3	391.2	945.1	970.5	10453.1	3093.9	30614.1
U. Kingdom	2084.8	0.0	223.9	575.4	559.5	615.4	766.8	607.8	554.0	379.5	4126.3	4182.0	14575.4
Japan	4051.4	357.5	0.0	151.5	77.6	399.5	281.8	73.2	92.3	70.1	6028.6	1193.9	12777.3
Netherlands	427.6	698.5	62.6	0.0	1169.6	57.4	2273.1	226.3	861.2	392.9	1155.8	853.0	8178.1
Belgium	747.7	346.5	53.7	1668.1	0.0	50.6	1659.7	136.7	147.1	300.1	858.3	633.8	7926.2
Canada	7546.1	1003.2	497.9	151.3	105.6	0.0	190.3	26.4	68.9	108.7	952.1	461.3	11111.8
Germany	2707.1	1004.5	349.2	2528.4	1862.5	275.8	0.0	962.9	3059.1	1889.7	4402.2	5801.0	24842.5
Sweden	365.3	692.5	40.3	216.4	144.1	66.5	548.0	0.0	219.0	147.2	656.1	1606.8	4702.2
France	721.8	569.6	95.6	602.3	1215.1	110.8	2223.0	194.2	0.0	1103.1	3428.1	1691.4	11955.0
Italy	1111.4	458.9	68.7	482.7	431.2	109.3	1941.6	164.6	1306.6	0.0	2427.1	1888.9	10391.0
Developing countries	8711.1	4822.5	5245.1	1441.7	1343.1	1029.1	4128.2	735.2	3181.4	2822.0	8693.0	5252.0	47404.4
Other developed countries	2425.1	4213.9	1428.1	606.6	458.6	294.4	2475.3	1184.2	993.9	1204.1	5172.2	2979.4	23435.6
Total imports	30899.3	15805.2	10691.6	9626.0	8051.0	10131.6	17966.1	4702.7	12761.6	9388.0	48352.9	29637.4	208013.4

Table 4

Market share of constant dollar world trade based on imports 1968

	U.S.	U.K.	Japan	Netherlands	Belgium	Canada	Germany	Sweden	France	Italy	Developing countries	Other developed countries
U.S.	0.0	0.1036	0.2457	0.1248	0.0850	0.7030	0.0823	0.0832	0.0748	0.1034	0.2162	0.1044
U. Kingdom	0.0675	0.0	0.0209	0.0598	0.0695	0.0607	0.0427	0.1292	0.0434	0.0404	0.0853	0.1411
Japan	0.1311	0.0226	0.0	0.0157	0.0096	0.0394	0.0157	0.0156	0.0072	0.0075	0.1247	0.0403
Netherlands	0.0138	0.0442	0.0059	0.0	0.1453	0.0057	0.1265	0.0481	0.0675	0.0419	0.0239	0.0288
Belgium	0.0242	0.0219	0.0050	0.1733	0.0	0.0050	0.0924	0.0291	0.1153	0.0320	0.0177	0.0214
Canada	0.2442	0.0635	0.0466	0.0157	0.0131	0.0	0.0106	0.0056	0.0054	0.0116	0.0197	0.0156
Germany	0.0876	0.0636	0.0327	0.2627	0.2313	0.0272	0.0	0.2048	0.2397	0.2013	0.0910	0.1957
Sweden	0.0118	0.0438	0.0038	0.0225	0.0179	0.0066	0.0305	0.0	0.0172	0.0157	0.0136	0.0542
France	0.0234	0.0360	0.0089	0.0626	0.1509	0.0109	0.1237	0.0413	0.0	0.1175	0.0709	0.0571
Italy	0.0360	0.0290	0.0064	0.0501	0.0536	0.0108	0.1081	0.0350	0.1024	0.0	0.0502	0.0637
Developing countries	0.2819	0.3051	0.4906	0.1498	0.1668	0.1016	0.2298	0.1563	0.2493	0.3006	0.1798	0.1772
Other developed countries	0.0785	0.2666	0.1336	0.0630	0.0570	0.0291	0.1378	0.2518	0.0779	0.1283	0.1070	0.1005
Total	1.0000	1.0000	1.0000	1.0000	1.0000	1.0000	1.0000	1.0000	1.0000	1.0000	1.0000	1.0000

In practice A_t is not constant, and a constant A_{t_0} matrix will not transform an import vector of an arbitrary period into an export vector of that period. The Hickman and Rhomberg papers show how various theoretical schemes can deal with this problem.

Our procedure in the applied work, while not disregarding the theoretical results, has used empirical and approximate methods to correct for the time drift in the A matrix. For the sample period 1950–68, we have computed

$$E_t - A_{68}M_t = r_t \tag{11}$$

where r_t is a vector of residuals between the actual vector of exports E_t and a computed vector

$$\hat{E}_t = A_{68}M_t \, . \tag{12}$$

We then estimate correction equations

$$E_{it} = \beta_{0i} + \beta_{1i}\,\hat{E}_{it} + \beta_{2i}\,(E_{i,\,t-1} - \hat{E}_{i,t-1}) + \beta_{3i}t + u_{it}. \tag{13}$$

Regression estimates of (13) are used to estimate the E_t from M_t in a way that allows for variation in A, either in the form of a trend drift or an autoregressive adjustment.

The LINK system is solved for an equilibrium import vector, as already discussed. Exports are then determined as linear functions of imports by eqs. (12) and (13). The export calculations in (13) will not exactly satisfy the trade restriction but come close to doing so in practice. Discrepancies can be distributed among countries in proportion to importance in trade and thus achieve complete balance between world exports and imports.

Instead of assuming that exports are a function of world trade as in (6), this method assumes that exports are given by a linear combination of imports, where the coefficients in the linear combination are derived from the matrix of the direction of trade. In (6) we add imports without weights to get WT, while in (12) [corrected for (13)], we weight the components of the world import vector in calculating exports. The two approaches are similar, but, in an approximate sense, the matrix approach through (12) and (13) preserves the world trade identity.

The whole calculation can be carried out in either current or constant prices. It is a question of the units in which the X_{ij} are measured. If the trade matrix is given in constant prices (1963 U.S. dollars) then E_t and M_t should also be measured in the same constant price system. If the X_{ij} are in current prices, then E_t and M_t should also be measured in current prices. We have experimented with both schemes, but lean towards the use of constant prices for deriving the A matrix with constant price measures of E and M.

The solution of the "Maxi-LINK" system involves the complete solution of models for each included industrial country, the small reduced form trade equation for blocks of developing countries, a single proportionality-type relation for the residual functions (last year's share of world trade for their imports) and the allocation of exports in a 12 × 12 system (with autoregressive/trend corrections) according to the trade matrix. All these calculations are done subject to the restriction that world imports and exports balance, that world trade is defined as world exports and that import prices move in each country proportionally to a weighted average of export prices.

This is a formidable calculation. It requires dealing with two complications: (1) Some of the country models are quarterly, while others are annual. (2) Solution variables for some models serve as predetermined variables in other models. This is particularly true of U.S. economic effects on Canada and Japan. There are also U.K. effects on Canada. The first complication necessitates solving the quarterly models first for four periods, averaging the quarterly values (at annual rates) and using the annual results together with the annual model results from the rest of the LINK system. The second complication introduces effective bilateral linkages and requires the solution of the U.S. model first for input values into other models and the U.K. model second.

Two iterations are required. First, each country model must be solved as a simultaneous system, usually by the Gauss-Seidel algorithm developed for the Wharton Model (U.S.). [5] Second, all the

[5] The programming generally follows the scheme presented in Klein, L.R., M.K. Evans and M. Hartley, *Econometric Gaming: A Computer Kit for Macroeconomic Analysis*, Macmillan, 1969.

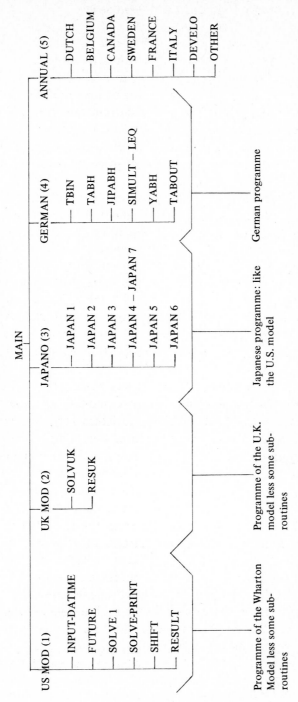

Fig. 3. Flow chart of the "Maxi-LINK" programme.

(1) USMOD: this subroutine is a modified version of the MAIN of the Wharton programme. (2) UKMOD: this subroutine is a modified version of the MAIN of the U.K. programme. (3) The Japanese programme was rewritten by Y. Ikeda – according to the Wharton programme. (4) German: this subroutine was the main of the programme of the University of Bonn for Germany, this model has just been reprogrammed. (5) The subroutine annual organises the solving of all the other annual models, each one being reduced to a subroutine containing only its set of equations.

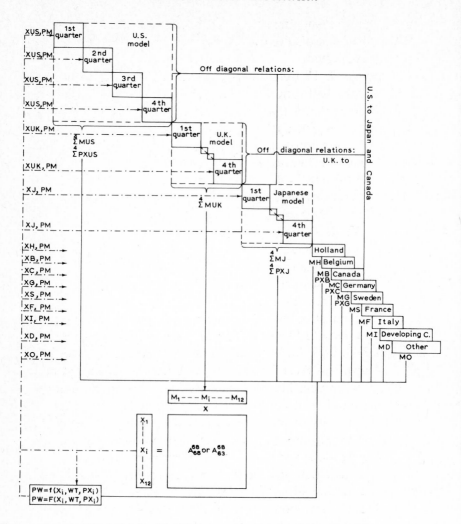

Fig. 4. Graph of the block recursive structure of "Maxi-LINK".

models and separate trade equations must be iterated by the procedures explained above to find a world trade equilibrium that
satisfies the volume and price constraints for exports and imports.
The flow chart and graphs of the block recursive structure of the
"Maxi-LINK" programme are given in figs. 3 and 4.

The entire system appears as a big block recursive model which is solved stepwise and iteratively. Each block which is, in fact, a country model is also solved iteratively at each iteration of the big block recursive system.

For example, if 17 iterations were required to find an equilibrium value for world trade — within an accuracy margin of $e = 0.01$ billion of U.S. $, that means that each country model must be solved 17 times. Since the country models are solved iteratively too, most of them must be iterated several hundred times. One quarterly model was iterated more than 2000 times.

In one "Maxi-LINK" calculation we required the following solutions for 17 iterations on the world trade equilibrium value.

$17 \times 4 \times 35 = 2380$ solutions of the U.S. model
  612 for the U.K. model
  612 for the Japanese model
  323 for the Belgian model
  612 for the Canadian model
  119 for the French model
  119 for the Italian model.

This required between 9 and 10 minutes of both CPU and channel time on an IBM 360/75. With the addition of programmes for the Dutch, Swedish and West German models, the size of the calculation will grow appreciably. The magnitude of the LINK solution programme should be evident from these citations.

To the complexity of solving simultaneously 10 or more models some of them having approximately 100 equations and being quarterly — in one programme with that double iterative process — we must add the fact that algorithms varied among countries. Every programming trick had to be exploited to reduce the memory requirements of each model and to enter them all together in a computer. Another complication is the fact that economic reporting delays are different in each country. Therefore, the periods for which models had to be solved in order to give a 1970 forecast were not the same. Lags in official statistics publications were such that some models had to be solved for 1969 first, or even for 1968, in order to generate a solution for 1970. The results of the "Maxi-LINK" experiments both at current and 1963 constant prices appear in tables 5 to 7.

Table 5

"Maxi-LINK" results of linkage of national econometric models: world trade forecasts for 1970
(Only non-communist countries)

Countries or group of countries		Year 1969 Control Solution		Year 1970 Control Solution		Year 1970 "Maxi-LINK" Equilibrium Solutions					
						Constant Prices and Current Prices Matrices "A"					
		Exports	Imports	Exports	Imports	$E = F(WT)$	M	$E = A*M$	$E = F(WT)$	M	$E = A*M$
		1	2	3	4	5	6	7	8	9	10
1. Belgium + Luxembourg											
Bil Bfr-'59	price-g + s-fob	374.34	376.98	407.95	414.07	436.55	474.30	471.48	434.90	472.74	467.63
Bil US $-'63	price-goods-fob	7.85	8.11	8.55	8.91	9.10	10.21	9.88	8.92	10.17	9.80
2. Canada											
Bil Ca $-'57	price-goods-fob	11.79	11.51	11.80	11.50	12.55	11.30	12.55	12.52	11.34	12.53
Bil US $-'63	price-goods-fob	11.75	12.02	11.76	12.00	12.51	11.79	12.51	12.48	11.84	12.48
3. France											
Bil Fr f-'63	price-g + s-cif	95.80	87.51	0.0	0.0	113.01	100.03	113.01	114.12	100.69	114.25
Bil US $-'63	price-goods-fob	14.03	12.31	0.0	0.0	15.36	13.07	15.36	15.51	13.16	15.55
4. Germany											
Bil DM-'70	price-g + s-cif	129.71	107.75	132.23	120.77	112.16	120.47	146.08	112.91	120.47	133.92
Bil US $-'63	price-goods-fob	22.98	17.60	26.36	22.78	22.36	23.47	32.36	22.51	23.47	29.66
5. Italy											
Bil Lira-'63	price-g + s-cif	10005.00	8301.70	0.0	0.0	11295.04	9563.05	11295.21	10917.20	9325.02	10924.84
Bil US $-'63	price-goods-fob	11.53	9.58	0.0	0.0	13.02	11.04	13.02	12.58	10.76	12.59
6. Japan											
Bil Yen-'65	price-g + s-cif	5440.70	5484.20	6497.30	6455.90	7462.05	9143.05	5869.76	7438.03	9050.72	5726.71
Bil US $-'63	price-goods-fob	14.73	13.22	17.59	15.57	20.21	22.05	15.89	20.14	21.82	15.51
7. Netherlands											
Bil Guld-'69	price-goods-cif	35.70	38.50	38.90	41.20	0.0	43.28	39.65	0.0	43.13	38.70
Bil US $-'63	price-goods-fob	9.39	9.51	10.23	10.18	0.0	10.69	10.42	0.0	10.65	10.17

Table 5 (continued)

Countries or group of countries	Year 1969 Control Solution		Year 1970 Control Solution		Year 1970 "Maxi-LINK" Equilibrium Solutions					
					Constant Prices and Current Prices Matrices "A"					
	Exports	Imports	Exports	Imports	$E =$ $F(WT)$	M	$E =$ $A*M$	$E =$ $F(WT)$	M	$E =$ $A*M$
	1	2	3	4	5	6	7	8	9	10
8. Sweden										
Bil Sv k-'59 price-goods-cif	29.11	29.74	31.61	32.13	0.0	27.85	32.14	0.0	27.83	30.60
Bil US $-'63 price-goods-fob	5.24	5.31	5.52	5.74	0.0	4.97	6.30	0.0	4.97	5.99
9. United Kingdom										
Bil £[a]	7.60	6.35	7.89	6.60	10.97	7.02	10.97	10.31	6.94	10.32
Bil US $-'63 price-goods-fob	13.06	14.55	13.56	15.12	18.86	16.09	18.86	17.72	15.91	17.73
10. United States										
Bil US $-'58 price[b]	48.00	32.67	53.13	33.24	53.64	33.15	53.64	53.13	33.12	53.16
Bil US $-'63 price-goods-fob	33.18	30.40	36.73	30.92	37.08	30.84	37.08	36.73	30.81	36.75
11. Total for the Separate Countries										
Bil US $-'63 price-goods-fob	143.74	132.61	130.30	121.22	0.0	154.22	171.68	0.0	153.56	166.23
12. Latin America Free Trade Association										
Bil US $-'63 price-goods-fob	0.0	8.20	0.0	0.0	0.0	8.80	0.0	0.0	8.77	0.0
13. Central America Common Market										
Bil US $-'63 price-goods-fob	0.0	1.07	0.0	0.0	0.0	1.24	0.0	0.0	1.23	0.0
14. Rest of Developing America										
Bil US $-'63 price-goods-fob	0.0	4.28	0.0	0.0	0.0	4.69	0.0	0.0	4.67	0.0
15. North Africa minus Libya										
Bil US $-'63 price-goods-fob	0.0	1.57	0.0	0.0	0.0	1.61	0.0	0.0	1.61	0.0
16. West Africa										
Bil US $-'63 price-goods-fob	0.0	2.04	0.0	0.0	0.0	2.28	0.0	0.0	2.27	0.0
17. Central Africa										
Bil US $-'63 price-goods-fob	0.0	0.57	0.0	0.0	0.0	0.59	0.0	0.0	0.59	0.0

Table 5 (continued)

Countries or group of countries

Year 1970

"Maxi-LINK" Equilibrium Solutions

	Year 1969 Control Solution		Year 1970 Control Solution		Constant Prices and Current Prices Matrices "A"					
	Exports	Imports	Exports	Imports	$E = F(WT)$	M	$E = A*M$	$E = F(WT)$	M	$E = A*M$
	1	2	3	4	5	6	7	8	9	10
18. East Africa Bil US $-'63 price-goods-fob	0.0	2.91	0.0	0.0	0.0	3.29	0.0	0.0	3.27	0.0
19. Middle East + Libya: Oil Producers Bil US $-'63 price-goods-fob	0.0	4.44	0.0	0.0	0.0	5.15	0.0	0.0	5.12	0.0
20. Middle East + U.A.R.: Non Oil Producers Bil US $-'63 price-goods-fob	0.0	2.47	0.0	0.0	0.0	2.76	0.0	0.0	2.75	0.0
21. South Asia Bil US $-'63 price-goods-fob	0.0	4.71	0.0	0.0	0.0	5.28	0.0	0.0	5.25	0.0
22. East Asia Bil US $-'63 price-goods-fob	0.0	13.16	0.0	0.0	0.0	14.86	0.0	0.0	14.79	0.0
23. Total for Developing Countries Bil US $-'63 price-goods-fob	0.0	45.42	0.0	0.0	0.0	50.55	55.74	0.0	50.32	58.25
24. Other non-communist countries Bil US $-'63 price-goods-fob	0.0	47.77	0.0	0.0	0.0	53.12	30.46	0.0	52.84	29.36
25. Total for non-communist world Bil US $-'63 price-goods-fob	225.80	225.80	0.0	0.0	0.0	257.89	257.88	0.0	256.72	253.84

Increase of world price in 1970, as a weighted average of each country export price

with the $X = A*M$ adjustment computed at 1963 prices 6.29 %.

with the $X = A*M$ adjustment computed at current prices 5.18 %.

[a] U.K. exports include goods and services at 1963 prices, while U.K. imports include only goods at 1958 prices f.o.b.

[b] U.S. exports include goods and services, while U.S. imports include only goods at 1958 prices c.i.f.

An entry 0.0 means that the corresponding figure was not used in the Maxi-LINK calculation.

Table 6

World trade matrix for 1970 at constant 1963 prices, non-communist countries only
(billions U.S. $ f.o.b.)

Countries and group of countries	Belgium*	Canada	France	Germany	Italy	Japan	Netherlands	Sweden	U.K.	U.S.	DC	ONCC	Total Exports
1. Belgium*	0.0	0.06	1.51	2.17	0.35	0.11	1.85	0.14	0.35	0.74	0.90	1.13	9.31
2. Canada	0.13	0.0	0.07	0.25	0.13	1.02	0.17	0.03	1.02	7.53	1.00	0.82	12.17
3. France	1.54	0.13	0.0	2.90	1.30	0.20	0.67	0.20	0.58	0.72	3.59	3.03	14.86
4. Germany	2.36	0.32	3.13	0.0	2.22	0.72	2.81	1.02	1.02	2.70	4.61	10.40	31.31
5. Italy	0.55	0.13	1.34	2.53	0.0	0.14	0.54	0.17	0.47	1.11	2.54	3.38	12.89
6. Japan	0.10	0.46	0.09	0.37	0.08	0.0	0.17	0.08	0.36	4.04	6.32	2.14	14.21
7. Netherlands	1.48	0.07	0.88	2.97	0.46	0.13	0.0	0.24	0.71	0.43	1.21	1.52	10.10
8. Sweden	0.18	0.08	0.22	0.72	0.17	0.08	0.24	0.0	0.70	0.36	0.69	2.88	6.33
9. United Kingdom	0.71	0.72	0.57	1.00	0.45	0.46	0.64	0.64	0.0	2.08	4.32	7.50	19.07
10. United States	0.87	8.29	0.98	1.93	1.14	5.41	1.33	0.41	1.67	0.0	10.95	5.54	38.53
11. Total for developing countries (DC)	1.70	1.20	3.26	5.39	3.32	10.81	1.60	0.78	4.91	8.69	8.99	9.41	60.06
12. Other non-communist countries (ONCC)	0.58	0.34	1.02	3.23	1.41	2.94	0.67	1.25	4.29	2.42	5.42	5.34	28.92
13. Total for non-communist world	10.20	11.79	13.07	23.45	11.03	22.03	10.69	4.97	16.08	30.83	50.54	53.09	257.77

Exports are listed horizontally and imports are listed vertically.
* Includes Luxembourg.

Table 7

World trade matrix for 1970 at current prices, non-communist countries only
(billions U.S. $ f.o.b.)

Countries and group of countries	Belgium*	Canada	France	Germany	Italy	Japan	Nether-lands	Sweden	U.K.	U.S.	DC	ONCC	Total Exports
1. Belgium*	0.0	0.06	1.70	2.38	0.38	0.12	2.01	0.17	0.38	0.86	0.96	1.23	10.26
2. Canada	0.16	0.0	0.09	0.30	0.15	1.19	0.20	0.04	1.21	9.54	1.17	0.99	15.04
3. France	1.72	0.14	0.0	3.27	1.45	0.21	0.75	0.25	0.65	0.86	3.94	3.40	16.65
4. Germany	2.49	0.34	3.42	0.0	2.34	0.73	2.96	1.17	1.08	3.03	4.78	10.99	33.35
5. Italy	0.57	0.13	1.43	2.64	0.0	0.14	0.55	0.20	0.48	1.22	2.58	3.51	13.46
6. Japan	0.11	0.43	0.11	0.40	0.09	0.0	0.18	0.09	0.39	4.63	6.68	2.31	15.40
7. Netherlands	1.60	0.07	0.98	3.22	0.50	0.13	0.0	0.28	0.76	0.49	1.28	1.65	10.97
8. Sweden	0.20	0.09	0.26	0.80	0.19	0.09	0.27	0.0	0.78	0.43	0.75	3.19	7.04
9. United Kingdom	0.76	0.77	0.63	1.08	0.47	0.48	0.68	0.75	0.0	2.36	4.53	8.01	20.51
10. United States	1.02	9.82	1.19	2.28	1.33	6.14	1.56	0.53	1.95	0.0	12.60	6.51	44.93
11. Total for developing countries (DC)	1.87	1.33	3.70	5.97	3.63	11.49	1.76	0.93	5.37	10.14	9.41	10.35	65.95
12. Other non-communist countries (ONCC)	0.63	0.37	1.16	3.57	1.57	2.90	0.73	1.49	4.50	2.73	5.80	5.83	31.27
13. Total for non-communist world	11.12	13.56	14.66	25.90	12.11	23.63	11.65	5.90	17.56	36.28	54.48	57.97	284.83

* Includes Luxembourg.

Together with the results for both price systems for each country or group of countries, table 5 presents also the "control solutions" results for 1969 and 1970 when available i.e. the solutions each model builder or user computed separately regardless of any total world trade consistency: these are in columns 1 to 4.

Again in this table, as in tables 1 and 2, for each country or group of countries we have two rows of results. The first one reproduces the results given by the models in local currency, c.i.f. or f.o.b., sometimes including services and in prices of different years, while the second row gives the same homogenised results in 1963 dollars, f.o.b., goods only.

Columns 5 to 7 of table 5 deal with the 1970 results computed with the 1963 priced market share matrix with 1963 priced imports and exports, while columns 8 to 10 give the same results, but use the current priced matrix and current priced exports and imports vectors.

The results of each country's second row are all in 1963 prices. In columns 8 to 10 the calculations were made with current priced matrices and import vectors, but the results are printed in 1963 prices for purposes of comparison. Table 7 is in current (1970) prices.

For both price systems, columns 6 and 9 – labeled "M" – reproduced imports given by each model solution, columns 7 and 10 – labeled $E = A*M$ – give exports computed by using the world trade market share matrices, which were values at 1963 constant prices (column 7) and at current prices (column 10).

Columns 5 and 8 – labeled "$E = F(WT)$" – are just "for show"; they present the value of each country's exports as they would have been computed by each model's own export function. They are not used in the "Maxi-LINK" exercise because exports, there, are given by redistribution of other countries imports through the market share matrices. Japanese exports are more reliably estimated in columns 5 and 8 than in 7 and 10.

For 1970, the equilibrium level of world trade at 1963 prices is equal to $ 257.89 billion when imports were redistributed at 1963 prices through a 1963 priced market share matrix, and equal to either 256.72 or 253.84 (1963 prices) when imports were redistributed at current prices through a current priced market share matrix. For this latter case the difference is due to inconsistencies among the imports and exports price indices used. Table 6 shows the world trade matrix at 1963 prices given by the exercise when all the computations were carried out at 1963 prices. The amount of world trade is the same as that appearing in table 5 — columns 6 and 7.

Table 7 shows the world trade matrix at 1970 current prices, given by the exercise when we used a market share matrix, export vector and import vector at current prices. The current priced *value* of world trade amounts to $ 284.85 billion. This figure corresponds to the $ 256.72 and $ 253.84 billion of 1963 prices of columns 4 and 10 of table 5. The totals look reasonable, but the Japanese exports and imports are out of line.

5. Proposed future developments

An interesting improvement of the LINK exercises will be for each country to have 4 import functions (for SITC 0 + 1, 2 + 4, 3 and 5 to 9) and a fifth for services, including the corresponding prices if possible, and for each country to have 4 export price functions — one for each SITC group.

With these features we should be able to link the models with 4 world trade equilibria and in the "Maxi-LINK" to have 4 trade matrices, one for each SITC group, linking country exports of each SITC group to imports of the same commodity for the other countries.

We could then use the same 4 matrices, but transposed, to compute for each importing country its 4 import prices — one for each SITC group — as weighted averages of its supplier export prices for that SITC group. This disaggregation would give us more meaningful relationships between import and export prices. The relationships could be worked out for the goods that a country actually imports.

To summarise, each country model *i* would give us import results for four SITC groups

$$M_{ijt} \qquad\qquad \begin{aligned} i &= 1, ..., 12 \\ j &= 1, ..., 4 \end{aligned}$$

and four export prices

$$Pe_{ijt} \qquad\qquad \begin{matrix} i &=& 1, ..., 12 \\ j &=& 1, ..., 4 \end{matrix}$$

For each SITC group we would compute the export vector

$$E_{jt} = A M_{jt} \qquad\qquad j = 1, ..., 4$$

from the four SITC world trade matrices (a_{ik}^{j}), and the import prices for country k for product j would be equal to

$$Pm_{kjt} = \sum_{i=1}^{12} \alpha_{ik}^{j} \, Pe_{ijt} \, .$$

This kind of double linkage – by exports and prices – would be an improvement to the actual treatment of the price linkage in the "Maxi-LINK". Of course, the trade matrices will not remain constant by commodity type any more than they do in the aggregate; thus it will be necessary to develop autoregressive/trend correction factors for individual commodity groups in the same way that we did this for total trade.

There is still the question of bringing the countries of the socialist world into the LINK system. The world trade matrix should have at least one row and one column for exports to, and imports from, the Centrally planned Economies. First steps in this direction are taken in the chapter by UNCTAD economists. This will be a major new achievement for trade linkage when the integration has been worked out.

INDEX

Amano, A., 59
Ando, A., 72, 395n
Argentinian economy,
   characteristics, 132–141
   model of, 113–131
Armington, P.S., 12n, 13n, 15, 16n, 22n,
   24n, 25, 28n, 190

Ball, R.J., 72, 97n, 232n
Barten, A.P., 54
Basevi, G., 329, 432
Behrman, J., 111n, 134n
Bell, P., 283n
Beltran del Rio, A., 111n
Berner, R., 252n
Bischoff, C.W., 403
Boatwright, B.D., 65n
Boissonneault, L., 335n, 367n
Branson, W.H., 289n

Capacity utilisation, 26, 30, 32, 232,
   246, 333, 415
Capital flows, 3, 59, 397
   long-term, 298, 304, 411
   short-term, 285, 302, 412
   and speculation, 295
Cohen, B., 283n
Common Market, 49, 53, 57
Conrad, A.H., 111
Consumer durables,
   effects of government grants, 73
Consumption,
   and income distribution, 73
   and monetary effects, 74, 401, 402
   and net worth, 72
   and permanent income, 72, 73
   treatment in LINK models, 72–77
Cost of capital, 17, 79, 81, 232, 403,
   419, 420
Crouch, R.L., 105n

Delivery lags, 16, 30, 229
Demand for labour,
   treatment in LINK models, 93–96
Domestic prices, 26, 33, 185
Drake, P.S., 72
Driehuis, W., 332, 335, 362n
Duesenberry, J.S., 72
Duffy, M., 97n, 332, 341

Eaton, J.R., 232n
Eckstein, O., 97n
Eshag, E., 157
Evans, M.K., 236n, 368n, 452n
Exchange markets,
   forward, 295, 299, 412
   spot, 299, 301
Export prices, 33, 185, 239
   of services, 333
      problems of construction, 334
      treatment in LINK models, 359–
      363
Exports, 27, 239
   of services, 332–335
   treatment in LINK models, 247–249

Felix, D., 137
Forte, F., 397n
Friedman, M., 72
Fromm, G., 97n, 403n

Ginsburg, A., 56
Goldfeld, S.M., 105n
Gordon, R.A., 1
Gregory, R.G., 229n, 232n, 252n
Grinwis, M., 61
Grubel, H.G., 287n

Hartley, M., 452n
Helliwell, J.F., 284n, 341n, 395n
Henderson, G., 329n

Hickman, B.G., 1, 9n, 184n
Holbrook, R., 425n
Housing investment,
    and starts, 86, 402
    treatment in LINK models, 85–87

Import prices, 26, 27
    and domestic prices, 98, 185
Imports,
    and domestic demand, 229–232
    and domestic supply, 232
    of services, 332–335
    treatment in LINK models, 243–247
    treatment in US and Japanese mod-
        els, 386–392
Income determination,
    and inflation, 100
    treatment in LINK models, 99–103
    and unemployment, 100
Indian economy,
    characteristics, 141–154
    model of, 154–161
Inventory investment,
    and excess demand, 186
    and gestation lags, 88
    and imports, 230, 231, 246
    and model solutions, 88–90
    treatment in LINK models, 88, 89
Investment,
    neo-classical theory of, 79
    and production functions, 80, 403
    treatment in LINK models, 80–85

Johnston, J., 90n
Jorgenson, D.W., 80, 84
Junz, H.B., 56

Kenen, P., 283n
Killingsworth, M.R., 91n
Klein, L.R., 1, 111, 134n, 368n, 452n
Koizumi, K., 283n
Kosuge, N., 283n
Kravis, I.B., 59, 60, 235n
Kuh, E., 78n

LAFTA, 137
Lau, L.J., 9n, 21n
Leamer, E.E., 10n, 235n, 283n
Lederer, W., 329n
Lipsey, R.E., 59, 60, 235n
Locke Anderson, W.H., 78n

McDougall, G.D.A., 56
Maisel, S., 86n
Marginal efficiency of capital, 75
Matsumoto, T., 283n
Maxi-LINK, 65, 170, 179, 446–462
Maxwell, T., 284n, 395n
Maynard, G., 139n
Meyer, J.R., 78n
Midi-LINK, 444–446
Miller, N.C., 291n
Mini-LINK, 46, 57, 58, 65, 170, 379,
    433–444
Modigliani, F., 82, 395n
Monetary movements, 59
Money,
    treatment in LINK models, 104–106
    in US and Canadian models, 409–
        411, 417–421
Moriguchi, C., 368n

Neild, R.R., 97n
Nigerian economy,
    characteristics, 166–169
    model of, 161–166

Okigbo, P.N.C., 166

Pani, P.K., 141n
Papanek, G.F., 111n, 139n
Patel, R.H., 160n
Portfolio selection, 284, 287, 412
Preston, R.S., 236n
Prices, 26, 33, 97
    treatment in LINK models, 97–99
Production functions, 79
    Cobb–Douglas, 81, 402, 403
    CES, 24, 81, 84, 403
Profit maximisation, 17, 78
Project LINK, 21, 45, 52, 57, 58, 61, 65,
    67, 75, 182
    enlarged group, 2, 5
    finance, 2
    initial aims, 1
    initial members, 1

Raj, K.N., 156n
Rasche, R., 395n
Renton, G.A., 332, 341
Rhomberg, R., 1, 12n, 21, 24, 45n, 53,
    54, 56, 184n, 187n, 335n, 367n, 372

Shapiro, H., 425n
Shares matrix, 16, 21, 28, 36, 54, 178, 212
  definition of, 23–25
  on forecasting, 190–192
  and international linkage, 54–56, 228
  non-price effects on, 30–33
Spiro, A., 72
Spraos, J., 295n, 299n
Stern, R.M., 10n, 235n, 283n
Steuer, M.D., 232n

Taplin, G.B., 45n, 184n
Tatemoto, M., 368n
Teigen, R., 105n
Tims, W., 54n
Traded goods,
  and bilateral linkage, 414–417
  demand for, 11, 13, 16
  problems of classification, 11, 12, 234–236

problems of valuation, 200–202
  supply of, 11, 13, 17
Tsiang, S.C., 285n, 299n
Two gap model, 110
Tyszinski, H., 54, 56

Uchida, M., 368n
UNCTAD, 65, 109, 429n
University of Pennsylvania, 2, 368
University of Stanford, 1, 2

Van der Beld, C.A., 60
Verdoorn, P.J., 9n, 21n, 192n, 241n
Vernon, R., 110

Waelbroeck, J., 21, 28n, 54n, 56
Whitman, M.v.N., 291n
Willett, D., 397n
Woolley, H.B., 329n

Zellner, A., 111n